Butterworths Guide to
THE COUNCIL TAX
IN SCOTLAND

Edited by
Butterworths Editorial Staff

with an Introduction by
T J Mullen LLB,
Senior Lecturer in Law at the University of Glasgow,
Convener of the Legal Services Agency

Butterworths
Edinburgh
1993

United Kingdom	Butterworth & Co (Publishers) Ltd, 4 Hill Street, EDINBURGH EH2 3JZ, 88 Kingsway, LONDON WC2B 6AB
Australia	Butterworths, SYDNEY, MELBOURNE, BRISBANE, ADELAIDE, PERTH, CANBERRA and HOBART
Belgium	Butterworth & Co (Publishers) Ltd, BRUSSELS
Canada	Butterworths Canada Ltd, TORONTO and VANCOUVER
Ireland	Butterworth (Ireland) Ltd, DUBLIN
Malaysia	Malayan Law Journal Sdn Bhd, KUALA LUMPUR
New Zealand	Butterworths of New Zealand Ltd, WELLINGTON and AUCKLAND
Puerto Rico	Equity de Puerto Rico, Inc, HATO REY
Singapore	Butterworths Asia, SINGAPORE
USA	Butterworth Legal Publishers, AUSTIN, Texas; BOSTON, Massachusetts; CLEARWATER, Florida (D & S Publishers); ORFORD, New Hampshire (Equity Publishing); ST PAUL, Minnesota; and SEATTLE, Washington

A CIP Catalogue record for this book is available from the British Library.

ISBN 0 406 02453 7

Printed by Thomson Litho Ltd, East Kilbride, Scotland

PREFACE

The aim of this guide is to make available in a convenient form the statutory texts relating to the council tax. The guide is divided into three sections. The first consists of a short narrative, which describes the background to the introduction of the council tax and summarises the main provisions of the legislation. There then follows those sections of the Local Government and Finance Act 1992 which apply to Scotland, and the final section consists of the text of the statutory instruments made thereunder by 31 January 1993. The statutory texts are set out in their current form with the latest amendments incorporated in the appropriate palces, and the source of any such amendments indicated in the notes at the end of the sections.

The material in this guide is, in general, up-to-date as at 1 February 1993, but it has been possible to take account of some later developments.

Butterworth Law Publishers
Edinburgh
February 1993

CONTENTS

Introduction 1

Local Government Finance Act 1992 (c14)
Parts II, III, IV, V, Schedules 21

Council Tax (Valuation of Dwellings) (Scotland) Regulations 1992 ,
SI 1992/1329 99

Council Tax (Contents of Valuation Lists) (Scotland) Regulations 1992,
SI 1992/1330 101

Council Tax (Liability of Owners) (Scotland) Regulations 1992,
SI 1992/1331 102

Council Tax (Administration and Enforcement) (Scotland)
Regulations 1992, SI 1992/1332 104

Council Tax (Exempt Dwellings) (Scotland) Order 1992,
SI 1992/1333 129

Council Tax (Dwellings) (Scotland) Regulations 1992, SI 1992/1334 133

Council Tax (Reduction for Disabilities) (Scotland) Regulations
1992, SI 1992/1335 134

Council Tax (Discounts) (Scotland) Order 1992, SI 1992/1408 136

Council Tax (Discounts) (Scotland) Regulations 1992, SI 1992/1409 143

Council Tax Benefit (General) Regulations 1992, SI 1992/1814 145

Council Tax Benefit (Transitional) Order 1992, SI 1992/1909 227

Non-Domestic Rating (Payment of Interest) (Scotland) Regulations
1992, SI 1992/2184 230

Council Tax (Dwellings and Part Residential Subjects) (Scotland)
Regulations 1992, SI 1992/2955 235

Local Government (District Council Tax) (Scotland) Regulations 1992,
SI 1992/3024 239

Non-Domestic Rating Contributions (Scotland) Regulations 1992,
SI 1992/3061 241

Council Tax (Transitional Reduction Scheme) (Scotland)
Regulations 1993, SI 1993/277 247

Council Tax (Alteration of Lists and Appeals) (Scotland)
Regulations 1993, SI 1993/355 254

Council Tax (Deductions from Income Support)
Regulations 1993, SI 1993/494 271

COUNCIL TAX

The Local Government Finance Act 1992 ('the 1992 Act') introduces the second major upheaval in Scottish local government finance in four years. The measure follows on the consultation document 'A New Tax For Local Government' published in April 1991. The previous upheaval took place in April 1989 when the Abolition of Domestic Rates Etc (Scotland) Act 1987 ('the 1987 Act') introduced the system of community charges to replace domestic rates, along with a revised non-domestic rate, and revenue support grants to replace the former rate support grants. The 1987 Act and with it the community charges are abolished with effect from 1 April 1993 on which date the new system of local government finance comes into effect. The 1992 Act applies in both England and Wales and Scotland. Most of the Scottish provisions came into force on 6 March 1992 (royal assent) but, in general, their effects are postponed until the beginning of the financial year 1993/94. This introduction gives an outline of the effects of the 1992 Act, in so far as it applies in Scotland, and subordinate legislation made thereunder. It is not a comprehensive account of the legislation, but is intended to give readers a basic understanding of the legislation, and assist them to find quickly the provisions relevant to any queries they may have.

The 1992 Act is a radical but not a complete overhaul of local government finance. It deals primarily with revenue finance and the law relating to capital expenditure is unaffected by the 1992 Act. Housing finance has always been separately regulated from general capital and revenue expenditure[1] and that separation is unaffected by the 1992 Act.

Under the 1987 Act, the three main sources of finance for local government expenditure were (1) government grants; (2) the non-domestic rate; (3) the community charges. These are given in descending order of the amount of their contribution to local government finance. Income was also derived from specific grants for particular services and purposes, and from rents, fees and charges for services. Except in the case of housing authorities, the amount derived from rents and other charges was comparatively unimportant.

The main features of the new system which will operate in the financial year 1993/94 and subsequent financial years are as follows:

* A revenue support grant.
* Non-domestic rates levied primarily on business premises, the amounts being prescribed by the Secretary of State, and the income pooled and redistributed amongst local authorities.
* The abolition of community charges and their replacement with a council tax levied on domestic property.
* Council water and sewerage charges levied on both domestic and business consumers.

Again, the components of the system are listed in descending order of their contribution to financing local expenditure. The council water and sewerage charges are earmarked for those particular services. The other three components of the system go to finance all other non-housing revenue expenditure. Specific grants will continue for certain purposes, for example, police services. Fees and charges will

---

1   Housing (Scotland) Act 1987, Parts IX and X.

continue to be levied for certain services but, except in the case of housing authorities, will make a negligible contribution to expenditure.

The centre-piece of the reform is the council tax which is an attempt to marry a property tax with elements of a personal tax. The tax bill is for a particular property, but the amount is based partly on the value of the property, and partly on the number of people living in it. Although it is the council tax which has been the focus of most discussion about the 1992 Act, significant changes have also been made to the arrangements for making government grants to local authorities, and for collection and distribution of non-domestic rate income. Since the components of local government finance cannot be understood properly in isolation from each other, this introduction covers each of the main sources of finance which have been affected by the 1992 Act.

GOVERNMENT GRANTS

Pre-1989 Grant System

Central government grants form the largest portion of local authority income. The legal provisions for payment of grant contained in the 1992 Act are best explained by comparison with the former arrangements. Before financial year 1989/90 the Secretary of State each year made grants (known as rate support grants) to local authorities under the Local Government (Scotland) Act 1966 along with specific grants, the former making up the bulk of grant support. The legislation provided that the rate support grant would be composed of three elements - the needs element, the resources element, and the domestic element. The needs element was intended to allow for variations in local authority spending needs. The resources element was intended to compensate for the differences in the rateable resources available to local authorities (which arose from the uneven distribution of commercial and industrial development in Scotland). The domestic element was simply a subsidy to domestic rate payers reducing the rate poundage which would otherwise have been payable. The Secretary of State had powers to impose grant penalties on local authorities whose expenditure exceeded the limits proposed by central government.

Grants: 1989-1993

A new system of revenue support grants was introduced in 1989/90 by the Abolition of Domestic Rates Etc (Scotland) Act 1987. As before, support of housing expenditure was excluded, with those authorities requiring such support receiving it through the separate system of housing support grants. The total grant was divided into two rather than three elements, described in the Green Paper which preceded the legislation as a needs grant and a standard grant. The needs grant was the larger of the two and was divided amongst local authorities according to the Secretary of State's estimate of their spending needs. In practice the needs element was apportioned on the basis of the same client group assessments of expenditure need as were used in distributing the former rate support grant. The standard grant was distributed solely on the basis of population size with each local authority receiving a fixed sum per head of adult population.

There was nothing in this structure corresponding to the domestic element of the rate support grant because of the abolition of domestic rates by the 1987 Act. Similarly there was no provision for a resources element because of the introduction of the changes made to the rating of business property. However, the changes made to business rating were only a step in the direction of the government's overall policy aim of a uniform national business rate, and in the short term, the uneven distribution of commercial and industrial property continued to affect the non-domestic rate income of local authorities. Local authorities with a small non-domestic rate base were compensated for this in the apportionment of the needs element of the revenue support grant.

The Secretary of State had no powers directly equivalent to the powers to impose grant penalties that he had possessed under the 1966 Act, but had in effect more comprehensive control over levels of local authority expenditure through his power to determine the amount of grant support, impose a maximum non-domestic rate, and reduce community charges.

1992 Act: Revenue Support Grants and Non-Domestic Rate Income

Under the 1992 Act the process of making revenue support grants is combined with distribution of non-domestic rate income. The non-domestic rate is discussed in more detail below. For the purposes of this discussion, it is enough to note that all non-domestic rate income collected by local authorities in Scotland is 'pooled' and re-distributed by the Secretary of State. Beginning with 1993/94, the Secretary of State is empowered to make revenue support grants and distribute non-domestic rate (NDR) income to local authorities in each financial year.[2] The allocation of grant and NDR income is effected by a local government finance order which requires the approval of the House of Commons and may be made only with the consent of the Treasury and after consultation with local authorities. The Secretary of State's powers to fix the amounts of revenue support grant and NDR payable to local authorities are highly discretionary and unrestricted by statements of statutory purpose or criteria for their exercise, and he may at any time amend or revoke a local government finance order, or replace it with a different order. More detailed provision is, however, made for the 'pooling', as opposed to the actual distribution of NDR.[3] The procedure for 'pooling' NDR is described below.

The combined total of revenue support grant, specific grants, and NDR income for all Scottish local authorities is known as aggregate external finance (AEF). In practice the total amount available for grant support is divided into two parts. The larger part is allocated amongst local authorities on the basis of the number of band D equivalent properties (see discussion of council tax banding below) which is used as a proxy for population size. The distribution of NDR income is also in proportion to the resident population size. The smaller part of revenue support grant is distributed according to spending needs.

Separate provision is made for council tax grants which are intended to compensate local authorities for the amount of income they lose as a result of provision for reduced amounts of council tax liability and the council tax transitional relief scheme.[4] The scheme for transitional relief places a limit on the amount by which a household's council tax bill for the year 1993/94 exceeds its community charge bill for 1992/93.

---

2   Local Government Finance Act 1992, s 108 and Sch 12.
3   Ibid, Sch 12, paras 10-12.
4   Ibid, s 109.

NON-DOMESTIC RATES

Progress Towards a Unified Business Rate

The government's main policy objective since 1986 has been to alter the impact of local taxation on business by the creation of a uniform business rate under which the local tax burden would be effectively the same for all businesses no matter where their location.[5] The intention was not only to equalise the tax burden across Scottish local authority areas, but also to harmonise rate poundages and valuation levels with those in England. Achieving this objective posed a number of technical and political difficulties, and no attempt was made to achieve the desired transformation in the course of a single financial year. To achieve a truly uniform business rate it is necessary (1) to remove differences in the rate poundage fixed by local authorities; (2) to remove any differences in valuation practice which would otherwise result in properties with similar characteristics, being assessed at substantially different rateable values in different local government areas.

The initial step taken by the 1987 Act was 'index-linking' of business rates. Local authorities were still legally responsible for setting the rate, but could only do so subject to a maximum prescribed by the Secretary of State who used his powers to restrict permissible increases in rate poundages in 1989/90 to the rate of inflation as measured by the retail price index. The second step was the replacement of the provisions imposing index-linking by more open-ended provisions requiring the Secretary of State directly to prescribe the non-domestic rate for each Scottish local authority beginning with financial year 1990/91. That too was an interim measure and was intended to be replaced, after a transitional period, by a provision requiring the Secretary of State to prescribe a single non-domestic rate to be levied throughout Scotland. The transitional period had not ended by the time legislation was introduced to replace the community charge with the council tax, so equivalent provisions have been included in the 1992 Act.[6] The Secretary of State will, therefore, continue to prescribe non-domestic rates for each local authority annually, until such time as the provision enacting the unified business rate is brought into force. The process of harmonising rate poundages and valuation levels with those in England will continue under the provisions currently in force.

Pooling of Non-Domestic Rate Income

Under the 1987 Act, each local authority in Scotland received the actual amount of non-domestic rate income levied by it. NDR income was not pooled as it was in England and Wales. However, a similar economic outcome was achieved through adjusting the distribution of the revenue support grant. The 1992 Act introduces direct provision for pooling NDR income. On the one hand, the Secretary of State has, as described above, an *ex facie* unfettered discretion to distribute NDR income amongst local authorities.[7] The distribution is in practice in proportion to the size of the resident population. On the other hand, a detailed procedure is laid down for the ingathering of NDR receipts by the Secretary of State into the central 'pool'.[8] The broad effect of these complex provisions is summarised below.

5   *Paying for Local Government*, Cmnd 9714 (1986).
6   Local Government Finance Act 1992, s 110(1) and (2), respectively substituting new s 7A in Local Government (Scotland) Act 1975, and providing for future substitution for that section of new section 7B.
7   Ibid, s 108 and Sch 12, paras 1-5.
8   Ibid, s 108 and Sch 12, paras 6-12.

The Secretary of State is required to keep a non-domestic rating account to which NDR collected by local authorities is credited, and from which NDR income distributed to local authorities is debited. Before the beginning of each financial year, the Secretary of State calculates the amount of NDR he expects each local authority to contribute to the non-domestic rating account in accordance with rules laid down by regulations,[9] and notifies them of that amount. The local authority is obliged to pay that amount (the 'provisional amount') to him. After the end of the financial year, the local authority calculates the amount of NDR it has collected and notifies that amount to the Secretary of State. If they have collected more than the provisional amount they must pay the excess to the Secretary of State. If they have collected less than the provisional amount, the Secretary of State repays the difference to the local authority. Provision is made for certification of the amounts collected by the Commission for Local Authority Accounts in Scotland and, if it disagrees with the amount notified by the local authority appropriate adjustments are made to the amounts payable to or repayable by the Secretary of State.

Separation of Rateable From Non-Rateable Property

When the community charge was introduced domestic rates were abolished, but rating continued for non-domestic subjects. With effect from 1 April 1993 the community charge is to be replaced by the council tax,[10] and rating continues for non-domestic subjects. It is necessary, therefore, to divide property into categories according to whether it is subject to the council tax, subject to non-domestic rates, or exempt from both. The general policy underlying the 1992 Act is to make domestic property subject to the council tax and other property subject to rates. The aim behind the policy is to ensure that all adults resident in an area (subject to exemptions and rebates) contribute to local tax revenue through the household of which they form part. However, because not all adults live in conventional households or conventional houses, a simple distinction between houses and commercial property is not possible. Complex provisions are, therefore, necessary to achieve the appropriate incidence of the different forms of local taxation. These provisions are discussed in more detail in the next section of this introduction which deals with the coverage of the council tax.

The categories of property which will be subject to non-domestic rates from April 1993 are broadly similar to those subject to rates from 1989 to 1993 under the previous system, but there are a number of changes. The most significant change of policy is in relation to certain types of communal living accommodation which had been subject to the collective community charge, but will instead be subject to rates, and certain types of commercial properties which had been divided into domestic and non-domestic parts for the purposes of the community charge legislation.

The concept used in the 1992 Act to distinguish rateable from non-rateable property is that of the 'dwelling' (see below). Dwellings are not to be entered in the valuation roll for the financial year 1993/94 or any subsequent year, and any dwellings entered in the valuation roll immediately before 1 April 1993 shall be deleted from the roll with effect from that date.[11] In general, dwellings which were not entered in the roll between 1989 and 1993 because they were domestic subjects for the purposes of the community charge legislation will remain off the roll. However, if such a property does not satisfy the definition of dwelling in the 1992 Act they will be entered in the roll with effect from 1 April 1993. Where any subjects cease to be

---

9   The Non-Domestic Rating Contributions (Scotland) Regulations 1992, SI 1992/3061.
10 Local Government Finance Act 1992, Part II and s 100.
11 Ibid, s 73.

dwellings after 1 April 1993 they must be entered in the valuation roll. Similarly, subjects which become dwellings after 1 April 1993 must be deleted from the roll.

The Assessor remains responsible for keeping the valuation roll up to date, and existing provisions for appeal remain in force. A proprietor, tenant, or occupier aggrieved by the entry of a property in the valuation roll may appeal to a valuation appeal committee.[12] In addition, a proprietor, tenant, or occupier aggrieved by the entry in the valuation roll, or amendment to, or deletion of an apportionment note in relation to part-residential subjects, may appeal to a valuation appeal committee.[13] Such appeals follow the procedure laid down under the Local Government (Scotland) Act 1975. Appeals disputing council tax liability follow a slightly different procedure under the 1992 Act (see below).

Valuation of Non-Domestic Subjects

The general body of valuation law remains in force in so far as it affects non-domestic subjects. A number of technical amendments have been required as a result of the introduction of the council tax, and the opportunity of the 1992 Act has been used to make other changes to valuation law, including provision for payment of interest on rates paid in error.[14]

Statutory and Other References to Rateable Values

The 1987 Act which abolished domestic rates contained provisions designed to render intelligible, references in deeds, legal documents, and statutes, to rateable values and other concepts in valuation law. Similar provisions have been included in the 1992 Act which repeal and replace the earlier provisions, and include a power to prescribe by regulations new meanings for statutory references to rates, rateable values, or other factors concerned with valuation or rating.[15]

THE COUNCIL TAX

As noted above, the council tax is primarily a property tax but includes elements of a personal tax. It occupies the same role in the new system of local government finance as the community charge did in the 1989-1993 system ie it is the element which balances the books, although it finances only a small portion of local expenditure. The main features of the council tax may be summarised as follows:

*   The council tax is levied on domestic properties and the tax is based on their value.
*   Unlike the rating system the valuation is based on bands of value rather than exact values. The amount of tax varies according to the band in which the house is valued.
*   There is a single bill per household, and the person liable to pay will be determined by the circumstances of its occupation.
*   Discounts are available to some taxpayers depending on the composition and characteristics of the household.

12   Local Government (Scotland) Act 1975, s 3.
13   Ibid, as applied by Local Government Finance Act 1992, s 72(8) and Sch 5, para 11.
14   Local Government Finance Act 1992, s 110(4), substituting new section 9A in Local Government (Scotland) Act 1975, and the Non-Domestic Rates (Payment of Interest) (Scotland) Regulations 1992, SI 1992/2184.
15   Ibid, s 111.

The revenue derived from the council tax supports local expenditure generally, however special provision is made for water and sewerage services. Expenditure on water is to be funded from a separate council water charge levied on the supply of water to dwellings and the non-domestic water rate levied on the supply of water to other property. Expenditure on sewerage is to be met from the general council tax and the non-domestic sewerage rate. There is no separate charge levied for sewerage services for domestic property.

Each local authority sets a council tax. Thus, in mainland Scotland, persons liable to pay the council tax will pay both a regional council tax and a district council tax. In Islands Council areas a single islands council tax is payable.[16]

Fixing the Level of the Council Tax

The expenses of local authorities in discharging their statutory functions, so far as not met from other sources, are to be met out of the council tax. Local authorities must, therefore, set a council tax sufficient to balance their books. The tax must be set for each financial year before 11 March of the preceding financial year.[17] Thus, the council taxes for 1993/94 were required to be set before 11 March 1993. This is the only element of local revenue funding which is controlled by local authorities themselves. Decisions by the Secretary of State on the level of grant support, and the distribution of NDR income are, therefore, crucial factors in determining the amount of the council tax. The scope of local autonomy is, however, further narrowed by the provisions which permit the Secretary of State to reduce the council tax actually set by a local authority (subject to Parliamentary approval) if he 'is satisfied ... that the total estimated expenses ... of a local authority are excessive or that an increase in those expenses is excessive'.[18] These provisions are similar to those in earlier legislation providing for the reduction of rates and community charge.

The council tax for an area is set by fixing the amount of tax payable in respect of a property in valuation band D. The amounts of tax appropriate to the other bands are than calculated in accordance with the proportion specified in section 74 of the 1992 Act (see below).

Valuation Bands and Amounts of Tax

For the purposes of the council tax properties are placed in one of eight valuation bands as specified below[19]:

Range of Values	Band
not more than £27000	A
£27001 - £35000	B
£35001 - £45000	C
£45001 - £58000	D
£58001 - £80000	E
£80001 - £106000	F
£106001 - £212000	G
more than £212000	H

The amounts of council tax for properties in these bands are in the proportion - 6: 7: 8: 9: 11: 13: 15: 18.[20] If, for example, a local authority were to set a council tax of £180 for properties in band D, the range of tax liability would be as shown below:

16 Local Government Finance Act 1992, s 70.
17 Ibid, s 93.
18 Ibid, s 94 and Sch 7.
19 Ibid, s 74.
20 Ibid.

Band	Council Tax
A	£120
B	£140
C	£160
D	£180
E	£220
F	£260
G	£300
H	£360

Other bands and proportions may be substituted by order. Liability is determined on a daily basis and, where a person is liable for only part of a financial year, he pays an amount proportionate to his period of liability. Thus, a person who was liable for 73 days would pay 20% of the appropriate annual amount.[21]

Valuation Lists and Assessor's Powers

The calculation of council tax liability is based on the value of dwellings as shown in the valuation lists made up under the 1992 Act. The local assessor for each regional and islands council area must compile and maintain a list for that council showing each dwelling in the area, the valuation band which applies to it and such other information as may be prescribed.[22] The valuation lists come into force on 1 April 1993. In order to compile the list the assessor must carry out a valuation of 'such of the dwellings in his area as he considers necessary or expedient' for the purpose of placing all properties in valuation bands. The valuation is carried out by reference to 1 April 1991 and is carried out according to prescribed assumptions which include that the valuation is at market value, and that the dwelling was in a reasonable state of repair.[23] The valuation must also be in accordance with such directions as may be given by the Commissioners of Inland Revenue.

There is provision for alteration of the lists,[24] and provision for determining the date at which new dwellings should be entered in the lists.[25] In order to carry out his functions, the assessor has power to enter property to carry out a valuation,[26] and has access to any information available to him under the Valuation Acts, and any information available to the community charges registration officer, or to the electoral registration officer.[27] He may require information from local authorities and public sector landlords, and levying authorities must pass on such information as comes to their attention in the exercise of their functions as they consider would assist the assessor in carrying out his functions.[28] He may also require any person who is or has been an owner or occupier of any dwelling in his area to supply information specified in a notice which he believes would assist him in carrying out his functions[29]. Failure to supply on request such information as is under a persons possession or control, and knowingly or recklessly making a false statement in response are offences.

---

[21] Local Government Finance Act 1992, ss 71 and 78.
[22] Ibid, s 84.
[23] Ibid, s 86 and Council Tax (Valuation of Dwellings) (Scotland) Regulations 1992, SI 1992/1329.
[24] Ibid, s 87.
[25] Ibid, s 83 and Sch 6.
[26] Ibid, s 89.
[27] Ibid, s 90.
[28] Ibid.
[29] Ibid.

Persons generally have certain rights of access to information gathered in connection with the making up of valuation lists.[30]

Liability to Pay Council Tax

Determination of liability to pay council tax has two aspects. The first issue is whether a particular property is a 'chargeable dwelling' ie subject to council tax. If it is accepted that a property is a chargeable dwelling, the second issue is that of who is liable to pay the tax.

Dwellings

The concept used in the 1992 Act to determine which property is subject to the council tax is that of the 'dwelling'. For the purposes of the 1992 Act 'dwelling' means 'any lands and heritages - (i) which consist of one or more dwelling houses with any garden, yard, garage, outhouse or pertinent belonging to and occupied with such dwelling house or dwelling houses ...' which but for this legislation would be entered separately in the valuation roll.[31] It does not include a caravan which is not a person's sole or main residence. Such a caravan would be valued for rating along with the caravan site. By implication, a caravan which is a person's sole or main residence is a dwelling and subject to the council tax. The expression 'dwelling house' is not further defined but some help in defining its meaning in cases of doubt may be gained from case law under the Valuation Acts. However, the Secretary of State's powers to vary the definition of domestic subjects by inclusion or exclusion have been used to prescribe the status of certain classes of property which might otherwise have caused difficulties of interpretation.[32]

The following are dwellings and, therefore, subject to the council tax (unless specifically exempted):

(1) private car parking and storage premises whose use is ancillary to, and which are used exclusively in connection with, a dwelling;
(2) bed and breakfast accommodation operated on a commercial basis by a person living there for letting to not more than six persons per night;
(3) student halls of residence which include shared facilities;
(4) military barracks;
(5) those parts of communal residential establishments with shared facilities for residents ie hostels, nursing homes, private hospitals, and residential care homes, which are used as living accommodation for employees. Those parts in which the ordinary residents live are not dwellings, and will be entered in the valuation roll, and be subject to rates;[33]
(6) school boarding accommodation.

The following are *not* dwellings[34] and, therefore, are not subject to the council tax, but may be subject to rates:

(1) huts, sheds, and bothies which are not living accommodation;
(2) certain self-catering holiday accommodation;

---

30 Local Government Finance Act 1992, ss 91-92.
31 Ibid, s 72.
32 Ibid, s 72(2), and the Council Tax (Dwellings) (Scotland) Regulations 1992, SI 1992/1334, and the Council Tax (Dwellings and Part Residential Subjects) (Scotland) Regulations 1992, SI 1992/2955.
33 Local Government Finance Act 1992, s 73(6).
34 Ibid, s 72(2) and the Council Tax (Dwellings and Part Residential Subjects) (Scotland) Regulations 1992, SI 1992/2955.

(3)   women's refuges (except for any part comprising accommodation for employees who live on the premises). A part of a women's refuge which does not fall
within the exclusion because it is living accommodation is likely to be treated
as a dwelling and, therefore, subject to council tax.

One of the difficulties in categorising property for the purposes of local taxation
is that much property although held on a single title is neither exclusively domestic,
nor exclusively non-domestic in use. One way round this difficulty is to divide such
a property into parts according to use and enter part only in the valuation roll. This
is the strategy adopted for private hospitals and nursing homes. Another approach
is to treat the property as a single valuation unit, but to apportion the value as between the residential and the non-residential use. The latter approach has been used
in relation to properties referred to in the 1992 Act as 'part residential subjects'.[35]
Essentially the same concept was employed for similar purposes in the community
charge legislation. Such subjects are rated but only on the portion of their value attributable to the non-residential use, and the apportionment is indicated on the valuation
roll by means of an apportionment note. The residential part of part residential subjects is a dwelling and will be liable to the council tax, unless exempt. The residential
part of any premises which had been apportioned under section 45 of the Water (Scotland) Act 1980 as at 1 April 1989 is also to be considered a dwelling.

'Part-residential subjects' are defined as 'lands and heritages which are used partly
as the sole or main residence of any person...' other than subjects which are technically dwellings and prescribed classes of subjects.[36] An example of subjects fitting
the general definition would be a hotel which accommodated both temporary guests
and long-term residents. The following have been prescribed as *not* being part-residential subjects:[37] (1) those parts of hostels, nursing homes, private hospitals, and
residential care homes, which are used as living accommodation for residents rather
than employees; (2) those parts of women's refuges used as temporary accommodation by the persons seeking refuge rather than as permanent accommodation for
staff.

Chargeable dwellings

The council tax is levied on 'dwellings' as defined in the 1992 Act. The precise
meaning of 'dwelling' has already been discussed. However, not all dwellings are
chargeable dwellings, as the Secretary of State may prescribe by order classes of
exempt dwellings. The classes prescribed as exempt from council tax are given below. In some cases the exemption is of specified duration. In other cases it is of in-
definite duration. For the sake of simplicity, persons who would have to pay council
tax but for the provisions of the relevant order are referred to as 'liable taxpayers'.
The exempted classes are:[38]

(1)   **Newly built dwellings.** Unoccupied and unfurnished dwellings whose effective date of first entry in the valuation list is after 1 April 1993 - for up to six
months.

---

[35]   Local Government Finance Act 1992, s 72(8) and Sch 5.
[36]   Ibid, s 99(1).
[37]   Ibid, and the Council Tax (Dwellings and Part Residential Subjects) (Scotland) Regulations 1992,
SI 1992/2955.
[38]   Local Government Finance Act 1992, s 72(6), and the Council Tax (Exempt Dwellings) (Scotland)
Order 1992, SI 1992/1333.

(2) **Newly built dwellings.** Unoccupied and unfurnished dwellings first entered in the valuation list with effect from 1 April 1993 having been completed recently before then - for up to six months from when potential for liability arose.

(3) **Disrepair etc.** Dwellings which are incapable of, and are not being lived in, because they are being structurally repaired, improved or reconstructed.

(4) **Dwellings owned by charities.** Unoccupied dwellings for which the liable taxpayer is a charitable body which had been occupied to further the objects of the charity - for up to six months.

(5) **Unoccupied and unfurnished dwellings.** Unoccupied and unfurnished dwellings which have been unoccupied for less than six months.

(6) **Prisoners, personal care etc.** Unoccupied dwellings if the former resident is the liable taxpayer and is no longer in occupation because he is in detention, or receiving treatment or personal care, or providing personal care to another.

(7) **Deceased persons.** Dwellings forming part of the estate of a deceased person up to six months from the grant of confirmation provided the estate would otherwise have the sole liability and the house is not the sole or main residence of any person.

(8) **Uninhabitable dwellings.** Dwellings occupation of which is prohibited by law or as a result of the exercise of statutory powers.

(9) **Dwellings awaiting demolition.** Dwellings owned by public sector housing authorities and kept unoccupied with a view to demolition.

(10) **Ministers' houses.** Dwellings which are not the sole or main residence of any person and are kept available by religious bodies as official residences for ministers of religion.

(11) **Students' houses.** Dwellings occupied by at least one student provided they are not the sole or main residence of any person who is not a student.

(12) **Unoccupied students' houses.** Unoccupied dwellings last occupied by students provided not the sole or main residence of any non-student - for up to four months.

(13) **Student as liable taxpayer.** Dwellings which are not the sole or main residence of any person and each liable taxpayer is a student.

(14) **Repossessed houses.** Dwellings which are not the sole or main residence of any person, of which the creditor in a heritable security has taken possession.

(15) **Agricultural workers.** Unoccupied and unfurnished dwellings on agricultural land last used in connection with such land.

(16) **'Trial' sheltered housing.** Certain dwellings which are not the sole or main residence of any person located in complexes of sheltered housing, and available for trial by disabled persons.

(17) **Student halls of residence.** Dwellings which comprise or are part of student halls of residence.

(18) **Armed forces accommodation.** Dwellings which are armed forces accommodation owned by the Secretary of State for Defence.

(19) **Young persons' houses.** Dwellings which are the sole or main residence only of persons under the age of 18.

(20) **Dwellings occupied with other dwellings.** Unoccupied dwellings which are either (a) part of premises which include another dwelling; or (b) situated within the curtilage of another dwelling, if the liable taxpayer has his sole or main residence in the other dwelling, and the unoccupied dwellings are difficult to let separately from the taxpayer's residence.

(21) **Lock-ups and domestic storage.** Private parking and storage premises whose use is ancillary to, and which are used exclusively in connection with, a dwelling.

(22) **Bankruptcy.** Dwellings which are not the sole or main residence of any person an interest in which is vested in a permanent trustee in bankruptcy where the trustee is the only liable taxpayer.

Persons liable

The person liable to pay the council tax on any dwelling is the person who falls into the first of the following categories to apply:[39]

(a) a resident owner of the whole or part of the dwelling
(b) a resident tenant of the whole or part of the dwelling
(c) a resident statutory tenant, resident statutory assured tenant, or resident secure tenant of the whole or part of the dwelling
(d) a resident sub-tenant of the whole or part of the dwelling
(e) a resident of the dwelling
(f) any of the following: (i) the sub-tenant of the whole or part of the dwelling under a sub-lease for a minimum term of six months; (ii) the tenant under a lease for a minimum term of six months, of any part of the dwelling which is not subject to a sub-lease granted for a minimum term of six months; (iii) the owner of any part of the dwelling which is not subject to a lease granted for a minimum term of six months

Thus, if there is no resident owner, it is necessary to consider whether there is a resident tenant. If there is neither a resident owner, nor a resident tenant, it is necessary to consider whether there is a resident statutory tenant, resident statutory assured tenant, or resident secure tenant, and so forth. Category (f) will be effective to determine liability in relation to dwellings which are not the main residence of any person. The liable person will be the owner if he has not granted a lease of the dwelling of at least six months duration. If such a lease has been granted, the liable person will be the tenant, unless he has granted a sub-lease of the dwelling of at least six months duration. If such a tenant has granted a sub-lease of at least six months duration, the sub-tenant will be the liable person.

Where two or more people fall into the first category to apply they are jointly and severally liable, unless one of them qualifies for the discount for the severely mentally impaired. Where only one of two spouses is liable under the preceding rules, the other is nonetheless jointly and severally liable where he or she is also a resident of the dwelling.[40] The same rule applies to unmarried persons who 'are living together as husband and wife'. Again, this rule does not apply so as to make liable a person who is severely mentally impaired.

The Secretary of State may make regulations using a different basis for attaching liability to prescribed classes of dwellings than that just described.[41] Regulations have been made prescribing the following classes of dwellings:[42] (1) residential care homes, nursing homes, private hospitals and hostels; (2) dwellings occupied by religious communities; (3) houses in multiple occupation; (4) dwellings occupied by domestic staff; (5) official residences of ministers of religion. In respect of the first four classes, the owner of the dwelling is liable. In respect of the fifth class, the person responsible for the remuneration of the minister is liable. The Secretary of State may also make regulations giving levying authorities the option of using a

---

[39] Local Government Finance Act 1992, s 75.
[40] Ibid, s 77.
[41] Ibid, s 76.
[42] The Council Tax (Liability of Owners) (Scotland) Regulations 1992, SI 1992/1331.

different basis for attaching liability to all dwellings in prescribed classes. If the option is exercised, the owner or other specified person is liable. If the option is not exercised liability is determined according to the rules given above.[43]

Meaning of resident

The 1992 Act defines 'resident', in relation to dwellings, as a person of at least 18 years of age who 'has his sole or main residence in the dwelling ...' and cognate expressions are construed accordingly.[44] The interpretation of this definition will be important not only in determining who is liable to pay council tax in respect of a dwelling, but also in determining whether there is any liability in respect of a dwelling, since many categories of exemption utilise the same concept of residence. Whereas a person may have more than one residence, it is clear that he can have only one main residence. Although strictly speaking not relevant, case law built up under the 1987 Act may be useful in predicting how 'sole or main residence' will be interpreted by the courts. It is probably necessary however, to distinguish cases relating to liability for the personal community charge, from cases relating to liability for the standard community charge, with the latter being more relevant.

Discounts and reduced amounts

In many cases liability to pay council tax is for an amount less than the full amount appropriate to a property's value. There is separate provision for discounts and other reductions. The amount of discount is 25% or 50% depending on the circumstances, although different percentages may be prescribed in substitution for these. Eligibility for discounts is calculated on a daily basis. The following discounts apply:[45]

1. *Sole residents.* There is a 25% discount where there is only one adult resident of a chargeable dwelling, or where all the residents except one are disregarded persons (see below).
2. *Dwellings without residents.* There is a 50% discount where no adult has his sole or main residence in the chargeable dwelling.
3. *Dwellings with only disregarded residents.* There is a 50% discount where all the residents of a chargeable dwelling are disregarded persons (see below).

The following persons are disregarded for the purposes of discount:

1. Persons in detention
2. The severely mentally impaired
3. Persons for whom child benefit is payable
4. Students, student nurses, apprentices, and youth training trainees
5. Hospital patients
6. Patients in residential care homes, nursing homes, private hospitals and hostels
7. Care workers providing care and support to others
8. Residents of hostels and night shelters for the homeless
9. Members of international headquarters and defence organisations
10. Members of religious communities
11. Certain school leavers for a limited period

---

[43] Local Government Finance Act 1992, s 76.
[44] Ibid, s 99(1).
[45] Ibid, s 79 and Sch 1.

The precise conditions under which persons in the above categories are disregarded are specified in Schedule 1 to the 1992 Act and in subordinate legislation.[46] Those under 18 are also ignored in determining the number of residents because they do not satisfy the statutory definition of 'resident'.

The Secretary of State has power to make regulations providing for a reduction in the amount of council tax payable which may be in addition to any discounts available. The power may be exercised in a variety of contexts. It has already been used to reduce council tax on houses specially adapted for the disabled.[47] The taxpayer(s) benefit from the reduction of the amount of tax to that eligible on houses in the band below the band within which the house has actually been valued ie if the house was valued in band D, the tax payable will be the amount for a band C house. There is, however, no reduction for houses in band A. It will also be used to give transitional relief which will limit the increase in household tax bills as compared to the community charge levied in 1992/93.

Administration and Appeals

The duty of classifying property into the statutory groups falls on the assessor. Other information relevant to quantifying liability is collected by the finance departments of levying authorities. If persons are aggrieved by decisions affecting their council tax liability they will generally have a right of appeal.[48] Firstly, a person aggrieved by a decision that a dwelling is a chargeable dwelling, may appeal to a valuation appeal committee. Secondly, a person may appeal against the decision that he is the person liable to pay council tax in respect of a dwelling.[49] In addition, a person may appeal against any calculation made by a levying authority of the amount of his liability. In order to make an appeal of either kind, [50] a person first serves notice on the levying authority which states the nature and grounds of his grievance. The appeal can then proceed once the person has received written notification from the levying authority stating that they believe his grievance is not well founded, or that steps have been taken to deal with it, but he is still aggrieved. If the aggrieved person has received no such notice he may continue the appeal two months after service of his notice on the levying authority.

An interested person may 'appeal' against the valuation band assigned to a property, but the process must be begun by his making a proposal for alteration of the valuation list.[51] The assessor will alter the valuation list if he thinks that the proposal is well founded. If he does not think the proposal is well founded, and the proposal is not withdrawn, he must refer the disagreement within six months to the local valuation panel and an appeal will be heard by the valuation appeal committee.

46   The Council Tax (Discounts) (Scotland) Order 1992, SI 1992/1408, and the the Council Tax (Discounts) (Scotland) Regulations 1992, SI 1992/1409.
47   Local Government Finance Act 1992, s 80, and the Council Tax (Reductions for Disabilities) (Scotland) Regulations 1992, SI 1992/1335.
48   Local Government Finance Act 1992, ss 81, 82, 87 and the Council Tax (Alteration of Lists and Appeals) (Scotland) Regulations 1993, SI 1993/355.
49   Ibid.
50   Ibid.
51   Ibid, s 72 and the Council Tax (Alteration of Lists and Appeals) (Scotland) Regulations 1993, SI 1993/355.

Levying, Collection and Payment of Council Tax

The levying authorities for the council tax are the regional and islands councils. It is their duty to collect the charges and, in the case of the district councils, distribute the appropriate amounts to the districts in their areas.[52] To that end, the regional council must, in relation to each financial year, estimate the amount that would be produced by each of the district council taxes for that year in its region, and notify each district council of the estimate made in relation to that district. The regional councils must make payment on account, in accordance with prescribed arrangements, of the council tax due to the district in the course of the financial year. If the amount actually produced in a district by the council tax differs from the amount paid on account by the regional council as a result of its estimate, an adjustment is effected after the end of the financial year.

Levying authorities have extensive powers to require information from persons for the purpose of identifying who are liable persons in relation to dwellings.[53] They have separate powers to require information from public bodies, and district registrars must supply to them particulars of deaths. They must take reasonable steps to ascertain whether dwellings are exempt dwellings and notify the persons concerned that dwellings are exempt. A liable person who has reason to believe that a dwelling is not entitled to an exemption that has been notified to him, or is only entitled to an exemption of shorter duration than that notified must notify the levying authority of that belief in writing within 21 days. Failure to do so attracts a civil penalty of £50. They must also calculate chargeable amounts, and where these are subject to discounts notify the liable person of the amount of discount and the basis on which it has been calculated. A person who has reason to believe that he is not entitled to a discount that he has been given, or has been given too large a discount, must notify the levying authority of that belief in writing within 21 days. Failure to do so attracts a civil penalty of £50. A person who disputes the amount, but not the fact of liability, may appeal to a valuation appeal committee.

The process of billing[54] for the council tax begins with the issue of demand notices containing prescribed matters. These must be issued in respect of all chargeable dwellings as soon as practicable after the amounts of council tax have been set. The normal method of payment is by ten (approximately) equal instalments, but the levying authority may agree with the liable person a different manner of payment. The authority is empowered to accept payment by a single lump sum, and to accept a reduced amount in such a case. If payments of instalments are late, the liable person may lose the right to pay by instalments. Civil penalties may be collected as if they were part of a person's liability to pay council tax, or by issue of a separate notice requiring payment of the penalty. A person aggrieved by the imposition of a civil penalty may appeal to a valuation appeal committee.

Unpaid arrears of council tax and unpaid civil penalties may be recovered by diligence following decree in an action of payment, or diligence authorised by a summary warrant.[55] To obtain a summary warrant, the local authority must make an application to the sheriff accompanied by a certificate containing prescribed particulars. If this is done, the sheriff must grant the warrant which authorises recovery of the unpaid tax along with a ten per cent surcharge by any of the following diligences: (a) a poinding and sale; (b) an earnings arrestment; (c) an arrestment and action of

52 Ibid, ss 93-96.
53 Ibid, s 97 and Sch 2, and the Council Tax (Administration and Enforcement) (Scotland) Regulations 1992, SI 1992/ 1332.
54 Ibid, and Sch 3.
55 Ibid, s 97(5) and Sch 8.

furthcoming or sale. The same diligences are available following an action of payment. Sheriff officers' fees and outlays in connection with the execution of a summary warrant are recoverable from the debtor. Where a summary warrant or decree for payment has been granted, the debtor comes under a duty to supply relevant information to the levying authority until such time as the whole amount due is paid. Regulations may provide for the deduction of social benefit at source from income support claimants who are in arrears, as an alternative to diligence.

Council Tax Benefit

For many years before April 1989 there was a system of rate rebates for those on low incomes. Latterly, this operated through the housing benefit system. From April 1990, a system of community charge benefit was introduced with similar purposes. With effect from 1 April 1993, a new benefit, known as council tax benefit, will provide relief for those on low income.[56] Although technically a benefit, in general it will be payable in the form of a rebate on the amount due to the levying authority. The benefit is administered by levying authorities. There are two sorts of rebate - 'ordinary' council tax benefit and 'second adult rebate'. The former is based on the income of the taxpayer. The latter applies where the taxpayer does not qualify for the ordinary benefit on income grounds, but there is another adult resident in the property who is on a low income.

'Ordinary' council tax benefit

The maximum amount of benefit is 100% of the council tax due, and will be available to those whose income does not exceed amounts equivalent to the applicable amounts for income support. As income rises above this level, benefit is withdrawn at the rate of 20 pence for each additional pound of weekly income.

Second adult rebate

This benefit is claimed by and paid to the liable taxpayer and provides a 25% rebate where the second adult's income is at or below income support level, a 15% rebate where the second adult's income is under £100 per week, or a 7.5% rebate where the second adult's income is £100-130 per week. The conditions are very restrictive and include that the second adult must stay there as their sole or main residence, and must not be jointly liable for council tax *in any way*, and the relationship be on a non-commercial basis, and no-one else be paying the liable taxpayer rent to live in his house.

Detailed regulations prescribe the exact conditions of entitlement to both benefits.[57]

Council Water Charge and Charges for Sewerage

Although local services generally (except housing) are funded from the combination of council tax, non-domestic rate and government grants, special provision is made for water and sewerage. Both of these are the responsibility of regional and islands councils. Before April 1989 water supply was funded from three sources: metering, the public water rate, and a separate domestic water rate. For the years

---

56   Local Government Finance Act 1992, s 103 and Sch 9, amending the Social Security Contributions and Benefits Act 1992, and the Social Security Administration Act 1992; the Council Tax Benefit (General) Regulations 1992, SI 1992/1814; the Council Tax Benefit (Transitional) Order 1992, SI 1992/1909.
57   Ibid.

from 1989/90 to 1992/93, water supply was funded from metering, three community water charges, and a non-domestic water rate. Further changes are made by the 1992 Act. For 1993/94 and subsequent financial years, metering will continue and will be the main method of charging business consumers. The remainder of the costs of water supply, in so far as not met from other sources, will be met from the council water charge, and from the non-domestic water rate.

The council water charge is payable in respect of any dwelling which is not an exempt dwelling which receives a public water supply (unless supplied wholly by meter), and will be payable by the person liable for the council tax in respect of that dwelling.[58] The general provisions for assessment, collection, and payment of council tax apply also to the council water charge.[59] The non-domestic water rate is due from non-domestic ratepayers who have a water supply to their premises, unless wholly supplied by meter.

Sewerage services are treated differently both from water supply and other services. Expenditure on sewerage, in so far as not otherwise met, is met from the council tax, and the non-domestic sewerage rate. The non-domestic sewerage rate is levied on non-domestic ratepayers whose drains or sewers are connected with public sewers or public sewage treatment works.[60] There is no separate council sewerage charge.

Tom Mullen
Senior Lecturer in Public Law
University of Glasgow

---

58   Ibid, s 107 and Sch 11.
59   Ibid, and the Council Water Charge (Scotland) Regulations 1992, SI 1992/1203.
60   Local Government Finance Act 1992, s 107 and Sch 11.

Local Government Finance Act 1992 (c14)

ARRANGEMENT OF SECTIONS

* * *

PART II. COUNCIL TAX: SCOTLAND

Preliminary

70. Council tax in respect of dwellings. 23
71. Liability to be determined on a daily basis. 23

Chargeable dwellings

72. Dwellings chargeable to council tax. 24
73. Alterations to valuation roll. 25
74. Different amounts for dwellings in different valuation bands. 26

Liability to tax

75. Persons liable to pay council tax. 26
76. Liability in prescribed cases. 27
77. Liability of spouses. 28

Amounts of tax payable

78. Basic amounts payable. 29
79. Discounts. 29
80. Reduced amounts. 30

Appeals

81. Appeal to valuation appeal committee. 31
82. Appeal procedure. 32

New dwellings

83. Completion of new dwellings. 33

Valuation lists

84. Compilation and maintenance of valuation lists. 33
85. Distribution of lists. 34
86. Valuation of dwellings. 35
87. Alteration of lists. 36
88. Compilation and maintenance of new lists. 37

Valuation lists: supplemental

89. Power of entry. 38

90. Information about properties. 38
91. Information about lists. 39
92. Information about proposals and appeals. 40

Setting of the tax

93. Setting of council tax. 41
94. Substituted and reduced settings. 41
95. District council tax: setting and collection. 42
96. Information. 43

Levying and collection of the tax

97. Levying and collection of council tax. 44

Miscellaneous and supplemental

98. Information required by Secretary of State. 44
99. Interpretation of Part II. 45

PART III. COMMUNITY CHARGES

100. Abolition of community charges. 46

* * *

PART IV. MISCELLANEOUS

Social security

103. Council tax benefit. 46

* * *

Scottish provisions

107. Water and sewerage charges. 47
108. Payments to local authorities by Secretary of State. 47
109. Council tax grants. 47
110. Amendments to the 1975 Act in relation to non-domestic rates. 48
111. Statutory and other references to rateable values etc. 50
112. Council tax and community charges: restrictions on voting. 52

PART V. SUPPLEMENTAL

113. Orders and regulations. 53
114. Power to make supplementary provision. 54
115. Financial provisions. 54
116. Interpretation: general. 54
117. Minor and consequential amendments and repeals. 55
118. Savings and transitional provisions. 55
119. Short title, commencement and extent. 56

SCHEDULES:

Schedule 1—Persons Disregarded for Purposes of Discount. 57
Schedule 2—Administration. 61
Schedule 3—Penalties. 70
Schedule 4—Enforcement: England and Wales. 72
Schedule 5—Part Residential Subjects: Scotland. 72
Schedule 6—Completion of New Buildings: Scotland. 74
Schedule 7—Reduction of Council Tax: Scotland. 75
Schedule 8—Enforcement: Scotland. 76
Schedule 9—Social Security: Council Tax Benefit. 78

* * *

Schedule 11—Water and Sewerage Charges: Scotland. 84
    Part I—Charges for Water Services. 84
    Part II—Charges for Sewerage Services. 86
    Part III—Miscellaneous Provisions. 89
    Part IV—Amendments to the 1980 Act. 89
Schedule 12—Payments to Local Authorities by Secretary of State: Scotland. . 92
    Part I—Payments to Local Authorities. 92
    Part II—Non-Domestic Rating Accounts. 93
    Part III-Contribution. 94

* * *

PART II. COUNCIL TAX: SCOTLAND

Preliminary

70. Council tax in respect of dwellings

(1) In respect of the financial year 1993-94 and each subsequent financial year, each local authority in Scotland shall impose a tax which—

  (a) shall be known as—

      (i)   the regional council tax;
      (ii) the islands council tax; or
      (iii) the district council tax,

  depending upon which local authority impose it; and

  (b) shall be payable in respect of dwellings situated in that authority's area.

(2) The expenses of a local authority in discharging functions under any public general Act, so far as not met otherwise or so far as not otherwise provided for in any Act, shall be met out of the council tax imposed by the local authority under this Part.

71. Liability to be determined on a daily basis

(1) Liability to pay council tax shall be determined on a daily basis.

(2) For the purposes of determining for any day—

(a) whether any property is a chargeable dwelling;
(b) which valuation band is shown in a valuation list as applicable to any chargeable dwelling;
(c) the person liable to pay council tax in respect of any such dwelling; or
(d) whether any amount of council tax is subject to a discount and (if so) the amount of the discount,

it shall be assumed that any state of affairs subsisting at the end of the day had subsisted throughout the day.

NOTE
Sub-ss(1), (2)(c) and (d): With respect to the council water charge, the words 'the council water charge' shall be substituted for the words 'council tax' by the Council Water Charge (Scotland) Regulations 1992, SI 1992/1203, Schedule, para 1(a).

Chargeable dwellings

72. Dwellings chargeable to council tax

(1) Council tax shall be payable in respect of any dwelling which is not an exempt dwelling.

(2) In this Part, "dwelling"—

(a) means any lands and heritages—

(i) which consist of one or more dwelling houses with any garden, yard, garage, outhouse or pertinent belonging to and occupied with such dwelling house or dwelling houses; and
(ii) which would, but for the provisions of section 73(1) below, be entered separately in the valuation roll;

(b) includes—

(i) the residential part of part residential subjects; and
(ii) that part of any premises which has, in terms of section 45 of the 1980 Act, been apportioned, as at 1st April 1989, as a dwelling house; and

(c) does not include a caravan which is not a person's sole or main residence.

(3) For the purposes of subsection (2) above "caravan" has the same meaning as it has in Part I of the Caravan Sites and Control of Development Act 1960.

(4) The Secretary of State may vary the definition of dwelling in subsection (2) above by including or excluding such lands and heritages or parts thereof or such class or classes of lands and heritages or parts thereof as may be prescribed.

(5) The Secretary of State may by order provide that in such cases as may be prescribed by or determined under the order—

(a) anything which would (apart from the order) be one dwelling shall be treated as two or more dwellings; and
(b) anything which would (apart from the order) be two or more dwellings shall be treated as one dwelling.

(6) In this Part—
"chargeable dwelling" means any dwelling in respect of which council tax is payable;

"exempt dwelling" means any dwelling of a class prescribed by an order made by the Secretary of State.

(7) For the purposes of subsection (6) above, a class of dwelling may be prescribed by reference to—

(a) the physical characteristics of dwellings;

(b) the fact that dwellings are unoccupied or are occupied for prescribed purposes or are occupied or owned by persons of prescribed descriptions; or

(c) such other factors as the Secretary of State thinks fit.

(8) Schedule 5 to this Act shall have effect in relation to part residential subjects.

NOTES

Sub-s (4): See the Council Tax (Dwellings) (Scotland) Regulations 1992, SI 1992/1334, and the Council Tax (Dwelling and Part Residential Subjects)(Scotland) Regulations 1992, SI 1992/2955.

Sub-ss (6), (7): See the Council Tax (Exempt Dwellings) (Scotland) Order 1992, SI 1992/1333.

---

73. Alterations to valuation roll

(1) Subject to subsection (7) below, dwellings shall not be entered in the valuation roll in respect of the financial year 1993-94 or any subsequent financial year.

(2) Dwellings in respect of which there is an entry in the valuation roll immediately before 1st April 1993 shall be deleted from the roll with effect from that date.

(3) Lands and heritages—

(a) in respect of which there is, by reason of the fact that they constitute domestic subjects within the meaning of section 2(3) of the Abolition of Domestic Rates Etc. (Scotland) Act 1987 ("the 1987 Act"), no entry on the roll immediately before 1st April 1993; and

(b) which are not dwellings within the meaning of section 72(2) above,

shall be entered on the valuation roll with effect from that date.

(4) Where, after 1st April 1993, any lands and heritages (including a caravan which constitutes a person's sole or main residence) or any parts of lands and heritages cease to be a dwelling, they shall be entered in the valuation roll with effect from the date on which they so cease.

(5) Where after 1st April 1993, by virtue of regulations made under section 72(4) above, any lands and heritages or any parts of lands and heritages—

(a) cease to be dwellings, they shall be entered in the valuation roll;

(b) become dwellings, any entry in the valuation roll in respect of such lands and heritages shall be deleted,

with effect from such date as may be prescribed by such regulations.

(6) Where a part of any lands and heritages falls within a class prescribed under section 72(4) above—

(a) the part so affected and the remainder shall be treated for the purposes of the Valuation Acts as separate lands and heritages, and

(b) the part of those lands and heritages which does not constitute a dwelling shall be entered in the valuation roll accordingly.

(7) Nothing in this section affects the entering in the valuation roll of part residential subjects.

74. Different amounts for dwellings in different valuation bands

(1) The amounts of regional, islands or district council tax payable in respect of dwellings situated in any local authority's area and listed in different valuation bands shall be in the proportion—

6: 7: 8: 9: 11: 13: 15: 18

where 6 is for dwellings listed in valuation band A, 7 is for dwellings listed in valuation band B, and so on.

(2) The valuation bands for dwellings are set out in the following Table—

Range of values	Valuation band
Values not exceeding £27,000	A
Values exceeding £27,000 but not exceeding £35,000	B
Values exceeding £35,000 but not exceeding £45,000	C
Values exceeding £45,000 but not exceeding £58,000	D
Values exceeding £58,000 but not exceeding £80,000	E
Values exceeding £80,000 but not exceeding £106,000	F
Values exceeding £106,000 but not exceeding £212,000	G
Values exceeding £212,000	H

(3) The Secretary of State may by order, as regards financial years beginning on or after such date as is specified in the order—

   (a) substitute another proportion for that which is for the time being effective for the purposes of subsection (1) above;
   (b) substitute other valuation bands for those which are for the time being effective for the purposes of subsection (2) above.

(4) No order under subsection (3) above shall be made unless a draft of the order has been laid before and approved by resolution of the House of Commons.

(5) Any reference in this Part to dwellings listed in a particular valuation band shall be construed as a reference to dwellings to which that valuation band is shown as applicable in the valuation list.

Liability to tax

75. Persons liable to pay council tax

(1) The person who is liable to pay council tax in respect of any chargeable dwelling and any day is the person who falls within the first paragraph of subsection (2) below to apply, taking paragraph (a) of that subsection first, paragraph (b) next, and so on.

(2) A person falls within this subsection in relation to any chargeable dwelling and any day if, on that day—

   (a) he is the resident owner of the whole or any part of the dwelling;
   (b) he is a resident tenant of the whole or any part of the dwelling;

(c) he is a resident statutory tenant, resident statutory assured tenant or resident secure tenant of the whole or any part of the dwelling;

(d) he is a resident sub-tenant of the whole or any part of the dwelling;

(e) he is a resident of the dwelling; or

(f) he is any of the following—

    (i) the sub-tenant of the whole or any part of the dwelling under a sub-lease granted for a term of 6 months or more;

    (ii) the tenant, under a lease granted for a term of 6 months or more, of any part of the dwelling which is not subject to a sub-lease granted for a term of 6 months or more;

    (iii) the owner of any part of the dwelling which is not subject to a lease granted for a term of 6 months or more.

(3) Where, in relation to any chargeable dwelling and any day, two or more persons fall within the first paragraph of subsection (2) above to apply, they shall be jointly and severally liable to pay the council tax payable in respect of the dwelling and that day.

(4) Subsection (3) above shall not apply as respects any day on which one or more of the persons there mentioned fall to be disregarded for the purposes of discount by virtue of paragraph 2 of Schedule 1 to this Act (the severely mentally impaired) and one or more of them do not; and liability to pay the council tax in respect of that dwelling and that day shall be determined as follows—

(a) if only one of those persons does not fall to be so disregarded, he shall be solely liable;

(b) if two or more of those persons do not fall to be so disregarded, they shall be jointly and severally liable.

(5) In this section—

"secure tenant" means a tenant under a secure tenancy within the meaning of Part III of the Housing (Scotland) Act 1987;

"statutory tenant" means a statutory tenant within the meaning of the Rent (Scotland) Act 1984;

"statutory assured tenant" means a statutory assured tenant within the meaning of the Housing (Scotland) Act 1988.

NOTES

Sub-s (1): With respect to the council water charge, the words 'the council water charge' shall be substituted for the words 'council tax' by the Council Water Charge (Scotland) Regulations 1992, SI 1992/1203, Schedule, para 1(b).

Sub-s (4): With respect to the council water charge, the words 'council water charge' shall be substituted for the words 'council tax' by the Council Water Charge (Scotland) Regulations 1992, SI 1992/1203, Schedule, para 2(a).

---

76. Liability in prescribed cases.

(1) Subsections (3) and (4) below shall have effect in substitution for section 75 above in relation to any chargeable dwelling of a class prescribed for the purposes of this subsection.

(2) Subsections (3) and (4) below shall have effect in substitution for section 75 above in relation to any chargeable dwelling of a class prescribed for the purposes of this

subsection, if the levying authority so determines in relation to all dwellings of that class which are situated in its area.

(3) Where on any day this subsection has effect in relation to a dwelling, the owner of the dwelling shall be liable to pay the council tax in respect of the dwelling and that day.

(4) Where on any day two or more persons fall within subsection (3) above, they shall each be jointly and severally liable to pay the council tax in respect of the dwelling and that day.

(5) Subsection (4) of section 75 above shall apply for the purposes of subsection (4) above as it applies for the purposes of subsection (3) of that section.

(6) Regulations prescribing a class of chargeable dwellings for the purposes of sub-section (1) or (2) above may provide that, in relation to any dwelling of that class, subsection (3) above shall have effect as if for the reference to the owner of the dwelling there were substituted a reference to the person falling within such descrip-tion as may be prescribed.

(7) Subsection (7) of section 72 above shall apply for the purposes of subsections (1) and (2) above as it applies for the purposes of subsection (6) of that section.

NOTES
Sub-ss (3), (4): With respect to the council water charge, the words 'council water charge' shall be substituted for the words 'council tax' by the Council Water Charge (Scotland) Regulations 1992, SI 1992/1203, Schedule, para 2(b).
Sub-ss (1), (6), (7): See the Council Tax (Liability of Owners) (Scotland) Regulations 1992, SI 1992/1331.

77. Liability of spouses

(1) Where—
   (a) a person who is liable to pay council tax in respect of any chargeable dwell-ing and any day is married to another person; and
   (b) that other person is also a resident of the dwelling on that day but would not, apart from this section, be so liable,

those persons shall be jointly and severally liable to pay the council tax payable in respect of that dwelling and that day.

(2) Subsection (1) above shall not apply as respects any day on which the other per-son there mentioned falls to be disregarded for the purposes of discount by virtue of paragraph 2 of Schedule 1 to this Act (the severely mentally impaired).

(3) For the purposes of this section two persons are married to each other if they are a man and a woman—
   (a) who are married to each other; or
   (b) who are not married to each other but are living together as husband and wife.

NOTES
Sub-s (1)(a): With respect to the council water charge, the words 'the council water charge' shall be substituted for the words 'council tax' by the Council Water Charge (Scotland) Regulations 1992, SI 1992/1203, Schedule, para 1(c).

Sub-s (1): With respect to the council water charge, the words 'council water charge' shall be substituted for the words 'council tax' by the Council Water Charge (Scotland) Regulations 1992, SI 1992/1203, Schedule, para 2(c).

Amounts of tax payable

78. Basic amounts payable

Subject to sections 79 and 80 below, a person who is liable to pay council tax in respect of any chargeable dwelling and any day shall, as respects the dwelling and the day, pay to the levying authority for the area in which the dwelling is situated an amount calculated in accordance with the formula—

$$\frac{A}{D}$$

where—

A   is the amount or, as the case may be, the aggregate of the amounts which, for the financial year in which the day falls and for dwellings in the valuation band listed for the dwelling, has or have been imposed by the local authority or authorities in whose area or areas the dwelling is situated;

D   is the number of days in the financial year.

NOTES

With respect to the council water charge, the words 'the council water charge' shall be substituted for the words 'council tax' by the Council Water Charge (Scotland) Regulations 1992, SI 1992/1203, Schedule, para 1(d).

With respect to the council water charge, the words 'or, as the case may be, the aggregate of the amounts' shall not apply: Council Water Charge (Scotland) Regulations 1992, SI 1992/ 1203, Schedule, para 3(a).

With respect to the council water charge, for the words from 'or have been' to the end of that definition, there shall be substituted the words 'been imposed by the levying authority': Council Water Charge (Scotland) Regulations 1992, SI 1992/1203, Schedule, para 3(b).

79. Discounts

(1) The amount of council tax payable in respect of a chargeable dwelling and any day shall be subject to a discount equal to the appropriate percentage of that amount if on that day—

(a) there is only one resident of the dwelling and he does not fall to be disregarded for the purposes of discount; or

(b) there are two or more residents of the dwelling and each of them except one falls to be disregarded for those purposes.

(2) The amount of council tax payable in respect of a chargeable dwelling and any day shall be subject to a discount equal to twice the appropriate percentage of that amount if on that day—

(a) there is no resident of the dwelling; or

(b) there are one or more residents of the dwelling and each of them falls to be disregarded for the purposes of discount.

(3) In this section "the appropriate percentage" means 25 per cent. or, if the Secretary of State by order so provides in respect of the financial year in which the day falls, such other percentage as is specified in the order.

(4) No order under subsection (3) above shall be made unless a draft of the order has been laid before and approved by resolution of the House of Commons.

(5) Schedule 1 to this Act shall have effect for determining who shall be disregarded for the purposes of discount.

NOTE

Sub-ss (1), (2): With respect to the council water charge, the words 'the council water charge' shall be substituted for the words 'council tax' by the Council Water Charge (Scotland) Regulations 1992, SI 1992/1203, Schedule, para 1(e).

80. Reduced amounts

(1) The Secretary of State may make regulations as regards any case where—

    (a) a person is liable to pay an amount to a levying authority in respect of council tax for any financial year which is prescribed; and

    (b) prescribed conditions are fulfilled.

(2) The regulations may provide that the amount he is liable to pay shall be an amount which—

    (a) is less than the amount it would be apart from the regulations; and

    (b) is determined in accordance with prescribed rules.

(3) This section applies whether the amount mentioned in subsection (1) above is determined under section 78 above or under that section read with section 79 above.

(4) The conditions mentioned in subsection (1) above may be prescribed by reference to such factors as the Secretary of State thinks fit; and in particular such factors may include the making of an application by the person concerned and all or any of—

    (a) the factors mentioned in subsection (5) below; or

    (b) the factors mentioned in subsection (6) below.

(5) The factors mentioned in subsection (4)(a) above are—

    (a) community charges for a period before 1st April 1993;

    (b) the circumstances of, or other matters relating to, the person concerned;

    (c) an amount—

        (i) relating to any local authority whose council tax constitutes all or part of the amount referred to in subsection (1) above; and

        (ii) which is specified, or is to be specified, in a report laid, or to be laid, before the House of Commons;

    (d) such other amounts as may be prescribed or arrived at in a prescribed manner.

(6) The factors referred to in subsection (4)(b) above are—

    (a) a disabled person having his sole or main residence in the dwelling concerned;

    (b) the circumstances of, or other matters relating to, that person;

    (c) the physical characteristics of, or other matters relating to, that dwelling.

(7) The rules mentioned in subsection (2) above may be prescribed by reference to such factors as the Secretary of State thinks fit; and in particular such factors may include all or any of the factors mentioned in subsection (5) or subsection (6) (b) or (c) above.

(8) Without prejudice to the generality of section 113(2) below, regulations under this section may include—

(a) provision requiring the Secretary of State to specify in a report, for the purposes of the regulations, an amount in relation to each local authority;
(b) provisions requiring him to lay the report before the House of Commons;
(c) provisions for the review of any prescribed decision of a levying authority relating to the application or operation of the regulations;
(d) provision that no appeal may be made to a valuation appeal committee in respect of such a decision, notwithstanding section 81(1) below.

(9) To the extent that he would not have power to do so apart from this subsection, the Secretary of State may—

(a) include in regulations under this section such amendments of any social security instrument as he thinks expedient in consequence of the regulations under this section;
(b) include in any social security instrument such provision as he thinks expedient in consequence of regulations under this section.

(10) In subsection (9) above "social security instrument" means an order or regulations made, or falling to be made, by the Secretary of State under the Social Security Acts.

NOTES

Sub-s (1)(a): With respect to the council water charge, the words 'the council water charge' shall be substituted for the words 'council tax' by the Council Water Charge (Scotland) Regulations 1992, SI 1992/1203, Schedule, para 1(f).

Sub-s (5)(a): With respect to the council water charge, after the word 'community' there shall be inserted the word 'water': Council Water Charge (Scotland) Regulations 1992, SI 1992/1203, Schedule, para 4(a)(i).

Sub-s (5)(c)(i): With respect to the council water charge, there shall be substituted the following sub-paragraph: '(i) relating to the levying authority concerned;': Council Water Charge (Scotland) Regulations 1992, SI 1992/1203, Schedule, para 4(a)(ii).

Sub-s (8)(a): With respect to the council water charge, for the word 'local' there shall be substituted the word 'levying': Council Water Charge (Scotland) Regulations 1992, SI 1992/1203, Schedule, para 4(b).

Sub-ss (1)-(4), (6), (7): See the Council Tax (Reductions for Disabilities) (Scotland) Regulations 1992, SI 1992/1335.

Appeals

81. Appeal to valuation appeal committee

(1) A person may appeal to a valuation appeal committee if he is aggrieved by—

(a) any decision of a levying authority that a dwelling is a chargeable dwelling, or that he is liable to pay council tax in respect of such a dwelling; or
(b) any calculation made by a levying authority of an amount which he is liable to pay to the authority in respect of council tax,

and the committee shall make such decision as they think just.

(2) In subsection (1) above the reference to any calculation of an amount includes a reference to any estimate of the amount.

(3) Subsection (1) above shall not apply where the grounds on which the person concerned is aggrieved fall within such category or categories as may be prescribed.

(4) No appeal may be made under subsection (1) above unless—

    (a) the aggrieved person serves a written notice under this subsection; and
    (b) one of the conditions mentioned in subsection (7) below is fulfilled.

(5) A notice under subsection (4) above must be served on the levying authority concerned.

(6) A notice under subsection (4) above must state the matter by which and the grounds on which the person is aggrieved.

(7) The conditions are that—

    (a) the aggrieved person is notified in writing, by the authority on which he served the notice, that the authority believes the grievance is not well founded, but the person is still aggrieved;
    (b) the aggrieved person is notified in writing, by the authority on which he served the notice, that steps have been taken to deal with the grievance, but the person is still aggrieved;
    (c) the period of two months, beginning with the date of service of the aggrieved person's notice, has ended without his being notified under paragraph (a) or (b) above.

(8) Where a notice under subsection (4) above is served on an authority, the authority shall—

    (a) consider the matter to which the notice relates;
    (b) include in any notification under subsection (7)(a) above the reasons for the belief concerned;
    (c) include in any notification under subsection (7)(b) above a statement of the steps taken.

NOTE

Sub-s (1)(a), (b): With respect to the council water charge, the words 'the council water charge' shall be substituted for the words 'council tax' by the Council Water Charge (Scotland) Regulations 1992, SI 1992/1203, Schedule, para 1(g).

82. Appeal procedure

(1) The Secretary of State may by regulations make provision for the procedure to be followed in appeals under this Part to a valuation appeal committee.

(2) Regulations under this section may include provision—

    (a) as to the time within which any proceedings before the committee are to be instituted;
    (b) for requiring persons to attend to give evidence and produce documents and for granting to any person such recovery of documents as might be granted by the Court of Session; and
    (c) as to the manner in which any decision of the committee is to be implemented.

(3) Any person who fails to comply with any requirement imposed by regulations under paragraph (b) of subsection (2) above shall be guilty of an offence and liable on summary conviction to a fine not exceeding level 1 on the standard scale.

(4) Any party to an appeal under this Part may appeal against a decision of the valuation appeal committee on a point of law to the Court of Session.

(5) Neither section 1(3A) of the Lands Tribunal Act 1949 nor section 5 of the Local Government (Financial Provisions) (Scotland) Act 1963 shall apply to appeals to or from a valuation appeal committee under this Part.

(6) It shall be a defence for a person charged with an offence under subsection (3) above to prove that he had a reasonable excuse for acting as he did.

New dwellings

83. Completion of new dwellings

(1) Schedule 6 to this Act (which makes provision with respect to the determination of a day as the completion day in relation to a new building which, or any part of which, will constitute or constitutes a dwelling) shall have effect.

(2) A dwelling in a new building shall be deemed for the purposes of this Part to have come into existence on the day determined under that Schedule as the completion day in respect of that building, whether or not the building is completed on that day.

(3) Where—

  (a) a day is determined under that Schedule as the completion day in relation to a new building; and
  (b) the building is one produced by the structural alteration of a building which consists of one or more existing dwellings,

the existing dwelling or dwellings shall be deemed for the purposes of this Part to have ceased to exist on that day.

(4) Any reference in this section or that Schedule to a new building includes a reference to a building produced by the structural alteration of an existing building where—

  (a) the existing building constitutes a dwelling which, by virtue of the alteration, becomes, or becomes part of, a different dwelling or different dwellings; or
  (b) the existing building does not, except by virtue of the alteration, constitute a dwelling.

(5) Any reference in this section or that Schedule to a building includes a reference to a part of a building.

Valuation lists

84. Compilation and maintenance of valuation lists

(1) In accordance with this Part, the local assessor for each regional and islands council shall compile, and then maintain, a list for that council (to be known as the "valuation list").

(2) A valuation list must show, for each day for which it is in force—

(a) each dwelling which is situated in the regional or islands council's area; and

(b) which of the valuation bands mentioned in section 74(2) above is applicable to the dwelling.

(3) A list must also contain such information about dwellings shown in it as may be prescribed.

(4) The omission from a list of any matter required to be included in it shall not of itself render the list invalid, so far as any other matter contained in it is concerned.

(5) Any rules as to Crown exemption which would have applied apart from this subsection shall not prevent a list showing a dwelling, showing the valuation band applicable to a dwelling and containing any prescribed information about a dwelling.

(6) A list must be compiled on 1st April 1993 and shall come into force on that day.

(7) Before a list is compiled the local assessor must take such steps as are reasonably practicable in the time available to ensure that it is accurately compiled on 1st April 1993.

(8) Any valuation of a dwelling carried out by the local assessor in pursuance of subsection (7) above shall be carried out in accordance with section 86(2) below.

(9) The local assessor shall maintain the valuation list for so long as is necessary for the purposes of this Part.

(10) In this Part "local assessor" means the assessor appointed under section 116(2) or (5) (appointment of assessors) of the 1973 Act for each region and islands area; and any depute assessor appointed under the said section 116(2) or (5) shall have all the functions of a local assessor under this Part.

NOTE

Sub-s (3): See the Council Tax (Contents of Valuation Lists) (Scotland) Regulation 1992, SI 1992/1330.

---

85. Distribution of lists.

(1) At the following times, namely—

(a) not later than 1st September 1992; and

(b) not earlier than 15th November 1992 and not later than 1st December 1992,

the local assessor shall send to each council for which he has been appointed to act as local assessor a copy of the list which he proposes (on the information then before him) to compile for that council's area.

(2) At the same time as he sends a copy of the valuation list to a council under subsection (1) above, the local assessor for a regional council shall send to each district council in the region a copy of so much of the regional valuation list as relates to dwellings in the area of that district.

(3) As soon as reasonably practicable after receiving a copy of a list under subsection (1)(b) above the regional or islands council shall deposit it at their principal office and take such steps as they think fit for giving notice of it.

(4) As soon as reasonably practicable after compiling a list the local assessor shall—

(a) send to each council for which he has been appointed to act as local assessor a copy of the list compiled for that council's area; and

(b) in the case of a regional council, send to each district council in the region a copy of so much of the list as relates to dwellings in the area of that district.

(5) As soon as reasonably practicable after receiving a copy of a list under subsection (4) above the regional or islands council shall deposit it at their principal office.

(6) The local assessor shall, as soon as is reasonably practicable after 1st April in each year, send a copy of the valuation list as in force on that date to the Keeper of the Records of Scotland for preservation by him.

86. Valuation of dwellings

(1) In order to enable him to compile a valuation list for his area under section 84 above, a local assessor shall, in accordance with the provisions of this Part, carry out a valuation of such of the dwellings in his area as he considers necessary or expedient for the purposes of determining which of the valuation bands mentioned in section 74(2) above applies to each dwelling in his area.

(2) The valuation shall be carried out by reference to 1st April 1991 and on such assumptions and in accordance with such principles as may be prescribed.

(3) Where it appears to a local assessor that, having regard to the assumptions and principles mentioned in subsection (2) above, and to any directions given under subsection (5) below, a dwelling falls clearly within a particular valuation band, he need not carry out an individual valuation of that dwelling.

(4) Subject to subsection (5) below, the local assessor shall carry out the valuation in the region or islands area for which he has been appointed as assessor.

(5) A local assessor shall comply with such directions as may be given in relation to the valuation by the Commissioners of Inland Revenue.

(6) The Commissioners of Inland Revenue may, for the purpose of preparing any directions under subsection (5) above, make such investigations and set up such facilities in Scotland as appear to them to be appropriate.

(7) A local assessor may appoint persons to assist him.

(8) A local assessor may disclose to a person appointed by him under subsection (7) above any information available to him or obtained by him in the exercise of the powers conferred by section 90 below.

(9) If any person to whom any information is disclosed by virtue of subsection (8) above uses or discloses the information, in whole or in part, otherwise than for the purposes of the valuation, he shall be guilty of an offence and liable—

(a) on conviction on indictment, to imprisonment for a term not exceeding two years or a fine or both; and

(b) on summary conviction, to imprisonment for a term not exceeding six months or a fine not exceeding the statutory maximum or both.

(10) A regional or islands council shall secure the provision of sufficient staff, accommodation and other resources (including sums for the payment of persons appointed by the local assessor to assist him) to enable the local assessor to carry out his functions.

(11) The Secretary of State may, with the consent of the Treasury, make grants of such amounts as he may, with such consent, determine to regional or islands councils towards such of their expenditure under this section as he considers to have been reasonably incurred.

NOTE

Sub-s (2): See the Council Tax (Valuation of Dwellings) (Scotland) Regulations, SI 1992/1329.

87. Alteration of lists

(1) The Secretary of State may make regulations about the alteration by local assessors of valuation lists which have been compiled under this Part; and subsections (2) to (10) below shall apply for the purposes of this subsection.

(2) The regulations may include provision that where a local assessor intends to alter the list with a view to its being accurately maintained, he shall not alter it unless prescribed conditions (as to notice or otherwise) are fulfilled.

(3) The regulations may include provision that any valuation of a dwelling carried out in connection with a proposal for the alteration of the list shall be carried out in accordance with section 86(2) above.

(4) The regulations may include provision that no alteration shall be made of a valuation band shown in the list as applicable to any dwelling unless—

    (a) since the valuation band was first shown in the list as applicable to the dwelling—

        (i) there has been a material increase in the value of the dwelling and it, or any part of it, has subsequently been sold; or

        (ii) there has been a material reduction in the value of the dwelling,

    and (in either case) prescribed conditions are fulfilled; or

    (b) the local assessor is satisfied that—

        (i) a different valuation band should have been determined by him as applicable to the dwelling; or

        (ii) the valuation band shown in the list is not that determined by him as so applicable; or

    (c) the assessor has, under Schedule 5 to this Act, added, amended or deleted an apportionment note relating to any lands and heritages included in the valuation roll; or

    (d) there has been a successful appeal under this Act against the valuation band shown in the list.

(5) The regulations may include provision—

    (a) as to who (other than a local assessor) may make a proposal for the alteration of the list with a view to its being accurately maintained;

    (b) as to the manner and circumstances in which a proposal may be made and the information to be included in a proposal;

    (c) as to the period within which a proposal must be made;

    (d) as to the procedure for and subsequent to the making of a proposal;

(e) as to the circumstances within which and the conditions upon which a proposal may be withdrawn; and

(f) requiring a local assessor to inform other prescribed persons of the proposal in a prescribed manner.

(6) The regulations may include provision that, where there is a disagreement between the local assessor and another person making a proposal for the alteration of a list—

(a) about the validity of the proposal; or

(b) about the accuracy of the list,

an appeal may be made to a valuation appeal committee.

(7) The regulations may include—

(a) provision as to the period for which or day from which an alteration of a list is to have effect (including provision that it is to have retrospective effect);

(b) provision requiring a list to be altered so as to indicate the effect (retrospective or otherwise) of the alteration;

(c) provision requiring the local assessor to inform prescribed persons of an alteration within a prescribed period;

(d) provision requiring the local assessor to keep for a prescribed period a record of the state of the list before the alteration was made.

(8) The regulations may include provision as to financial adjustments to be made as a result of alterations, including—

(a) provision requiring payments or repayments to be made; and

(b) provision as to the recovery (by deduction or otherwise) of sums due.

(9) The regulations may include provision that where—

(a) a local assessor has informed a regional or islands council of an alteration to a list; and

(b) a copy of the list has been deposited by that authority under section 85(5) above,

the authority must alter the copy accordingly.

(10) In this section—

"material increase", in relation to the value of a dwelling, means any increase which is caused (in whole or in part) by any building, engineering or other operation carried out in relation to the dwelling, whether or not constituting development for which planning permission is required;

"material reduction", in relation to the value of a dwelling, means any reduction which is caused (in whole or in part) by the demolition of any part of the dwelling, any change in the physical state of the dwelling's locality or any adaptation of the dwelling to make it suitable for use by a physically disabled person.

88. Compilation and maintenance of new lists

(1) This section applies where the Secretary of State makes an order under subsection (3)(b) of section 74 above providing that, as regards financial years beginning on or after such date as is specified in the order, valuation bands so specified shall

be substituted for those for the time being effective for the purposes of subsection (2) of that section.

(2) For the purpose of—

(a) requiring local assessors to compile, and then maintain, new valuation lists for those financial years; and
(b) facilitating the compilation and maintenance by the local assessors of those lists,

the provisions of this Part shall have effect with the modifications mentioned in subsection (3) below.

(3) The modifications are—

(a) for the date specified in section 84(6) and (7) above there shall be substituted the date specified in the order; and
(b) for the dates specified in sections 85(1) and 86(2) above there shall be substituted such dates as are specified in an order made by the Secretary of State under this subsection.

Valuation lists: supplemental

89. Powers of entry

(1) Subject to subsection (2) below, if a local assessor needs to value a property for the purpose of carrying out any functions conferred or imposed on him by or under this Part, he may enter on, survey and value the property.

(2) At least three clear days' notice in writing of the proposed exercise of the power must be given to the occupier; and there shall be disregarded for this purpose any day which is—

(a) a Saturday, a Sunday, Christmas Day or Good Friday; or
(b) a day which is a bank holiday under the Banking and Financial Dealings Act 1971 in Scotland.

(3) Any person who wilfully delays or obstructs a person in the exercise of a power under this section shall be guilty of an offence and liable on summary conviction to a fine not exceeding level 2 on the standard scale.

90. Information about properties.

(1) This section makes provision in relation to the carrying out by the local assessor of any functions conferred or imposed on him by or under this Part.

(2) The local assessor shall have access to and the use of any information available to—

(a) the assessor for the purposes of the Valuation Acts;
(b) the community charges registration officer; or
(c) the electoral registration officer,

for his area.

(3) In any case where—

(a) a notice is served by a local assessor on a regional, islands or district council, a housing body or on any other person prescribed for the purposes of this section; and

    (b) the notice requests the supply of information of a description specified in the notice; and

    (c) the information relates to property and is information which the local assessor reasonably believes will assist him in carrying out any of his functions under this Part,

the council or other person shall supply the information requested, and shall do so in such form and manner and at such time as the local assessor specifies in the notice.

(4) For the purpose of carrying out any of his functions under this Part, a local assessor may serve on a person who is or has been an owner or occupier of any dwelling in his area a notice—

    (a) requesting him to supply to the local assessor information which is of a description specified in the notice; and

    (b) stating that the local assessor believes the information requested will assist him in carrying out those functions.

(5) A person on whom a notice is served under subsection (4) above shall supply the information requested if it is in his possession or control, and shall do so in such form and manner as is specified in the notice and within the period of 21 days beginning with the day on which the notice is served.

(6) If a person on whom a notice has been served under subsection (4) above fails to comply with subsection (5) above, he shall be guilty of an offence and liable on summary conviction to a fine not exceeding level 2 on the standard scale.

(7) If, in supplying information in purported compliance with subsection (5) above, a person on whom a notice has been served under subsection (4) above—

    (a) makes a statement which he knows to be false in a material particular; or

    (b) recklessly makes a statement which is false in a material particular,

he shall be guilty of an offence and liable on summary conviction to imprisonment for a term not exceeding 3 months or a fine not exceeding level 3 on the standard scale or both.

(8) if in the course of the exercise of their functions any information comes to the notice of a levying authority which they consider would assist the local assessor in carrying out any of his functions under this Part, they shall give him that information.

(9) It shall be a defence for a person charged with an offence under subsection (6) above to prove that he had a reasonable excuse for acting as he did.

91. Information about lists

(1) A person may require a local assessor to give him access to such information as will enable him to establish what is the state of a list, or has been its state at any time since it came into force, if—

    (a) the local assessor is maintaining the list; and

    (b) the list is in force or has been in force at any time in the preceding 5 years.

(2) A person may require a levying authority to give him access to such information as will enable him to establish what is the state of a copy of a list, or has been its state at any time since it was deposited, if—

    (a) the authority has deposited the copy under section 85(5) above; and

    (b) the list is in force or has been in force at any time in the preceding 5 years.

(3) A person may require a levying authority to give him access to such information as will enable him to establish what is the state of a copy of a proposed list if—

    (a) the authority has deposited the copy under section 85(3) above; and

    (b) the list itself is not yet in force.

(4) A requirement under subsection (1), (2) or (3) above must be complied with at a reasonable time and place and without payment being sought; but the information may be in documentary or other form, as the person or authority of whom the requirement is made thinks fit.

(5) Where access is given under this section to information in documentary form the person to whom access is given may—

    (a) make copies of (or of extracts from) the document;

    (b) require a person having custody of the document to supply to him a photographic copy of (or of extracts from) the document.

(6) Where access is given under this section to information in a form which is not documentary the person to whom access is given may—

    (a) make transcripts of (or of extracts from) the information;

    (b) require a person having control of access to the information to supply to him a copy in documentary form of (or of extracts from) the information.

(7) If a reasonable charge is required for a facility under subsection (5) or (6) above, the subsection concerned shall not apply unless the person seeking to avail himself of the facility pays the charge.

(8) If a person having custody of a document containing, or having control of access to, information access to which is sought under this section—

    (a) intentionally obstructs a person in exercising a right under subsection (1), (2), (3), (5)(a) or (6)(a) above; or

    (b) refuses to comply with a requirement under subsection (5)(b) or (6)(b) above,

he shall be guilty of an offence and liable on summary conviction to a fine not exceeding level 2 on the standard scale.

(9) It shall be a defence for a person charged with an offence under subsection (8) above to prove that he had a reasonable excuse for acting as he did.

92. Information about proposals and appeals

(1) A person may, at a reasonable time and without making payment, inspect any proposal made or notice of appeal given under regulations made under section 87 above, if made or given as regards a list which is in force when inspection is sought or has been in force at any time in the preceding five years.

(2) A person may—

    (a) make copies of (or extracts from) a document mentioned in subsection (1) above; or

    (b) require a person having custody of such a document to supply to him a photographic copy of (or of extracts from) the document.

(3) If a reasonable charge is required for a facility under subsection (2) above, that subsection shall not apply unless the person seeking to avail himself of the facility pays the charge.

(4) If a person having custody of a document mentioned in subsection (1) above—

    (a) intentionally obstructs a person in exercising a right under subsection (1) or (2)(a) above; or

    (b) refuses to supply a copy to a person entitled to it under subsection (2)(b) above,

he shall be guilty of an offence and liable on summary conviction to a fine not exceeding level 2 on the standard scale.

(5) It shall be a defence for a person charged with an offence under subsection (4) above to prove that he had a reasonable excuse for acting as he did.

Setting of the tax

93. Setting of council tax

(1) In respect of the financial year 1993–94 and each subsequent financial year, a local authority shall—

    (a) set an amount of regional, islands or district council tax, as appropriate, to be paid in respect of a chargeable dwelling in their area listed in valuation band D (whether or not there is such a dwelling in their area) as specified in section 74(2) above;

    (b) determine the amount of council tax to be paid in respect of a chargeable dwelling in each of the other valuation bands specified in that section in accordance with the proportion mentioned in subsection (1) of that section,

and references in this Part to the setting of a council tax or of an amount of council tax shall be construed as references to the setting of the amount mentioned in paragraph (a) above.

(2) A local authority shall set its council tax before 11th March in the financial year preceding that for which it is set but it is not invalid merely because it is set on or after that date.

(3) The amounts mentioned in paragraphs (a) and (b) of subsection (1) above shall be such as will provide sufficient money to meet such part of the total estimated expenses to be incurred by that authority during the financial year in respect of which the amount is set as falls to be met out of their council tax, together with such additional sum as is, in their opinion, required—

    (a) to cover expenses previously incurred;

    (b) to meet contingencies;

    (c) to meet any expenses which may fall to be met before the money to be received in respect of their council tax for the next following financial year will become available.

(4) In calculating, for the purposes of subsection (3) above, such part of the total estimated expenses to be incurred by a local authority as falls to be met out of council tax, account shall be taken of any means by which those expenses may otherwise be met or provided for.

94. Substituted and reduced settings

(1) Subject to subsection (3) below, a local authority may set, in substitution for an amount of council tax already set or deemed to have been set, a lesser amount of council tax for the same financial year.

(2) Schedule 7 to this Act has effect for the purpose of making provision as to the reduction of council tax where the Secretary of State is satisfied, in accordance with that Schedule, that the total estimated expenses mentioned in section 93(3) above of a local authority are excessive or that an increase in those expenses is excessive.

(3) A local authority may not set a substitute amount of council tax during the period between the approval by the House of Commons of a report in respect of that authority made by the Secretary of State under paragraph 1 of that Schedule and the setting or deemed setting of a reduced amount of council tax under paragraph 3 of that Schedule.

(4) Section 93(2) above shall not apply for the purposes of this section.

(5) A local authority who, in respect of any financial year, set (or are deemed to have set) a substituted or reduced council tax shall neither wholly nor partially offset the difference between—

(a) the amount produced by that substituted or reduced setting; and
(b) the amount which would have been produced had they not substituted or reduced their setting,

with sums advanced from their loans fund established under Schedule 3 to the 1975 Act:

Provided that such offsetting may nevertheless be permitted by the Secretary of State in any case on such terms and conditions as he considers appropriate.

(6) If the Secretary of State is of the opinion that subsection (5) above, or any term or condition imposed under the proviso thereto, has been contravened, the local authority shall, on such opinion being intimated to them, reimburse their loans fund forthwith or within such time as the Secretary of State may allow.

(7) Anything paid by reference to one setting of council tax shall be treated as paid by reference to a substitute setting under subsection (1) above or a reduced setting or deemed setting by virtue of paragraph 3 of Schedule 7 to this Act.

(8) Where a person has paid by reference to one setting of council tax more than is due under a substituted or reduced setting—

(a) the balance shall be repaid to the person if he so requires;
(b) in any other case the balance shall (as the levying authority determine) either be repaid to the person or be credited against any subsequent liability of the person to pay in respect of any council tax due to the authority.

(9) Where—

(a) a substitute amount of council tax has been set under subsection (1) above; or
(b) a reduced amount of council tax has been set or been deemed to have been set under paragraph 3 of that Schedule,

the regional council shall levy and collect that substituted or reduced amount in place of the previous amount of council tax and may recover from the district council any administrative expenses incurred in so doing in relation to a substituted or reduced amount of district council tax.

95. District council tax: setting and collection

(1) In relation to each financial year, a regional council shall estimate the amount which would be produced by each of the district council taxes for that year in each district in their region as that amount falls to be ascertained in pursuance of regulations made under subsection (6) below.

(2) For the purpose of making the estimate mentioned in subsection (1) above, the regional council shall assume that in respect of the financial year concerned both the regional council and the district council set £1, or such other amount as may be prescribed, as the amount mentioned in section 93(1)(a) above.

(3) The regional council shall, before such date as may be prescribed in relation to each financial year, notify the council of each district in their region of the estimate made under subsection (1) above in relation to that district for that financial year.

(4) In respect of the financial year 1993-94 and each subsequent financial year, every district council shall, within two days of the date mentioned in section 93(2) above, intimate to the regional council within whose region their district falls—

   (a) the amount of district council tax they have set; and
   (b) such further information with respect to the district council tax as may reasonably be needed by the regional council for the purpose of issuing notices in accordance with regulations made under paragraph 2 of Schedule 2 to this Act.

(5) A regional council shall be liable to pay to the council of each district in their region, in respect of the district council tax for any financial year, the amount produced in the district by that tax; and shall, in accordance with such arrangements as may be prescribed, make payments to the district council on account of that liability.

(6) For the purposes of subsection (5) above, the amount produced in a district by the district council tax for a financial year shall, subject to subsection (7) below, be ascertained after the end of that year in such manner as may be prescribed, and—

   (a) if that amount exceeds the aggregate amount of payments on account made under subsection (5) above, the balance shall be paid by the regional council to the district council; and
   (b) if that amount is less than the said aggregate amount, the balance shall be set off against payments on account under subsection (5) above in respect of the next following financial year.

(7) The Secretary of State may prescribe what deductions are to be made in estimating and ascertaining the amount produced by each of the regional and district council taxes levied by a regional council.

(8) There shall be taken into account, in the calculation of the amount which a regional council are liable, under subsection (5) above, to pay to a district council, the amount of any council tax and council water charge which has been collected by the district council under paragraph 19 of Schedule 2 to this Act and is due but has not been paid to the regional council.

(9) The amount which a regional council are liable to pay under subsection (5) above to a district council shall, if not paid by such a date as may be prescribed, attract interest at such rate as may be prescribed.

NOTE
Sub-s (3): See the Local Government (District Council Tax)(Scotland) Regulations 1992, SI 1992/ 3024.

96. Information

(1) Within 21 days after setting a council tax, a local authority shall publish in at least one newspaper circulating in their area a notice of—

   (a) the provision of this Act under which the council tax has been set; and

(b)   the amounts payable in respect of chargeable dwellings in each valuation band.

(2) Failure to comply with subsection (1) above does not make the setting of an amount invalid.

NOTES
Sub-s (1): With respect to the council water charge, the words 'council water charge' shall be substituted for the words 'council tax' (in the first place where they appear) by the Council Water Charge (Scotland) Regulations 1992, SI 1992/1203, Schedule, para 2(d); for the word 'local' there shall be substituted the word 'levying': Council Water Charge (Scotland) Regulations 1992, SI 1992/1203, Schedule, para 5(a).
Sub-s (1)(a): With respect to the council water charge, this paragraph shall not apply: Council Water Charge (Scotland) Regulations 1992, SI 1992/1203, Schedule, para 5(b).

Levying and collection of the tax

97. Levying and collection of council tax

(1) An islands authority shall levy and collect the islands council tax set by them in respect of their area.

(2) A regional authority shall levy and collect—

(a)   the regional council tax set by them in respect of their area; and
(b)   the district council tax set by each district in their area.

(3) Schedule 2 to this Act (which contains provisions about administration, including collection) shall have effect.

(4) Schedule 3 to this Act (which contains provisions about civil penalties) shall have effect.

(5) Schedule 8 to this Act (which contains provisions about the recovery of sums due, including sums due as penalties) shall have effect.

NOTES
Sub-s (1): With respect to the council water charge, the words 'council water charge' shall be substituted for the words 'council tax' by the Council Water Charge (Scotland) Regulations 1992, SI 1992/1203, Schedule, para 2(e).
Sub-s (2): With respect to the council water charge, for paragraphs (a) and (b) there shall be substituted the words 'the regional council water charge set by them in respect of their area.': Council Water Charge (Scotland) Regulations 1992, SI 1992/1203, Schedule, para 6.

Miscellaneous and supplemental

98. Information required by Secretary of State.

(1) Subsection (2) below applies where—

(a)   the Secretary of State serves a notice on a levying authority requiring them to supply to the Secretary of State information specified in the notice;
(b)   the information is in the possession or control of the authority and was obtained by them for the purpose of carrying out their functions under this Act; and
(c)   the information is not personal information.

(2) The authority shall supply the information required, and shall do so in such form and manner and at such time as the Secretary of State specifies in the notice.

(3) Personal information is information which relates to an individual (living or dead) who can be identified from that information or from that and other information supplied by the authority; and personal information includes any expression of opinion about the individual and any indication of the intentions of any person in respect of the individual.

99. Interpretation of Part II.

(1) In this Part and in sections 107 to 112 below, unless the context otherwise requires—
"the 1947 Act" means the Local Government (Scotland) Act 1947;
"the 1956 Act" means the Valuation and Rating (Scotland) Act 1956;
"the 1968 Act" means the Sewerage (Scotland) Act 1968;
"the 1973 Act" means the Local Government (Scotland) Act 1973;
"the 1975 Act" means the Local Government (Scotland) Act 1975;
"the 1980 Act" means the Water (Scotland) Act 1980;
"the Valuation Acts" means the Lands Valuation (Scotland) Act 1854, the Acts amending that Act, and any other enactment relating to valuation;
"apportionment note" has the meaning assigned to it in paragraph 1 of Schedule 5 to this Act;
"council tax" shall be construed in accordance with the provisions of section 70(1) above;
"council water charge" shall be construed in accordance with the provisions of paragraph 6 of Schedule 11 to this Act;
"levying authority" means a regional or islands council;
"local authority", except in Schedule 11, means a regional, islands or district council;
"housing body" means—
    (a) a district council;
    (b) a development corporation (within the meaning of the New Towns (Scotland) Act 1968); or
    (c) Scottish Homes;
"part residential subjects" means lands and heritages which are used partly as the sole or main residence of any person, other than—
    (a) dwellings (except the residential part of part residential subjects);
    (b) such other class or classes of lands and heritages as may be prescribed;
"public sewage treatment works" has the meaning assigned to it in section 59(1) of the 1968 Act;
"public sewer" has the meaning assigned to it in section 59(1) of the 1968 Act;
"rateable value" shall be construed in accordance with the provisions of section 6 of the 1956 Act;
"resident", in relation to any dwelling, means an individual who has attained the age of 18 years and has his sole or main residence in the dwelling; and cognate expressions shall be construed accordingly;
"valuation appeal committee" means a valuation appeal committee established under section 4 of the 1975 Act;
"water authority" has the meaning assigned to it in section 3 of the 1980 Act.

(2) In this Part and sections 107 to 112 below and in any other enactment, whether passed or made before or after the passing of this Act, and unless the context otherwise requires—

- (a) the word "rate" shall mean—
  - (i) the non-domestic rate;
  - (ii) the non-domestic water rate; and
  - (iii) the non-domestic sewerage rate;
- (b) the expression "non-domestic rate" shall be construed in accordance with the provisions of section 37 of the 1975 Act;
- (c) the expression "non-domestic water rate" shall be construed in accordance with the provisions of section 40 of the 1980 Act; and
- (d) the expression "non-domestic sewerage rate" shall be construed in accordance with the provisions of paragraph 19 of Schedule 11 to this Act, and cognate expressions shall be construed accordingly.

(3) In this Part—

- (a) any reference to dwellings listed in a particular valuation band shall be construed in accordance with section 74(5) above; and
- (b) any reference to an amount payable in respect of council tax for any financial year includes a reference to an amount payable in respect of council tax for any period falling within that year.

NOTE

Sub-s (3)(b): With respect to the council water charge, the words 'the council water charge' shall be substituted for the words 'council tax' by the Council Water Charge (Scotland) Regulations 1992, SI 1992/1203, Schedule, para 1(h).

PART III. COMMUNITY CHARGES

100. Abolition of community charges

(1) No person shall be subject to a community charge in respect of any day falling after 31st March 1993.

(2) In this section "community charge" means—

- (a) in relation to England and Wales, any community charge provided for by the 1988 Act;
- (b) in relation to Scotland, any community charge or community water charge provided for by the 1987 Act.

[*Sections 101–102 apply to England and Wales only.*]

PART IV. MISCELLANEOUS

Social security

103. Council tax benefit.

Schedule 9 to this Act (which amends the Social Security Acts so as to make provision for benefit in respect of council tax in Great Britain) shall have effect.

NOTE
See the Council Tax Benefit Regulations 1992, SI 1992/1814.

English and Welsh provisions

[*Sections 104–106 apply to England and Wales only.*]

Scottish provisions

107. Water and sewerage charges.

(1) Parts I to III of Schedule 11 to this Act shall have effect in relation to water and sewerage charges in respect of the financial year 1993-94 and subsequent financial years.

(2) The 1980 Act shall have effect subject to the amendments made in Part IV of that Schedule.

108. Payments to local authorities by Secretary of State.

(1) The Secretary of State may, in respect of the financial year 1993-94 and each subsequent financial year—

    (a) make grants, (to be known as "revenue support grants") to local authorities; and

    (b) distribute among local authorities the money recovered by way of non-domestic rates ("non-domestic-rate income") in that financial year.

(2) Schedule 12 to this Act has effect in relation to revenue support grant and the recovery and distribution of non-domestic rate income.

109. Council tax grants.

(1) If regulations under section 80 above have effect in respect of a financial year the Secretary of State may, with the consent of the Treasury, pay a grant to a levying authority as regards that financial year.

(2) The amount of the grant shall be such as the Secretary of State may with the consent of the Treasury determine.

(3) A grant under this section shall be paid at such time, or in instalments of such amounts and at such times, as the Secretary of State may with the consent of the Treasury determine.

(4) In making any payment of grant under this section the Secretary of State may impose such conditions as he may with the consent of the Treasury determine; and the conditions may relate to the repayment in specified circumstances of all or part of the amount paid.

(5) In deciding whether to pay a grant under this section, and in determining the amount of any such grant, the Secretary of State shall have regard to his estimate of any amount which, in consequence of the regulations, the authority might reasonably be expected to lose, or to have lost, by way of payments in respect of council tax as it has effect for the financial year concerned.

110. Amendments to the 1975 Act in relation to non-domestic rates.

(1) After section 7 of the 1975 Act there shall be inserted the following section—

" 7A. Provisions as to setting of non-domestic rates.

(1) The Secretary of State shall, in respect of the financial year 1993-94 and each subsequent financial year, prescribe for each local authority a rate which shall be their non-domestic rate in respect of that year.

(2) Non-domestic rates shall be levied in accordance with section 7 of this Act by each rating authority in respect of lands and heritages—

    (a)   which are subjects (other than part residential subjects) in respect of which there is an entry in the valuation roll, according to their rateable value or, where a rateable value has been prescribed or determined in respect of the lands and heritages under section 128 of the Local Government Finance Act 1988, according to that rateable value; or

    (b)   which are part residential subjects, according to that part of their rateable value which is shown in the apportionment note as relating to the non-residential use of those subjects or, where a rateable value has been prescribed or determined in respect of the lands and heritages under section 128 of the Local Government Finance Act 1988, according to that part of that rateable value which is so shown in the apportionment note.

(3) The rates prescribed under subsection (1) above shall be known—

    (a)   in the case of the regional council, as the non-domestic regional rate;
    (b)   in the case of the district council, as the non-domestic district rate; and
    (c)   in the case of the islands council, as the non-domestic islands rate.

(4) References (however expressed) in any enactment to the non-domestic rate determined by a local authority shall be construed as references to the non-domestic rate prescribed for the local authority under this section.

(5) A statutory instrument containing any order under this section shall be subject to annulment in pursuance of a resolution of either House of Parliament."

(2) For section 7A of the 1975 Act there shall be substituted the following section—

" 7B. Provisions as to setting of non-domestic rates.

(1) The Secretary of State shall, in respect of the financial year following that in which this subsection comes into force and each subsequent financial year, prescribe a rate which shall be the non-domestic rate to be levied throughout Scotland in respect of that financial year.

(2) Subject to subsection (3) below, non-domestic rates shall be levied in accordance with section 7 of this Act by each rating authority in respect of lands and heritages in their area, being lands and heritages—

    (a)   which are subjects (other than part residential subjects) in respect of which there is an entry in the valuation roll, according to their rateable value or, where a rateable value has been prescribed or determined in respect of the lands and heritages under section 128 of the Local Government Finance Act 1988, according to that rateable value; or

(b) which are part residential subjects, according to that part of their rateable value which is shown in the apportionment note as relating to the non-residential use of those subjects or, where a rateable value has been prescribed or determined in respect of the lands and heritages under section 128 of the Local Government Finance Act 1988, according to that part of that rateable value which is so shown in the apportionment note.

(3) In the application of section 7 of this Act to the levying of the non-domestic rate prescribed under this section, for the words 'to which the rate relates' in each of subsections (1) and (2) of that section there shall be substituted the words 'of the rating authority'.

(4) References (however expressed) in any enactment to the non-domestic rate determined by a local authority shall be construed as references to the non-domestic rate prescribed under this section.

(5) A statutory instrument containing any order under this section shall be subject to annulment in pursuance of a resolution of either House of Parliament."

(3) In section 37 (interpretation) of the 1975 Act, in the definition of "non-domestic rate", for "section 7A" there shall be substituted "section 7B".

(4) For section 9A of the 1975 Act (as inserted by paragraph 13 of Schedule 12 to the 1988 Act) there shall be substituted the following section—

" 9A. Interest on rates paid in error.

(1) Subject to regulations made under this section—

(a) where any amount has been paid to a rating authority in respect of rates either—

(i) in error; or
(ii) in consequence of the entry on to the valuation roll of a valuation which is subsequently reduced,

and the rating authority repay the amount, the authority shall also pay to the person to whom the repayment is made interest on the amount; and

(b) where any amount has been paid to any person by a rating authority either—

(i) in error; or
(ii) in consequence of the entry on to the valuation roll of a valuation which is subsequently increased,

and the rating authority recover the amount, the authority may also recover from that person any interest paid on that amount.

(2) The Secretary of State may by regulations make provision as to—

(a) the circumstances in which interest is to be payable or recoverable by a rating authority;

(b) the rate at which any interest is to be paid, or the manner in which such rate is to be determined; and

(c) the date or dates from which, or by reference to which, any payment of interest is to run.

(3) This section applies to any payments such as are mentioned in subsection (1) which were made—

(a) after 1st April 1990; and

(b) before the coming into force of this section,

as it applies to such payments made after the coming into force of this section; but does not entitle any person to receive any payment of interest in respect of any such payment made before 1st April 1990.

(4) Regulations made under this section may provide for the deduction from any sum paid by way of interest under or by virtue of this section of any sum previously paid under or by virtue of any other enactment by way of interest in respect of the same payment.

(5) Regulations under this section—

(a) may make different provision in relation to different cases or descriptions of case;

(b) may include such transitional provisions as appear to the Secretary of State to be necessary or expedient and

(c) shall be made by statutory instrument subject to annulment in pursuance of a resolution of either House of Parliament."

NOTE

Sub-s (4): See the Non-Domestic Rating (Payment of Interest) (Scotland) Regulations 1992, SI 1992/2184.

---

111. Statutory and other references to rateable values etc.

(1) Where—

(a) in any deed relating to heritable property executed before 1st April 1989 there is any provision which apportions any liability according to the assessed rental or, as the case may be, the gross annual net annual or rateable value of any properties; and

(b) all the properties involved in the apportionment appear in the valuation roll in force immediately before 1st April 1989; and

(c) one or more of the properties constitute dwellings,

then, with effect from 1st April 1989, any reference to the assessed rental or, as the case may be, to any of those values in any such deed shall, unless the context otherwise requires, be construed as a reference to the net annual value or, as the case may be, to the gross annual, net annual or rateable value which appears in relation to any of those properties in the valuation roll in force immediately before that date.

(2) Where in any document executed before 1st April 1989 there is a reference to the assessed rental or, as the case may be, to the gross annual, net annual or rateable value of any property which—

(a) constitutes a dwelling; and

(b) appears in the valuation roll in force immediately before 1st April 1989,

then, with effect from that date that reference shall, unless the context otherwise requires, be construed as a reference to the net annual value or, as the case may be, to the gross annual, net annual or rateable value which appears in relation to that property in the valuation roll in force immediately before that date.

(3) Subject to subsection (4) below, where in any enactment (including an enactment contained in a subordinate instrument) there is a reference to the gross annual value, net annual value or rateable value of any property which constitutes a dwelling, then, with effect from 1st April 1989, that reference shall, unless the context otherwise requires, be construed as a reference to the gross annual value, net annual value or rateable value—

(a) subject to subsection (6) below, which appears in relation to that property in the valuation roll in force immediately before that date; or

(b) subject to subsection (7) below, in the case of such property which does not come into existence or occupancy as a dwelling until after that date, which would have appeared in the roll in respect of it had it been in existence or occupancy as such immediately before that date.

(4) Where in any enactment (including an enactment contained in a subordinate instrument or an enactment which falls to be construed in accordance with subsection (3) above) there is a reference to a rate or rateable value or to any factor connected with rating, or valuation for rating, the Secretary of State may make regulations providing that the reference shall instead be such as is prescribed.

(5) Regulations may provide as mentioned in subsection (4) above—

(a) as regards such enactment, or enactments of such description, as may be prescribed;

(b) in such way as the Secretary of State thinks fit (whether by amending enactments or otherwise).

(6) Where, before or after 1st April 1989, there is a material change of circumstances, within the meaning of section 37(1) of the 1975 Act—

(a) in relation to any such property as is mentioned in subsection (3)(a) above; and

(b) in respect of which no alteration has been made to the valuation roll in force immediately before that date,

references in that subsection to the gross annual, net annual or rateable value of that property which appears in the roll in force immediately before that date shall be construed as references to the gross annual, net annual or rateable value which would have so appeared had the roll been altered to take account of that material change of circumstances.

(7) Where there is a material change of circumstances, with the meaning of section 37(1) of the 1975 Act, in relation to any such property as is mentioned in subsection (3)(b) above, references in that subsection to the gross annual, net annual or rateable value of that property which would have appeared in respect of it in the roll in force immediately before 1st April 1989 shall be construed as references to the gross annual, net annual or rateable value which would have so appeared had that material change of circumstances been taken into account.

(8) The assessor shall, at the request of any person and on payment of such fee as may be prescribed, certify—

(a) what would have appeared in the valuation roll in force immediately before 1st April 1989 as the gross annual value, net annual value or rateable value of any such property as is mentioned in subsection (3)(b) above; or

(b) what would have appeared in that roll as the gross annual value, net annual value or rateable value of any such property as is mentioned in subsection (3) above had that roll been altered to take account of any material change of circumstances, within the meaning of section 37(1) of the 1975 Act, occurring before or after that date.

(9) An appeal shall lie—

(a) against any certificate issued by the assessor under subsection (8) above; or

(b) against any refusal by the assessor to issue a certificate under that subsection,

and the provisions of the Valuation Acts in regards to appeals and complaints shall apply, subject to such modifications and adaptations as may be prescribed, for the purposes of this subsection.

(10) Without prejudice to section 35 of the Lands Valuation (Scotland) Act 1854 (which relates to the preservation of valuation rolls by the Keeper of the Records of Scotland), the assessor for each valuation area shall retain a copy of the valuation roll in force immediately before 1st April 1989 for the purposes of this Act; and the copy so retained shall be made available for public inspection at the assessor's offices during ordinary business hours.

(11) Where the net annual value of any property does not appear, or would not have appeared, in the valuation roll in force immediately before 1st April 1989, references in this section to the appearance in that roll of the net annual value of that property shall be taken as references to the appearance of its rateable value.

(12) For the purposes of this section "gross annual value", "net annual value" and "rateable value" shall continue to be construed in accordance with the provisions of section 6 of the 1956 Act as those provisions had effect immediately before 1st April 1989.

112. Council tax and community charges: restrictions on voting.

(1) This section applies at any time to a member of a local authority, or a member of a committee of a local authority or of a joint committee of two or more local authorities (including in either case a sub-committee), if at that time—

(a) a sum falling within paragraph 1(1)(a) of Schedule 8 to this Act (including a sum falling within that paragraph by virtue of paragraph 11 of Schedule 11 to this Act) has become payable by him and has remained unpaid for at least two months; or

(b) a sum falling within paragraph—

(i) 4 or 5 of Schedule 2 (collection etc. of community charges); or

(ii) 11 of Schedule 5 (as read with the said paragraphs 4 and 5),

to the 1987 Act has become payable by him and has remained unpaid for at least three months.

(2) Subject to subsection (4) below, if a member to whom this section applies is present at a meeting of the authority or committee at which any of the following matters is the subject of consideration, namely—

(a) the setting of council tax under section 93(1)(a) above;
(b) the substitute setting of council tax under section 94(1) above;
(c) a reduced or deemed setting under paragraph 3 of Schedule 7 to this Act;
(d) the setting of council water charge under paragraph 9(a) of Schedule 11 to this Act; or
(e) the exercise of any functions under Schedule 2, 3 or 8 or paragraph 11 of Schedule 11 to this Act, or Schedule 2 or paragraph 11 of Schedule 5 to the 1987 Act,

he shall at the meeting and as soon as practicable after its commencement disclose the fact that this section applies to him and shall not vote on any question with respect to the matter.

(3) If a person fails to comply with subsection (2) above, he shall be guilty of an offence, and shall for each offence be liable on summary conviction to a fine not exceeding level 3 on the standard scale, unless he proves that he did not know—

(a) that this section applied to him at the time of the meeting; or
(b) that the matter in question was the subject of consideration at the meeting.

(4) Subsections (1) to (3) of section 41 (removal or exclusion of disability) of the 1973 Act shall apply in relation to this section and any disability imposed by it as they apply in relation to section 38 (provision as to disability of members of authorities from voting) of that Act and any disability imposed by that section.

Part V. Supplemental

113. Orders and regulations.

(1) Any power of the Secretary of State or the Treasury under this Act to make orders or regulations (other than the power to make orders under section 54(6) above) may be so exercised as to make different provision for different cases or descriptions of case, including different provisions for different areas or for different authorities.

(2) Any power of the Secretary of State or the Treasury under this Act to make orders or regulations includes power to make such incidental, consequential, transitional or supplementary provision as he or they think necessary or expedient.

(3) Any power of the Secretary of State or the Treasury under this Act to make orders or regulations shall be exercisable by statutory instrument which, except in the case of orders, under—

(a) section 5(4), 11(3), 54(6), 57(2), 59(2), 74(3) or 79(3) above;
(b) section 119(2) below; or
(c) paragraph 1 of Schedule 12 to this Act,

shall be subject to annulment in pursuance of a resolution of either House of Parliament.

NOTES

Sub-s (1): See the Council Tax (Valuation of Dwellings) (Scotland) Regulations 1992, SI 1992/1329; the Council Tax (Contents of Valuation Lists) (Scotland) Regulations 1992, SI 1992/1330; the Council Tax (Administration and Enforcement) (Scotland) Regulations 1992, SI 1992/1332; the Council Tax (Reductions for Disabilities) (Scotland) Regulations 1992,

SI 1992/1335; the Council Tax (Discounts) (Scotland) Order 1992, SI 1992/1408; the Council Tax (Discounts) (Scotland) Regulations 1992, SI 1992/1409.

114. Power to make supplementary provision.

(1) The Secretary of State may at any time by order make such supplementary, incidental, consequential or transitional provision as appears to him to be necessary or expedient for the general purposes or any particular purposes of this Act or in consequence of any of its provisions or for giving full effect to it.

(2) An order under this section may in particular make provision for amending, repealing or revoking (with or without savings) any provision of an Act passed before or in the same session as this Act, or of an instrument made under an Act before the passing of this Act, and for making savings or additional savings from the effect of any amendment or repeal made by this Act.

(3) Any provision that may be made under this section shall be in addition and without prejudice to any other provision of this Act.

(4) No other provision of this Act shall be construed as prejudicing the generality of the powers conferred by this section.

(5) In this section "Act" includes a private or local Act.

NOTE
See the Council Tax Benefit (Transitional) Order 1992, SI 1992/1909.

115. Financial provisions.

(1) There shall be paid out of money provided by Parliament—

    (a) any sums required to enable valuations to be carried out in accordance with Part I or II of this Act;

    (b) any expenses of the Secretary of State incurred in consequence of this Act; and

    (c) any increase attributable to this Act in the sums payable out of money so provided under any other enactment.

(2) There shall be paid into the Consolidated Fund—

    (a) any sums received by the Secretary of State in consequence of this Act; and

    (b) any increase attributable to this Act in the sums payable into that Fund under any other enactment.

116. Interpretation: general.

(1) In this Act, unless the context otherwise requires—
    "the 1987 Act" means the Abolition of Domestic Rates Etc. (Scotland) Act 1987;
    "the 1988 Act" means the Local Government Finance Act 1988;
    "the Social Security Acts" means the Social Security Contributions and Benefits Act 1992 and the Social Security Administration Act 1992;
    "financial year" means any period of twelve months beginning with 1st April;
    "information" includes accounts, estimates and returns;

"prescribed" means prescribed by regulations made by the Secretary of State.

(2) Nothing in any private or local Act (whenever passed) shall in any way affect the operation of this Act or of anything done under it.

NOTES

Sub-s (1): See the Council Tax (Valuation of Dwellings) (Scotland) Regulations 1992, SI 1992/1329; the Council Tax (Contents of Valuation Lists) (Scotland) Regulations 1992, SI 1992/1330; the Council Tax (Liability of Owners) (Scotland) Regulations 1992, SI 1992/1331; the Council Tax (Administration and Enforcement) (Scotland) Regulations 1992, SI 1992/1332; the Council Tax (Dwellings) (Scotland) Regulations 1992, SI 1992/1334; the Council Tax (Reductions for Disabilities) (Scotland) Regulations 1992, SI 1992/1335; the Council Tax (Discounts) (Scotland) Regulations 1992, SI 1992/1409.

117. Minor and consequential amendments and repeals.

(1) The enactments mentioned in Schedule 13 to this Act shall have effect subject to the amendments there specified (being minor amendments and amendments consequential on the provisions of this Act).

(2) The enactments mentioned in Schedule 14 to this Act (which include some that are spent or no longer of practical utility) are hereby repealed to the extent specified in the third column of that Schedule.

118. Savings and transitional provisions.

(1) Nothing in this Act (except sections 101 and 102) shall affect the operation of the 1988 Act in relation to any community charge in respect of a day falling before 1st April 1993; and nothing in this Act (except paragraphs 1 to 4 and 6(11) of Schedule 10) shall affect the operation of that Act in relation to any financial year beginning before that date.

(2) Nothing in this Act (except section 101) shall affect the operation of the 1987 Act in relation to any community charge in respect of a day falling before 1st April 1993.

(3) The repeal by this Act of the 1987 Act shall not affect any amendment made by that Act to any other enactment; and the repeal by this Act of any enactment amending that Act shall not affect any amendment so made to that Act.

(4) Nothing in this Act shall affect the operation of the Social Security Acts in relation to any community charge benefit in respect of a day falling before 1st April 1993.

(5) In relation to any time before the commencement of the Social Security Acts, this Act and the repealed enactments shall have effect as if—

   (a) any reference in this Act to those Acts were a reference to those enactments;

   (b) any reference in this Act (except paragraph 4 of Schedule 9) to either of those Acts, or to any provision of those Acts, were a reference to the corresponding provisions or provision of those enactments;

   (c) subsections (1) to (7) of the section set out in paragraph 4 of Schedule 9 to this Act were substituted for subsections (8A), (8AA) and (8B) to (8F), and subsection (11) of that section were substituted for subsections (8G) and (8H), of section 20 of the Social Security Act 1986; and

(d) subsections (8) and (9) of the section so set out were substituted for subsections (5A) and (5B), and paragraphs (a) and (b) of subsection (10) of that section were substituted for paragraph (c) of subsection (6), of section 21 of that Act.

(6) The provisions of any regulations or orders relating to council tax benefit which—

(a) are made before the commencement of the Social Security Acts; and

(b) are expressed to come into force after that commencement,

may refer to any relevant provisions of those Acts rather than to the corresponding provisions of the repealed enactments.

(7) In this section—

"community charge" has the same meaning as in section 100 above;

"the repealed enactments" means the enactments repealed by the Social Security (Consequential Provisions) Act 1992;

and any reference to an enactment includes a reference to any regulations or orders made (or having effect as if made) under that enactment.

119. Short title, commencement and extent

(1) This Act may be cited as the Local Government Finance Act 1992.

(2) The following provisions of this Act, namely—

(a) sections 99(2), 110 and 111;

(b) paragraphs 1 to 4 of Schedule 10;

(c) paragraphs 29(a), 30, 31(b), 32 to 37 and 38(a), (b), (c) and (e) of Schedule 11;

(d) Schedule 13 except paragraphs 15 to 25, 31, 42, 44(c), 45 to 47, 59 to 74, 76 to 88, 92, 99 and 100; and

(e) Schedule 14 except the repeals in the 1988 Act (other than the repeals in Schedule 12) and the repeals in the Social Security Acts,

shall not come into force until such days as the Secretary of State may by order appoint; and different days may be appointed for different provisions or for different purposes.

(3) Part I of this Act, sections 102 and 104 to 106 above and Schedule 10 to this Act extend to England and Wales only.

(4) Part II of this Act, sections 107 to 112 above and Schedules 11 and 12 to this Act extend to Scotland only.

(5) This Act does not extend to Northern Ireland.

SCHEDULES
SCHEDULE 1
PERSONS DISREGARDED FOR PURPOSES OF DISCOUNT
Persons in detention

1. (1) A person shall be disregarded for the purposes of discount on a particular day if on the day—

- (a) he is detained in a prison, a hospital or any other place by virtue of an order of a court to which sub-paragraph (2) below applies;
- (b) he is detained under paragraph 2 of Schedule 3 to the Immigration Act 1971 (deportation);
- (c) he is detained under Part II or section 46, 47, 48 or 136 of the Mental Health Act 1983; or
- (d) he is detained under Part V or section 69, 70, 71 or 118 of the Mental Health (Scotland) Act 1984.

(2) The sub-paragraph applies to the following courts—

- (a) a court in the United Kingdom; and
- (b) a Standing Civilian Court established under the Armed Forces Act 1976.

(3) If a person—

- (a) is temporarily discharged under section 28 of the Prison Act 1952, or temporarily released under rules under section 47(5) of that Act; or
- (b) is temporarily discharged under section 27 of the Prisons (Scotland) Act 1989, or temporarily released under rules under section 39(6) of that Act,

for the purposes of sub-paragraph (1) above he shall be treated as detained.

(4) Sub-paragraph (1) above does not apply where the person—

- (a) is detained under regulations made under paragraph 8 of Schedule 4 to this Act;
- (b) is detained under section 76 of the Magistrates' Courts Act 1980, or section 9 of the Criminal Justice Act 1982, for default in payment of a fine; or
- (c) is detained only under section 407 of the Criminal Procedure (Scotland) Act 1975.

(5) In sub-paragraph (1) above "order" includes a sentence, direction, warrant or other means of giving effect to the decision of the court concerned.

(6) The Secretary of State may by order provide that a person shall be disregarded for the purposes of discount on a particular day if—

- (a) on the day he is imprisoned, detained or in custody under the Army Act 1955, the Air Force Act 1955 or the Naval Discipline Act 1957; and
- (b) such conditions as may be prescribed by the order are fulfilled.

The severely mentally impaired

2. (1) A person shall be disregarded for the purposes of discount on a particular day if—

- (a) on the day he is severely mentally impaired;
- (b) as regards any period which includes the day he is stated in a certificate of a registered medical practitioner to have been or to be likely to be severely mentally impaired; and
- (c) as regards the day he fulfils such conditions as may be prescribed by order made by the Secretary of State.

(2) For the purposes of this paragraph a person is severely mentally impaired if he has a severe impairment of intelligence and social functioning (however caused) which appears to be permanent.

(3) The Secretary of State may by order substitute another definition for the definition in sub-paragraph (2) above as for the time being effective for the purposes of this paragraph.

Persons in respect of whom child benefit is payable

3. (1) A person shall be disregarded for the purposes of discount on a particular day if on the day he—

- (a) has attained the age of 18 years; but
- (b) is a person in respect of whom another person is entitled to child benefit, or would be so entitled but for paragraph 1(c) of Schedule 9 to the Social Security Contributions and Benefits Act 1992.

(2) The Secretary of State may by order substitute another provision for sub-paragraph (1)(b) above as for the time being effective for the purposes of this paragraph.

Students etc.

4. (1) A person shall be disregarded for the purposes of discount on a particular day if—

- (a) on the day he is a student, student nurse, apprentice or youth training trainee; and
- (b) such conditions as may be prescribed by order made by the Secretary of State are fulfilled.

(2) In this paragraph "apprentice", "student", "student nurse" and "youth training trainee" have the meanings for the time being assigned to them by order made by the Secretary of State.

5. (1) An institution shall, on request, supply a certificate under this paragraph to any person who is following or, subject to sub-paragraph (3) below, has followed a course of education at that institution as a student or student nurse.

(2) A certificate under this paragraph shall contain such information about the person to whom it refers as may be prescribed by order made by the Secretary of State.

(3) An institution may refuse to comply with a request made more than one year after the person making it has ceased to follow a course of education at that institution.

(4) In this paragraph—
"institution" means any such educational establishment or other body as may be prescribed by order made by the Secretary of State; and
"student" and "student nurse" have the same meanings as in paragraph 4 above.

Hospital patients

6. (1) A person shall be disregarded for the purposes of discount on a particular day if on the day he is a patient who has his sole or main residence in a hospital.

(2) In this paragraph "hospital" means—

- (a) a health service hospital within the meaning of the National Health Service Act 1977 or section 108(1) (interpretation) of the National Health Service (Scotland) Act 1978; and
- (b) a military, air-force or naval unit or establishment at or in which medical or surgical treatment is provided for persons subject to military law, air-force law or the Naval Discipline Act 1957.

(3) The Secretary of State may by order substitute another definition for the definition in sub-paragraph (2) above as for the time being effective for the purposes of this paragraph.

Patients in homes in England and Wales

7. (1) A person shall be disregarded for the purposes of discount on a particular day if on the day—

    (a) he has his sole or main residence in a residential care home, nursing home, mental nursing home or hostel in England and Wales; and

    (b) he is receiving care or treatment (or both) in the home or hostel.

(2) In this paragraph—

"hostel" means anything which falls within any definition of hostel for the time being prescribed by order made by the Secretary of State under this sub-paragraph;

"mental nursing home" means anything which is a mental nursing home within the meaning of the Registered Homes Act 1984;

"nursing home" means anything which is a nursing home within the meaning of the Registered Homes Act 1984 or would be but for section 21(3)(a) of that Act;

"residential care home" means—

    (a) an establishment in respect of which registration is required under Part I of the Registered Homes Act 1984 or would be so required but for section 1(4) or (5)(j) of that Act; or

    (b) a building or part of a building in which residential accommodation is provided under section 21 of the National Assistance Act 1948.

    (3) The Secretary of State may by order substitute another definition for any definition of "mental nursing home", "nursing home" or "residential care home" for the time being effective for the purposes of this paragraph.

Patients in homes in Scotland

8. (1) A person shall be disregarded for the purposes of discount on a particular day if on the day—

    (a) he has as his sole or main residence a residential care home, nursing home, private hospital or hostel in Scotland; and

    (b) he is receiving care or treatment (or both) in the home, hospital or hostel.

(2) In this paragraph—

"hostel" means anything which falls within any definition of hostel for the time being prescribed by order made by the Secretary of State under this sub-paragraph;

"nursing home" means—

    (a) a nursing home within the meaning of section 10(2) of the Nursing Homes Registration (Scotland) Act 1938 in respect of which a person is registered; or

    (b) any premises in respect of which an exemption has been granted under section 6 or 7 of that Act;

"private hospital" means a private hospital within the meaning of section 12 (registration of private hospitals) of the Mental Health (Scotland) Act 1984;

"residential care home" means—

    (a) a residential establishment provided and maintained by a local authority in respect of their functions under section 13B (provision of care and after-care) of the Social Work (Scotland) Act 1968; or

    (b) a residential establishment to which Part IV of the said Act of 1968 applies; or

    (c) residential accommodation provided and maintained by a local authority under section 7 (functions of local authorities) of the Mental Health (Scotland) Act 1984, where the sole or main function of the establishment or accommodation is to provide personal care or support, combined with board, to persons who are solely or mainly resident in the establishment or accommodation.

(3) In the definition of "residential care home" in sub-paragraph (2) above—

"personal care" includes the provision of appropriate help with physical and social needs; and

"support" means counselling or other help provided as part of a planned programme of care.

(4) The Secretary of State may by order substitute another definition for any definition of "nursing home", "private hospital" or "residential care home" for the time being effective for the purposes of this paragraph.

Care workers

9. (1) A person shall be disregarded for the purposes of discount on a particular day if—

(a) on the day he is engaged in providing care or support (or both) to another person or other persons; and

(b) such conditions as may be prescribed are fulfilled.

(2) Without prejudice to the generality of sub-paragraph (1)(b) above the conditions may—

(a) require the care or support (or both) to be provided on behalf of a charity or a person fulfilling some other description;

(b) relate to the period for which the person is engaged in providing care or support (or both);

(c) require his income for a prescribed period (which contains the day concerned) not to exceed a prescribed amount;

(d) require his capital not to exceed a prescribed amount;

(e) require him to be resident in prescribed premises;

(f) require him not to exceed a prescribed age;

(g) require the other person or persons to fulfil a prescribed description (whether relating to age, disablement or otherwise).

Residents of certain dwellings

10. (1) A person shall be disregarded for the purposes of discount on a particular day if on the day he has his sole or main residence in a dwelling to which sub-paragraph (2) below applies.

(2) This sub-paragraph applies to any dwelling if—

(a) it is for the time being providing residential accommodation, whether as a hostel or night shelter or otherwise; and

(b) the accommodation is predominantly provided—

(i) otherwise than in separate and self-contained sets of premises;

(ii) for persons of no fixed abode and no settled way of life; and

(iii) under licences to occupy which do not constitute tenancies.

Persons of other descriptions

11. A person shall be disregarded for the purposes of discount on a particular day if—

(a) on the day he falls within such description as may be prescribed; and

(b) such conditions as may be prescribed are fulfilled.

NOTES
Paras 1, 2, 4, 5, 8,: See the Council Tax (Discounts) (Scotland) Order 1992, SI 1992/1408.
Paras 9, 11: See the Council Tax (Discounts) (Scotland) Regulations 1992, SI 1992/1409.

SCHEDULE 2

ADMINISTRATION

Introduction

1. (1) The Secretary of State may make regulations containing such provision as he thinks fit in relation to—

    (a) the collection of amounts persons are liable to pay in respect of council tax; and

    (b) other aspects of administration as regards council tax.

(2) Any reference in this Schedule to an authority is a reference to a billing authority or a levying authority.

Collection of council tax

2. (1) In the following provisions of this paragraph—

    (a) any reference to the liable person is a reference to a person who is solely liable to pay to an authority, in respect of a particular dwelling, an amount in respect of council tax for a financial year, and includes, unless the context otherwise requires, a reference to a person who in the opinion of the authority will be so liable; and

    (b) any reference to the chargeable amount is a reference to the amount the liable person is or will be liable to pay.

(2) Regulations under this Schedule may include provision—

    (a) that the liable person is to make payments on account of the chargeable amount, which may include payments during the course of the financial year concerned;

    (b) that payments on account must be made in accordance with an agreement between the liable person and the authority or a prescribed scheme for payment by instalments or a scheme for such payment made by the authority in accordance with prescribed rules;

    (c) that in prescribed circumstances payments on account must be calculated by reference to an estimate of the chargeable amount; and

    (d) that an estimate must be made on prescribed assumptions.

(3) Regulations under this Schedule may include provision—

    (a) that any person appearing to an authority to be a resident, owner or managing agent of a particular dwelling shall supply to the authority such information as fulfils the following conditions—

        (i) it is in the possession or control of the person concerned;

        (ii) the authority requests the person concerned to supply it; and

        (iii) it is requested by the authority for the purpose of identifying the person who, in respect of any period specified in the request, is or will be the liable person in relation to the dwelling;

    (b) that the information is to be supplied within a prescribed period of the request being made and, if the authority so requires, in a form specified in the request; and

    (c) that a request may be served on the person concerned either by name or by such description as may be prescribed.

(4) Regulations under this Schedule may include provision—

    (a)   that the authority must serve a notice or notices on the liable person stating the charge-able amount or its estimated amount and what payment or payments he is required to make (by way of instalment or otherwise);

    (b)   that no payment on account of the chargeable amount need be made unless a notice requires it;

    (c)   that a notice may be served on the liable person either by name or by such descrip-tion as may be prescribed;

    (d)   that a notice must be in a prescribed form;

    (e)   that a notice must contain prescribed matters;

    (f)   that a notice must not contain other prescribed matters;

    (g)   that where a notice is invalid because it does not comply with regulations under paragraph (d) or (e) above, and the circumstances are such as may be prescribed, a requirement contained in the notice by virtue of regulations under paragraph (a) or (b) above shall nevertheless have effect as if the notice were valid;

    (h)   that where a notice is invalid because it does not comply with regulations under paragraph (d) above, and a requirement has effect by virtue of regulations under paragraph (g) above, the authority must take prescribed steps to issue to the liable person a document in the form which the notice would have taken had it complied with regulations under paragraph (d) above;

    (i)   that where a notice is invalid because it does not comply with regulations under paragraph (e) above, and a requirement has effect by virtue of regulations under paragraph (g) above, the authority must take prescribed steps to inform the liable person of such of the matters prescribed under paragraph (e) above as were not con-tained in the notice; and

    (j)   that the authority must supply prescribed information to the liable person when it serves a notice.

(5) Regulations under this Schedule may include provision—

    (a)   that if the liable person fails to pay an instalment in accordance with the regulations, the unpaid balance of the chargeable amount or its estimated amount is to be pay-able on the day after the end of a prescribed period which begins with the day of the failure; and

    (b)   that any amount paid by the liable person in excess of his liability (whether the ex-cess arises because an estimate turns out to be wrong or otherwise) must be repaid or credited against any subsequent liability.

3. (1) Regulations under this Schedule may include provision as to the collection of amounts persons are jointly and severally liable to pay in respect of council tax.

(2) The regulations may include provision equivalent to that included under paragraph 2 above subject to any modifications the Secretary of State thinks fit.

(3) The regulations may include rules for determining whether any payment made by a per-son jointly and severally liable as to a fraction of an amount is (or is not) made towards sat-isfaction of his liability as to that fraction.

4. (1) In the following provisions of this paragraph—

    (a)   any reference to the chargeable amount is a reference to an amount which, in re-spect of a particular dwelling, a person is solely liable to pay to an authority in re-spect of council tax for a financial year, and includes, unless the context otherwise requires, an amount which in the opinion of the authority a person will be so liable to pay; and

    (b)   any reference to any calculation of the chargeable amount includes a reference to any estimate of the amount.

(2) Regulations under this Schedule may include provision that, before making any calculation of the chargeable amount for the purposes of regulations under this Schedule, the authority shall take reasonable steps to ascertain whether that amount is subject to any discount, and if so, the amount of that discount.

(3) The regulations may include provision that—

(a) where (having taken such steps) the authority has no reason to believe that the chargeable amount is subject to a discount, it shall assume, in making any calculation of the chargeable amount for the purposes of regulations under this Schedule, that the chargeable amount is not subject to any discount; and

(b) where (having taken such steps) the authority has reason to believe that the chargeable amount is subject to a discount of a particular amount, it shall assume, in making any such calculation, that the chargeable amount is subject to a discount of that amount.

(4) The regulations may include provisions that the authority must inform the person who is or will be liable to pay the chargeable amount of that assumption.

(5) The regulations may include provision that where—

(a) in accordance with any provision included under sub-paragraph (4) above the authority informs the person concerned that it has assumed that the chargeable amount is subject to a discount of a particular amount; and

(b) at any time before the end of the financial year following the financial year concerned, the person has reason to believe that the chargeable amount is not in fact subject to any discount, or is subject to a discount of a smaller amount,

the person shall, within such period as may be prescribed, notify the authority of his belief.

(6) In construing the reference in sub-paragraph (5)(b) above to the chargeable amount, the fact that the person concerned has wholly or partly discharged his liability to pay the amount shall be ignored.

5. Regulations under this Schedule may include, as regards a case where persons are or will be jointly and severally liable to pay to an authority, in respect of a particular dwelling, an amount in respect of council tax for a financial year, provision equivalent to that included under paragraph 4 above subject to any modifications the Secretary of State thinks fit.

Reductions for lump sum payment etc.

6. (1) Regulations under this Schedule may include provision empowering an authority, subject to such conditions as may be prescribed, to accept, in such cases as the authority may determine and in satisfaction of a person's sole liability to pay in respect of a dwelling an amount ("the chargeable amount") in respect of council tax for a financial year, an amount which—

(a) is determined by the authority; and

(b) is payable in a single lump sum; and

(c) is less than the authority's estimate of the chargeable amount.

(2) The regulations may include provision empowering or requiring the authority to make such adjustments (whether by way of an additional sum due to the authority or by way of repayment or credit by the authority or otherwise) as may be prescribed where the chargeable amount is subsequently estimated to be or proves to be greater or less than the amount originally (or last) estimated.

(3) The regulations may include, as regards a case where persons are jointly and severally liable to pay the chargeable amount, provision equivalent to that included under sub-paragraphs (1) and (2) above subject to any modifications the Secretary of State thinks fit.

(4) The regulations may include provision that, in a case where an authority has made provision by virtue of any of sub-paragraphs (1) to (3) above, any provision which is included in regulations under this Schedule by virtue of paragraph 2 or 3 above and is prescribed under this sub-paragraph shall not apply.

7. (1) Regulations under this Schedule may include provision that where—

    (a)   a person has sole liability to pay to an authority a sum on account in respect of council tax;

    (b)   a sum smaller than that sum is paid; and

    (c)   such conditions as may be prescribed are fulfilled;

the authority may accept the smaller sum in satisfaction of the liability to pay the sum on account.

(2) The regulations may include provision that—

    (a)   for prescribed purposes the sum on account shall be treated as having been paid in full;

    (b)   for other prescribed purposes the fact that only the smaller sum has been paid shall be taken into account.

(3) The regulations may include, as regards a case where persons are jointly and severally liable to pay to an authority a sum on account in respect of council tax, provision equivalent to that included under sub-paragraphs (1) and (2) above subject to any modifications the Secretary of State thinks fit.

8. (1) Regulations under this Schedule may include provision that an authority which has received a copy of a proposed list sent to it under section 22(5)(b) or 85(1)(b) of this Act shall, as respects each dwelling shown in the copy which in the opinion of the authority will be a relevant dwelling on the day when the list comes into force, notify the person concerned of such matters relating to the dwelling's entry in the copy as may be prescribed.

(2) Regulations under this Schedule may include provision that in any case where—

    (a)   a dwelling is not shown in the copy of a proposed list sent to an authority under section 22(5)(b) or 85(1)(b) of this Act but is shown in the copy of the list sent to the authority under section 22(7) or 85(4) of this Act; and

    (b)   in the opinion of the authority the dwelling was a relevant dwelling on the day when the list came into force,

the authority shall notify the person concerned of such matters relating to the dwelling's entry in the copy of the list sent to the authority under section 22(7) or 85(4) of this Act as may be prescribed.

(3) Regulations under this Schedule may include provision that in any case where—

    (a)   the valuation band shown as applicable to a dwelling in the copy of a proposed list sent to an authority under section 22(5)(b) or 85(1)(b) of this Act is different from that shown as applicable to it in the copy of the list sent to the authority under section 22(7) or 85(4) of this Act; and

    (b)   in the opinion of the authority the dwelling was a relevant dwelling on the day when the list came into force,

the authority shall notify the person concerned of such matters relating to the dwelling's entry in the copy of the list sent to the authority under section 22(7) or 85(4) of this Act as may be prescribed.

(4) The regulations may include provision—

    (a)   as to the period within which or time at which any notification must be given;

    (b)   prescribing additional information which the notification must contain;

(c) that if at the time when a person is notified under any provision included in regulations under sub-paragraph (2) or (3) above the authority has not yet given him a notification under any provision included in regulations under sub-paragraph (1) above, the authority shall not be required to give him such a notification.

(5) For the purposes of this paragraph a dwelling is a relevant dwelling on any day if—

(a) on the day the dwelling is an exempt dwelling; or
(b) in respect of the financial year in which the day falls and the dwelling, the amount set under section 30 or 93 of this Act or, where the authority is a regional council, each amount set under section 93 of this Act is nil.

(6) In this paragraph any reference to the person concerned is a reference to a person who, in respect of the particular dwelling, would be solely liable to pay to the authority an amount in respect of council tax for the particular day if the dwelling were not or had not been a relevant dwelling on that day.

9. (1) Regulations under this Schedule may include provision that, as regards each financial year, an authority shall take reasonable steps to ascertain whether any dwellings will be or were exempt dwellings for any period during the year.

(2) The regulations may include provision that—

(a) where (having taken such steps) the authority has no reason to believe that a particular dwelling will be or was an exempt dwelling for any period during the year, it shall assume, for the purposes of regulations under this Schedule, that the dwelling will be or was a chargeable dwelling for that period; and
(b) where (having taken such steps) the authority has reason to believe that a particular dwelling will be or was an exempt dwelling for any period during the year, it shall assume, for those purposes, that the dwelling will be or was an exempt dwelling for that period.

(3) The regulations may include provision—

(a) that the authority must inform the relevant person of that assumption;
(b) prescribing additional information which the authority must give to that person;
(c) as to the period within which or time at which any information must be given.

(4) The regulations may include provision that where—

(a) in accordance with any provision included under sub-paragraph (3) above the authority informs the relevant person that it has assumed that the dwelling will be or was an exempt dwelling for a particular period during the year; and
(b) at any time before the end of the following financial year, the person has reason to believe that in fact the dwelling will not be or was not an exempt dwelling for that period, or will be or was an exempt dwelling for a shorter period,

the person shall, within such period as may be prescribed, notify the authority of his belief.

(5) Regulations under this Schedule may include provision—

(a) that any person appearing to an authority to be a resident, owner or managing agent of a particular dwelling shall supply to the authority such information as fulfils the following conditions—
  (i) it is in the possession or control of the person concerned;
  (ii) the authority requests the person concerned to supply it; and
  (iii) it is requested by the authority for the purpose of identifying the person who, in respect of any period specified in the request, is or will be the relevant person in relation to the dwelling;
(b) that the information is to be supplied within a prescribed period of the request being made and, if the authority so requires, in a form specified in the request; and
(c) that a request may be served on the person concerned either by name or by such description as may be prescribed.

(6) In this paragraph any reference to the relevant person is a reference to a person who, in respect of the particular dwelling—

    (a) is or will be solely liable to pay to the authority an amount in respect of council tax for the period to which the assumption relates; or

    (b) would be so liable if the dwelling were not or had not been an exempt dwelling for that period.

10. (1) Regulations under this Schedule may include, as regards a case where, in respect of a particular dwelling, persons would be jointly and severally liable to pay to an authority an amount in respect of council tax for a particular day if the dwelling were not or had not been on that day a relevant dwelling for the purposes of paragraph 8 above, provision equivalent to that included under that paragraph subject to any modifications the Secretary of State thinks fit.

(2) Regulations under this Schedule may include, as regards a case where, in respect of a particular dwelling, persons—

    (a) are or will be jointly and severally liable to pay to an authority an amount in respect of council tax for a particular period; or

    (b) would be so liable if the dwelling were not or had not been an exempt dwelling for that period,

provision equivalent to that included under paragraph 9 above subject to any modifications the Secretary of State thinks fit.

Supply of information to authorities

11. (1) Regulations under this Schedule may include provision that any person mentioned in sub-paragraph (2) below shall supply to a billing authority such information as fulfils the following conditions—

    (a) it is in the possession or control of the person concerned;

    (b) the authority requests the person concerned to supply it;

    (c) it is requested by the authority for the purpose of carrying out its functions under Part I of this Act; and

    (d) it does not fall within any prescribed description of information which need not be supplied.

(2) The persons referred to in sub-paragraph (1) above are—

    (a) any other authority;

    (b) any precepting authority;

    (c) the electoral registration officer for any area in Great Britain; and

    (d) any community charges registration officer.

(3) The regulations may include provision that the information is to be supplied in a prescribed form and within a prescribed period of the request being made.

(4) In this paragraph and paragraph 12 below references to any community charges registration officer shall be construed—

    (a) in relation to such officers in England or Wales, in accordance with section 26 of the 1988 Act; and

    (b) in relation to such officers in Scotland, in accordance with section 12 of the 1987 Act.

12. (1) Regulations under this Schedule may include provision that any person mentioned in sub-paragraph (2) below shall supply to a levying authority such information as fulfils the following conditions—

    (a) it is in the possession or control of the person concerned;

    (b) the authority request the person concerned to supply it;

    (c) it is requested by the authority for the purpose of carrying out their functions under Part II of this Act; and

    (d) it does not fall within any prescribed description of information which need not be supplied.

(2) The persons referred to in sub-paragraph (1) above are—

    (a) any other authority;

    (b) any district council;

    (c) the electoral registration officer for any area in Great Britain;

    (d) any community charges registration officer;

    (e) the local assessor for the levying authority's area; and

    (f) any housing body operating in the levying authority's area.

(3) The regulations may include provision that the information is to be supplied in a prescribed form and within a prescribed period of the request being made.

13. (1) Regulations under this Schedule may include provision that—

    (a) a registrar of births and deaths in England and Wales shall supply to any appropriate billing authority which is prescribed such particulars of such deaths as may be prescribed;

    (b) the Registrar General for England and Wales shall supply to any billing authority which is prescribed such particulars of such deaths as may be prescribed.

(2) Regulations under this Schedule may include provision that—

    (a) a district registrar in Scotland shall supply to any appropriate levying authority which is prescribed such particulars of such deaths as may be prescribed;

    (b) the Registrar General for Scotland shall supply to any levying authority which is prescribed such particulars of such deaths as may be prescribed.

(3) The regulations may include provision as to the times at which and the manner in which the particulars are to be supplied.

(4) For the purposes of this paragraph—

    (a) an appropriate billing authority, in relation to a registrar of births and deaths, is a billing authority whose area includes all or part of, or falls within, the registrar's sub-district;

    (b) an appropriate levying authority, in relation to a district registrar, is a levying authority whose area includes all or part of, or falls within, the registrar's registration district.

14. (1) Where regulations under this Schedule impose a duty on a billing authority to supply information to any person, they may also require—

    (a) the Secretary of State;

    (b) any appropriate precepting authority; or

    (c) any appropriate levying body,

to supply the billing authority with prescribed information if the Secretary of State considers it to be information the billing authority needs in order to fulfil its duty.

(2) Where regulations under this Schedule contain provision about the contents or form of a notice to be served by a billing authority, they may also require the Secretary of State or any appropriate precepting authority to supply the billing authority with prescribed information if the Secretary of State considers it to be information the billing authority needs to ensure that the provision is met.

(3) Where any person other than the Secretary of State fails to supply information to a billing authority in accordance with regulations made by virtue of sub-paragraph (1) or (2) above, he shall be liable to indemnify the authority against any loss or damage which the authority sustains in consequence of the failure.

Para 8(5)(b): With respect to the council water charge, for the words 'the financial year in which the day falls' there shall be substituted the words 'the day': Council Water Charge (Scotland) Regulations 1992, SI 1992/1203, Schedule, para 7(b)(i); and for the words from 'for the amount' to the end of that sub-paragraph, there shall be substituted the words 'the qualifying conditions specified in paragraph 8 of Schedule 11 to this Act are not met': Council Water Charge (Scotland) Regulations 1992, SI 1992/1203, Schedule, para 7(b)(ii).

Paras 11-18: With respect to the council water charge, these paragraphs shall not apply: Council Water Charge (Scotland) Regulations 1992, SI 1992/1203, Schedule, para 7(c).

Paras 1(1); 2(2), (3), (4)(a)-(c), (e), (g), (i), (5); 3-10; 12; 13(2)(a), (3); 16; 18: See the Council Tax (Administration and Enforcement) (Scotland) Regulations 1992, SI 1992/1332.

SCHEDULE 3

PENALTIES

Failure to supply information to or notify billing authority

1. (1) Where a person is requested by a billing authority to supply information under any provision included in regulations under paragraph 2, 3, 9 or 10(2) of Schedule 2 to this Act, the authority may impose a penalty of £50 on him if—

   (a) he fails to supply the information in accordance with the provision; or
   (b) in purported compliance with the provision he knowingly supplies information which is inaccurate in a material particular.

(2) In any case where—

   (a) a person is required by any provision included in regulations under paragraph 4, 5, 9 or 10(2) of Schedule 2 to this Act to notify a billing authority; and
   (b) he fails without reasonable excuse to notify the authority in accordance with the provision,

the authority may impose a penalty of £50 on him.

(3) Where a penalty has been imposed on a person under sub-paragraph (1) above and he is requested by the authority again to supply the same information under the same provision, the authority may impose a further penalty of £200 on him if—

   (a) he fails to supply the information in accordance with the provision; or
   (b) in purported compliance with the provision he knowingly supplies information which is inaccurate in a material particular.

(4) Sub-paragraph (3) above applies each time the authority repeats a request.

(5) A penalty under this paragraph shall be paid to the authority imposing it.

(6) An authority may quash a penalty imposed by it under this paragraph.

Failure to supply information to or notify levying authority

2. (1) Where a person is requested by a levying authority to supply information under any provision included in regulations under paragraph 2, 3, 9 or 10(2) of Schedule 2 or paragraph 5 of Schedule 8 to this Act, the authority may impose a penalty of £50 on him if—

   (a) he fails to supply the information in accordance with the provision; or
   (b) in purported compliance with the provision he knowingly supplies information which is inaccurate in a material particular.

(2) In any case where—

   (a) a person is required by any provision included in regulations under paragraph 4, 5, 9 or 10(2) of Schedule 2 to this Act to notify a levying authority; and

   (b) he fails to notify the authority in accordance with the provision,

the authority may impose a penalty of £50 on him.

(3) Where a penalty has been imposed on a person under sub-paragraph (1) above and he is requested by the authority again to supply the same information under the same provision, the authority may impose a further penalty of £200 on him if—

   (a) he fails to supply the information in accordance with the provision; or

   (b) in purported compliance with the provision he knowingly supplies information which is inaccurate in a material particular.

(4) Sub-paragraph (3) above applies each time the authority repeats a request.

(5) A penalty under this paragraph shall be paid to the authority imposing it.

(6) If, after the imposition of a penalty under this paragraph but before the making of an appeal under paragraph 3 below against that imposition, the levying authority are satisfied that the person upon whom the penalty was imposed had a reasonable excuse for his failure, they may revoke the imposition of the penalty.

General

3. (1) A person may appeal to a valuation tribunal if he is aggrieved by the imposition on him of a penalty under paragraph 1 above.

(2) A person may appeal to a valuation appeal committee if he is aggrieved by the imposition on him of a penalty under paragraph 2 above.

(3) Where a penalty is imposed on a person under paragraph 1 or 2 above, and he alleges that there is no power in the case concerned to impose a penalty of the amount imposed, he may appeal under sub-paragraph (1) or (2) above against the imposition.

4. Where a person is convicted of an offence, the conduct by reason of which he is convicted shall not also allow a penalty to be imposed under paragraph 1 or 2 above.

5. (1) If it appears to the Treasury that there has been a change in the value of money since the passing of this Act or (as the case may be) the last occasion when the power conferred by this paragraph was exercised, they may by order substitute for any sum for the time being specified in paragraph 1 or 2 above such other sum as appears to them to be justified by the change.

(2) An order under this paragraph shall not apply in relation to any failure which began or anything done before the date on which the order comes into force.

6. (1) The Secretary of State may make regulations containing provision as to the collection of amounts payable as penalties under paragraph 1 or 2 above.

(2) The regulations may include provision for the collection of such amounts (including provision about instalments and notices) which is equivalent to that made in regulations under paragraphs 2 and 3 of Schedule 2 to this Act for the collection of amounts persons are liable to pay in respect of council tax subject to any modifications the Secretary of State thinks fit.

(3) The regulations may include provision that, where the imposition of a penalty is subject to an appeal, no amount shall be payable in respect of the penalty while the appeal is outstanding.

(4) The regulations may include rules for ascertaining whether an imposition is subject to an appeal, and whether an appeal is outstanding; and the regulations may treat an appeal as outstanding unless it is finally disposed of or abandoned or fails for non-prosecution.

(5) The regulations may include provisions dealing with any case where a penalty under paragraph 1 or 2 above is quashed or revoked, and may in particular provide for the repayment of an amount or the allowance of an amount by way of deduction against a sum due.

(6) In the application of this paragraph to England and Wales, any reference to an appeal includes a reference to an arbitration in pursuance of regulations made under paragraph 4 of Schedule 11 to the 1988 Act (valuation tribunals).

NOTE

Para 6: See the Council Tax (Administration and Enforcement) (Scotland) Regulations 1992, SI 1992/1332.

SCHEDULE 4

ENFORCEMENT: ENGLAND AND WALES

[*Schedule 4 applies to England and Wales only.*]

SCHEDULE 5

PART RESIDENTIAL SUBJECTS: SCOTLAND

Addition, deletion or amendment of apportionment notes

1. Where, on or after 1st April 1993, the assessor alters the valuation roll by entering therein lands and heritages which are part residential subjects, he shall apportion the net annual value and the rateable value of those lands and heritages as between the residential and non-residential use made of them and shall include in the entry an apportionment note.

2. Subject to paragraph 6 below, where, on or after 1st April 1993—

    (a)   lands and heritages included in the valuation roll become or cease to be part residential subjects; or

    (b)   there is such a change as between the residential and non-residential use of lands and heritages that the apportionments of the net annual value and the rateable value shown in the valuation roll are incorrect,

the assessor shall apportion or, as the case may be, re-apportion the net annual value and the rateable value of those lands and heritages as between the residential and non-residential use made of them, and shall alter the roll by adding an apportionment note to the entry in respect of those lands and heritages or, as the case may be, by deleting or amending the existing note.

3. Subject to paragraph 6 below, where, under any of the provisions of section 2(1) of the 1975 Act (which provides for the alteration of the valuation roll in certain circumstances), the assessor alters the net annual value and the rateable value of any lands and heritages which are part residential subjects, he shall apportion the new net annual value and the new rateable value as between the residential and the non-residential use of the subjects, and shall amend the apportionment note accordingly.

Date of coming into effect of addition, deletion or amendment of apportionment note

4. Where an apportionment note is included under paragraph 1 above as part of an entry relating to any land and heritages in the valuation roll, the note shall take effect from—

(a) the date when the lands and heritages to which the entry relates come into existence or occupancy; or

(b) the beginning of the financial year in which the entry is made,

whichever is the later.

5. Subject to paragraph 6 below, where the valuation roll is altered by the addition or deletion of, or by an amendment to, an apportionment note under paragraph 2 above, or by an amendment to an apportionment note under paragraph 3 above, the alteration shall take effect from—

(a) the date of the event by reason of which the addition, deletion or amendment is made, or

(b) the beginning of the financial year in which the addition, deletion or amendment is made,

whichever is the later.

6. No alteration to the valuation roll consisting of an amendment to an apportionment note shall be made or take effect until three months, or such other period as may be prescribed, after the date when that apportionment note is made or takes effect, whichever is the later.

Revaluation

7. Where the assessor makes up a valuation roll in respect of a financial year which is a year of revaluation within the meaning of section 37(1) of the 1975 Act (which defines terms used in that Act), he shall apportion the new net annual value and the new rateable value of any lands and heritages which are part residential subjects as between the residential and non-residential use of the subjects, and shall include in the entry relating to those lands and heritages a new apportionment note.

General

8. For the purposes of this Schedule the extent to which subjects are used residentially shall be determined by reference to the use made of the subjects as the sole or main residence of any person, and criteria may be prescribed by reference to which any apportionment or re-apportionment of net annual values and rateable values under this Schedule is to be carried out.

9. No rates shall be leviable in respect of such part of their rateable value as relates to the residential use of any lands and heritages which are part residential subjects.

Noting of date on which alterations take effect

10. Where the assessor has altered the entry in the valuation roll relating to any lands and heritages by adding, deleting or amending an apportionment note, he shall also alter the entry by adding thereto a note of the date on which the alteration takes effect.

Notification of addition, deletion or alteration of apportionment notes

11. Section 3 of the 1975 Act (which requires the assessor to notify the rating authority and other person affected of any alterations in the roll, and provides for a right of appeal against any such alterations) shall apply to any addition, deletion or amendment of apportionment notes made under this Schedule as it applies to deletions and alterations made under section 1 or 2 of that Act.

    (b) the Secretary of State may deduct such sums and pay them to the authority towards satisfaction of any such outstanding sum.

(2) Regulations made under this paragraph may include—

    (a) provision allowing or enquiring adjudication as regards an application and provision as to appeals and reviews;

    (b) a scheme containing provision as to the circumstances and manner in which and times at which sums are to be deducted and paid, provision about the calculation of such sums (which may include provision to secure that amounts payable to the debtor by way of income support do not fall below prescribed figures), and provision as to the circumstances in which the Secretary of State is to cease making deductions;

    (c) provision requiring the Secretary of State to notify the debtor, in a prescribed manner and at any prescribed time, of the total amount of sums deducted up to the time of the notification;

    (d) provision that, where the whole amount to which the application relates has been paid, the authority shall give notice of that fact to the Secretary of State.

NOTE

Paras 2(2), 5: See the Council Tax (Administration and Enforcement) (Scotland) Regulations 1992, SI 1992/1332.

SCHEDULE 9

SOCIAL SECURITY: COUNCIL TAX BENEFIT

Social Security Contributions and Benefits Act 1992 (c. 4)

1. (1) In subsection (1) of section 123 of the Social Security Contributions and Benefits Act 1992 (income-related benefits), for paragraph (e) there shall be substituted the following paragraph—

    "(e) council tax benefit."

(2) For subsections (4) to (6) of that section there shall be substituted the following subsection—

    "(4) Each billing or levying authority—

        (a) shall take such steps as appear to it appropriate for the purpose of securing that any person who may be entitled to council tax benefit in respect of council tax payable to the authority becomes aware that he may be entitled to it; and

        (b) shall make copies of the council tax benefit scheme, with any modifications adopted by it under the Administration Act, available for public inspection at its principal office at all reasonable hours without payment."

2. In subsection (2)(a) of section 129 of that Act (disability working allowance), for the words "community charge benefit" there shall be substituted the words "council tax benefit".

3. In subsection (2) of section 130 of that Act (housing benefit), for the words from "mortgage payments" to the end there shall be substituted the following paragraphs—

    "(a) payments to a billing or levying authority in respect of council tax; or

    (b) mortgage payments, or, in relation to Scotland, payments under heritable securities."

4. For section 131 of that Act there shall be substituted the following section—

"Council tax benefit

131. Council tax benefit.

(1) A person is entitled to council tax benefit in respect of a particular day falling after 31st March 1993 if the following are fulfilled, namely, the condition set out in subsection (3) below and either—

    (a) each of the two conditions set out in subsections (4) and (5) below; or

    (b) the condition set out in subsection (6) below.

(2) Council tax benefit—

    (a) shall not be allowed to a person in respect of any day falling before the day on which his entitlement is to be regarded as commencing for that purpose by virtue of paragraph (1) of section 6(1) of the Administration Act; but

    (b) may be allowed to him in respect of not more than 6 days immediately following the day on which his period of entitlement would otherwise come to an end, if his entitlement is to be regarded by virtue of that paragraph as not having ended for that purpose.

(3) The main condition for the purposes of subsection (1) above is that the person concerned—

    (a) is for the day liable to pay council tax in respect of a dwelling of which he is a resident; and

    (b) is not a prescribed person or a person of a prescribed class.

(4) The first condition for the purposes of subsection (1)(a) above is that there is an appropriate maximum council tax benefit in the case of the person concerned.

(5) The second condition for the purposes of subsection (1)(a) above is that—

    (a) the day falls within a week in respect of which the person concerned has no income;

    (b) the day falls within a week in respect of which his income does not exceed the applicable amount; or

    (c) neither paragraph (a) nor paragraph (b) above is fulfilled in his case but amount A exceeds amount B where—

        (i) amount A is the appropriate maximum council tax benefit in his case; and

        (ii) amount B is a prescribed percentage of the difference between his income in respect of the week in which the day falls and the applicable amount.

(6) The condition for the purposes of subsection (1)(b) above is that—

    (a) no other resident of the dwelling is liable to pay rent to the person concerned in respect of the dwelling; and

    (b) there is an alternative maximum council tax benefit in the case of that person which is derived from the income or aggregate incomes of one or more residents to whom this subsection applies.

(7) Subsection (6) above applies to any other resident of the dwelling who—

    (a) is not a person who, in accordance with Schedule 1 to the Local Government Finance Act 1992, falls to be disregarded for the purposes of discount; and

    (b) is not a prescribed person or a person of a prescribed class.

(8) Subject to subsection (9) below, where a person is entitled to council tax benefit in respect of a day, the amount to which he is entitled shall be—

17. (1) In subsection (2) of section 116 of that Act (legal proceedings), for the words "community charge benefits", in both places where they occur, there shall be substituted the words "council tax benefit".

(2) In subsection (5) of that section, for the words "community charge benefits" there shall be substituted the words "council tax benefit".

18. (1) In subsection (1) of section 128 of that Act (information for purposes of community charge benefits), for the words "charging authorities" there shall be substituted the words "billing authorities" and for the words "community charge benefits" there shall be substituted the words "council tax benefit".

(2) In subsection (2) of that section, for the words "Charging authorities" there shall be substituted the words "Billing authorities" and for the words "community charge benefits" there shall be substituted the words "council tax benefit".

(3) In subsection (3) of that section—

  (a) for the words "charging authority" there shall be substituted the words "billing authority";
  (b) for the words "community charge benefits", in both places where they occur, there shall be substituted the words "council tax benefit"; and
  (c) for the words "community charge benefit subsidy" there shall be substituted the words "council tax benefit subsidy".

19. (1) For subsections (1) and (2) of section 138 of that Act (nature of benefits) there shall be substituted the following subsection—

  "(1) Regulations shall provide that where a person is entitled to council tax benefit in respect of council tax payable to a billing authority or levying authority the benefit shall take such of the following forms as is prescribed in the case of the person—

  (a) a payment or payments by the authority to the person;
  (b) a reduction in the amount the person is or becomes liable to pay to the authority in respect of the tax for the relevant or any subsequent financial year;
  (c) both such payment or payments and such reduction."

(2) Subsections (3) and (4) of that section shall cease to have effect.

(3) In subsection (5) of that section, for the words "subsections (1) and (2)" there shall be substituted the words "subsection (1)" and for the words "chargeable financial year", in both places where they occur, there shall be substituted the words "financial year".

(4) Subsections (6) to (8) of that section shall cease to have effect.

(5) In subsection (9) of that section, the words "or (2) or (3)" shall cease to have effect and for the words "the 1987 Act or the 1988 Act" there shall be substituted the words "Part I or II of the Local Government Finance Act 1992".

20. (1) In subsection (1) of section 139 of that Act (arrangements for community charge benefits), for the words "Any community charge benefit" there shall be substituted the words "Council tax benefit" and for the words "community charge benefit scheme" there shall be substituted the words "council tax benefit scheme".

(2) For subsections (2) and (3) of that section there shall be substituted the following subsection—

  "(2) For the purposes of this section the appropriate authority is the billing authority or levying authority which levied the council tax as regards which a person is entitled to the benefit."

(3) In subsection (4) of that section, for the words "Charging authorities" there shall be substituted the words "Billing authorities" and for the words "community charge benefits" there shall be substituted the words "council tax benefit".

(4) In subsection (5) of that section, for the words "community charge benefits" there shall be substituted the words "council tax benefit".

(5) In subsection (6) of that section, for the words "charging authority" there shall be substituted the words "billing authority" and for the words "community charge benefit scheme" there shall be substituted the words "council tax benefit scheme".

(6) In subsection (7) of that section, for the word "benefits", in both places where it occurs, there shall be substituted the word "benefit".

(7) In subsection (9) of that section—

    (a) for the words "community charge benefit scheme" there shall be substituted the words "council tax benefit scheme";

    (b) for the words "community charge benefits" there shall be substituted the words "council tax benefit"; and

    (c) for the word "benefits", in the second and third places where it occurs, there shall be substituted the word "benefit".

(8) In subsection (10) of that section, for the word "benefits" there shall be substituted the word "benefit".

21. In subsection (1) of section 140 of that Act (community charge benefit finance), for the words "community charge benefit subsidy" there shall be substituted the words "council tax benefit subsidy" and for the words "charging authority" there shall be substituted the words "billing authority".

(2) In subsection (2) of that section, for the words "community charge benefit subsidy to be paid to a charging authority" there shall be substituted the words "council tax benefit subsidy to be paid to a billing authority".

(3) In subsection (3) of that section, for the words "community charge benefits" there shall be substituted the words "council tax benefit".

(4) In subsection (4) of that section, for the words "to a charging or levying authority by way of community charge benefit subsidy" there shall be substituted the words "to a billing or levying authority by way of council tax benefit subsidy".

(5) In subsection (5) of that section, for the words "community charge benefit subsidy" there shall be substituted the words "council tax benefit subsidy" and for the words "community charge benefits" there shall be substituted the words "council tax benefit".

(6) In subsection (6) of that section, for the words "community charge benefits" there shall be substituted the words "council tax benefit".

(7) In subsection (7) of that section, for the words "charging authority" there shall be substituted the words "billing authority".

22. In subsection (2)(d) of section 163 of that Act (general financial arrangements), for the words "community charge benefit subsidy" there shall be substituted the words "council tax benefit subsidy".

23. In subsection (1) of section 176 of that Act (consultation with representative organisations), for the words "community charge benefits" there shall be substituted the words "council tax benefit".

24. In subsection (7) of section 189 of that Act (regulations and orders: general), for the words "community charge benefits" there shall be substituted the words "council tax benefit".

25. In section 191 of that Act (interpretation: general)—

    (a) for the definitions of "chargeable financial year" and "charging authority" there shall be substituted the following definition—

> "'billing authority' has the same meaning as in Part I of the Local Government Finance Act 1992;";

(b)　after the definition of "dwelling" there shall be inserted the following definition—

> "'financial year' has the same meaning as in the Local Government Finance Act 1992;";

(c)　in the definition of "income-related benefit", for paragraph (e) there shall be substituted the following paragraph—

> "(e) council tax benefit."; and

(d)　for the definition of "levying authority" there shall be substituted the following definition—

> "'levying authority' has the same meaning as in Part II of the Local Government Finance Act 1992;".

26. A statutory instrument containing (alone or with other provisions) regulations or an order relating to council tax benefit and made by virtue of section 6, 7, 63, 76, 77, 128, 138 or 139 of that Act shall not be made before 1st April 1993 unless a draft of the instrument has been laid before and has been approved by a resolution of each House of Parliament.

NOTE
See the Council Tax Benefit Regulations, 1992, SI 1992/1814.

---

* * *

SCHEDULE 11

WATER AND SEWERAGE CHARGES: SCOTLAND

Part I. Charges for Water Services

1. Subject to the provisions of this Part of this Schedule, the expenditure incurred by the council of a region or islands area (in this Schedule referred to as a "local authority") in meeting any requisition under Part IV or VIII of the 1980 Act and in the exercise of any of their functions under any enactment (within the meaning of section 109(1) of that Act) in relation to water supply in their area shall, insofar as not otherwise met, be met out of—

(a)　the charges (hereinafter in this Schedule referred to as "direct charges") made under section 49 (payment of water supplies by meter) of the 1980 Act;

(b)　the council water charge mentioned in paragraph 6 below; and

(c)　the non-domestic water rate mentioned in paragraph 12 below.

Estimation and apportionment of expenditure

2. In respect of the financial year 1993-94 and each subsequent financial year, each local authority shall, before such date as may be prescribed in relation to each of those years—

(a)　subject to paragraph 3 below, estimate the amount of the expenditure mentioned in paragraph 1 above which they will incur in respect of that year; and

(b)　subject to paragraph 4 below, determine what proportion of that expenditure is to be met from each of the sources mentioned in sub-paragraphs (a) to (c) of paragraph 1 above.

NOTE
The prescribed date is 11 March: Water (Timetable) (Scotland) Regulations 1992, SI 1992/1202, Schedule 2.

---

3. In estimating the expenditure mentioned in paragraph 1 above which they will incur in respect of any financial year a local authority shall take into account—

(a) such additional sum as is in their opinion required—

    (i) to cover expenses previously incurred;

    (ii) to meet contingencies; and

    (iii) to meet any expenses which may fall to be met before the money to be received from the sources mentioned in paragraph 1 above in respect of the next following financial year will become available; and

(b) any means by which any part of that expenditure may otherwise be met or provided for.

4. A local authority may apportion their estimated expenditure under paragraph 2 above on whatever basis they consider appropriate, but they shall ensure that the apportionment is not such as to show undue preference to, or discriminate unduly against, any class or classes of person liable to pay—

(a) the direct charges;

(b) the council water charge; or

(c) the non-domestic water rate,

respectively.

Direct charges

5. After a local authority have, under paragraph 2 above, determined what proportion of their estimated expenditure in respect of a particular financial year is to be met out of direct charges, they shall, before such date as may be prescribed in relation to that year, determine such rate or rates of direct charges in respect of that year as will, when calculated in accordance with the provisions of section 49 (payment for water supplied by meter) of the 1980 Act, produce sufficient money to meet the said proportion; and different rates of direct charges may be determined for different circumstances.

NOTE

The prescribed date is 11 March: Water (Timetable) (Scotland) Regulations 1992, SI 1992/ 1202, Schedule 2.

Council water charge

6. Each local authority shall impose a water charge, which—

(a) shall be known as the regional council water charge or the islands council water charge, depending upon which authority impose it; and

(b) shall be payable in respect of dwellings situated in that authority's area.

Liability to pay council water charge

7.—(1) The council water charge shall be payable in respect of any dwelling which is not an exempt dwelling and in respect of which the qualifying conditions are met.

(2) For the purposes of this Schedule—

"dwelling" has the meaning assigned to it by section 72(2) of this Act;

"chargeable dwelling" means any dwelling in respect of which council water charge is payable; and

"exempt dwelling" means any dwelling of a class prescribed by an order made by the Secretary of State.

(3) For the purposes of sub-paragraph (2) above, a class of dwelling may be prescribed by reference to—

(a) the physical characteristics of dwellings;

  (b) the fact that dwellings are unoccupied or are occupied for prescribed purposes or
       are occupied or owned by persons of prescribed descriptions; or
  (c) such other factors as the Secretary of State thinks fit.

8. The qualifying conditions for the purposes of paragraph 7 above are—

  (a) that a water authority provide a supply of water to that dwelling;
  (b) that the water is not supplied wholly by meter; and
  (c) that the supply is not one which the water authority—

       (i)   were, immediately before 16th May 1949; and
       (ii) continue to be,

under an obligation to provide free of charge.

Setting of council water charge

9. After a local authority have, under paragraph 2 above, determined what proportion of their
estimated expenditure in respect of a particular financial year is to be met out of the council
water charge, they shall, before such date as may be prescribed in relation to that year—

  (a) set an amount of regional council water charge or islands council water charge, as
       appropriate, to be paid for that year in respect of a chargeable dwelling in their area
       listed in valuation band D (whether or not there is such a dwelling in their area) as
       specified in section 74(2) of this Act;
  (b) determine the amount of council water charge to be paid in respect of a chargeable
       dwelling in each of the other valuation bands specified in that section in accordance
       with the proportion mentioned in subsection (1) of that section,

and references in this Schedule to the setting of an amount of council water charge shall be
construed as references to the setting of the amount mentioned in paragraph (a) above.

NOTE
The prescribed date is 11 March: Water (Timetable) (Scotland) Regulations 1992, SI 1992/
1202, Schedule 2.

10. The amounts mentioned in paragraph 9(a) and (b) above shall be such as will provide
sufficient money to meet such proportion of the authority's estimated expenditure for that
year as they have determined under paragraph 2 above is to be met out of the council water
charge.

Application of provisions relating to council tax

11. The provisions of sections 71, 75 to 81, 96, 97 and 99(3) of this Act shall have effect,
subject to such adaptations, exceptions and modifications as may be prescribed, in relation
to the council water charge as they have effect in relation to the council tax.

Non-domestic water rate

12. The provisions of section 40 of the 1980 Act shall continue to have effect in relation to
the non-domestic water rate.

Part II. Charges for Sewerage Services

13. The expenditure incurred by a local authority in carrying out any of their functions under the 1968 Act shall, insofar as not otherwise met, be met out of—

  (a) the council tax; and
  (b) the non-domestic sewerage rate described in paragraphs 19 to 22 below.

Estimation and apportionment of expenditure

14. In respect of the financial year 1993-94 and each subsequent financial year, each local authority shall, before such date as may be prescribed in relation to each of those years—

    (a)   subject to paragraph 15 below, estimate the amount of the expenditure mentioned in paragraph 13 above which they will incur in respect of that year; and

    (b)   subject to paragraphs 16 and 17 below, determine what proportion of that expenditure is to be met out of—

        (i)   the council tax; and

        (ii)   the said non-domestic sewerage rate,

respectively.

NOTE
The prescribed date is 11 March: Water (Timetable) (Scotland) Regulations 1992, SI 1992/1202, Schedule 2.

---

15. In estimating the expenditure mentioned in paragraph 13 above which they will incur in respect of any financial year a local authority shall take into account—

    (a)   such additional sum as is in their opinion required—

        (i)   to cover expenses previously incurred;

        (ii)   to meet contingencies; and

        (iii)   to meet any expenses which may fall to be met before the money to be received from the sources mentioned in paragraph 13 above in respect of the next following financial year will become available; and

    (b)   any means by which any part of that expenditure may otherwise be met or provided for.

16. The proportion of the expenditure mentioned in paragraph 13 above which is to be met out of the council tax shall be such proportion as the local authority consider to be reasonably attributable to the provision by them of the sewerage services mentioned in section 1(1) of the 1968 Act to dwellings in their area, and no part of that proportion shall be met out of any other charge or rate leviable by the local authority.

17. Subject to paragraph 16 above, a local authority may apportion their estimated expenditure mentioned in paragraph 14(a) above on whatever basis they consider appropriate, but they shall ensure that the apportionment is not such as to show undue preference to, or discriminate unduly against, any class or classes of person liable to pay—

    (a)   the council tax; or

    (b)   the non-domestic sewerage rate,

respectively.

18. Where a local authority have determined in respect of any financial year what proportion of their estimated expenditure under the 1968 Act falls to be met out of the council tax, that amount shall form part of the total estimated expenses in respect of that year which are mentioned in section 93(3) of this Act.

Non-domestic sewerage rate

19. Each local authority shall, in respect of the financial year 1993-94 and each subsequent financial year, determine, before such date as may be prescribed in relation to each of those years, such amount of the non-domestic sewerage rate as will provide sufficient money to meet the proportion of their estimated expenditure under the 1968 Act for that year which they have determined under paragraph 14 above is to be met out of that rate.

NOTE
The prescribed date is 11 March: Water (Timetable) (Scotland) Regulations 1992, SI 1992/
1202, Schedule 2.

20. Subject to paragraphs 21 and 23 below, the non-domestic sewerage rate shall be levied
in respect of lands and heritages whose drains or private sewers are connected with public
sewers or public sewage treatment works and which are—

   (a) subjects (other than part residential subjects) in respect of which there is an entry in
the valuation roll, according to the rateable value of those subjects; or
   (b) part residential subjects, according to that part of their rateable value which is shown
in the apportionment note as relating to the non-residential use of those subjects.

21.—(1) Where, in respect of a financial year, the non-domestic sewerage rate is leviable
under paragraph 20 above in respect of lands and heritages which are both—

   (a) church or charity premises; and
   (b) premises to which, by virtue of subsection (4) of section 41 of the 1980 Act, that
section applies, whether or not they are premises in respect of which the non-domestic water rate is leviable,

the non domestic sewerage rate shall be levied not according to the rateable value of those
lands and heritages or that part thereof which is shown in the apportionment note as relating
to their non-residential use but instead in accordance with sub-paragraph (2) below.

(2) Where—

   (a) the water authority, in a resolution under subsection (1) of the said section 41, made
with respect to the lands and heritages mentioned in sub-paragraph (1) above or to
a class of premises which includes those lands and heritages, have specified for the
purposes of that subsection in respect of that year a fraction of net annual value
smaller than one half, then the non-domestic sewerage rate shall be levied according to that smaller fraction of the rateable value of those lands and heritages or, as
the case may be, that part thereof; and
   (b) the water authority have not so specified a smaller fraction, then the non-domestic
sewerage rate shall be levied according to one half of the rateable value of those
lands and heritages or, as the case may be, that part thereof.

(3) In sub-paragraph (1) above "church or charity premises" means—

   (a) premises to the extent to which, under section 22(1) of the 1956 Act (exemption from
non-domestic rates of church premises etc.), no non-domestic rate is leviable on them
in respect of the financial year; or
   (b) lands and heritages in respect of which relief in respect of the non-domestic rate is
given in respect of the financial year under subsection (2) of section 4 of the Local
Government (Financial Provisions etc.) (Scotland) Act 1962 (relief for premises
occupied by charities); or
   (c) lands and heritages in respect of which a reduction of or remission from the non-
domestic rate has effect in respect of the financial year under subsection (5) of the
said section 4.

22. The person who is liable to pay the non-domestic sewerage rate in respect of any premises
shall be the person who is liable to pay the non-domestic rate in respect of those premises,
or who would be liable to pay the non-domestic rate but for any enactment which exempts
those premises from the rate or by or under which relief or remission from liability for that
rate is given.

23. The provisions of—

   (a) Part XI of the 1947 Act;
   (b) Part VII of the 1973 Act; and
   (c) sections 7, 8, 9 and 10 of the 1975 Act,

(all of which relate to rating) shall apply, subject to such adaptations and modifications as may be prescribed, to the levying, collection and recovery of the non-domestic sewerage rate.

Part III. Miscellaneous Provisions

Accounts

24. Without prejudice to section 96(1) of the 1973 Act (which relates to the keeping of accounts by local authorities), each local authority shall prepare and maintain separate accounts in respect of its functions under the 1968 and 1980 Acts respectively.

25. The provisions of sections 96(2) to (4) (which impose requirements as to the accounts mentioned in section 96(1)) and 105(1) (which empowers the Secretary of State to make regulations as to the said accounts) of the 1973 Act shall apply in relation to the accounts mentioned in paragraph 24 above as they apply to the accounts mentioned in the said section 96(1).

Tariff of charges

26. Each local authority shall, in respect of the financial year 1993-94 and each subsequent financial year, and before such date as may be prescribed in relation to each of those years, prepare a statement, to be known as a tariff of charges, indicating—

    (a)   the basis upon which they have apportioned their estimated expenditure under paragraph 2 above as between—

        (i)   the direct charges,
        (ii) the council water charge, and
        (iii) the non-domestic water rate;

    (b)   the amount determined or set by them in respect of that year as—

        (i)   the rate or rates of the direct charges under paragraph 5 above,
        (ii) the council water charge under paragraph 9 above, and
        (iii) the non-domestic water rate under section 40 of the 1980 Act;

    (c)   the basis upon which they have apportioned their estimated expenditure for that year under paragraph 14 as between—

        (i)   the council tax, and
        (ii) the non-domestic sewerage rate; and

    (d)   the amount determined by them for that year as the non-domestic sewerage rate.

NOTE
The prescribed date is 31 March: Water (Timetable) (Scotland) Regulations 1992, SI 1992/1202, Schedule 2.

27. Each local authority shall make their tariff of charges available for public inspection at all reasonable hours at such places within their area as they may determine, and shall send a copy of the tariff to the Secretary of State.

Part IV. Amendments to the 1980 Act

28. The 1980 Act shall be amended in accordance with the following provisions of this Part.

29. In section 9A (which relates to the exemption from charges of water for fire fighting)—

(a) for the words "community water charges" there shall be substituted the words "council water charge"; and

(b) for paragraphs (a) and (b) there shall be substituted the following paragraphs—

> "(a) water taken for the purpose of extinguishing fires or taken by a fire authority for any other emergency purposes;
>
> (b) water taken for the purpose of testing apparatus installed or equipment used for extinguishing fires or for the purpose of training persons for fire-fighting; or
>
> (c) the availability of water for any purpose mentioned in paragraph (a) or (b) above:".

30. In section 35 (which relates to the power to supply water fittings)—

(a) in subsection (1) the words "by way either of sale or hire" shall cease to have effect;

(b) in subsection (2), for the words "let for hire" there shall be substituted the words "supplied otherwise than by sale"; and

(c) for subsection (5) there shall be substituted the following subsection—

> "(5) If any person—
>
> (a) so interferes with a meter used by the authority in determining the amount of any charges fixed in relation to any premises as intentionally or recklessly to prevent the meter from showing, or from accurately showing, the volume of water supplied to those premises; or
>
> (b) carries out, without the consent of the water authority, any works which he knows are likely to affect the operation of such a meter or which require the disconnection of such a meter; or
>
> (c) otherwise wilfully or negligently injures or suffers to be injured any water fitting belonging to the authority,
>
> he shall be guilty of an offence and liable on summary conviction to a fine not exceeding level 3 on the standard scale."

31. In section 40 (which provides for liability to the non-domestic water rate)—

(a) in subsection (2)(a), for the words "the water authority" there shall be substituted the words "a water authority"; and

(b) in subsection (4), for the words "5 to the Abolition of Domestic Rates Etc. (Scotland) Act 1987" there shall be substituted the words "11 to the 1992 Act".

32. After section 41 there shall be inserted—

"41A. Supply of water by meter.

(1) Where premises to which water is supplied are premises in respect of which there is an entry on the valuation roll, the occupier shall have the option of taking the supply by meter.

(2) Where premises to which water is supplied constitute a dwelling within the meaning of section 72(2) of the 1992 Act—

(a) the owner of the dwelling; or

(b) the person or persons who, in terms of section 75 of that Act—

> (i) are liable to pay council tax on the dwelling; or
> (ii) would have been so liable had the building not been exempt from council tax under section 72(6) of that Act,

shall have the option of taking the supply by meter.

(3) Neither of the parties mentioned in paragraph (a) or (b) of subsection (2) above may exercise the option mentioned in that subsection without the consent of the other.

(4) The exercise of the option mentioned in subsections (1) and (2) above is subject to—

(a) the payment by the person exercising the option of any reasonable charges made by the authority under section 35 of this Act; and

(b) the acceptance by him of such reasonable terms and conditions as may be published by the authority under section 55(1) of this Act,

and any question as to whether any such charges or terms and conditions are reasonable shall, in default of agreement, be referred to the Secretary of State who may determine it himself or, if he thinks fit, refer it for arbitration."

33. In section 46(2) (which relates to transport hereditaments), for the words "community water charge" there shall be substituted the words "council water charge".

34. For section 49 (which relates to payment for water supplied by meter) there shall be substituted—

"49. Payment for supplies by meter.

(1) Subject to the provisions of this section, where water is supplied by meter by a water authority, they may make—

(a) such a standing charge as they may from time to time consider appropriate, irrespective of whether any water is consumed on the premises; and

(b) charges calculated on the amount of water, if any, actually so consumed.

(2) Charges payable under this section shall be payable—

(a) in the case of premises (other than premises constituting the residential part of part residential subjects) in respect of which there is an entry on the valuation roll, by the occupier of the premises in respect of which they are due; or

(b) in the case of a dwelling within the meaning of section 72(2) of the 1992 Act, by the person or persons who—

(i) are liable to pay council tax on the dwelling; or

(ii) would have been so liable had the building not been exempt from council tax under section 72(6) of that Act.

(3) Charges payable under this section, including charges for any meter supplied by the authority, shall be recoverable in the manner in which non-domestic rates are recoverable.

(4) No charges shall be made under this section in relation to any lands and heritages such as are mentioned in section 5 (rebates for institutions in Scotland for the disabled) of the Rating (Disabled Persons) Act 1978 during any rebate period (within the meaning of section 6(2) of that Act)".

35. After section 56 there shall be inserted—

"56A. Regulations as to meters.

The Secretary of State may make regulations under this Act as to the installation, connection, use, maintenance, authentication and testing of meters, and as to any related matters."

36. In section 58(3) (which relates to the termination of the right to the supply of water on special terms), for the words "community water charge" there shall be substituted the words "council water charge".

37. In section 61(1)(b) (which relates to the calculation of the amount to be requisitioned by water authorities), for the words "community water charges" there shall be substituted the words "the council water charge".

38. In section 109(1) (which defines terms used in the Act)—

    (a) before the definition of "agricultural lands and heritages" there shall be inserted—
        "'the 1992 Act' means the Local Government Finance Act 1992;

    (b) in the definition of "apportionment note", for the words "2 of Schedule 1 to the Abolition of Domestic Rates Etc. (Scotland) Act 1987" there shall be substituted the words "1 of Schedule 5 to the 1992 Act";

    (c) after the definition of "contributing authority" there shall be inserted—
        "'council water charge' shall be construed in accordance with the provisions of paragraph 6 of Schedule 11 to the 1992 Act:";

    (d) after the definition of "enactment" there shall be inserted—
        "'fire authority' has the same meaning as in the Fire Services Act 1947;";

    (e) in the definition of "part residential subjects" for the words from "section" to the end there shall be substituted the words "section 99 (interpretation of Part II etc) of the 1992 Act;"; and

    (f) in the definition of "prescribed", after "prescribed by" there shall be inserted the words "or determined under".

NOTE
Para 7(2), (3): See the Council Tax (Exempt Dwellings) (Scotland) Order 1992, SI 1992/1333.
Para 11: See the Council Water Charge (Scotland) Regulations 1992, SI 1992/1203.

SCHEDULE 12

PAYMENTS TO LOCAL AUTHORITIES BY SECRETARY OF STATE: SCOTLAND

PART I. PAYMENTS TO LOCAL AUTHORITIES

General

1. (1) The local authorities—

    (a) to which revenue support grant is payable; and

    (b) among whom the distributable amount (within the meaning of paragraph 9 below) of non-domestic rate income is distributed,

in respect of a financial year shall be such local authorities as are specified in an order made by the Secretary of State; and different provision may be made for the purposes of sub-paragraphs (a) and (b) of this paragraph in respect of the same authority.

(2) The amount of revenue support grant payable in respect of a financial year to a local authority so specified shall be such amount as is determined in relation to that authority by order made by the Secretary of State.

(3) The amount of non-domestic rate income distributed in respect of a financial year to a local authority so specified shall be such part of the distributable amount for that year as is determined in relation to that authority by order made by the Secretary of State.

(4) Subject to paragraph 4 below, the Secretary of State may at any time by order—

    (a) make such amendments as he thinks fit to; or

    (b) revoke; or

    (c) revoke and replace with a different order,

any order made under this paragraph; and any amount of revenue support grant or non-domestic rate income which has been paid and which, in consequence of anything done under this paragraph, falls to be repaid may be recovered by the Secretary of State whenever and however he thinks fit.

(5) An order under this paragraph shall be known as a local government finance order.

2. (1) A local government finance order shall be made only with the consent of the Treasury.

(2) Before making a local government finance order the Secretary of State shall consult such associations of local authorities as appear to him to be appropriate.

(3) A local government finance order together with a report of the considerations which led to its provisions shall be laid before the House of Commons but shall have no effect until approved by a resolution of that House.

Payment of revenue support grant and non-domestic rate income

3. Revenue support grant and non-domestic rate income shall be paid to a local authority in such instalments and at such times as the Secretary of State may, with the consent of the Treasury, determine.

4. The Secretary of State may determine that the amount of revenue support grant or non-domestic rate income which has been paid to a local authority in respect of a financial year shall be final and, where he does so, he shall have no power to redetermine that amount.

Secretary of State's power on local authority's failure to provide information

5. Where under section 199 of the 1973 Act (which provides for reports and returns being made by local authorities and others) the Secretary of State requires a local authority to give information for the purposes of his functions in relation to revenue support grants or non-domestic rate income payable for the financial year 1993-94 or for any subsequent financial year, but that information is not given timeously—

    (a)   he may make an estimate as regards any element of the required information; and

    (b)   without prejudice to section 211 of that Act (which makes general provision concerning failure by a local authority to do what is required of them), for the said purposes any such estimate shall be deemed to be information given by the local authority.

PART II. NON-DOMESTIC RATING ACCOUNTS

The accounts

6. (1) In accordance with this Part of this Schedule the Secretary of State shall keep, in respect of the financial year 1993-94 and each subsequent financial year, an account (to be called a non-domestic rating account).

(2) The Secretary of State—

    (a)   shall keep each account in such form as the Treasury may direct; and

    (b)   shall at such time as the Treasury may direct send copies of each account to the Comptroller and Auditor General.

(3) The Comptroller and Auditor General shall examine, certify and report on any account of which copies are sent to him under sub-paragraph (2) above and shall lay copies of the account and of his report before each House of Parliament.

Credits and debits

7. (1) For each financial year there shall be credited (as items of account) to the account kept for the year any sums received by the Secretary of State in the year under paragraph 11 below.

(2) Any amount of non-domestic rate income distributed by the Secretary of State in a financial year under—

(a)   paragraph 3 above;
(b)   paragraph 11(9) and (10) below; or
(c)   regulations made under paragraph 12(5) below,

shall be debited (as items of account) to the account kept for the year

8. (1) As soon as is reasonably practicable after the end of each financial year the Secretary of State shall calculate the following—

(a)   the aggregate of the items of account credited to the account kept for the year; and
(b)   the aggregate of the items of account debited to the account kept for the year.

(2) If the aggregate mentioned in sub-paragraph (1)(a) above exceeds that mentioned in sub-paragraph (1)(b) above, a sum equal to the excess shall be—

(a)   debited (as an item of account) to the account kept for the year; and
(b)   credited (as an item of account) to the account kept for the next financial year.

(3) If the aggregate mentioned in sub-paragraph (1)(b) above exceeds that mentioned in sub-paragraph (1)(a) above, a sum equal to the excess shall be—

(a)   credited (as an item of account) to the account kept for the year; and
(b)   debited (as an item of account) to the account kept for the next financial year.

Distributable amount

9. (1) Before a financial year begins the Secretary of State shall estimate—

(a)   the aggregate of the items of account which will be credited to the account kept for that year; and
(b)   the aggregate of the items of account which will be debited to the account kept for that year under paragraphs 7(2)(b) and (c) and 8(3)(b) above.

(2) In making any estimate under sub-paragraph (1) above the Secretary of State may make such assumptions as he thinks fit.

(3) If the aggregate estimated under sub-paragraph (1)(a) above exceeds the aggregate estimated under sub-paragraph (1)(b) above the Secretary of State shall calculate the amount equal to the difference.

(4) In any local government finance order in respect of that year the Secretary of State shall specify the amount arrived at under this paragraph (the distributable amount for the year).

Part III. Contribution

Non-domestic rating contributions

10. (1) The Secretary of State may make regulations containing rules for the calculation of an amount for a financial year in relation to each levying authority (to be called its non-domestic rating contribution for the year).

(2) Subject to sub-paragraph (3) below, the rules shall be so framed that the amount calculated under them in relation to an authority is broadly the same as the total which would be payable to that authority if there were added—

(a) any sum paid to them by way of a contribution in aid made in respect of lands and heritages which, but for any rule of law relating to Crown exemption, would be liable to non-domestic rates; and

(b) the sum which, if the authority acted diligently, would be payable to them in respect of non-domestic rates for that year.

(3) The Secretary of State may incorporate in the rules provision for deductions (of such extent (if any) as he thinks fit) as regards—

(a) the operation of—

(i) section 243A (relief of rates in respect of lands and heritages occupied only for a short time) of the 1947 Act;

(ii) section 244 (remission of rates on account of poverty) of the 1947 Act; and

(iii) section 4(5) (reduction and remission of rates payable by charitable and other organisations) of the Local Government (Financial Provisions) (Scotland) Act 1962;

(b) the costs of collection and recovery; and

(c) such other matters (if any) as he thinks fit.

(4) Regulations under this paragraph in their application to a particular financial year (including regulations amending or revoking others) shall not be effective unless they come into force before 1st January in the preceding financial year.

11. (1) This paragraph applies where regulations under paragraph 10 above are in force in respect of a financial year, and has effect subject to any such regulations.

(2) Before the beginning of the relevant financial year, the Secretary of State shall calculate the amount of each levying authority's non-domestic rating contribution for that year, and shall inform each authority of the amount so calculated in respect of them.

(3) The authority shall be liable to pay to the Secretary of State an amount (the "provisional amount") equal to that calculated and notified to them under sub-paragraph (2) above.

(4) The authority shall pay the provisional amount during the course of the year, in such instalments and at such times as the Secretary of State may with the consent of the Treasury direct.

(5) Within such period after the year ends as the Secretary of State may direct the authority shall—

(a) calculate, in such manner as may be prescribed, the amount of its non-domestic rating contribution for the year;

(b) notify the amount so calculated to the Secretary of State; and

(c) arrange for the calculation and the amount to be certified under arrangements made by the Commission for Local Authority Accounts in Scotland.

(6) The Commission shall send a copy of the certification of the calculation and the amount to the Secretary of State.

(7) When the Secretary of State receives notification from an authority under sub-paragraph (5)(b) above he shall—

(a) calculate the amount of the difference (if any) between that amount (the "notified amount") and the provisional amount; and

(b) if there is a difference, inform the authority of the amount of the difference.

(8) If the notified amount exceeds the provisional amount the authority shall pay an amount equal to the difference to the Secretary of State at such time as he may direct.

(9) If the notified amount is less than the provisional amount the Secretary of State shall pay an amount equal to the difference to the authority; and the amount shall be paid at such time as he decides with the Treasury's approval.

(10) When the Secretary of State receives notification of the certified amount from the Commission under sub-paragraph (6) above he shall inform the authority of the amount of any difference between the certified amount and the notified amount, and sub-paragraphs (8) and (9) above shall apply in relation to differences between the certified amount and the notified amount as they apply in relation to differences between the provisional amount and the notified amount.

(11) If the authority fail to comply with sub-paragraph (5) above the Secretary of State may suspend payments which would otherwise fall to be made to the authority under—

   (a) paragraph 3 above;
   (b) sub-paragraph (9) or (10) above; or
   (c) regulations made under paragraph 12(5) below,

but if the authority then comply with the sub-paragraph he shall resume payments falling to be made to the authority under those provisions and make payments to them equal to those suspended.

(12) Where the Secretary of State has suspended payments under sub-paragraph (9) above by reason of the authority's failure to make the calculation required under sub-paragraph (5)(a) above in the manner prescribed, for the purposes of sub-paragraph (10) above sub-paragraphs (8) and (9) above shall apply to differences between the provisional amount and the certified amount as they apply to differences between the provisional amount and the notified amount.

12. (1) Any calculation under paragraph 11 above of the amount of an authority's non-domestic rating contribution for a year shall be made on the basis of the information before the person making the calculation at the time he makes it; but regulations under paragraph 10 above may include provision—

   (a) requiring a calculation under paragraph 11(2) above to be made on the basis of that information read subject to prescribed assumptions;
   (b) enabling a calculation under paragraph 11(5)(a) above to be made without taking into account any information as regards which the following conditions are satisfied—

       (i)   it is not reasonably practicable for the person making the calculation to take it into account; and
       (ii) it was received by the authority after the prescribed date (which may be before or after the end of the year in question).

(2) Regulations under paragraph 10 above may incorporate in the rules provision for adjustments to be made in the calculation of the amount of an authority's non-domestic rating contribution under paragraph 11(2) or (5) above, being adjustments to take account of relevant changes affecting the amount of the authority's non-domestic rating contribution for an earlier year.

(3) For the purposes of sub-paragraph (2) above, a change is a relevant change if it results from a decision, determination or other matter which (whether by reason of the time at which it was taken, made or occurred or otherwise) was not taken into account by the authority in the calculation under paragraph 11(5) above of the amount of their non-domestic rating contribution for the earlier year in question.

(4) The power to give directions under paragraph 11 above—

   (a) includes power to revoke or amend a direction given under the power;
   (b) may be exercised differently for different authorities.

(5) The Secretary of State may make regulations providing that, once the provisional amount has been arrived at under paragraph 11 above as regards an authority for a financial year and if prescribed conditions are fulfilled, the provisional amount is to be treated for the purposes of that paragraph as being an amount smaller than it would otherwise be.

(6) Regulations under sub-paragraph (5) above may include—

    (a) provision as to the re-calculation of the provisional amount, including provision for the procedure to be adopted for re-calculation if the prescribed conditions are fulfilled;

    (b) provision as to financial adjustments to be made as a result of any re-calculation, including provision for the making of reduced payments under paragraph 11 above or of repayments.

NOTE

Paras 10–12: See the Non-Domestic Rating Contributions (Scotland) Regulations 1992, SI 1992/3061.

The Council Tax (Valuation of Dwellings) (Scotland) Regulations 1992

(SI 1992/1329)

NOTES
Made: 2nd June 1992
Laid before Parliament: 10th June 1992
Coming into force: 1st July 1992

Citation, commencement and interpretation

1.—(1) These Regulations may be cited as the Council Tax (Valuation of Dwellings) (Scotland) Regulations 1992 and shall come into force on 1st July 1992.

(2) In these Regulations—
   "agricultural lands and heritages" means—

   (a) any lands and heritages used for agricultural or pastoral purposes only (disregarding any use of the lands and heritages for the purpose of the breeding, rearing, grazing or exercising of horses (within the meaning of section 6(4) of the Riding Establishments Act 1964, if the only other use of the lands and heritages is a substantial use for agricultural or pastoral purposes);

   (b) any lands and heritages used as woodlands, market gardens, orchards, reed beds, allotments or allotment gardens; and

   (c) any lands exceeding one tenth of a hectare used for the purpose of poultry farming;

but does not include any land kept or preserved mainly or exclusively for sporting purposes;

   "common parts", in relation to a dwelling, means any part of a building containing the dwelling and any land or premises which the owner or occupier of the dwelling is entitled to use in common with the owners or occupiers of other premises in the immediate locality;

   "cottar", "croft" and "crofter" have the same meanings as they have in the Crofters (Scotland) Act 1955 and "the crofting counties" means the former counties to which that Act applies;

   "fish farming" means the breeding or rearing of fish or the cultivation of shellfish (including crustaceans and molluscs of any description) for the purpose of producing food for human consumption or for transfer to other waters, but does not include the breeding, rearing or cultivation of any fish or shellfish—

   (a) which are purely ornamental; or
   (b) which are bred, reared or cultivated for exhibition;

   "permitted development" means development—

   (a) for which planning permission is not required; or
   (b) for which an application for planning permission is not required.

Valuation of dwellings

2.—(1) For the purposes of valuations under section 86(2) of the Local Government Finance Act 1992 [and valuations carried out in connection with proposals for the alteration of a valuation list], the value of any dwelling shall be taken to be the amount which the dwelling might reasonably have been expected to realise if it had been sold in the open market by a willing seller on 1st April 1991, having applied the assumptions mentioned in paragraph (2) below and, where applicable, the additional assumption mentioned in sub-paragraph (a), (b) or (c) of paragraph (1) of regulation 3 below, as the case may be.

(2) The assumptions referred to in paragraph (1) above are—

    (a) that the sale was with vacant possession;

    (b) that the dwelling was sold free from any heritable security;

    (c) that the size and layout of the dwelling, and the physical state of its locality, were the same as at the time when the valuation of the dwelling is made [or, in the case of a valuation carried out in connection with a proposal for the alteration of a valuation list, as at the date from which that alteration would have effect];

    (d) that the dwelling was in a state of reasonable repair;

    (e) in the case of a dwelling the owner or occupier of which is entitled to use common parts, that those parts were in a like state of repair and the purchaser would be liable to contribute towards the cost of keeping them in such a state;

    (f) in the case of a dwelling which contains fixtures to which paragraph (4) below applies, that the fixtures were not included in the dwelling;

    (g) that the use of the dwelling would be permanently restricted to use as a private dwelling; and

    (h) that the dwelling had no development value other than value attributable to permitted development.

(3) In determining what is "reasonable repair" in relation to a dwelling for the purposes of paragraph (2) above, the age and character of the dwelling and its locality shall be taken into account.

(4) This paragraph applies to any fixtures which—

    (a) are designed to make the dwelling suitable for use by a person who is physically disabled; and

    (b) add to the value of the dwelling.

NOTE

Regs 2(1), 2(2): Words added by the Council Tax (Valuation of Dwellings)(Scotland) Amendment Regulations 1993, SI 1993/354.

Dwellings occupied in connection with agriculture or fish farming

3.—(1) The additional assumptions referred to in regulation 2(1) above are—

    (a) if the dwelling is, at the time when the valuation of it is made [or, in the case of a valuation carried out in connection with a proposal for the alteration of a valuation list, as at the date from which that alteration would have effect]—

        (i) occupied in connection with agricultural lands and heritages;

        (ii) used as living accommodation by a person engaged primarily in carrying on or directing agricultural operations on those lands and heritages or employed as an agricultural worker thereon; and

        (iii) suitable in character and size for such use in connection with those lands and heritages;

    that the dwelling could not be occupied and used otherwise than as stated;

    (b) if the dwelling is, at the time when the valuation of it is made [or, in the case of a valuation carried out in connection with a proposal for the alteration of a valuation list, as at the date from which that alteration would have effect]—

    (i)   not a dwelling falling within sub-paragraph (a) above;

    (ii) occupied in connection with lands and heritages used solely for or in connection with fish farming (disregarding any time in the year during which they are used in any other way, if that time does not amount to a substantial part of the year);

    (iii) used as living accommodation by a person engaged primarily in carrying on or directing fish farming operations on those lands and heritages or employed in connection with fish farming thereon; and

    (iv) suitable in character and size for such use in connection with those lands and heritages;

that the dwelling could not be occupied and used otherwise than as stated; and

(c) if the dwelling is, at the time when the valuation of it is made [or, in the case of a valuation carried out in connection with a proposal for the alteration of a valuation list, as at the date from which that alteration would have effect]—

    (i)   not a dwelling falling within sub-paragraph (a) or (b) above;

    (ii) situated in the crofting counties;

    (iii) occupied in connection with agricultural lands and heritages to which paragraph (2) below applies;

    (iv) used as living accommodation by a person who is the owner or tenant of those lands and heritages or is a cottar in respect of the dwelling or who has no right or title to occupy the dwelling and is engaged in the like activities and occupations as a crofter; and

    (v) suitable in character and size for such use in connection with those lands and heritages;

that the dwelling could not be occupied otherwise than as stated and could not be used otherwise than as living accommodation by a person engaged in carrying on or directing agricultural operations on those lands and heritages.

(2) This paragraph applies to agricultural lands and heritages—

(a) which form all or part of a croft; or

(b) the area of which does not exceed thirty hectares and any rent in respect of which does not exceed £100 *per annum*.

NOTE

Reg 3(1)(a), (b), (c): Words added by the Council Tax (Valuation of Dwellings)(Scotland) Amendment Regulations 1993, SI 1993/354.

Revocations

4. The Domestic Property (Valuation) (Scotland) Regulations 1991 and the Domestic Property (Valuation) (Scotland) Amendment Regulations 1991 are hereby revoked.

The Council Tax (Contents of Valuation Lists) (Scotland) Regulations 1992

(SI 1992/1330)

NOTES

Made: 2nd June 1992

Laid before Parliament: 10th June 1992

Coming into force: 1st July 1992

Citation, commencement and interpretation

1.—(1) These Regulations may be cited as the Council Tax (Contents of Valuation Lists) (Scotland) Regulations 1992 and shall come into force on 1st July 1992.

(2) In these Regulations—
"the Act" means the Local Government Finance Act 1992;
"list" means a valuation list compiled under section 84 of the Act.

Information in valuation lists

2. For each day on which a dwelling is shown in the list, the list must contain (in addition to the matters required to be shown by section 84(2) of the Act)—

(a) the reference number ascribed to the dwelling by the local assessor;
(b) where the list is altered as regards the dwelling—

    (i) a note of the day from which the alteration has effect; and
    (ii) if it be the case, a note that the alteration was made pursuant to an order of a valuation appeal committee or the Court of Session; and

(c) where the dwelling falls within either of the classes of lands and heritages specified in paragraphs (2) and (3) of regulation 2 of the Council Tax (Dwellings) (Scotland) Regulations 1992, a note that that is the case.

The Council Tax (Liability of Owners) (Scotland) Regulations 1992

(SI 1992/1331)

NOTES
Made: 2nd June 1992
Laid before Parliament: 10th June 1992
Coming into force: 1st July 1992

Citation, commencement and interpretation

1.—(1) These Regulations may be cited as the Council Tax Regulations 1992 and shall come into force on 1st July 1992.

(2) In these Regulations—
"the Act" means the Local Government Finance Act 1992;
"minister" means a minister of any religious denomination;
"tenant" includes a secure tenant, statutory tenant or statutory assured tenant (within the meanings assigned by section 75(5) of the Act).

Liability in prescribed cases

2. The classes of dwelling specified in the Schedule to these Regulations are prescribed for the purposes of section 76(1) of the Act.

3. In relation to a dwelling within the class specified in paragraph 5 of the Schedule to these Regulations, section 76(3) of the Act shall have effect as if, for the reference to the owner of the dwelling, there were substituted a reference to the person liable for the remuneration of the minister.

SCHEDULE   Regulations 2 and 3

PRESCRIBED CLASSES OF DWELLING

Residential care homes, etc.

1. A dwelling which constitutes all or part of a residential care home, nursing home, private hospital or hostel (within the meanings given by paragraph 8 of Schedule 1 to the Act).

Religious communities

2. A dwelling occupied by a religious community whose principal occupation—

    (a) is prayer, contemplation, education or the relief of suffering; or

    (b) consists of two or more of these occupations.

Houses in multiple occupation, etc.

3. A dwelling [which]—

    (a) [was originally constructed or subsequently adapted for occupation by persons] who do not constitute a single household; and

    (b) [is occupied by one or more persons] each of whom—

        (i) is a tenant of, or has a licence to occupy, part only of the dwelling; or

        (ii) has a licence to occupy, but is not liable (whether alone or jointly with other persons) to pay rent or a licence fee in respect of, the dwelling as a whole.

Resident staff

4. A dwelling—

    (a) at least one of the residents of which is employed in domestic service and resides in the dwelling wholly or mainly for the purposes of his employment;

    (b) any other resident of which is either so employed or is a member of the family of a resident so employed; and

    (c) which is from time to time occupied by the employer of the person referred to in sub-paragraph (a).

Ministers of religion

5. A dwelling—

    (a) which is the sole or main residence of a minister for whose remuneration a person is liable; and

    (b) from which the minister performs the duties of his office.

[School boarding accommodatiion

6. Premises which fall to be treated as a dwelling by virtue of regulation 4 of, and paragraph 5 of Schedule 1 to, the Council Tax (Dwellings and Part Residential Subjects)(Scotland) Regulations 1992.]

NOTES

Para 3: amended by Council Tax (Liability of Owners)(Scotland) Amendment Regulations 1993, SI 1993/344.

Para 6: added by SI 1993/344.

The Council Tax (Administration and Enforcement) (Scotland) Regulations 1992
(SI 1992/1332)

NOTES
Made: 2nd June 1992
Laid before Parliament: 10th June 1992
Coming into force: 1st July 1992

ARRANGEMENT OF REGULATIONS

PART I. GENERAL

1. Citation, commencement and interpretation

PART II. INFORMATION

2. Information as to liable persons, etc.
3. Information from public bodies
4. Information as to deaths
5. Use of information by levying authority

PART III. EXEMPT DWELLINGS, ETC.

6. Information for owners of exempt dwellings, etc.
7. Inquiries as to dwellings
8. Assumptions as to dwellings
9. Notification of assumptions
10. Correction of assumptions

PART IV. DISCOUNTS

11. Interpretation of Part IV
12. Ascertainment of entitlement to discount
13. Assumptions as to discount
14. Notification of discount assumptions
15. Correction of discount assumptions

PART V. BILLING

16. Interpretation of Part V
17. The requirement for demand notices
18. Payments required: general
19. Notices: general
20. Demand notices: payments required

21. Council tax and the council water charge: payments
22. Failure to pay instalments
23. Payments: adjustments
24. Lump sum payments
25. Non-cash payments
26. Collection of penalties
27. Final adjustment of sums payable

PART VI. CONTENTS OF DEMAND NOTICES

28. Contents of demand notices
29. Invalid notices

PART VII. ENFORCEMENT

30. Certificates with application for a summary warrant
31. Duty of debtor to supply information

SCHEDULES

1. Council Tax and Council Water Charge Instalments—
    Part I — Payment of the aggregate amount: monthly instalments
    Part II — Cessation and adjustment of instalments
2. Contents of Demand Notices—
    Part I — Matters to be contained in all demand notices
    Part II — Matters to be contained in demand notices so far as not already notified

PART I. GENERAL

Citation, commencement and interpretation

1.—(1) These Regulations may be cited as the Council Tax (Administration and Enforcement) (Scotland) Regulations 1992 and shall come into force on 1st July 1992.

(2) In these Regulations—
  "the Act" means the Local Government Finance Act 1992;
  "chargeable amount" means an amount which, in respect of a particular dwelling, a person is liable to pay (whether solely or jointly and severally with another person or persons) to a levying authority in respect of council tax and the council water charge for a financial year and includes, unless the context otherwise requires, an amount which in the opinion of the authority a person will be so liable to pay;
  "demand notice" means a notice served under regulation 17;
  "liable person" means a person who is liable (whether solely or jointly and severally with another person or persons) to pay to a levying authority, in respect of a particular dwelling, an amount in respect of council tax or the council water charge for a financial year, and includes, unless the context otherwise requires, a reference to a person who in the opinion of the authority will be so liable;
  "relevant valuation band" in relation to a dwelling, means the valuation band shown as applicable to the dwelling—

    (a) in the levying authority's valuation list; or

    (b) if no such list is in force, in the copy of the proposed list sent to the authority under section 85(1)(b) of the Act;

"relevant year", in relation to a notice, means the financial year to which the notice relates.

(3) Any reference in these Regulations to the day on, or time at which, a notice is issued, served or given by a levying authority is a reference to the day on, or time at which, the notice is, in accordance with the terms of section 192 of the Local Government (Scotland) Act 1973, posted, delivered or affixed.

(4) Unless otherwise stated, in these Regulations any reference—

    (a) to a numbered regulation or Schedule is a reference to the regulation or Schedule so numbered in these Regulations;

    (b) in a regulation or Schedule to a numbered paragraph is a reference to the paragraph so numbered in that regulation or Schedule; and

    (c) in a paragraph to a sub-paragraph is a reference to the appropriate sub-paragraph of that paragraph.

Part II. Information

Information as to liable persons, etc.

2.—(1) Any person appearing to a levying authority to be a resident, owner or managing agent of a particular dwelling shall supply to the authority in accordance with paragraph (2) such information as fulfils the following conditions:—

    (a) it is in the possession or control of the person concerned;

    (b) the authority request the person to supply it, by serving a notice addressed—

        (i) to him by name; or

        (ii) to "The Resident" or, as the case may be, "the Owner" or "The Managing Agent" of the dwelling concerned (naming the dwelling) without further name or designation; and

    (c) it is requested by the authority for the purpose of identifying the person who, in respect of any period specified in the notice—

        (i) is the liable person in relation to the dwelling; or

        (ii) would be such a liable person if the dwelling were not or had not been an exempt dwelling.

(2) Information shall be supplied within the period of 21 days beginning on the day on which the notice was served and, if the authority so require, in a form specified in the request.

(3) In paragraph (1), the reference to a managing agent of a particular dwelling is to a person authorised to arrange lettings of the dwelling.

Information from public bodies

3.—(1) A levying authority may, for the purpose of carrying out their functions under Part II of the Act, by notice request—

(a) a person mentioned in paragraph (3) to supply to them such information as is specified in the notice and does not fall within paragraph (2)[; or

(b) a person mentioned in paragraph (3B) to supply to them such information as is specified in the notice and does not fall within paragraph (3A).]

(2) Information falls within this paragraph if—

(a) it was obtained by the person concerned in that person's capacity as an employer;

(b) where it is requested from a billing authority, it was obtained by that authority, or by a committee of that authority—

  (i) in its capacity as police authority; or

  (ii) in its capacity as a constituent council of such an authority; or

(c) it consists of other than—

  (i) the name, address and any past or present place of residence of any person;

  (ii) the dates during which he is known or thought to have resided at that place; and

  (iii) the nature of any present or past interest which any person may have or have had in a dwelling which is or has been owned by the person to whom the request for information is made.

(3) The persons referred to in paragraph [(1)(a)] are—

(a) any other levying authority;

(b) any district council;

(c) any billing authority;

(d) the electoral registration officer for any area in Great Britain;

(e) ...

(f) the local assessor for the levying authority's area; and

(g) any housing body operating in the levying authority's area.

[(3A) Information falls within this paragraph if it consists of other than—

(a) the name, address and any past or present place of residence of any person;

(b) the dates during which he is known or thought to have resided at that place;

(c) information relevant to the status of any person as an exempt individual; and

(d) the days on which any person was an exempt individual.

(3B) The person referred to in paragraph (1)(b) is any community charges registration officer.]

(4) If information requested under paragraph (1) is in the possession or control of the person requested to supply it, that person shall supply it to the levying authority within the period of 21 days beginning on the day on which the notice was served.

(5) A levying authority may (so far as they do not have the power to do so apart from these Regulations) supply relevant information to another levying authority or to a billing authority even if they are not requested to supply the information.

(6) Information is relevant information for the purposes of paragraph (5) if—

(a) it was obtained by the first-mentioned authority in exercising their functions under Part II of the Act; and

(b) that authority believe that it would be useful to the other authority in exercising their functions under that Part or, in the case of a billing authority, Part I of the Act.

[(6A) The references to an exempt individual in paragraph (3A) shall be construed—

(a) as regards any period during which the sole or main residence of the person concerned is or was in England or Wales, in accordance with section 2 of, and Schedule 1 to, the Local Government Finance Act 1988; and

(b) as regards any period during which a person was solely or mainly resident in Scotland, in accordance with section 8(8) of, and Schedule 1 to, the Abolition of Domestic Rates Etc (Scotland) Act 1987.]

(7) The reference to a community charges registration officer in [paragraph (3B)] shall be construed—

(a) in relation to such officers in England and Wales, in accordance with section 26 of the Local Government Finance Act 1988; and

(b) in relation to such officers in Scotland, in accordance with section 12 of the Abolition of Domestic Rates Etc. (Scotland) Act 1987.

NOTES

Reg 3: Para (1): Words added by the Council Tax (Administration and Enforcement)(Scotland) Regulations 1992, SI 1992/3290, reg 2(2)(a) and (b).
Para (3): Words substituted by SI 1992/3290, reg 2(3)(a).
Para (3)(e): Sub-paragraph deleted by SI 1992/3290, reg 2(3)(b).
Paras (3A) and (3B): Paragraphs inserted by SI 1992/3290, reg 2(4).
Para (6A): Paragraph inserted by SI 1992/3290, reg 2(5).
Para (7); Words substituted by SI 1992/3290, reg 2(6).

Information as to deaths

4.—(1) Within 7 days of the registration in a registration district in Scotland of the death of any person aged 18 or over, the district registrar for that district shall, in accordance with paragraph (2), supply to any levying authority within the area of which the registration district wholly or partly falls the following particulars of the death:-

(a) the name and surname of the deceased;
(b) the date of his death;
(c) his usual address; and
(d) the district where the death was registered.

(2) The registrar shall supply the particulars specified in paragraph (1) by sending such form as is from time to time approved by the Registrar General for such purposes with these particulars duly entered thereon.

Use of information by levying authority

5.—(1) In carrying out their functions under Part II of the Act, a levying authority may use information which—

(a) is obtained under any other enactment; and
(b) does not fall within paragraph (2) below.

(2) Information falls within this paragraph if it is information obtained under, and held for the purposes of, or in connection with, the functions of the authority under the Social Work (Scotland) Act 1968 (other than information as to the names and addresses of persons or addresses of premises).

PART III. EXEMPT DWELLINGS, ETC.

Information for owners of exempt dwellings, etc.

6.—(1) Subject to paragraph (5), a levying authority who have received a copy of a proposed list sent to them under section 85(1)(b) of the Act shall, as respects each dwelling shown in the copy which in the opinion of the authority will be a relevant dwelling on the day when the list comes into force, notify the person concerned of the valuation band shown in the copy as applicable to the dwelling.

(2) Where—

    (a) a dwelling is not shown in the copy of a proposed list sent as mentioned in paragraph (1) but is shown in the copy of the list sent to the authority under section 85(4) of the Act; and

    (b) in the opinion of the authority the dwelling was a relevant dwelling on the day when the list came into force;

the authority shall notify the person concerned of the valuation band shown in the copy of the list as applicable to the dwelling.

(3) Where—

    (a) the valuation band shown as applicable to a dwelling in the copy of a proposed list sent to a levying authority under section 85(1)(b) of the Act is different from that shown as applicable to it in the copy of the list sent to the authority under section 85(4) of the Act; and

    (b) in the opinion of the authority the dwelling was a relevant dwelling on the day when the list came into force;

the authority shall notify the person concerned of the valuation band shown in the copy of the list sent under section 85(4) of the Act as applicable to the dwelling.

(4) A notification required to be given—

    (a) by paragraph (1), shall be given within the period of 6 months beginning on the day on which the authority received the copy of the proposed list;

    (b) by paragraph (2) or (3), shall be given within the period of 4 months beginning on the day on which the authority received the copy of the list.

(5) If at the time when a person is notified as mentioned in paragraph (3) the authority have not yet given him a notification under paragraph (1), they shall not be required to give him such a notification.

(6) Any notification given by a levying authority under this regulation shall contain a statement—

    (a) specifying, in respect of the financial year commencing on 1st April 1993 and dwellings in the valuation band applicable to the dwelling in question—

        (i) the amounts set by the authority as council tax under section 93(1) of the Act and as the council water charge under paragraph 7 of Schedule 11 to the Act; and

        (ii) where the dwelling is situated within the area of a district council, the amount set by that council as council tax under section 93(1) of the Act;

    (b) summarising the effect of any regulations under section 87 of the Act relevant to the making by a person (other than a levying authority) of a proposal for alteration to the authority's valuation list;

(c) summarising the classes of dwelling which are for the time being exempt dwellings for the purposes of Part II of the Act; and

(d) if the amount set under section 93(1) of the Act for the financial year commencing on 1st April 1993—

    (i) where the levying authority is an islands council, by that council; or

    (ii) where the levying authority is a regional council, by both that council and the district council within the area of which the dwelling in question is situated;

is nil, that, if the dwelling is a chargeable dwelling on any day of that year, no council tax will be payable for that year in respect of the dwelling.

(7) For the purposes of this regulation—

(a) a dwelling is a relevant dwelling on any day if—

    (i) on the day the dwelling is an exempt dwelling [(other than a dwelling which is exempt by virtue of paragraph 18 or 21 of the Schedule to the Council Tax (Exempt Dwellings)(Scotland) Order 1992]; or

    (ii) the qualifying conditions specified in paragraph 8 of Schedule 11 to the Act are not met in respect of the dwelling on the day, and the day falls within a financial year in respect of which the levying authority, and (where that authority is a regional council) the district council within the area of which the dwelling is situated, have set an amount of nil under section 93(1) of the Act; and

(b) any reference to the person concerned, in relation to a dwelling, is a reference to a person who would be liable (whether solely or jointly and severally with another person or persons) to pay to the authority an amount in respect of council tax or the council water charge for the particular day if the dwelling were not or had not been a relevant dwelling on that day.

NOTES

Reg 6: Para (7)(a)(i): Words inserted by the Council Tax (Administration and Enforcement)(Scotland) Regulations 1992, SI 1992/3290. reg 3.

Inquiries as to dwellings

7. A levying authority shall, as regards each financial year commencing with the financial year beginning on 1st April 1993, take reasonable steps to ascertain whether any dwellings in their area will be or were exempt dwellings for any period during the year.

Assumptions as to dwellings

8.—(1) Where a levying authority, having taken such steps as are referred to in regulation 7, have no reason to believe that a particular dwelling will be or was an exempt dwelling for any period during the year, they shall assume, for the purposes of Part V of these Regulations, that the dwelling will be or was a chargeable dwelling for that period.

(2) Where a levying authority, having taken such steps as are referred to in regulation 7, have reason to believe that a particular dwelling will be or was an exempt

dwelling for a period during the year, they shall assume, for the purposes of the said Part V, that the dwelling will be or was an exempt dwelling for that period.

Notification of assumptions

9.—(1) Subject to paragraphs (3) and (4), as soon as reasonably practicable after a levying authority have made such an assumption as is mentioned in regulation 8(2) in respect of a period commencing after 1st April 1993, they shall by notice inform the relevant person of the assumption made in his case.

(2) Subject to paragraph (5), a levying authority shall supply with any such notice a statement—

   (a) specifying the valuation band shown in the authority's valuation list as applicable to the dwelling;
   (b) specifying, in respect of the financial year in question and dwellings in that valuation band—

   (i) the amounts set by the authority as council tax under section 93(1) of the Act and as the council water charge under paragraph 9 of Schedule 11 to the Act; and
   (ii) where the dwelling is situated within the area of a district council, the amount set by that council as council tax under section 93(1) of the Act;

   (c) summarising the effect of any regulations under section 87 of the Act relevant to the making by a person (other than a levying authority) of a proposal for the alteration of that list;
   (d) summarising the classes of dwelling which are for the time being exempt dwellings for the purposes of Part II of the Act;
   (e) if the amount last set under section 93(1) of the Act for the financial year in question—

   (i) where the levying authority is an islands council, or
   (ii) where the levying authority is a regional council, by both that council and the district council within the area of which the dwelling in question is situated;

is nil, that, if the dwelling is a chargeable dwelling on any day of that year, no council tax will be payable for that year in respect of the dwelling; and,

   (f) summarising the contents of regulation 10 and advising the relevant person that a penalty of £50 may be imposed on him under paragraph 2(2) of Schedule 3 to the Act if he fails to comply with the obligation contained in that regulation.

(3) Where, as regards a particular dwelling and period, there is more than one relevant person, nothing in paragraph (1) shall require a notice to be served, as regards that dwelling and period, on more than one of them.

(4) No notice under paragraph (1) need be served as regards a dwelling and a period if—

   (a) the only relevant person as regards that dwelling and period is a housing body; or
   [(b) the levying authority have made an assumption that the dwelling will be or was exempt for that period by virtue of paragraph 18 or 21 of the Schedule to the Council Tax (Exempt Dwellings)(Scotland) Order 1992.]

(5) Information need not be given under paragraph (2) insofar as it would be repetitive of information already given to a relevant person under these Regulations.

(6) In this regulation, "relevant person" means a person who, in respect of the particular dwelling, would be liable (whether solely or jointly and severally with another person or persons) to pay to the authority an amount in respect of council tax or the council water charge for the period to which the assumption relates if the dwelling were not or had not been an exempt dwelling for that period.

NOTES

Reg 9: Para (4)(b): Sub-paragraph substituted by the Council Tax (Administration and Enforcement)(Scotland) Regulations 1992, SI 1992/3290, reg 4.

Correction of assumptions

10.—(1) Subject to paragraph (2), where a person—

   (a) has been informed of an assumption under regulation 8(2) made in his case; and
   (b) at any time before the end of the financial year following the financial year in respect of which the assumption is made, has reason to believe that in fact the dwelling concerned will not be or was not an exempt dwelling for the period concerned, or will be or was an exempt dwelling for a shorter period;

he shall, within the period of 21 days beginning on the day on which he first has reason so to believe, notify the authority in writing of his belief.

(2) The duty to notify specified in paragraph (1) may be discharged, in respect of all persons who are jointly and severally liable to pay council tax and the council water charge in respect of the dwelling and period concerned and who have been informed as specified in sub-paragraph (a) of that paragraph, by one of those persons providing the notification on behalf of all of them.

(3) References in paragraphs (1) and (2) to the dwelling and period concerned are to the dwelling and period to which the relevant assumption relates.

Part IV. Discounts

Interpretation of Part IV

11. In this Part, any reference to any calculation of the chargeable amount includes a reference to any estimate of the amount.

Ascertainment of entitlement to discount

12. A levying authority shall, before making any calculation for the purposes of Part V of these Regulations of the chargeable amount in respect of any dwelling in their area, take reasonable steps to ascertain whether that amount is subject to any discount under section 79 of the Act or under that section as read with paragraph 11 of Schedule 11 to the Act and, if so, the amount of that discount.

Assumptions as to discount

13.—(1) Where a levying authority, having taken such steps as are referred to in regulation 12, have no reason to believe that the chargeable amount for the financial year concerned is subject to a discount, they shall assume, in making any calculation of the chargeable amount for the purposes of Part V of these Regulations, that the chargeable amount is not subject to any discount.

(2) Where a levying authority, having taken such steps as are referred to in regulation 12, have reason to believe that the chargeable amount for the financial year concerned is subject to a discount of a particular amount, they shall assume, in making any such calculation as is mentioned in paragraph (1), that the chargeable amount is subject to a discount of that amount.

Notification of discount assumptions

14.—(1) Subject to paragraphs (3) to (5), as soon as reasonably practicable after a levying authority have made such an assumption as is mentioned in regulation 13(2), they shall by notice inform the relevant person of the assumption made in his case.

(2) Subject to paragraph (4), a levying authority shall supply with any such notice a statement—

    (a) of the basis on which the authority assumed that the chargeable amount was or should be subject to a discount; and

    (b) summarising the contents of regulation 15 and advising the relevant person that a penalty of £50 may be imposed on him under paragraph 2(2) of Schedule 3 to the Act if he fails to comply with the obligation contained in that regulation.

(3) Where there is more than one relevant person, nothing in paragraph (1) shall require a notice to be served on more than one of them.

(4) Information need not be given under this regulation insofar as it would be repetitive of information already given to a relevant person under these Regulations.

(5) No notice under paragraph (1) need be served as regards a dwelling if the only relevant person is a housing body.

(6) In this regulation "relevant person" means a person who is liable (whether solely or jointly and severally with another person or persons) to pay to the authority the chargeable amount in respect of which the assumption in question is made, and includes a person who in the opinion of the authority will be so liable.

Correction of discount assumptions

15.—(1) Subject to paragraph (3), where a person—

    (a) has been informed of an assumption under regulation 13(2) made in his case; and

    (b) at any time before the end of the financial year following the financial year in respect of which the assumption is made, has reason to believe that the chargeable amount is not in fact subject to any discount, or is subject to a discount of a smaller amount;

he shall, within the period of 21 days beginning on the day on which he first has reason so to believe, notify the authority in writing of his belief.

(2) For the purposes of paragraph (1), the fact that the person concerned has wholly or partly discharged his liability to pay the amount shall be ignored.

(3) The duty to notify specified in paragraph (1) may be discharged, in respect of all persons who are jointly and severally liable to pay the chargeable amount and who have been informed as specified in sub-paragraph (a) of that paragraph, by one of those persons providing the notification on behalf of all of them.

PART V. BILLING

Interpretation of Part V

16. The provisions of this Part which provide for the repayment or crediting of any amount or the adjustment of payments due under a notice shall have effect subject to section 94(8) of the Act.

The requirement for demand notices

17.—(1) Subject to paragraph (5), in respect of each financial year commencing with the financial year beginning on 1st April 1993, a levying authority shall serve, in accordance with paragraph (2) or (3), a demand notice as regards every dwelling in their area appearing to them likely to be, or to have been, a chargeable dwelling on 1st April in the year in question.

(2) A levying authority which is an islands council shall serve any demand notice required by paragraph (1) as soon as practicable after they have both—

    (a) first set an amount of islands council tax for the relevant year; and
    (b) set an amount of islands council water charge for that year.

(3) A levying authority which is a regional council shall, in respect of chargeable dwellings situated within the area of each district council within the region, serve any demand notice required by paragraph (1) as soon as practicable after—

    (a) they have received intimation of the district council tax first set by that district council for the relevant year; and
    (b) they have both—

        (i) first set an amount of regional council tax for that year; and
        (ii) set an amount of regional council water charge for that year.

(4) Subject to paragraph (5), a levying authority shall serve a demand notice as regards a dwelling in their area if it appears to them, at any time after the beginning of a financial year, that—

    (a) a sum in respect of council tax or the council water charge for that year remains to be paid as regards that dwelling; and
    (b) any part of that sum is attributable to a period in that year in respect of which all the liable persons are persons—

        (i) on whom no demand notice as regards that dwelling and that year has yet been served; and

(ii) who have at no point in that year been jointly and severally liable with a person on whom such a demand notice has been served to pay council tax or the council water charge in respect of that dwelling.

(5) No demand notice need be served under paragraph (1) or (4) as regards a dwelling and a period in any case where the only liable person in respect of that dwelling and period is—

(a) a housing body; or
(b) a person who is liable in respect of that dwelling and period by virtue of—

    (i) being the owner of the dwelling; or
    (ii) the Council Tax (Liability of Owners) (Scotland) Regulations 1992;

and who has agreed with the levying authority that no demand notice need be served on him.

Payments required: general

18.—(1) Subject to paragraphs (2) and (3), no payment on account of the chargeable amount (whether interim, final or sole) need be made unless a notice served under this Part requires it.

(2) Where a notice under this Part is addressed to a liable person or liable persons, any other person who is, in terms of section 75(3) or (4), 76(4) or (5) or 77(1) or (2) of the Act or in terms of those provisions as read with paragraph 11 of Schedule 11 to the Act, jointly and severally liable with that person or those persons for payment of council tax and the council water charge in respect of the dwelling and the period to which the notice relates shall be jointly and severally liable to make any payments required by the notice.

(3) Paragraph (1) shall not apply where payment is due in terms of such an agreement as is referred to in paragraph (7) of regulation 21.

Notices: general

19.—(1) A notice under this Part shall relate to a particular dwelling and a particular financial year only.

(2) If the levying authority have not after reasonable inquiry been able to ascertain the name of a liable person in respect of a dwelling and they wish to serve a notice under this Part pertaining to that dwelling, they may do so by addressing it to the "The Council Tax Payer(s)" of the dwelling concerned (naming the dwelling) without further name or designation.

(3) If at the time of serving a notice under this Part it appears to the levying authority that there are persons jointly and severally liable to make any payments to which the notice relates, they shall address the notice in the joint names of those persons and may, where all such persons appear to the authority to be resident at the same address, effect service by sending or delivering only one copy of the notice to that address.

Demand notices: payments required

20.—(1) Subject to paragraph (4), if a demand notice is issued before or during the relevant year, it shall require the making of payments on account of the amount referred to in paragraph (2).

(2) The amount is—

(a) the levying authority's estimate of the chargeable amount, made as respects the relevant year or part, as the case may be, on the assumptions referred to in paragraph (3); or

(b) where an amount falls to be credited by the levying authority against the chargeable amount, the amount (if any) by which the amount estimated as mentioned in sub-paragraph (a) exceeds the amount falling to be so credited.

(3) The assumptions are—

(a) that the person will be liable to pay the council tax and the council water charge to which the notice relates on every day after the issue of the notice;

(b) that, as regards the dwelling concerned, the relevant valuation band on the day the notice is issued will remain the relevant valuation band for the dwelling as regards every day after the issue of the notice;

(c) if on the day the notice is issued the person satisfies conditions prescribed for the purposes of regulations under section 80 of the Act (and consequently the chargeable amount in his case is less than it would otherwise be), that he will continue to satisfy those conditions as regards every day after the issue of the notice;

(d) if, by virtue of regulation 8(1), the dwelling to which the notice relates is assumed to be a chargeable dwelling on the day the notice is issued, that it will continue to be a chargeable dwelling as regards every day after the issue of the notice;

(e) if, by virtue of regulation 13(1), the chargeable amount is assumed not to be subject to a discount on the day the notice is issued, that it will not be subject to a discount as regards any day after the issue of the notice;

(f) if, by virtue of regulation 13(2), the chargeable amount is assumed to be subject to a discount on the day the notice is issued, that it will continue to be subject to the same rate of discount as regards every day after the issue of the notice;

(g) if on the day the notice is issued a determination as to council tax benefit to which the person is entitled is in effect, and by virtue of regulations under section 138(1) of the Social Security Administration Act 1992 the benefit allowed as regards that day takes the form of a reduction in the amount the person is liable to pay in respect of council tax for the relevant year, that as regards every day after that day he will be allowed the same reduction in that amount;

(h) if on the day the notice is issued the qualifying conditions mentioned in paragraph 8 of Schedule 11 to the Act are met in respect of the dwelling concerned, that they will continue to be met as regards every day after the issue of the notice; and

(i) if on the day the notice is issued those qualifying conditions are not met in respect of the dwelling concerned, that they will continue not to be met as regards every day after the issue of the notice.

(4) If a demand notice is issued during the relevant year and the liable person is not liable to pay an amount by way of council tax or the council water charge in respect of the day on which the notice is issued and the dwelling to which the notice relates, the notice shall require payment of—

    (a) the chargeable amount for the period in the year up to the last day in respect of which he was so liable; or

    (b) where an amount falls to be credited by the levying authority against that chargeable amount, an amount equal to the amount (if any) by which that chargeable amount exceeds the amount falling to be so credited.

(5) If a demand notice is issued after the end of the relevant year, it shall require payment of—

    (a) the chargeable amount; or

    (b) where an amount falls to be credited by the levying authority against the chargeable amount, an amount equal to the amount (if any) by which the chargeable amount exceeds the amount falling to be so credited.

Council tax and the council water charge: payments

21.—(1) Unless an agreement under paragraph (4) in relation to the relevant year has been reached between the levying authority and the liable person before a demand notice is issued, a demand notice to which paragraph (1) of regulation 20 applies shall require the amount mentioned in paragraph (2) of that regulation to be paid by instalments in accordance with Part I of Schedule 1.

(2) Where instalments are required to be paid under Part I of Schedule 1, Part II of that Schedule applies for their cessation or adjustment in the circumstances described in that Part.

(3) If an agreement under paragraph (4) in relation to the relevant year has been reached between the levying authority and the liable person before a demand notice is issued, a demand notice to which paragraph (1) of regulation 20 applies shall require the amount mentioned in paragraph (2) of that regulation to be paid in accordance with that agreement.

(4) A levying authority and a liable person may agree that the amount mentioned in paragraph (2) of regulation 20 which is required to be paid under a notice to which paragraph (1) of that regulation applies shall be paid in such manner as is provided by the agreement.

(5) Notwithstanding the foregoing provisions of this regulation, such an agreement may be entered into either before or after the demand notice concerned is issued, and may make provision for the cessation or adjustment of payments, and for the making of fresh estimates, in the event of the estimate mentioned in sub-paragraph (a) of regulation 20(2) turning out to be wrong; and if it is entered into after the demand notice has been issued, it may make provision dealing with the treatment for the purposes of the agreement of any sums paid in accordance with Part I of Schedule 1 before it was entered into.

(6) A demand notice to which paragraph (4) or (5) of regulation 20 applies shall (as the levying authority determine) require payment of the amount concerned—

    (a) on the expiry of such period (being not less than 14 days) after the day of issue of the notice as is specified in it; or

    (b) by instalments of such amounts as are specified in the notice, payable at such intervals and on such day in each interval as is so specified.

(7) Where, under paragraph (5) of regulation 17, a demand notice is not served in respect of a dwelling and a period in a financial year, any sum that would have been payable to a levying authority had such a notice been served shall instead be payable to them in terms of any agreement entered into between them and the liable person.

Failure to pay instalments

22.—(1) Subject to paragraph (2), where—

    (a) a notice under this Part has been served by a levying authority on a liable person;

    (b) instalments in respect of the council tax and the council water charge to which the notice relates are payable in accordance with Schedule 1 or an agreement under paragraph (4) of regulation 21; and

    (c) any such instalment is not paid in accordance with that Schedule or that agreement;

the levying authority shall serve a notice ("reminder notice") on the liable person stating—

    (i)   the instalments required to be paid;

    (ii) the effect of paragraph (3) below; and

    (iii) where the notice is the second such notice as regards the relevant year, the effect of paragraph (4) below.

(2) Nothing in paragraph (1) shall require the service of a reminder notice—

    (a) where all the instalments have fallen due; or

    (b) in the circumstances mentioned in paragraph (4).

(3) If, within the period of 7 days beginning with the day on which a reminder notice is issued, the liable person fails to pay any instalments which are or will become due before the expiry of that period, the unpaid balance of the estimated amount specified in the notice referred to in sub-paragraph (a) of paragraph (1) shall become payable by him at the expiry of a further period of 7 days beginning with the day of the failure.

(4) If, after making a payment in accordance with a reminder notice which is the second such notice as regards the relevant year, the liable person fails to pay any subsequent instalment as regards that year on or before the day on which it falls due, the unpaid balance of the estimated amount specified in the notice referred to in sub-paragraph (a) of paragraph (1) shall become payable by him on the day following the day of the failure.

Payments: adjustments

23.—(1) This regulation applies for the purpose of adjusting amounts payable under this Part, but shall not apply in the circumstances specified in paragraph 5(1) or 6(1) of Schedule 1.

(2) If the chargeable amount proves to be greater than the estimated amount, an additional sum equal to the difference between the two shall, on the service by the

levying authority on the liable person of a notice stating the chargeable amount, be due from him to the authority on the expiry of such period (being not less than 14 days) after the day of issue of the notice as is specified in it.

(3) If the chargeable amount proves to be less than the estimated amount, the levying authority shall notify the liable person in writing of the chargeable amount; and any overpayment of the chargeable amount shall, to the extent that it exceeds any other outstanding liability of that person to the levying authority in respect of council tax or the council water charge—

    (a) subject to paragraph (4), be repaid to him if he so requires; or

    (b) in any other case (as the levying authority determine) either be repaid to him or be credited against any subsequent liability of his to make a payment in respect of any council tax or council water charge to the authority.

(4) If the chargeable amount is less than the estimated amount in consequence of the liable person ceasing during the relevant year to be a liable person in respect of the dwelling to which the estimated amount relates, and he becomes liable, in respect of a different chargeable dwelling, to make a payment to the same levying authority by way of council tax or the council water charge in respect of the same day as that on which he so ceases, the levying authority may require that the amount of any overpayment mentioned in paragraph (3) shall, instead of being repaid, be credited against his liability in respect of the different dwelling.

(5) In this regulation, "the estimated amount" means the amount last estimated under paragraph (2) of regulation 20 for the purposes of a demand notice or any subsequent notice served under paragraph 6(3)(b) of Schedule 1.

Lump sum payments

24.—(1) A levying authority may, subject to the conditions set out in paragraph (2), accept an amount payable in a single lump sum in such cases as they may determine and in satisfaction of any liability of a liable person under a demand notice to which paragraph (1) of regulation 20 applies to pay the estimated amount, being a lump sum which is of an amount determined by the authority and less than the estimated amount.

(2) The conditions are that—

    (a) the determinations under paragraph (1) as to the cases where a lump sum will be accepted and as to the basis of calculation of the amount of the sum in those cases must be made by the authority on or before the day on which they first set an amount for the relevant year under section 93(1) of the Act;

    (b) under those determinations persons liable to pay the same number of instalments in the relevant year must be treated alike, and so that in particular the proportion that the amount of the single lump sum to be accepted from a liable person bears to the estimated amount payable by him must be the same as that applicable to all other liable persons liable to pay the same number of instalments in the relevant year; and

    (c) for a lump sum to be accepted under those determinations as they have effect in any case—

        (i) at least two instalments must fall to be paid under the demand notice concerned in accordance with Part I of Schedule 1 or any agreement under paragraph (4) of regulation 21; and

(ii) the single lump sum payment must be made on or before the day on which the first instalment falls due under the notice.

(3) A determination under paragraph (1) may be revoked at any time, and if revoked may (but only on or before the day mentioned in sub-paragraph (a) of paragraph (2)) be replaced by a fresh determination.

(4) If the chargeable amount proves to be greater than the estimated amount, an additional sum equal to the difference between the two, proportionately reduced in accordance with paragraph (9), shall, on the service by the levying authority on the liable person of a notice stating the chargeable amount, be due from him to the authority on the expiry of such period (being not less than 14 days) after the day of issue of the notice as is specified in it.

(5) If the chargeable amount proves to be less than the estimated amount, the levying authority shall notify the liable person in writing of the chargeable amount; and any overpayment of the chargeable amount (proportionately reduced in accordance with paragraph (9)) shall, to the extent that it exceeds any other outstanding liability of that person to the levying authority in respect of council tax or the council water charge—

(a) be repaid to him if he so requires; or
(b) in any other case (as the levying authority determine) either be repaid to him or be credited against any subsequent liability of his to make a payment in respect of any council tax or council water charge to the authority.

(6) If any assumption by reference to which the estimated amount was calculated is shown to be false before the chargeable amount is capable of final determination for the purposes of paragraphs (4) and (5), the levying authority may, and if so required by the liable person shall, make a calculation of the appropriate amount with a view to adjusting that person's liability in respect of the estimated amount and (as appropriate) to—

(a) requiring an interim payment from the liable person (proportionately reduced in accordance with paragraph (9)) if the appropriate amount is greater than the estimated amount, or
(b) making an interim repayment to the liable person (proportionately reduced in accordance with paragraph (9)) if the appropriate amount is less than the amount of the estimated amount paid.

(7) The appropriate amount for the purposes of paragraph (6) is the amount which would be required to be paid under a demand notice if such a notice were issued with respect to the relevant year on the day that the notice under paragraph (8) is issued; and more than one calculation of the appropriate amount and interim adjustment may be made under paragraph (6) according to the circumstances.

(8) On calculating the appropriate amount the levying authority shall notify the liable person in writing of it; and a payment required under sub-paragraph (a) of paragraph (6) shall be due from the liable person to the levying authority on the expiry of such period (being not less than 14 days) after the day of issue of the notice as is specified in it.

(9) The proportion by reference to which a payment or repayment (or sum to be credited) under paragraph (4), (5) or (6) is to be reduced is to be the proportion determined under sub-paragraph (b) of paragraph (2) in respect of the lump sum concerned in that case; but in determining whether there has been an overpayment of

the chargeable amount or appropriate amount (and the amount of any sum to be re-paid or credited before reduction as aforementioned) one payment of the lump sum shall be treated as a payment of the estimated amount in full, and any other propor-tionately reduced payment or repayment already made shall be treated as not hav-ing been so reduced.

(10) In this regulation—

"the appropriate amount" has the meaning given in paragraph (7); and

"the estimated amount" means the amount last estimated under paragraph (2) of regulation 20 for the purposes of a demand notice or any subsequent notice given under paragraph 6(3)(b) of Schedule 1 prior to the payment of the single lump sum mentioned in paragraph (1) above; save that if in any case an interim adjustment has been made under paragraph (6), in re-lation to the next payment, repayment or interim adjustment in that case under this regulation (if any) it means (except in paragraph (9)) the appro-priate amount by reference to which the previous interim adjustment was so made.

Non-cash payments

25.—(1) A levying authority may, subject to the conditions set out in paragraph (2), accept an amount ("discounted amount") in such cases as they may determine and in satisfaction of any liability of a person to pay to them any instalment or other payment on account due under a notice given under this Part, being an amount de-termined by the authority and less than the amount of the instalment or other pay-ment due.

(2) The conditions are that—

(a) the discounted amount is paid to the authority otherwise than by either bank notes or coin; and

(b) the determinations under paragraph (1) as to the cases where a discounted amount will be accepted and as to the proportion that the amount is to bear to the amount of the instalment or other payment due in those cases must be made by the authority on or before the day on which they first set an amount for the relevant year under section 93(1) of the Act.

(3) Subject to paragraph (5), a determination under paragraph (1) may be revoked at any time, and if revoked may (but only on or before the day mentioned in sub-para-graph (b) of paragraph (2)) be replaced by a fresh determination.

(4) For the purpose of determining whether an adjustment of any amount paid (whether by way of repayment, crediting or otherwise) falls to be made under this Part where a discounted amount has been accepted, the instalment or other payment by reference to which the discounted amount was accepted shall be treated as hav-ing been paid in full; but any amount to be repaid or credited against any subsequent liability in any case shall, insofar as it is attributable to such an instalment or other payment, be reduced in accordance with the proportion determined under sub-para-graph (b) of paragraph (2) in respect of that case.

(5) Paragraph (4), and the power to revoke under paragraph (3), have effect in any case subject to any agreement to the contrary between the levying authority and the person liable to pay the instalment or other payment concerned.

Collection of penalties

26.—(1) Subject to paragraphs (2) and (4), where a penalty is payable by a person to a levying authority under any of sub-paragraphs (1) to (3) of paragraph 2 of Schedule 3 to the Act, it may be collected, as the authority to which it is payable determine, either—

(a) by treating the penalty for the purposes of regulations 20 and 21 and Schedule 1 as if it were part of the amount that the person is or will be liable to pay in respect of any council tax or council water charge as regards any demand notice issued after the penalty is imposed; or

(b) by the service by the authority on the person of a notice requiring payment of the penalty on the expiry of such period (being not less than 14 days) after the issue of the notice as is specified in it.

(2) Where the imposition of a penalty is subject to an appeal, no amount shall be payable in respect of the penalty while the appeal is outstanding.

(3) The imposition of a penalty is to be treated as subject to an appeal for the purposes of this regulation until such time as the appeal is finally disposed of in accordance with regulations under section 82 of the Act or is abandoned or fails for non-prosecution; and the circumstances in which an appeal is to be treated as failing for non-prosecution include the expiry of any time prescribed under such regulations in consequence of which any such appeal would require to be dismissed by a valuation appeal committee.

(4) A demand notice making provision for the recovery of a penalty which is subject to appeal may not be issued under sub-paragraph (a) of paragraph (1) during the period that the appeal concerned is outstanding; and where a penalty becomes subject to appeal after the issue of a demand notice which makes such provision, such proportion of the sum due under it as is attributable to the penalty shall not fall due until the appeal is finally disposed of, abandoned or fails for non-prosecution.

(5) Where an amount has been paid by a person in respect of a penalty which is quashed under paragraph 2(6) of Schedule 3 to the Act or pursuant to the order of a valuation appeal committee or the Court of Session, the levying authority which imposed the penalty may allow the amount to him by way of deduction against any other sum which has become due from him under this Part (whether in respect of another penalty or otherwise); and any balance shall be repaid to him.

Final adjustment of sums payable

27.—(1) This regulations applies where—

(a) a notice has been issued by a levying authority under this part requiring a payment or payments to be made by a person in respect of his liability to pay council tax and the council water charge for a financial year or part of a financial year;

(b) the payment of payments required to be made are found to be in excess of or less than his liability for the year or the part; and

(c) provision for adjusting the amounts payable under the notice and (as appropriate) for the making of additional payments or the repaying or crediting of any amount overpaid is not made by any other provision of this Part, of the Act or of any agreement entered into under paragraph (4) of regulation 21.

(2) The levying authority shall as soon as practicable after the expiry of the year or the part of a year serve a further notice on the person stating the amount of his liability for the year or the part, and adjusting (by reference to that amount) the amounts required to be paid under the notice referred to in sub-paragraph (a) of paragraph (1).

(3) If the amount stated in the further notice is greater than the amount required to be paid under the notice referred to in sub-paragraph (a) of paragraph (1), the amount of the difference for which such other provision as is mentioned in sub-paragraph (c) of that paragraph is not made shall be due from the person to the levying authority on the expiry of such period (being not less than 14 days) after the day of issue of the notice as is specified in it.

(4) If there has been an overpayment, the amount overpaid for which such other provision as is mentioned in sub-paragraph (c) of paragraph (1) is not made shall, to the extent that it exceeds any other outstanding liability of the person to the levying authority in respect of council tax or the council water charge—

    (a) be repaid to him if he so requires; or

    (b) in any other case (as the levying authority determine) either be repaid to him or be credited against any subsequent liability of his to make a payment in respect of any council tax or council water charge to the authority.

Part VI. Contents of Demand Notices

Contents of demand notices

28.—(1) Any demand notice issued by a levying authority must contain the matters specified in Part I of Schedule 2.

(2) Any demand notice issued by a levying authority must contain the matters specified in Part II of Schedule 2, except to the extent that previous notification of those matters has already been given (whether under these Regulations or otherwise) to the person, or any one of the persons, to whom the notice is addressed.

(3) Nothing in this regulation requires a demand notice to be given on a single sheet of paper, but if more than one sheet is used, the sheets shall be issued together, whether or not attached, so as to comprise one notice.

Invalid notices

29.—(1) Where—

    (a) a demand notice is invalid because it does not comply with regulation 28;

    (b) the failure so to comply was due to a mistake; and

    (c) the amounts required to be paid under the notice were demanded in accordance with Part V of these Regulations;

the requirement to pay those amounts shall apply as if the notice were valid.

(2) Where a requirement to pay an amount under an invalid notice subsists by virtue of paragraph (1), the levying authority shall as soon as practicable after the mistake is discovered issue to the liable person or persons concerned a statement of the matters which were not contained in the notice and which should have been so contained.

Part VII. Enforcement

Certificates with application for a summary warrant

30.—(1) For the purposes of paragraph 2(2) of Schedule 8 to the Act, the certificate from a levying authority accompanying their application for a summary warrant shall contain the following particulars:—

(a) a statement that the persons specified in the application have not paid sums falling within sub-paragraph (1) of paragraph 1 of that Schedule;

(b) a statement that the authority have served a notice ("a final notice") on each such person requiring him to make payment of the amount due by him within the period of 14 days beginning with the day on which the notice was served;

(c) a statement that that period of 14 days has expired without full payment of the said amount;

(d) a statement that, in respect of each of the persons specified in the application, either—

    (i) that period of 14 days has expired without the person having served a written notice on the authority under subsection (4) of section 81 of the Act stating that he is aggrieved by a matter which is one of those specified in subsection (1) of that section and which is relevant to the requirement contained in the final notice; or

    (ii) where such a notice has been served by a person, the authority have notified him in writing as specified in paragraph (a) or (b) of subsection (7) of that section or the period of two months specified in paragraph (c) of that subsection has expired; and

(e) specification of the amount due and unpaid by each such person.

(2) For the avoidance of doubt, where two or more persons are jointly and severally liable to pay to a levying authority a sum falling within sub-paragraph (1) of paragraph 1 of Schedule 8 to the Act, nothing in paragraph (1) above shall preclude the authority from seeking the granting of a warrant—

(a) which shows those persons as jointly and severally liable for that sum; or

(b) which shows them as individually liable for that sum.

Duty of debtor to supply information

31.—(1) Where, under Schedule 8 to the Act, a summary warrant or a decree in an action for payment has been granted, the debtor against whom it was granted shall, during such time as the amount in respect of which the warrant or decree was granted remains wholly or partly unpaid, be under a duty to supply, in accordance with paragraph (5), relevant information to the levying authority on whose application the warrant or decree was granted.

(2) Relevant information is such information as fulfils the following conditions:-

(a) it is in the debtor's possession or control;

(b) the levying authority request him by notice to supply it; and

(c) it falls within paragraph (3).

(3) Information falls within this paragraph if it is specified in the notice mentioned in sub-paragraph (b) of paragraph (2) and is information as to—

(a) the name of any employer of the debtor;

(b) the address of the employer's premises at or from which the debtor works;

(c) where there are in Scotland no such premises, the address of any one place of business of the employer within Scotland;

(d) the national insurance number of the debtor;

(e) the name of any bank having a place of business in Great Britain with which the debtor maintains an account (either in his own name or in the names of himself and another person or persons);

(f) the address of the office at which any such account is maintained and, if that office is outside Scotland, the address of the principal office in Scotland, or (if none) in Great Britain, of the bank in question;

(g) the number of any such account;

(h) the name and address of any other person or persons who are jointly and severally liable with the debtor to make payment of the whole or any part of the amount in respect of which the warrant or decree was granted.

(4) In paragraph (3), "bank" means any institution authorised under the Banking Act 1987.

(5) Information must be supplied in writing within 14 days of the day on which the request is made by the levying authority.

SCHEDULE 1   Regulation 21

COUNCIL TAX AND COUNCIL WATER CHARGE INSTALMENTS

PART I. PAYMENT OF THE AGGREGATE AMOUNT: MONTHLY INSTALMENTS

1.—(1) This paragraph applies where a demand notice is issued on or before 31st December in the relevant year, but has effect subject to paragraph 2 below.

(2) The aggregate amount is to be payable in monthly instalments—

(a) beginning—

(i)   where the demand notice is issued prior to the beginning of the relevant year, in May of that year; or

(ii) in any other case, in the month following that in which the demand notice is issued;

(b) ending in the penultimate month of the relevant year; and

(c) falling due on such day in each month as is specified in the notice.

(3) If the aggregate amount divided by the number of instalments gives an amount which is a multiple of £1, the instalments shall be of that amount.

(4) If the aggregate amount so divided would not give such an amount, all but the first instalment shall be of an amount equal to A and the first instalment shall be of an amount equal to B, where—

$A = \dfrac{C}{D}$, rounded up or down (as the levying authority shall determine) to a multiple of £1;

$B = C - ((D - 1) \times A)$;

C is equal to the aggregate amount; and

D is equal to the number of instalments to be paid.

2.—(1) If amounts calculated in accordance with paragraph 1 would produce an amount for an instalment of less than £5, a demand notice may require the aggregate amount to be paid—

   (a) where the aggregate amount is less than £10, in a single instalment payable on such day as is specified in the notice; or

   (b) where the aggregate amount is equal to or greater than £10, by a number of monthly instalments equal to the greatest whole number by which £5 can be multiplied to give a product which is less than or equal to the aggregate amount.

(2) The months in which the instalments under sub-paragraph (1)(b) are payable must be uninterrupted but subject to that are to be such of the months in which, but for this paragraph, the instalments would have been payable under paragraph 1 as are specified in the demand notice; and the instalments are to be payable on such day in each month as is so specified.

(3) Sub-paragraphs (3) and (4) of paragraph 1 apply to instalments under sub-paragraph (1)(b) as they apply to instalments under that paragraph.

3. Where a demand notice is issued between 1st January and 31st March in the relevant year, the aggregate amount is to be payable in a single instalment on such day as is specified in the notice.

4. In this Part, "the aggregate amount" means the amount referred to in paragraph (2) of regulation 20.

Part II. Cessation and Adjustment of Instalments

5.—(1) This paragraph applies where—

   (a) a demand notice has been served on a liable person by a levying authority;

   (b) the notice requires instalments to be paid in accordance with Part I of this Schedule; and

   (c) after the issue of the notice, but before the date on which the final instalment under it is payable, it comes to the attention of the authority that the person has ceased to be the liable person in respect of the dwelling and the period to which the notice relates.

(2) Subject to sub-paragraph (5), no payments of instalments falling due after the relevant day shall be payable under the notice.

(3) The levying authority shall, as soon as practicable after they are satisfied that this paragraph applies in a particular case, serve a notice on the liable person stating the amount of his liability in respect of the council tax and the council water charge to which the demand notice relates as it has effect for the period in the relevant year up to the date on which he ceased to be so liable.

(4) If the amount stated under sub-paragraph (3) is less than the aggregate amount of any instalments which have fallen due on or before the relevant day, the difference shall go in the first instance to discharge any liability to pay the instalments (to the extent that they remain unpaid); and any residual overpayment shall, to the extent that it exceeds any other outstanding liability of the liable person to the levying authority in respect of council tax or the council water charge—

   (a) be repaid to him if he so requires, or

   (b) in any other case (as the levying authority determine) either be repaid to him or credited against any subsequent liability of his to make a payment in respect of any council tax or council water charge to the authority.

(5) If the amount stated under sub-paragraph (3) is greater than the aggregate amount of any instalments which have fallen due on or before the relevant day, the difference between the two shall be due from the liable person to the levying authority on the expiry of such period

(being not less than 14 days) after the relevant day as is specified in the notice issued under sub-paragraph (3).

(6) In this paragraph "the relevant day" means the day on which the notice referred to in sub-paragraph (3) is issued.

6.—(1) This paragraph applies where—

    (a)   a demand notice has been served on a liable person by a levying authority;

    (b)   the notice requires instalments to be paid in accordance with Part I of this Schedule;

    (c)   after the issue of the notice, but before the date on which the final instalment under it is payable, it comes to the attention of the authority that one or more of the events specified in sub-paragraph (2) has occurred; and

    (d)   the person on whom the demand notice was served remains the liable person in respect of the dwelling and the period to which the notice relates.

(2) The events specified in this sub-paragraph are that—

    (a)   the demand notice was served by reference to an amount set by the levying authority for the relevant year and, after the issue of the notice, the authority have set a different amount in substitution for that amount under section 94 of the Act, or have set, or are deemed to have set, a reduced amount under paragraph 3 of Schedule 7 to the Act;

    (b)   the demand notice was served on the assumption that, as regards any day in the period to which the notice relates, the dwelling concerned would be or was a chargeable dwelling and the dwelling was not or has ceased to be a chargeable dwelling as regards any such day;

    (c)   the demand notice was served on the assumption that, as regards any day in the period to which the notice relates, the dwelling concerned would be or was in a particular valuation band and the dwelling was not or has ceased to be in that band as regards any day in that period;

    (d)   the demand notice was served on the assumption that, as regards any day in the period to which the notice relates, the person would be or was entitled to a discount and he was not or has ceased to be so entitled or was or is entitled to a discount of a smaller amount than had been assumed;

    (e)   the demand notice was served on the assumption that, as regards any day in the period to which the notice relates, the person was not or would not be entitled to a discount and he was or is so entitled;

    (f)   the demand notice was served on the assumption that, as regards any day in the period to which the notice relates, the person was or would be liable to pay an amount in respect of council tax or the council water charge and he was or is, by virtue of regulations made under section 80 of the Act, liable to pay a greater or lesser amount than the amount stated in the notice;

    (g)   the demand notice was served on the assumption that, as regards any day in the period to which the notice relates, the person was or would be entitled to a reduction in the amount he is liable to pay in respect of council tax under regulations made under section 138(1) of the Social Security Administration Act 1992, and he was or is allowed a larger or smaller reduction than had been so assumed;

  [(gg) the demand notice was served on the assumption that, as regards any day in the period to which the notice relates, the person was not or would not be entitled to such a reduction, and he was or is so entitled;]

    (h)   the demand notice was served on the assumption that, as regards any day in the period to which the notice relates, the dwelling concerned was an exempt dwelling and the dwelling was not an exempt dwelling as regards any such day;

    (i)   the demand notice was served on the assumption that, as regards any day in the period to which the notice relates, the qualifying conditions mentioned in paragraph 8 of Schedule 11 to the Act were or would be met in respect of the dwelling concerned and those conditions were not or have ceased to be met;

(j)   the demand notice was served on the assumption that, as regards any day in the period to which the notice relates, those qualifying conditions were not or would not be met in respect of the dwelling concerned and those conditions were or are now met.

(3) The levying authority shall, as soon as practicable after they are satisfied that this paragraph applies in a particular case—

(a)   adjust any instalments payable on or after the adjustment day ("the remaining instalments") in accordance with sub-paragraph (5); and

(b)   serve a notice on the liable person which is to state—

(i)   the revised amount; and

(ii)   the amount of any remaining instalments.

(4) The revised amount is the revised estimate of the levying authority of the amount that the person is liable to pay in respect of council tax and the council water charge for the relevant year, made on the assumptions mentioned in paragraph (3) of regulation 20 and as if the notice mentioned in that provision were the notice referred to in sub-paragraph (3) above.

(5) The aggregate amount of the remaining instalments payable shall be equal to the total of—

(a)   the amount by which the revised amount exceeds the aggregate amount of the instalments payable under the demand notice before the adjustment day; and

(b)   any amount which the levying authority decide to add to the remaining instalments in terms of sub-paragraph (6);

and the amount of each remaining instalment (if there are more than one) shall be such as the levying authority may determine.

(6) Where at the date of issue of the notice referred to in sub-paragraph (3)(b) there remains unpaid any sum in respect of an instalment or instalments payable under the demand notice before the adjustment day, the levying authority may decide to add all or part of that sum to the remaining instalments, and any sum so added shall subsequently be treated for all purposes of these Regulations as being payable as part of the remaining instalments.

(7) If the revised amount is less than the aggregate amount of the instalments payable before the adjustment day, any overpayment shall, to the extent that it exceeds any other outstanding liability of the liable person to the levying authority in respect of council tax or the council water charge—

(a)   be repaid to him if he so requires; or

(b)   in any other case (as the levying authority determine) either be repaid to him or credited against any subsequent liability of his to make a payment in respect of any council tax or council water charge to the authority.

(8) More than one adjustment of amounts paid or payable under a demand notice may be made under this paragraph as the circumstances require.

(9) Where a notice has been given under sub-paragraph (3), in the operation of this paragraph as respects any further notice that may fall to be given under it, references in this paragraph to the demand notice and to amounts in respect of instalments payable under it shall be construed (so far as the context permits) as references to the notice, and amounts in respect of instalments payable under the notice, as from time to time previously served or adjusted under this paragraph.

(10) In this paragraph—

"the adjustment day" means the day 14 days after the day of issue of the notice under sub-paragraph (3); and

"the revised amount" has the meaning assigned to it in sub-paragraph (4).

NOTES
Sch 1: Para 6(2)(gg): Paragraph inserted by the Council Tax (Administration and Enforcement)(Scotland) Regulations 1992, SI 1992/3290, reg5.

SCHEDULE 2

CONTENTS OF DEMAND NOTICES

PART I. MATTERS TO BE CONTAINED IN ALL DEMAND NOTICES

1. A statement of the address of the dwelling to which the notice relates ("the relevant dwelling").

2. A statement of the valuation band shown in the valuation list as applicable to the relevant dwelling ("the relevant valuation band") and, where the Council Tax (Reductions for Disabilities) (Scotland) Regulations 1992 apply, a statement of the valuation band applicable in terms of paragraph (1) of regulation 4 of those Regulations ("the alternative valuation band").

3. A statement, as regards the relevant year and the relevant valuation band or, where applicable, the alternative valuation band, of—

    (a) where the relevant dwelling is situated within the area of a regional council, the amounts last set or determined—

        (i) as council tax by that council and by the district council within the area of which the dwelling is situated; and

        (ii) as council water charge by that regional council; or

    (b) where the relevant dwelling is situated within the area of an islands council, the amounts last set or determined as council tax and council water charge by that council.

4. A statement of the period within the relevant year to which the notice relates.

5. A statement of the total amounts payable under the notice in respect of—

    (a) council tax; and

    (b) the council water charge;

showing itemised separately in each case the amount of any reductions or additions attributable to—

        (i) any regulations under section 80 of the Act, or under that section as read with paragraph 11 of Schedule 11 to the Act, other than the Council Tax (Reductions for Disabilities) (Scotland) Regulations 1992;

        (ii) discounts under section 79 of the Act, or under that section as read with paragraph 11 of Schedule 11 to the Act;

        (iii) council tax benefit;

        (iv) credits in respect of previous overpayments;

        (v) penalties under Schedule 3 to the Act; and

        (vi) any excess council tax benefit being recovered otherwise than by allowing, for the purposes of calculating the total amount payable under the notice, a smaller reduction in respect of council tax benefit than would have been applicable but for the previous over-allowance of such benefit.

6. A statement of the instalments or other payments required to be paid under the notice and of the dates on which, and the manner in which, those payments are to be made.

7. The name, address and telephone number of the department or unit of the levying authority to which enquiries may be directed as to any matter of which a statement is required to be given by any of the foregoing paragraphs, together with a note of the hours during which persons may attend at that department or unit with enquiries or during which they may make enquiries by telephone.

8. Explanatory notes, which shall include—

    (a) a general indication of the circumstances in which—

        (i) a dwelling may be an exempt dwelling for the purposes of Part II of the Act;

        (ii) a person may be an eligible person for the purposes of the Council Tax (Reductions for Disabilities) (Scotland) Regulations 1992 or of any other regulations under section 80 of the Act;

        (iii) an amount may be subject to a discount under section 79 of the Act; and

        (iv) a person may be entitled to council tax benefit;

    (b) a statement as to the procedures to be followed by a person who wishes to establish whether any matter referred to in sub-paragraph (a) is applicable in his case;

    (c) a statement as to the effect of paragraph (2) of regulation 18;

    (d) a general indication of the principles and assumptions relevant to the compilation of the authority's valuation list; and

    (e) a statement as to the procedures to be followed by a person who wishes to dispute—

        (i) any matter shown in relation to the relevant dwelling in the authority's valuation list;

        (ii) the calculation of the amount specified in the notice as that which he is liable to pay; or

        (iii) the fact that he is liable to pay council tax or the council water charge in respect of the relevant dwelling for any period to which the notice relates, or that that dwelling is a chargeable dwelling for any such period.

PART II. MATTERS TO BE CONTAINED IN DEMAND NOTICES SO FAR AS NOT ALREADY NOTIFIED

9. A statement to the same effect as the statement mentioned in paragraph (2) of regulation 14 (if the demand notice shows a deduction attributable as specified in sub-paragraph (ii) of paragraph 5 above).

10. A general explanation of how the amount of any reduction attributable to the Council Tax (Reductions for Disabilities) (Scotland) Regulations 1992 or to the matters specified in sub-paragraph (i) or (iii) of paragraph 5 above has been determined.

The Council Tax (Exempt Dwellings) (Scotland) Order 1992

(SI 1992/1333)

NOTES
Made: 2nd June 1992
Laid before Parliament: 10th June 1992
Coming into force: 1st July 1992

Citation and commencement

1. This Order may be cited as the Council Tax (Exempt Dwellings) (Scotland) Order 1992 and shall come into force on 1st July 1992.

Interpretation

2. In this Order—

"the Act" means the Local Government Finance Act 1992;

"charitable" shall be construed in the same way as if it were contained in the Income Tax Acts;

"the last occupation day" with respect to an unoccupied dwelling means the day on which the dwelling concerned was last occupied, save that where a dwelling which was unoccupied becomes occupied on any day and becomes unoccupied again at the expiry of a period of less than 6 weeks beginning with that day, for the purpose of determining the last occupation day (and only for that purpose) the dwelling shall be treated as having remained unoccupied during that period;

"personal care" includes the provision of appropriate help with physical and social needs;

"qualifying person" means a person who would be liable (either solely or jointly and severally with another person or persons) for council tax in respect of the dwelling concerned, but for the provisions of this Order;

"registered housing association" has the same meaning as it has for the purposes of the Housing Associations Act 1985;

"relevant person" means a person who—

    (a) is disregarded for the purposes of discount by virtue of paragraph 1, 6, 7 or 8 of Schedule 1 to the Act;

    (b) has his sole or main residence in a place (other than the dwelling concerned or a place referred to in paragraph 6(1), 7(1)(a) or 8(1)(a) of that Schedule) for the purpose of receiving personal care which he requires by reason of old age, disablement, illness, past or present alcohol or drug dependence or past or present mental disorder; or

    (c) has his sole or main residence in a place (other than the dwelling concerned) for the purpose of providing, or better providing, personal care for a person who requires such care by reason of old age, disablement, illness, past or present alcohol or drug dependence or past or present mental disorder;

"student" has the same meaning as in paragraph 4(2) of Schedule 1 to the Act;

"valuation list" means a list maintained by a levying authority under section 84 of the Act.

Exempt dwellings

3. The classes of dwelling specified in the Schedule to this Order are prescribed as exempt dwellings for the purposes of section 72(6) of, and paragraph 7(2) of Schedule 11 to, the Act.

SCHEDULE   Article 3

EXEMPT DWELLINGS

1. An unoccupied and unfurnished dwelling in respect of which—

    (a) the effective date for the first entry in the valuation list is later than 1st April 1993;

    (b) there was no entry in the valuation roll immediately prior to the effective date for the first entry in that list; and

(c) less than 6 months have elapsed since that effective date.

2. An unoccupied and unfurnished dwelling—

(a) which is entered in the valuation list with effect from 1st April 1993; and
(b) in respect of which less than 6 months have elapsed since the date on which it would first have been entered in that list had that list been in force from 1st October 1992.

3. A dwelling which is incapable of, and is not, being lived in because it is being structurally repaired, improved or reconstructed.

4. An unoccupied dwelling—

(a) in respect of which—

(i) a body established for charitable purposes only is a qualifying person; and
(ii) less than 6 months have elapsed since the last occupation day; and

(b) which was on that day occupied in furtherance of the objects of the body in question.

[**5.** A dwelling—

(a) which is both unoccupied and unfurnished; and
(b) in respect of which less than 6 months have elapsed since the end of the last period of 6 weeks or more throughout which it was continually occupied or furnished.]

6. An unoccupied dwelling which on the last occupation day was the sole or main residence of a person who—

(a) is, and has throughout the period since that day been, a relevant person; and
(b) is a qualifying person.

7. A dwelling—

(a) which is not the sole or main residence of any person; and
(b) in respect of which any liability to pay council tax (but for the terms of this Order) would fall to be met [solely] out of the estate of a deceased person and either—

(i) no grant of confirmation to the estate of that person has been made; or
(ii) no more than 6 months have passed since such a grant was made.

8. A dwelling—

(a) the occupation of which is prohibited by law; or
(b) which is kept unoccupied by reason of action taken under powers conferred by or under any Act of Parliament, with a view to prohibiting its occupation or to acquiring it.

9. A dwelling which—

(a) is owned by a housing body; and
(b) is kept unoccupied with a view to having it demolished.

10. A dwelling which—

(a) is not the sole or main residence of any person; and
(b) is held by or on behalf of a religious body for the purpose of being available for occupation by a minister of religion as a residence from which to perform the duties of his office.

[**11.** A dwelling which—

(a) is occupied by at least one person who is—

(i) a student;
(ii) a person disregarded for the purposes of discount in terms of paragraph 3 of the Schedule to the Council Tax (Discounts)(Scotland) Regulations 1992; or
(iii) a person under the age of 18 years; and

(b) is not the sole or main residence of any person other than a person described in sub-paragraph (a)(i) to (iii).]

12. An unoccupied dwelling—

(a) which is not the sole or main residence of any person other than a student;

(b) which, when last occupied, was occupied by a student or students; and

(c) in respect of which less than 4 months have passed since the last occupation day.

13. A dwelling—

(a) which is not the sole or main residence of any person; and

(b) in respect of which each qualifying person is a student.

14. A dwelling—

(a) which is not the sole or main residence of any person;

(b) in respect of which the qualifying person (or, where there is more than one such person, one or more of them) is a debtor, or one of the joint debtors, in a heritable security secured over the dwelling; and

(c) lawful possession of which has been entered into by the creditor in that heritable security.

15. An unoccupied and unfurnished dwelling which—

(a) is situated on lands and heritages used for agricultural or pastoral purposes only, or as woodlands, market gardens, orchards, allotments or allotment gardens, or on lands exceeding one tenth of a hectare used for the purpose of poultry farming; and

(b) when last occupied and used, was occupied together with and used in connection with the lands and heritages on which the dwelling is situated.

16. A dwelling which—

(a) is not the sole or main residence of any person;

(b) falls within the description mentioned in paragraph (a) of section 61(4) of the Housing (Scotland) Act 1987; and

(c) is held by a registered housing association for the purpose of being available for occupation by persons of pensionable age or disabled persons who are likely in future to have their sole or main residences in other dwellings falling within the same description which are provided by the association.

17. A dwelling which is, or is part of, a hall of residence provided predominantly for the accommodation of students, and which—

(a) is owned and managed by an institution within the meaning of paragraph 5(4) of Schedule 1 to the Act; or

(b) is the subject of an agreement allowing such an institution to nominate [the majority of the persons who are to occupy] the accommodation so provided.

18. A dwelling—

(a) of which the Secretary of State for Defence is the owner; and

(b) which is held for the purposes of armed forces accommodation.

19. A dwelling which is the sole or main residence of one or more persons under the age of 18 years and of no other person.

20. An unoccupied dwelling—

(a) which either—

(i)   forms part of premises which include another dwelling; or

(ii) is situated within the curtilage of another dwelling;

(b) which is difficult to let separately from that other dwelling; and

(c) in respect of which a qualifying person has his sole or main residence in that other dwelling.

21. A dwelling which falls within either of the classes of lands and heritages specified in paragraphs (2) and (3) of regulation 2 of the Council Tax (Dwellings) (Scotland) Regulations 1992.

[**22.** A dwelling—

   (a)   which is not the sole or main residence of any person;
   (b)   an interest in which is vested in a permanent trustee by virtue of subsection (1) or (10) of section 31, or subsection (6) of section 32, of the Bankruptcy (Scotland) Act 1985; and
   (c)   in respect of which that trustee is the only qualifying person.]

[**23.** A dwelling in respect of which any of the qualifying persons is a person who has a relevant association, within the meaning of Part I of the Visiting Forces Act 1952, with a body, contingent or detachment of the forces of a country to which any provision in that Part applies.]

NOTES
Para 5: Paragraph substituted by the Council Tax (Exempt Dwellings) (Scotland) Amendment Order 1992, SI 1992/2796, para 2(2).
Para 7(b): Word added by SI 1992/2796, para 2(3).
Para 11: Substituted by SI 1993/345.
Para 17(b): Amended by SI 1993/345.
Para 22: Added by SI 1992/2796, para 2(4).
Para 23: Added by SI 1993/345.

The Council Tax (Dwellings) (Scotland) Regulations 1992
(SI 1992/1334)

NOTES
Made: 2nd June 1992
Laid before Parliament: 10th June 1992
Coming into force: 1st July 1992

Citation, commencement and interpretation

1. (1) These Regulations may be cited as the Council Tax (Dwellings) (Scotland) Regulations 1992 and shall come into force on 1st July 1992.

(2) In these Regulations, "the Act" means the Local Government Finance Act 1992 [and "private motor vehicle" means a mechanically propelled vehicle not falling within Schedules 2, 3 and 4 to the Vehicles (Excise) Act 1971].

NOTE
Reg 1(2): Words added by the Council Tax (Dwellings and Part Residential Subjects) (Scotland) Regulations 1992, SI 1992/2955, reg 7(a).

Variation of definition of dwelling

2. (1) The definition of dwelling in section 72(2) of the Act is hereby varied by including as a dwelling any lands and heritages—

   (a)   which fall within the class specified in paragraph (2) or that specified in paragraph (3); and

(b) which would, but for the provisions of section 73(1) of the Act, be entered separately in the valuation roll.

(2) The class specified in this paragraph is lands and heritages which are a garage, a carport or, as the case may be, a car parking stance—

(a) the use of which is ancillary to, and which is used wholly in connection with, another dwelling; and
(b) which is used wholly or mainly for the accommodation of one or more private motor vehicles.

(3) The class specified in this paragraph is lands and heritages—

(a) the use of which is ancillary to, and which are used wholly in connection with, another dwelling; and
(b) which are used wholly or mainly for the storage of articles of domestic use (including cycles and other similar vehicles).

[(4) Lands and heritages which are not in use shall nevertheless be treated as falling within the class specified in paragraph (2) or that specified in paragraph (3) if, when last in use, they were used as specified in those paragraphs.]

NOTE
Reg 2: Paragraph (4) added by the Council Tax (Dwellings and Part Residential Subjects) (Scotland) Regulations 1992, SI 1992/2955, reg 7(b).

The Council Tax (Reduction for Disabilities) (Scotland) Regulations 1992
(SI 1992/1335)

NOTES
Made: 2nd June 1992
Laid before Parliament: 10th June 1992
Coming into force: 1st July 1992

Citation, commencement and interpretation

1. (1) These Regulations may be cited as the Council Tax (Reductions for Disabilities) (Scotland) Regulations 1992 and shall come into force on 1st July 1992.

(2) In these Regulations—
   "the Act" means the Local Government Finance Act 1992;
   "qualifying individual" means a person who is substantially and permanently disabled (whether by illness, injury, congenital deformity or otherwise); and
   "relevant valuation band", in relation to a dwelling, means the valuation band shown as applicable to the dwelling in the levying authority's valuation list.

(3) Any reference in these Regulations to a liable person is a reference to a person who is liable (whether his liability is sole or joint and several) to pay to a levying

authority, in respect of a particular dwelling, an amount in respect of council tax or the council water charge and includes, unless the context otherwise requires, a reference to a person who in the opinion of the authority will be so liable.

Prescribed years

2. The financial year commencing on 1st April 1993 and any subsequent financial years are prescribed as the years for which these Regulations apply.

Eligible persons

3. (1) Subject to paragraph (4), a person is an eligible person for the purposes of these Regulations if—

  (a) he is a liable person as regards a dwelling which is the sole or main residence of at least one qualifying individual and in which there is provided—

   (i)   a room which is not a bathroom, a kitchen or a lavatory and which is predominantly used (whether for providing therapy or otherwise) by, and is required for meeting the needs of, any qualifying individual resident in the dwelling; or
   (ii) a bathroom or kitchen which is not the only bathroom or kitchen within the dwelling and which is required for meeting the needs of any qualifying individual resident in the dwelling; or
   (iii) sufficient floor space to permit the use of a wheelchair required for meeting the needs of any qualifying individual resident in the dwelling; and

  (b) as regards the financial year in question, an application in writing is made to the levying authority within the area of which that dwelling is situated—

   (i)   by him or on his behalf; or
   (ii) by or on behalf of another person jointly and severally liable with him for council tax or the council water charge in respect of that dwelling.

(2) For the purposes of paragraph (1), and subject to paragraph (3), references to anything being required for meeting the needs of a qualifying individual are references to its being essential or of major importance to his well-being by reason of the nature and extent of his disability.

(3) A wheelchair is not required for meeting an individual's needs if he does not need to use it within the living accommodation comprising or included in the dwelling concerned.

(4) A person is not an eligible person for the purposes of these Regulations if the relevant valuation band as regards the dwelling in respect of which he is a liable person is valuation band A.

Calculation of amount payable

4. (1) Subject to paragraph (2), the amount of council tax and council water charge payable by an eligible person in respect of the dwelling in question and each day on which the condition referred to in regulation 3(1)(a) is satisfied shall be calculated as if, instead of the relevant valuation band, there had been shown in the valuation list the band which appears immediately above the relevant valuation band in the Table set out in section 74(2) of the Act.

(2) Where, as regards an eligible person, the dwelling in question and a day on which the condition referred to in regulation 3(1)(a) is satisfied—

  (a) regulations under section 80 of the Act (other than these Regulations) apply; or
  (b) the amount of any council tax benefit to which he is entitled takes the form of a reduction in the amount which he is liable to pay as regards that day;

the amount payable shall be calculated in accordance with these Regulations as read with those regulations or, as the case may be, regulations relating to that reduction.

The Council Tax (Discounts) (Scotland) Order 1992

(SI 1992/1408)

NOTES
Made: 12th June 1992
Laid before Parliament: 24th June 1992
Coming into force: 1st April 1993

Citation, commencement and extent

1.—(1) This Order may be cited as the Council Tax (Discounts) (Scotland) Order 1992 and shall come into force on 1st April 1993.

(2) This Order extends to Scotland only.

Interpretation

2. In this Order, except where the context otherwise requires—
  "the Act" means the Local Government Finance Act 1992;
  "central institution" has the same meaning as in section 135(1) of the Education (Scotland) Act 1980;
  "designated institution" has the same meaning as in section 44(2) of the Further and Higher Education (Scotland) Act 1992;
  "District Health Authority" and "Regional Health Authority" have the same meanings as in section 8 of the National Health Service Act 1977;
  "further education", in relation to Scotland, has the same meaning as in section 1(5)(b) of the Education (Scotland) Act 1980, in relation to England and Wales, has the same meaning as in section 41 of the Education Act 1944, and, in relation to Northern Ireland, has the same meaning as in article 5(c) of the Education and Libraries (Northern Ireland) Order 1986;
  "Health Board" has the same meaning as in section 2 of the National Health Service (Scotland) Act 1978;
  "qualifying course of education" has the meaning assigned to it by Schedule 1 to this Order;

"relevant activities" with respect to a qualifying course of education means the receipt of tuition, the undertaking of supervised study or examination, and the taking part (as part of the curriculum of the course) in any supervised exercise, experiment, project or practical work;

"the relevant number of hours per week" in relation to such a course means the average number of hours per week a person undertaking it would normally require to spend, in the period during which the course subsists, on relevant activities (excluding for the purpose of calculating that average any part of that period which is a period of vacation);

"the relevant period" for a programme or course means the period commencing with the day on which a person begins that programme or course and ending with the day ("the last day") on which he completes it, abandons it or is dismissed from it (which period includes any period of vacation between terms and before the last day);

and any reference to a paragraph in Schedule 1 to the Act includes a reference to that paragraph as read with paragraph 11 of Schedule 11 to the Act.

Persons in detention

3. (1) Under sub-paragraph (6) of paragraph 1 of Schedule 1 to the Act, a person shall be disregarded for the purposes of discount on a particular day if—

  (a) on the day he is imprisoned, detained or in custody under the Army Act 1955, the Air Force Act 1955 or the Naval Discipline Act 1957; and
  (b) the conditions prescribed in paragraph (2) below are fulfilled where they are applicable.

(2) The conditions are that, where a person is in custody under arrest under any of the Acts mentioned in paragraph (1) above—

  (a) he is not in custody under open arrest; and
  (b) the custody forms part of a continuous period exceeding 48 hours during which he is under arrest.

(3) A person is to be treated as in custody under open arrest for the purposes of sub-paragraph (a) of paragraph (2) above if he is so treated for the purposes of Queen's Regulations for the Navy, Army or Air Force.

The severely mentally impaired

4.—(1) The condition prescribed for the purposes of paragraph 2(1)(c) of Schedule 1 to the Act is that the person in question is entitled to one or more of the qualifying benefits listed in paragraph (2) below.

(2) The qualifying benefits are—

  (a) an invalidity pension under section 33, 40 or 41 of the Social Security Contributions and Benefits Act 1992;
  (b) an attendance allowance under section 64 of that Act;
  (c) a severe disablement allowance under section 68 of that Act;
  (d) the care component of a disability living allowance under section 71 of that Act, payable at the highest rate under section 72(4)(a) or at the middle rate under section 72(4)(b) of that Act;
  (e) an increase in the rate of disablement pension under section 104 of that Act (increase where constant attendance needed);

(f) a disability working allowance under section 129 of that Act for which the qualifying benefit is one falling within subsection (2)(a)(i) or (ii) of that section, or is a corresponding Northern Ireland benefit;

(g) an unemployability supplement under Part I of Schedule 7 to that Act;

(h) a constant attendance allowance under—

 (i) article 14 of the Personal Injuries (Civilians) Scheme 1983; or

 (ii) article 14 of the Naval, Military and Air Forces etc. (Disablement and Death) Service Pensions Order 1983 (including that provision as applied, whether with or without modifications, by any other instrument);

(i) an unemployability allowance under—

 (i) article 18(1) of the Personal Injuries (Civilians) Scheme 1983; or

 (ii) article 18(1) of the Naval, Military and Air Forces etc. (Disablement and Death) Service Pensions Order 1983 (including that provision as applied, whether with or without modifications, by any other instrument).

Apprentices

5. (1) For the purposes of paragraph 4 of Schedule 1 to the Act, "apprentice" means a person who, on a particular day, is—

(a) employed for the purpose of learning a trade, business, profession, office, employment or vocation;

(b) for that purpose undertaking a programme of training leading to a qualification accredited by the National Council for Vocational Qualifications or the Scottish Vocational Educational Council; and

(c) employed at a salary or in receipt of an allowance which is, or (if both) which are in total—

 (i) substantially less than the salary he would be likely to receive if he had achieved the qualification in question; and

 (ii) no more than £130 per week.

(2) A person is undertaking a programme for the purposes of paragraph (1) above on a particular day if the day falls within the relevant period for that programme.

Students

6.—(1) For the purposes of paragraph 4 of Schedule 1 to the Act, "student" means a person who, on a particular day, is not a student nurse (in terms of article 7 of this Order) and is—

(a) registered with the Central Bureau for Educational Visits and Exchanges as a foreign language assistant, provided that the day falls within the period of his appointment as such an assistant at a school or other educational institution in Great Britain;

(b) aged under 20 and undertaking with a single educational establishment (otherwise than in consequence of an office or employment held by him)—

 (i) a qualifying course of education in respect of which the relevant number of hours per week exceeds 12; or

 (ii) two or more qualifying courses of education in respect of which the aggregate of the relevant number of hours per week for all those courses exceeds 12; or

   (c) undertaking a course of education—

     (i)   which is specified in Schedule 2 to this Order;

     (ii) which is provided by an institution specified in Schedule 3 to this Order;

     (iii) which is required by the institution to attend for a period of at least 24 weeks within each academic year of the institution required to complete the course; and

     (iv) in respect of which, in the opinion of the institution, a person would ordinarily require to undertake periods of study or tuition (including any periods of industrial, professional or commercial experience associated with the course which he requires to undertake to complete the course) which amount, in the aggregate, to an average of at least 21 hours a week during the period mentioned in head (iii) above.

(2) A person is to be regarded for the purposes of sub-paragraph (b) of paragraph (1) above as undertaking a qualifying course of education on a particular day if—

   (a) the day falls within the relevant period for that course; and

   (b) he is not on that day an apprentice or a youth training trainee (in terms of article 5 or 8 of this Order).

(3) A person is to be regarded for the purposes of sub-paragraph (c) of paragraph (1) above as undertaking a course of education on a particular day if—

   (a) on the day he is enrolled with the institution providing the course for the purpose of attending that course; and

   (b) the day falls within the relevant period for that course.

Student nurses

7. (1) For the purposes of paragraph 4 of Schedule 1 to the Act, "student nurse" means a person who, on a particular day—

   (a) is undertaking a course which would (if successfully completed) lead to registration on any of Parts 1 to [9] or 11 of the Register maintained under section 10 of the Nurses, Midwives and Health Visitors Act 1979, as a first inclusion on that Register; or

   (b) is—

     (i)   undertaking a course which would (if successfully completed) lead to registration on Part 10 of that Register as a first inclusion on that Register; and

     (ii) employed by a Health Board or by a Regional or a District Health Authority.

(2) A person is undertaking a course for the purposes of paragraph (1) above on a particular day if the day falls within the relevant period for that course.

NOTE

Art 7(1)(a): Amended by the Council Tax (Discounts)(Scotland) Amendment Order 1993, SI 1993/343.

Youth training trainees

8. (1) For the purposes of paragraph 4 of Schedule 1 to the Act, "youth training trainee" means a person who, on a particular day, is—

(b) a degree, certificate or diploma granted by a designated institution, a central institution or any other institution for the provision of any form of further education.

Courses in further education

2. A course in further education leading to an award of the Scottish Certificate of Education, the General Certificate of Education, the General Certificate of Secondary Education or the International Baccalaureate.

3. A course in further education leading to the National Certificate, the Higher National Certificate or Higher National Diploma of the Scottish Vocational Education Council, or a Scottish Vocational Qualification, or any other course in further education leading to a comparable award.

4. A course in further education required by an education establishment to be undertaken prior to any other course mentioned in this Schedule being undertaken.

Teacher training and other courses

5. A course at undergraduate or postgraduate level for the initial training of teachers, social workers or youth and community workers.

Vocational courses at postgraduate level

6. A course at postgraduate level leading to a certificate or diploma in professional studies or to any other comparable award.

Courses at higher degree level

7. A course leading to the award of the degree of Doctor of Philosophy or a Master's degree or to any other comparable award.

SCHEDULE 3   Articles 6(1)(c)(ii) and 9(b)

INSTITUTIONS

1. A university in the United Kingdom and any college, school, hall or other institution of such a university.

2. A central institution.

3. A designated institution.

4. A college of nursing and midwifery or a college of health, established by a Health Board or by a Regional or District Health authority.

5. Any other institution in Scotland for the provision of any form of further education (other than a Ministry of Defence training establishment for the armed forces).

6. An establishment of further education in England or Wales maintained or assisted by a local education authority within the meaning of the Education Act 1944 or in receipt of grants made under regulations made under section 100 of that Act.

7. Any other institution in England or Wales which is—

(a) within the further education sector (in terms of subsection (3) of section 91 of the Further and Higher Education Act 1992; or

(b) within the higher education sector (in terms of subsection (5) of that section).

8. A college of education within the meaning of article 2(2) of the Education and Libraries (Northern Ireland) Order 1986.

9. An institution of further education in Northern Ireland provided by an Education and Library Board constituted in accordance with Schedule 1 to that Order.

10. A theological college.

11. An institution of a Research Council established by Royal Charter under section 1 of the Science and Technology Act 1965.

The Council Tax (Discounts) (Scotland) Regulations 1992

(SI 1992/1409)

NOTES
Made: 12th June 1992
Laid before Parliament: 24th June 1992
Coming into force: 1st April 1993

Citation, commencement, extent and interpretation

1. (1) These Regulations may be cited as the Council Tax (Discounts) (Scotland) Regulations 1992 and shall come into force on 1st April 1993.

(2) These Regulations extend to Scotland only.

(3) In these Regulations—
"the Act" means the Local Government Finance Act 1992;
"charitable" shall be construed in the same way as if it were contained in the Income Tax Acts; and
"relevant body" means—

(a) a regional, islands or district council;
(b) the Crown;
(c) a body established for charitable purposes only.

Care workers

2. (1) For the purposes of paragraph 9 of Schedule 1 to the Act (disregard for the purposes of discount of persons providing care or support (or both) to other persons, if prescribed conditions are fulfilled), and of that paragraph as read with paragraph 11 of Schedule 11 to the Act, it is prescribed that either the conditions set out in paragraph (2) below or those set out in paragraph (3) below must be fulfilled.

(2) The conditions set out in this paragraph are that the person—

(a) either—

(i) is providing care or support (or both) on behalf of a relevant body; or
(ii) is employed to provide care or support (or both) by the person to whom it is provided and to whom he was introduced by a body established for charitable purposes only;

(b) is engaged or employed to provide care or support (or both) for at least 24 hours per week;

(c) receives no more than £30 per week as remuneration in respect of the hours which he is required to work under the terms of his engagement or employment; and

(d) is resident in premises which—

(i) if sub-paragraph (a)(i) above applies, are provided by or on behalf of the relevant body; or

(ii) if sub-paragraph (a)(ii) above applies, are provided by his employer;

for the better performance of his work.

(3) The conditions set out in this paragraph are that the person—

(a) is providing care or support (or both) for an average of at least 35 hours per week;

(b) is providing care or support (or both) to a young person who is not his spouse or a child of his under the age of 18 years;

(c) is providing care or support (or both) to a person who is in receipt of—

(i) a higher rate attendance allowance under section 65 of the Social Security Contributions and Benefits Act 1992;

(ii) the highest rate of the care component of a disability living allowance under section 72(4)(a) of that Act;

(iii) an increase in the rate of his disablement pension under section 104 of that Act; or

(iv) an increase in a constant attendance allowance under the proviso to article 14 of the Personal Injuries (Civilians) Scheme 1983, or under article 14(1)(b) of the Naval, Military and Air Forces etc. (Disablement and Death) Service Pensions Order 1983 (including that provision as applied, whether with or without modifications, by any other instrument); and

(d) is resident in the same dwelling as that in which the person to whom he is providing care or support (or both) is resident.

(4) For the purposes of sub-paragraph (b) of paragraph (3) above, a person is the spouse of another if they are a man and a woman—

(a) who are married to each other; or

(b) who are not married to each other but are living together as husband and wife.

Persons of other descriptions

3. The Schedule to these Regulations, which makes provision as to persons who are to be disregarded for the purposes of discount in terms of paragraph 11 of Schedule 1 to the Act and in terms of that paragraph as read with paragraph 11 of Schedule 11 to the Act, shall have effect.

SCHEDULE

PERSONS DISREGARDED FOR PURPOSES OF DISCOUNT

International headquarters and defence organisations

1. (1) A person shall be disregarded for the purposes of discount on a particular day if on the day he is a member of a headquarters or a dependant of such a member.

(2) A headquarters, in relation to a particular day, is a headquarters or organisation designated on that day by an Order in Council under section 1 of the international Headquarters and Defence Organisations Act 1964.

(3) A person is, on a particular day, a member of a headquarters or a dependant of such a member if he is on that day such a member or dependant within the meanings of the Schedule to that Act.

Religious communities

2. (1) A person shall be disregarded for the purposes of discount on a particular day if on the day—

- (a) he is a member of a relevant religious community; and
- (b) he has no income (disregarding any pension in respect of former employment) or capital of his own and is dependent on the community concerned for his material needs.

(2) A relevant religious community is a religious community whose principal occupation—

- (a) is prayer, contemplation, education or the relief of suffering; or
- (b) consists of two or more of these occupations.

School leavers

3. A person shall be disregarded for the purposes of discount on a particular day if—

- (a) he is aged under 20 on the day;
- (b) the day falls no earlier than 1st May and no later than 31st October in a year; and
- (c) on 30th April in the year in question he was a student by virtue of article 6(1)(b) of the Council Tax (Discounts) (Scotland) Order 1992 and he has since ceased to be such a student.

[Visiting Forces

4. —(1) A person shall be disregarded for the purposes of discount on a particular day if on that day he has a relevant association with a visiting force.

(2) A visiting force, in relation to a particular day, is any body, contingent or detachment of the forces of a country to which any provision in Part I of the Visiting Forces Act 1952 applies on that day.

(3) A person has, on a particular day, a relevant association with a visitng force if he has on that day such an association within the meaning of that Part.]

NOTE
Para 4 inserted by the Council Tax (Discounts)(Scotland) Amendment Regulations 1993, SI 1993/3442.

The Council Tax Benefit (General) Regulations 1992

(SI 1992/1814)

NOTES
Made: 20th July 1992
Coming into force:
    (a) for the purposes of regulations 1, 2, 61 to 65, 92 and 93: 17th August 1992
    (b) for all other purposes: 1st April 1993

ARRANGEMENT OF REGULATIONS

PART I. GENERAL

1. Citation and commencement
2. Interpretation
3. Definition of non-dependant
4. Remunerative work

PART II. MEMBERSHIP OF A FAMILY

5. Persons of prescribed description for the definition of family in section 137(1) of the Contributions and Benefits Act 1992
6. Circumstances in which a person is to be treated as responsible or not responsible for another
7. Circumstances in which a person is to be treated as being or not being a member of the household

PART III. APPLICABLE AMOUNTS

8.   Applicable amounts
9.   Polygamous marriages
10. Patients

PART IV. INCOME AND CAPITAL

Chapter I. General

11. Calculation of income and capital of members of claimant's family and of a polygamous marriage
12. Circumstances in which income of non-dependant is to be treated as claimant's

Chapter II. Income

13. Calculation of income on a weekly basis
14. Average weekly earnings of employed earners
15. Average weekly earnings of self-employed earners
16. Average weekly income other than earnings
17. Calculation of weekly income
18. Disregard of changes in tax, contributions etc

Chapter III. Employed Earners

19. Earnings of employed earners
20. Calculation of net earnings of employed earners

Chapter IV. Self-employed Earners

21. Earnings of self-employed earners
22. Calculation of net profit of self-employed earners
23. Deduction of tax and contributions for self-employed earners

Chapter V. Other Income

24. Calculation of income other than earnings

25. Capital treated as income
26. Notional income
27. Modifications in respect of child and young person

Chapter VI. Capital

28. Capital limit
29. Calculation of capital
30. Disregard of capital of child or young person
31. Income treated as capital
32. Calculation of capital in the United Kingdom
33. Calculation of capital outside the United Kingdom
34. Notional capital
35. Diminishing notional capital rule
36. Capital jointly held
37. Calculation of tariff income from capital

PART V. STUDENTS

Chapter I. General

38. Interpretation
39. Treatment of students
40. Students who are excluded from entitlement to council tax benefit
41. Further provision with respect to students entering the United Kingdom from abroad

Chapter II. Income

42. Calculation of grant income
43. Calculation of covenant income where a contribution is assessed
44. Covenant income where no grant income or no contribution is assessed
45. Relationship with amounts to be disregarded under Schedule 4
46. Other amounts to be disregarded
47. Treatment of student loans
48. Disregard of contribution
49. Income treated as capital
50. Disregard of changes occurring during summer vacation

PART VI. AMOUNT OF BENEFIT

51. Maximum council tax benefit
52. Non-dependant deductions
53. Council tax benefit taper
54. Alternative maximum council tax benefit
55. Residents of a dwelling to whom section 131(6) of the Contributions and Benefits Act 1992 does not apply

PART VII. BENEFIT PERIODS AND CHANGES OF CIRCUMSTANCES AND INCREASES FOR EXCEPTIONAL CIRCUMSTANCES

56. Date on which entitlement is to begin
57. Benefit period
58. Date on which benefit period is to end

59. Date on which change of circumstance is to take effect
60. Increases of weekly amounts for exceptional circumstances

PART VIII. CLAIMS

61. Who may claim
62. Time and manner in which claims are to be made
63. Evidence and information
64. Amendment and withdrawal of claim
65. Duty to notify changes of circumstances

PART IX. DETERMINATION OF QUESTIONS

66. Who is to make a determination
67. Notification of determinations
68. Time and manner of making notifications, requests or representations
69. Review of determinations
70. Further review of determinations
71. Procedure on further review
72. Decisions upon further review
73. Effect of revising a determination
74. Correction of accidental errors in determinations and decisions
75. Setting aside of determinations and decisions on certain grounds
76. Provisions common to regulations 74 and 75

PART X. AWARDS OR PAYMENTS OF BENEFIT

77. Time and manner of granting council tax benefit
78. Person to whom benefit is to be paid
79. Shortfall in benefit
80. Withholding of benefit
81. Payment on death of the person entitled
82. Offsetting

PART XI. EXCESS BENEFIT

83. Meaning of excess benefit
84. Recoverable excess benefit
85. Authority by which recovery may be made
86. Person from whom recovery may be sought
87. Methods of recovery
88. Further provision as to recovery of excess benefit
89. Diminution of capital
90. Sums to be deducted in calculating recoverable excess benefit
91. Recovery of excess benefit from prescribed benefits

PART XII. INFORMATION

92. Information to be supplied by the Secretary of State to an appropriate authority
93. Information to be supplied by an appropriate authority to the Secretary of State

SCHEDULES

Schedule 1. Applicable amounts
Schedule 2. Amount of alternative maximum council tax benefit
Schedule 3. Sums to be disregarded in the calculation of earnings
Schedule 4. Sums to be disregarded in the calculation of income other than earnings
Schedule 5. Capital to be disregarded
Schedule 6. Matters to be included in the notice of determination
Schedule 7. Constitution of review boards

PART I. GENERAL

Citation and commencement

1. These Regulations may be cited as the Council Tax Benefit (General) Regulations 1992 and shall come into force—

(a) for the purposes of regulations 1, 2, 61 to 65, 92 and 93 on 17th August 1992;
(b) for all other purposes on 1st April 1993.

Interpretation

2. (1) In these Regulations, unless the context otherwise requires—
  "the 1992 Act" means the Local Government Finance Act 1992;
  "the Administration Act 1992" means the Social Security Administration Act 1992;
  "the Contributions and Benefits Act 1992" means the Social Security Contributions and Benefits Act 1992;
  "alternative maximum council tax benefit" means the amount determined in accordance with regulation 54 and Schedule 2;
  "appropriate authority" means—

(a) in England and Wales, the billing authority to which Part I of the 1992 Act refers,
(b) in Scotland, the levying authority to which Part II of the 1992 Act refers;

  "appropriate social security office" means an office of the Department of Social Security which is normally open to the public for the receipt of claims for income support and includes an office of the Department of Employment which is normally open to the public for the receipt of claims for unemployment benefit;
  "assessment period" means such period as is prescribed in regulations 14 to 16 over which income falls to be calculated;
  "attendance allowance" means—

(a) an attendance allowance under Part III of the Contributions and Benefits Act 1992;
(b) an increase of disablement pension under section 104 of that Act;
(c) a payment under regulations made in exercise of the power conferred by paragraph 7(2)(b) of Schedule 8 to that Act (constant attendance allowance);
(d) an increase of an allowance which is payable in respect of constant attendance under paragraph 4 of Schedule 8 to that Act;

    (e) a payment by virtue of article 14, 15, 16, 43 or 44 of the Personal Injuries (Civilians) Scheme 1983 or any analogous payment;

    (f) any payment based on need for attendance which is paid as part of a war disablement pension;

"benefit period" has the meaning prescribed in regulation 57;

"benefit week" means a period of 7 consecutive days commencing on a Monday and ending on a Sunday;

"boarder" means a person who pays a charge for his accommodation and at least some cooked or prepared meals which are both prepared and consumed in that accommodation or associated premises;

"child" means a person under the age of 16;

"claim" means a claim for council tax benefit;

"claimant" means a person claiming council tax benefit;

"close relative" means a parent, parent-in-law, son, son-in-law, daughter, daughter-in-law, step-parent, step-son, step-daughter, brother, sister or the spouse of any of the preceding persons or, if that person is one of an unmarried couple, the other member of that couple;

"community charge benefit" means the benefit to which section 123(1)(e) of the Contributions and Benefits Act 1992 refers;

"concessionary payment" means a payment made under arrangements made by the Secretary of State with the consent of the Treasury which is charged either to the National Insurance Fund or to a Departmental Expenditure Vote to which payments of benefit under the Contributions and Benefits Act 1992 are charged;

"council tax benefit" means council tax benefit under Part VII of the Contributions and Benefits Act 1992;

"designated office" means the office designated by the appropriate authority, by way of notice upon a form approved by them, for the purpose of claiming council tax benefit and for the receipt of claims to council tax benefit;

"disability living allowance" means a disability living allowance under Part III of the Contributions and Benefits Act 1992;

"disability working allowance" means a disability working allowance under section 123 of the Contributions and Benefits Act 1992;

"dwelling" has the same meaning as in section 3 or 72 of the 1992 Act;

"earnings" has the meaning prescribed in regulation 19 or, as the case may be, 21;

"eligible rent" shall be construed in accordance with regulation 10 of the Housing Benefit (General) Regulations 1987 (rent);

"employed earner" is to be construed in accordance with section 2(1)(a) of the Contributions and Benefits Act 1992;

"family" has the meaning assigned to it by section 137(1) of the Contributions and Benefits Act 1992;

"housing benefit" means housing benefit under Part VII of the Contributions and Benefits Act 1992;

"invalid carriage or other vehicle" means a vehicle propelled by a petrol engine or by electric power supplied for use on the road and to be controlled by the occupant;

"lone parent" means a person who has no partner and who is responsible for and a member of the same household as a child or young person;

"married couple" has the meaning assigned to it by section 137(1) of the Contributions and Benefits Act 1992;

"member of a couple" means a member of a married or unmarried couple;

"mobility supplement" means a supplement to which paragraph 7 of Schedule 3 refers;

"net earnings" means such earnings as are calculated in accordance with regulation 20;

"net profit" means such profit as is calculated in accordance with regulation 22;

"non-dependant" has the meaning prescribed in regulation 3;

"occupational pension" means any pension or other periodical payment under an occupational pension scheme but does not include any discretionary payment out of a fund established for relieving hardship in particular cases;

"partner", means—

    (a) where a claimant is a member of a married or unmarried couple, the other member of that couple; or

    (b) where a claimant is polygamously married to two or more members of his household, any such member to whom he is married;

"payment" includes part of a payment;

"person affected" means any person (including the appropriate authority) whose rights, duties or obligations are affected by a determination, whether or not on review, or by a decision on further review;

"person on income support" means a person in receipt of income support;

"policy of life insurance" means any instrument by which the payment of money is assured on death (except death by accident only) or by the happening of any contingency dependent on human life, or any instrument evidencing a contract which is subject to payment of premiums for a term dependent on human life;

"polygamous marriage" means a marriage to which section 133(1) of the Contributions and Benefits Act 1992 refers;

"qualifying person" means a person in respect of whom payment has been made from the Fund;

"remunerative work" has the meaning prescribed in regulation 4;

"resident" has the meaning as in Part I or II of the 1992 Act;

"review board" means a board constituted in accordance with regulation 70(3) and Schedule 7;

"second adult" has the meaning given to it in Schedule 2;

"self-employed earner" is to be construed in accordance with section 2(1)(b) of the Contributions and Benefits Act 1992;

"single claimant" means a claimant who neither has a partner nor is a lone parent;

"student" has the meaning prescribed in regulation 38;

"supplementary benefit" means a supplementary pension or allowance under section 1 or 4 of the Supplementary Benefit Act 1976;

"the Fund" means moneys made available from time to time by the Secretary of State for the benefit of persons eligible for payment in accordance with the provisions of a scheme established by him on 24th April 1992 or, in Scotland, on 10th April 1992;

"the Independent Living Fund" means the charitable trust established out of funds provided by the Secretary of State for the purpose of providing financial assistance to those persons incapacitated by or otherwise suffering from very severe disablement who are in need of such assistance to enable them to live independently;

"the Trusts" means

(a) "the Macfarlane Trust", established partly out of funds provided by the Secretary of State to the Haemophilia Society, for the relief of poverty or distress among those suffering from haemophilia;

(b) "the Macfarlane (Special Payments) Trust" established on 29th January 1990 partly out of funds provided by the Secretary of State, for the benefit of certain persons suffering from haemophilia;

(c) "the Macfarlane (Special Payments) (No 2) Trust", established on 3rd May 1991 partly out of funds provided by the Secretary of State, for the benefit of certain persons suffering from haemophilia and other beneficiaries;

"training allowance" means an allowance (whether by way of periodical grants or otherwise) payable—

(a) out of public funds by a Government department or by or on behalf of the Secretary of State, Scottish Enterprise or Highlands and Islands Enterprise;

(b) to a person for his maintenance or in respect of a member of his family; and

(c) for the period, or part of the period, during which he is following a course of training or instruction provided by, or in pursuance of arrangements made with, that department or approved by that department in relation to him or so provided or approved by or on behalf of the Secretary of State, Scottish Enterprise or Highlands and Islands Enterprise,

but it does not include an allowance paid by any Government department to or in respect of a person by reason of the fact that he is following a course of full-time education other than under arrangements made under section 2 of the Employment and Training Act 1973 or is training as a teacher;

"unmarried couple" has the meaning assigned to it by section 137(1) of the Contributions and Benefits Act 1992;

"water charges" means—

(a) as respects England and Wales, any water charges under Chapter IV of Part II of the Water Act 1989,

(b) as respects Scotland, any water charges under Schedule 11 to the 1992 Act,

in so far as such charges are in respect of the dwelling which a person occupies as his home;

"year of assessment" has the meaning prescribed in section 832(1) of the Income and Corporation Taxes Act 1988;

"young person" has the meaning prescribed in regulation 5(1).

(2) In Schedule 5 references to a claimant occupying a dwelling or premises as his home shall be construed in accordance with regulation 5 of the Housing Benefit (General) Regulations 1987.

(3) In these Regulations, where an amount is to be rounded to the nearest penny, a fraction of a penny shall be disregarded if it is less than half a penny and shall otherwise be treated as a whole penny.

(4) For the purposes of these Regulations, two persons shall be taken to be estranged only if their estrangement constitutes a breakdown of the relationship between them.

(5) In these Regulations, unless the context otherwise requires, a reference—

(a) to a numbered Part is to the Part of these Regulations bearing that number;
(b) to a numbered regulation or Schedule is to the regulation in, or the Schedule to, these Regulations bearing that number;
(c) in a regulation or Schedule to a numbered paragraph is to the paragraph in that regulation or Schedule bearing that number;
(d) in a paragraph to a lettered or numbered sub-paragraph is to the sub-paragraph in that paragraph bearing that letter or number.

Definition of non-dependant

3. (1) In these Regulations, "non-dependant" means any person, except someone to whom paragraph (2) applies, who normally resides with a claimant.

(2) This paragraph applies to—

(a) any member of the claimant's family;
(b) if the claimant is polygamously married, any partner of his and any child or young person who is a member of his household and for whom he or one of his partners is responsible;
(c) a child or young person who is living with the claimant but who is not a member of his household by virtue of regulation 7 (membership of the same household);
(d) subject to paragraph (3), any person who, with the claimant, is jointly and severally liable to pay council tax in respect of a dwelling for any day under sections 6, 7 or 75 of the 1992 Act (persons liable to pay council tax);
(e) subject to paragraph (3), any person who is liable to make payments on a commercial basis to the claimant or the claimant's partner in respect of the occupation of the dwelling;
(f) a person who lives with the claimant in order to care for him or a partner of his and who is engaged by a charitable or voluntary body (other than a public or local authority) which makes a charge to the claimant or his partner for the services provided by that person.

(3) Excepting persons to whom paragraph (2)(a) to (c) and (f) refer, a person to whom any of the following sub-paragraphs applies shall be a non-dependant—

(a) a person who resides with the person to whom he is liable to make payments in respect of the dwelling and either—

(i) that person is a close relative of his or his partner, or
(ii) the tenancy or other agreement between them is other than on a commercial basis;

(b) a person whose liability to make payments in respect of the dwelling appears to the appropriate authority to have been created to take advantage of the council tax benefit scheme except someone who was, for any period within the eight weeks prior to the creation of the agreement giving rise to the liability to make such payments, otherwise liable to make payments of rent in respect of the same dwelling;

(c) a person who becomes jointly and severally liable with the claimant for council tax in respect of a dwelling and who was, at any time during the period of eight weeks prior to his becoming so liable, a non-dependant of one or more of the other residents in that dwelling who are so liable for the tax, unless the appropriate authority is satisfied that the change giving rise to the new liability was not made to take advantage of the council tax benefit scheme.

Remunerative work

4. (1) Subject to the following provisions of this regulation, a person shall be treated for the purposes of these Regulations as engaged in remunerative work if he is engaged, or, where his hours of work fluctuate, he is engaged on average, for not less than 16 hours a week, in work for which payment is made or which is done in expectation of payment.

(2) In determining the number of hours for which a person is engaged in work where his hours of work fluctuate, regard shall be had to the average of hours worked over—

    (a) if there is a recognisable cycle of work, the period of one complete cycle (including, where the cycle involves periods in which the person does no work, those periods but disregarding any other absences);

    (b) in any other case, the period of 5 weeks immediately prior to the date of claim, or such other length of time as may, in the particular case, enable the person's weekly average hours of work to be determined more accurately.

(3) Where no recognisable cycle has been established in respect of a person's work, regard shall be had to the number of hours or, where those hours will fluctuate, the average of the hours, which he is expected to work in a week.

(4) A person shall be treated as engaged in remunerative work during any period for which he is absent from work referred to in paragraph (1) if the absence is either without good cause or by reason of a recognised, customary or other holiday.

(5) A person on income support for more than 3 days in any benefit week shall be treated as not being in remunerative work in that week.

PART II. MEMBERSHIP OF A FAMILY

Persons of prescribed description for the definition of family in section 137(1) of the Contributions and Benefits Act 1992

5. (1) Subject to paragraph (2), a person of a prescribed description for the purposes of section 137(1) of the Contributions and Benefits Act 1992 (definition of family) as it applies to council tax benefit is a person aged 16 or over but under 19 who is treated as a child for the purposes of section 142 of that Act (meaning of child), and in these Regulations such a person is referred to as a "young person".

(2) Paragraph (1) shall not apply to a person who is on income support or to a person who is receiving advanced education within the meaning of regulation 12(2) of the Income Support (General) Regulations 1987 (relevant education).

Circumstances in which a person is to be treated as responsible or not responsible for another

6. (1) Subject to the following provisions of this regulation a person shall be treated as responsible for a child or young person who is normally living with him.

(2) Where a child or young person spends equal amounts of time in different households, or where there is a question as to which household he is living in, the child or young person shall be treated for the purposes of paragraph (1) as normally living with—

    (a) the person who is receiving child benefit in respect of him; or

(b) if there is no such person—

    (i) where only one claim for child benefit has been made in respect of him, the person who made that claim, or

    (ii) in any other case the person who has the primary responsibility for him.

(3) For the purposes of these Regulations a child or young person shall be the responsibility of only one person in any benefit week and any person other than the one treated as responsible for the child or young person under this regulation shall be treated as not so responsible.

Circumstances in which a person is to be treated as being or not being a member of the household

7. (1) Subject to paragraphs (2) and (3), the claimant and any partner and, where the claimant or his partner is treated as responsible by virtue of regulation 6 (circumstances in which a person is to be treated as responsible or not responsible for another) for a child or young person, that child or young person and any child of that child or young person shall be treated as members of the same household notwithstanding that any of them is temporarily absent from that household.

(2) A child or young person shall not be treated as a member of the claimant's household where he is—

(a) placed with the claimant or his partner by a local authority under section 23(2)(a) of the Children Act 1989 or by a voluntary organisation under section 59(1)(a) of that Act, or in Scotland boarded out with the claimant or his partner under a relevant enactment; or

(b) placed, or in Scotland boarded out, with the claimant or his partner prior to adoption; or

(c) placed for adoption with the claimant or his partner pursuant to a decision under the Adoption Agencies Regulations 1983 or the Adoption Agencies (Scotland) Regulations 1984.

(3) Subject to paragraph (4), paragraph (1) shall not apply to a child or young person who is not living with the claimant and he—

(a) is being looked after by, or in Scotland is in the care of, a local authority under a relevant enactment; or

(b) has been placed, or in Scotland boarded out, with a person other than the claimant prior to adoption; or

(c) has been placed for adoption pursuant to a decision under the Adoption Agencies Regulations 1983 or the Adoption Agencies (Scotland) Regulations 1984.

(4) An authority shall treat a child or young person to whom paragraph (3)(a) applies as being a member of the claimant's household in any benefit week where—

(a) that child or young person lives with the claimant for part or all of that benefit week; and

(b) the authority considers that it is reasonable to do so taking into account the nature and frequency of that child's or young person's visits.

(5) In this regulation "relevant enactment" means the Army Act 1955, the Air Force Act 1955, the Naval Discipline Act 1957, the Matrimonial Proceedings (Children) Act 1958, the Social Work (Scotland) Act 1968, the Family Law Reform Act 1969, the Children and Young Persons Act 1969, the Matrimonial Causes Act 1973, The

Guardianship Act 1973, the Children Act 1975, the Domestic Proceedings and Magistrates Courts Act 1978, the Adoption (Scotland) Act 1978, the Family Law Act 1986 and the Children Act 1989.

PART III. APPLICABLE AMOUNTS

Applicable amounts

8. Subject to regulations 9 and 10 (polygamous marriages and patients), a claimant's weekly applicable amount shall be the aggregate of such of the following amounts as may apply in his case—

(a) an amount in respect of himself or, if he is a member of a couple, an amount in respect of both of them, determined in accordance with paragraph 1(1), (2) or (3), as the case may be, of Schedule 1;

(b) an amount determined in accordance with paragraph 2 of Schedule 1 in respect of any child or young person who is a member of his family, except a child or young person whose capital, if calculated in accordance with Chapter VI of Part IV (income and capital) in like manner as for the claimant would exceed £3,000;

(c) if he is a member of a family of which at least one member is a child or young person, an amount determined in accordance with Part II of Schedule 1 (family premium);

(d) the amount of any premiums which may be applicable to him determined in accordance with Parts III and IV of Schedule 1 (premiums).

Polygamous marriages

9. Subject to regulation 10 (patients), where a claimant is a member of a polygamous marriage, his weekly applicable amount shall be the aggregate of such of the following amounts as may apply in his case—

(a) the amount applicable to him and one of his partners determined in accordance with paragraph 1(3) of Schedule 1 (applicable amounts) as if he and that partner were a couple;

(b) an amount equal to the difference between the amounts specified in sub-paragraphs (3) and (1)(b) of paragraph 1 of Schedule 1 in respect of each of his other partners;

(c) an amount determined in accordance with paragraph 2 of Schedule 1 (applicable amounts) in respect of any child or young person for whom he or a partner of his is responsible and who is a member of the same household, except a child or young person whose capital, if calculated in accordance with Chapter VI of Part IV (income and capital) in like manner as for the claimant would exceed £3,000;

(d) if he or another partner of the polygamous marriage is responsible for a child or young person who is a member of the same household, the amount specified in Part II of Schedule 1 (family premium);

(e) the amount of any premiums which may be applicable to him determined in accordance with Part III and IV of Schedule 1 (premiums).

Patients

10. (1) Where a person is a patient and has been a patient for a period of more than 6 weeks—

(a) in a case of a single claimant, his applicable amount shall be £13.55;

(b) in the case of a lone parent, his applicable amount shall be £13.55 plus any amount applicable to him under regulation 8(a) or (c) or (d) (applicable amounts) by virtue of his satisfying the condition specified in paragraph 8 or 15 of Schedule 1;

(c) in the case of a married or unmarried couple—

    (i) where the other member is not a patient, or, if a patient, has not been a patient for more than six weeks, his or, if he is not the claimant, the claimant's applicable amount shall be the amount applicable under regulation 8 (applicable amounts) reduced by £10.85,

    (ii) where the other member is also a patient and has been a patient for more than six weeks, his or, as the case may be, the claimant's applicable amount shall be £27.10 plus any amounts applicable under regulation 8(b) or (c) or (d) by virtue of his satisfying the condition specified in paragraph 15 of Schedule 1;

(d) if he is polygamously married—

    (i) where at least one member of the polygamous marriage is not a patient, or, if a patient, has not been a patient for more than six weeks, the applicable amount under regulation 9 (polygamous marriages) shall be reduced by £10.85 in respect of each member who is a patient and has been a patient for more than 6 weeks;

    (ii) where all members of a polygamous marriage are patients and have been patients for more than six weeks, the applicable amount shall be £13.55 in respect of each member plus any amounts applicable under regulation 9(c) or (d) or (e) by virtue of his satisfying the condition specified in paragraph 15 of Schedule 1.

(2) In paragraph (1), "patient" means a person (other than a person who is serving a sentence of imprisonment or detention in a youth custody institution) who is regarded as receiving free in-patient treatment within the meaning of the Social Security (Hospital In-Patients) Regulations 1975.

(3) For the purposes of calculating the period of 6 weeks referred to in paragraph (1), where a person has been maintained free of charge while undergoing medical or other treatment as an in-patient in a hospital or similar institution for two or more distinct periods separated by one or more intervals each not exceeding 28 days, he shall be treated as having been so maintained for a period equal in duration to the total of those distinct periods.

Part IV. Income and Capital

Chapter I. General

Calculation of income and capital of members of claimant's family and of a polygamous marriage

11. (1) The income and capital of a claimant's partner and, subject to paragraph (2) and to regulation 27 (modifications in respect of a child and young person), the income of a child or young person which by virtue of section 136(1) of the Contributions and Benefits Act 1992 is to be treated as income and capital of the claimant, shall be calculated or estimated in accordance with the following provisions of this Part in like manner as for the claimant; and any reference to the "claimant" shall,

except where the context otherwise requires, be construed for the purposes of this Part as if it were a reference to his partner or that child or young person.

(2) Regulation 20(2) and 22(2), so far as they relate to paragraphs 1 to 10 of Schedule 3 (sums to be disregarded in the calculation of earnings), and regulation 25(1) (capital treated as income) shall not apply to a child or young person.

(3) Where a claimant or the partner of a claimant is married polygamously to two or more members of his household—

(a) the claimant shall be treated as possessing capital and income belonging to each such member and the income of any child or young person who is one of that member's family; and

(b) the income and capital of that member or, as the case may be, the income of that child or young person shall be calculated in accordance with the following provisions of this Part in like manner as for the claimant or, as the case may be, as for any child or young person who is a member of his family.

Circumstances in which income of non-dependant is to be treated as claimant's

12. (1) Where it appears to the appropriate authority that a non-dependant and the claimant have entered into arrangements in order to take advantage of the council tax benefit scheme and the non-dependant has more capital and income than the claimant, that authority shall, except where the claimant is on income support, treat the claimant as possessing capital and income belonging to that non-dependant and, in such a case, shall disregard any capital and income which the claimant does possess.

(2) Where a claimant is treated as possessing capital and income belonging to a non-dependant under paragraph (1) the capital and income of that non-dependant shall be calculated in accordance with the following provisions of this Part in like manner as for the claimant and any reference to "the claimant" shall, except where the context otherwise requires, be construed for the purposes of this Part as if it were a reference to that non-dependant.

Chapter II. Income

Calculation of income on a weekly basis

13. (1) Subject to regulation 18 (disregard of changes in tax, contributions etc), for the purposes of section 131(5) of the Contributions and Benefits Act 1992 (conditions of entitlement to council tax benefit) the income of a claimant shall be calculated on a weekly basis—

(a) by estimating the amount which is likely to be his average weekly income over the benefit period in accordance with this Chapter and Chapters III to V of this Part and Part V; and

(b) by adding to that amount the weekly income calculated under regulation 37 (calculation of tariff income from capital).

(2) For the purposes of paragraph (1) "income" includes capital treated as income under regulation 25 (capital treated as income) and income which a claimant is treated as possessing under regulation 26 (notional income).

Average weekly earnings of employed earners

14. (1) Where a claimant's income consists of earnings from employment as an employed earner his average weekly earnings shall be estimated by reference to his earnings from that employment—

  (a) over a period immediately preceding the benefit week in which the claim is made or treated as made and being a period of—

   (i) 5 weeks, if he is paid weekly, or
   (ii) 2 months, if he is paid monthly; or

  (b) whether or not sub-paragraph (a)(i) or (ii) applies, where a claimant's earnings fluctuate, over such other period preceding the benefit week in which the claim is made or treated as made may, in any particular case, enable his average weekly earnings over the benefit period to be estimated more accurately.

(2) Where the claimant has been in his employment for less than the period specified in paragraph (1)(a)(i) or (ii)—

  (a) if he has received any earnings for the period that he has been in that employment and those earnings are likely to represent his average weekly earnings from that employment his average weekly earnings shall be estimated by reference to those earnings;

  (b) in any other case, the appropriate authority shall require the claimant's employer to furnish an estimate of the claimant's likely weekly earnings over such period as the appropriate authority may require and the claimant's average weekly earnings shall be estimated by reference to that estimate.

(3) Where the amount of a claimant's earnings changes during a benefit period the appropriate authority shall estimate his average weekly earnings by reference to his likely earnings from the employment over the remainder of the benefit period.

(4) For the purposes of this regulation the claimant's earnings shall be calculated in accordance with Chapter III of this Part.

Average weekly earnings of self-employed earners

15. (1) Where a claimant's income consists of earnings from employment as a self-employed earner his average weekly earnings shall be estimated by reference to his earnings from that employment over such period as is appropriate in order that his average weekly earnings over the benefit period may be estimated accurately but the length of the period shall not in any case exceed 52 weeks.

(2) For the purposes of this regulation the claimant's earnings shall be calculated in accordance with Chapter IV of this Part.

Average weekly income other than earnings

16. (1) A claimant's income which does not consist of earnings shall, except where paragraph (2) applies, be estimated over such period as is appropriate in order that his average weekly income over the benefit period may be estimated accurately but the length of the period shall not in any case exceed 52 weeks; and nothing in this paragraph shall authorise an authority to disregard any such income other than that specified in Schedule 4.

(2) The period over which any benefit under the Contributions and Benefits Act 1992 is to be taken into account shall be the period in respect of which that benefit is payable.

(3) For the purposes of this regulation income other than earnings shall be calculated in accordance with Chapter V of this Part.

Calculation of weekly income

17. For the purposes of regulations 14 to 16 (average weekly income), where the period in respect of which a payment is made—

(a) does not exceed a week, the weekly amount shall be the amount of that payment;

(b) exceeds a week, the weekly amount shall be determined—

(i) in a case where that period is a month, by multiplying the amount of the payment by 12 and dividing the product by 52,

(ii) in any other case, by dividing the amount of the payment by the number equal to the number of days in the period to which it relates and multiplying the quotient by 7.

Disregard of changes in tax, contributions etc

18. In calculating the claimant's income the appropriate authority may disregard any legislative change—

(a) in the basic or other rates of income tax;

(b) in the amount of any personal tax relief;

(c) in the rates of social security contributions payable under the Contributions and Benefit Act 1992 or in the lower earnings limit or weekly earnings figures for Class 1 contributions under that Act;

(d) in the amount of tax payable as a result of an increase in the weekly rate of Category A, B, C or D retirement pension or any addition thereto or any graduated pension payable under that Act,

for a period not exceeding 30 benefit weeks beginning with the benefit week immediately following the date from which the change is effective.

Chapter III. Employed Earners

Earnings of employed earners

19. (1) Subject to paragraph (2), "earnings" means in the case of employment as an employed earner, any remuneration or profit derived from that employment and includes—

(a) any bonus or commission;

(b) any payment in lieu of remuneration except any periodic sum paid to a claimant on account of the termination of his employment by reason of redundancy;

(c) any payment in lieu of notice or any lump sum payment intended as compensation for the loss of employment but only in so far as it represents loss of income;

(d) any holiday pay except any payable more than 4 weeks after termination or interruption of the employment;

(e) any payment by way of a retainer;

(f) any payment made by the claimant's employer in respect of expenses not wholly, exclusively and necessarily incurred in the performance of the duties of the employment, including any payment made by the claimant's employer in respect of—

(i) travelling expenses incurred by the claimant between his home and place of employment,

(ii) expenses incurred by the claimant under arrangements made for the care of a member of his family owing to the claimant's absence from home;

(g) any award of compensation made under section 68(2) or 71(2)(a) of the Employment Protection (Consolidation) Act 1978 (remedies and compensation for unfair dismissal);

(h) any such sum as is referred to in section 112 of the Contributions and Benefits Act 1992 (certain sums to be earnings for social security purposes);

(i) any statutory sick pay under Part XI of the Contributions and Benefits Act 1992 or statutory maternity pay under Part XII of that Act.

(2) Earnings shall not include—

(a) any payment in kind;

(b) any payment in respect of expenses wholly, exclusively and necessarily incurred in the performance of the duties of the employment;

(c) any occupational pension.

Calculation of net earnings of employed earners

20. (1) For the purposes of regulation 14 (average weekly earnings of employed earners), the earnings of a claimant derived or likely to be derived from employment as an employed earner to be taken into account shall, subject to paragraph (2), be his net earnings.

(2) There shall be disregarded from a claimant's net earnings, any sum, where applicable, specified in paragraphs 1 to 12 of Schedule 3.

(3) For the purposes of paragraph (1) net earnings shall, except where paragraph (4) applies, be calculated by taking into account the gross earnings of the claimant from that employment over the assessment period, less—

(a) any amount deducted from those earnings by way of—

(i) income tax,

(ii) primary Class 1 contributions under the Contributions and Benefits Act 1992; and

(b) one-half of any sum paid by the claimant by way of a contribution towards an occupational or personal pension scheme.

(4) Where the earnings of a claimant are estimated under paragraph (2) of regulation 14 (average weekly earnings of employed earners), his net earnings shall be

calculated by taking into account those earnings over the assessment period, less—

(a) an amount in respect of income tax equivalent to an amount calculated by applying to those earnings the basic rate of tax in the year of assessment in which the claim was made less only the personal relief to which the claimant is entitled under sections 257(1), (6) and (7) and 259(1)(a) and (2) of the Income and Corporation Taxes Act 1988 (personal relief) as is appropriate to his circumstances but, if the assessment period is less than a year, the amount of the personal relief deductible under this sub-paragraph shall be calculated on a pro-rata basis;

(b) an amount in respect of primary Class 1 contributions payable under the Contributions and Benefits Act 1992 in respect of those earnings; and

(c) one-half of any sum payable by the claimant by the way of a contribution towards an occupational or personal pensions scheme.

Chapter IV. Self-Employed Earners

Earnings of self-employed earners

21. "Earnings", in the case of employment as a self-employed earner, means the gross income of the employment and shall include any allowance paid under section 2 of the Employment and Training Act 1973 or section 2 of the Enterprise and New Towns (Scotland) Act 1990 to the claimant for the purpose of assisting him in carrying on his business.

Calculation of net profit of self-employed earners

22. (1) For the purposes of regulation 15 (average weekly earnings of self-employed earners) the earnings of a claimant to be taken into account shall be—

(a) in the case of a self-employed earner who is engaged in employment on his own account, the net profit derived from that employment;

(b) in the case of a self-employed earner whose employment is carried on in partnership or is that of a share fisherman within the meaning of the Social Security (Mariners' Benefits) Regulations 1975, his share of the net profit derived from that employment, less—

  (i) an amount in respect of income tax and of social security contributions payable under the Contributions and Benefits Act 1992 calculated in accordance with regulation 23 (deduction of tax and contributions for self-employed earners), and

  (ii) one-half of any qualifying premium payable.

(2) There shall be disregarded from a claimant's net profit, any sum, where applicable, specified in paragraphs 1 to 12 of Schedule 3.

(3) For the purposes of paragraph (1)(a) the net profit of the employment shall, except where paragraph (9) applies, be calculated by taking into account the earnings of the employment over the assessment period less—

(a) subject to paragraphs (5) to (7), any expenses wholly and exclusively incurred in that period for the purposes of that employment;

(b) an amount in respect of—

  (i) income tax, and

  (ii) social security contributions payable under the Contributions and Benefits Act 1992, calculated in accordance with regulation 23 (deduction of tax and contributions for self-employed earners); and
 (c) one-half of any qualifying premium payable.

(4) For the purposes of paragraph (1)(b) the net profit of the employment shall be calculated by taking into account the earnings of the employment over the assessment period less, subject to paragraphs (5) to (7), any expenses wholly and exclusively incurred in that period for the purposes of the employment.

(5) Subject to paragraph (6), no deduction shall be made under paragraph (3)(a) or (4), in respect of—

 (a) any capital expenditure;
 (b) the depreciation of any capital asset;
 (c) any sum employed or intended to be employed in the setting up or expansion of the employment;
 (d) any loss incurred before the beginning of the assessment period;
 (e) the repayment of capital on any loan taken out for the purposes of the employment;
 (f) any expenses incurred in providing business entertainment; and
 (g) any debts, except bad debts proved to be such, but this sub-paragraph shall not apply to any expenses incurred in the recovery of a debt.

(6) A deduction shall be made under paragraph (3)(a) or (4) in respect of the repayment of capital on any loan used for—

 (a) the replacement in the course of business of equipment or machinery; and
 (b) the repair of an existing business asset except to the extent that any sum is payable under an insurance policy for its repair.

(7) The appropriate authority shall refuse to make a deduction in respect of any expense under paragraph (3)(a) or (4) where it is not satisfied given the nature and the amount of the expense that it has been reasonably incurred.

(8) For the avoidance of doubt—

 (a) a deduction shall not be made under paragraph (3)(a) or (4) in respect of any sum unless it has been expended for the purposes of the business;
 (b) a deduction shall be made thereunder in respect of—

  (i) the excess of any value added tax paid over value added tax received in the assessment period,
  (ii) any income expended in the repair of an existing business asset except to the extent that any sum is payable under an insurance policy for its repair;
  (iii) any payment of interest on a loan taken out for the purposes of the employment.

(9) Where a claimant is engaged in employment as a child minder the net profit of the employment shall be one-third of the earnings of that employment, less—

 (a) an amount in respect of—

  (i) income tax, and
  (ii) social security contributions payable under the Contributions and Benefits Act 1992, calculated in accordance with regulation 23 (deduction of tax and contributions for self-employed earners); and

 (b) one-half of any qualifying premium payable.

(10) For the avoidance of doubt, where a claimant is engaged in employment as a self-employed earner and he is also engaged in one or more other employments as a self-employed earner or employed earner any loss incurred in any one of his employments shall not be offset against his earnings in any other of his employments.

(11) In this regulation "qualifying premium" means any premium or other consideration payable under an annuity contract for the time being approved by the Board of Inland Revenue as having for its main object the provision for the claimant of a life annuity in old age or the provision of an annuity for his partner or for any one or more of his dependants and in respect of which relief for income tax may be given.

Deduction of tax and contributions for self-employed earners

23. (1) The amount to be deducted in respect of income tax under regulation 22(1)(b)(i), (3)(b)(i) or (9)(a)(i) (calculation of net profit of self-employed earners) shall be calculated on the basis of the amount of chargeable income and as if that income were assessable to income tax at the basic rate of tax in the year of assessment in which the claim was made less only the personal relief to which the claimant is entitled under sections 257(1), (6) and (7) and 259(1)(a) and (2) of the Income and Corporation Taxes Act 1988 (personal relief) as is appropriate to his circumstances; but, if the assessment period is less than a year, the amount of the personal relief deductible under this paragraph shall be calculated on a pro-rata basis.

(2) The amount to be deducted in respect of social security contributions under regulation 22(1)(b)(i), (3)(b)(ii) or (9)(a)(ii) shall be the total of—

(a) the amount of Class 2 contributions payable under section 11(1) or, as the case may be, (3) of the Contributions and Benefits Act 1992 except where the claimant's chargeable income is less than the amount for the time being specified in section 11(4) of that Act (small earnings exception); and

(b) the amount of Class 4 contributions (if any) which would be payable under section 15 of that Act (Class 4 contributions recoverable under Tax Acts) in respect of profits or gains equal to the amount of that income.

(3) In this regulation "chargeable income" means—

(a) except where sub-paragraph (b) applies, the earnings derived from the employment less any expenses deducted under paragraph (3)(a) or, as the case may be, (4) of regulation 22;

(b) in the case of employment as a child minder, one third of the earnings of that employment.

Chapter V. Other Income

Calculation of income other than earnings

24. (1) For the purposes of regulation 16 (average weekly income other than earnings), the income of a claimant which does not consist of earnings to be taken into account shall, subject to paragraphs (2) to (4), be his gross income and any capital treated as income under regulation 25 (capital treated as income).

(2) There shall be disregarded from the calculation of a claimant's gross income under paragraph (1) any sum, where applicable, specified in Schedule 4.

(3) Where the payment of any benefit under the Contributions and Benefits Act 1992 is subject to any deduction by way of recovery the amount to be taken into account under paragraph (1) shall be the gross amount payable.

(4) Where a loan is made to a person pursuant to arrangements made under section 1 of the Education (Students Loans) Act 1990 or Article 3 of the Education (Student Loans) (Northern Ireland) Order 1990 and that person ceases to be a student before the end of the academic year in respect of which the loan is payable or, as the case may be, before the end of his course, a sum equal to the weekly amount apportionable under paragraph (2) of regulation 47 shall be taken into account under paragraph (1) for each week, in the period over which the loan fell to be apportioned, following the date on which that person ceases to be a student; but in determining the weekly amount apportionable under paragraph (2) of regulation 47 so much of that paragraph as provides for a disregard shall not have effect.

(5) For the avoidance of doubt there shall be included as income to be taken into account under paragraph (1) any payment to which regulation 19(2) applies (payments not earnings).

Capital treated as income

25. (1) Any capital payable by instalments which are outstanding at the date on which the claim is made or treated as made, or at the date of any subsequent review, shall, if the aggregate of the instalments outstanding and the amount of the claimant's capital otherwise calculated in accordance with Chapter VI exceeds £16,000, be treated as income.

(2) Any payment received under an annuity shall be treated as income.

(3) Any earnings to the extent that they are not a payment of income shall be treated as income.

Notional income

26. (1) A claimant shall be treated as possessing income of which he has deprived himself for the purpose of securing entitlement to council tax benefit or increasing the amount of that benefit.

(2) Except in the case of a discretionary trust or a trust derived from a payment made in consequence of a personal injury, any income which would become available to the claimant upon application being made, but which has not been acquired by him, shall be treated as possessed by the claimant but only from the date on which it could be expected to be acquired were an application made.

(3) Any payment of income, other than a payment of income made under the Trusts, the Fund or the Independent Living Fund, made—

(a) to a third party in respect of a single claimant or in respect of a member of the family (but not a member of the third party's family) shall be treated as possessed by that single claimant or by that member to the extent that it is used for the food, ordinary clothing or footwear, household fuel, or eligible rent to which regulation 10 of the Housing Benefit (General) Regulations 1987 refers, of that single claimant or, as the case may be, of any member of that

family or is used for any council tax, or water charges for which that claimant or member is liable;

(b) to a single claimant or a member of the family in respect of a third party (but
not in respect of another member of that family) shall be treated as possessed
by that single claimant or, as the case may be, that member of the family to
the extent that it is kept or used by him or used by or on behalf of any member of the family.

(4) Where a claimant is in receipt of any benefit (other than council tax benefit) under
the Contributions and Benefits Act 1992 and the rate of that benefit is altered with
effect from a date on or after 1st April in any year but not more than 14 days thereafter, the appropriate authority shall treat the claimant as possessing such benefit at
the altered rate from either 1st April or the first Monday in April in that year whichever date the appropriate authority shall select to apply in its area, to the date on
which the altered rate is to take effect.

(5) Where—

(a) a claimant performs a service for another person; and

(b) that person makes no payment of earnings or pays less than that paid for a
comparable employment in the area,

the appropriate authority shall treat the claimant as possessing such earnings (if any)
as is reasonable for that employment unless the claimant satisfies the authority that
the means of that person are insufficient for him to pay or to pay more for the service; but this paragraph shall not apply to a claimant who is engaged by a charitable
or voluntary body or is a volunteer if the appropriate authority is satisfied that it is
reasonable for him to provide his services free of charge.

(6) Where a claimant is treated as possessing any income under any of paragraphs
(1) to (3), the foregoing provisions of this Part shall apply for the purposes of calculating the amount of that income as if a payment had actually been made and as if it
were actual income which he does possess.

(7) Where a claimant is treated as possessing any earnings under paragraph (5), the
foregoing provisions of this Part shall apply for the purposes of calculating the amount
of those earnings as if a payment had actually been made and as if they were actual
earnings which he does possess except that paragraph (3) of regulation 20 (calculation of net earnings of employed earners) shall not apply and his net earnings shall be
calculated by taking into account those earnings which he is treated as possessing, less—

(a) an amount in respect of income tax equivalent to an amount calculated by
applying to those earnings the basic rate of tax in the year of assessment in
which the claim was made less only the personal relief to which the claimant
is entitled under sections 257(1), (6) and (7) and 259(1)(a) and (2) of the
Income and Corporation Taxes Act 1988 (personal relief) as is appropriate
to his circumstances; but, if the assessment period is less than a year the
amount of the personal relief deductible under this sub-paragraph shall be
calculated on a pro-rata basis;

(b) an amount in respect of primary Class 1 contributions payable under the
Contributions and Benefits Act 1992 in respect of those earnings; and

(c) one-half of any sum payable by the claimant by way of a contribution towards an occupational or personal pension scheme.

(8) In paragraph (3), the expression "ordinary clothing or footwear" means clothing
or footwear for normal daily use, but does not include school uniforms, or clothing
or footwear used solely for sporting activities.

Modifications in respect of child or young person

27. (1) Where the income of a child or young person, other than income consisting of any payment of maintenance whether under a court order or not, calculated in accordance with the foregoing provisions of this Part exceeds the amount included under Schedule 1 in the calculation of the claimant's applicable amount for that child or young person by way of the personal allowance and disabled child premium, if any, the excess shall not be treated as income of the claimant.

(2) Where the capital of a child or young person, if calculated in accordance with Chapter VI in like manner as for the claimant would exceed £3,000, any income of that child or young person shall not be treated as income of the claimant.

(3) In calculating the net earnings or net profit of a child or young person there shall be disregarded (in addition to any sum which falls to be disregarded under paragraphs 11 and 12) any sum specified in paragraphs 13 and 14 of Schedule 3.

(4) Any income of a child or young person which is to be disregarded under Schedule 4 shall be disregarded in such manner as to produce the result most favourable to the claimant.

Chapter VI. Capital

Capital limit

28. For the purposes of section 134(1) of the Contributions and Benefits Act 1992 as it applies to council tax benefit (no entitlement to benefit if capital exceeds prescribed amount), the prescribed amount is £16,000.

Calculation of capital

29. (1) For the purposes of Part VII of the Contributions and Benefits Act 1992 as it applies to council tax benefit, the capital of a claimant to be taken into account shall, subject to paragraph (2), be the whole of his capital calculated in accordance with this Part and any income treated as capital under regulation 31 (income treated as capital).

(2) There shall be disregarded from the calculation of a claimant's capital under paragraph (1), any capital, where applicable, specified in Schedule 5.

Disregard of capital of child or young person

30. The capital of a child or young person who is a member of the claimant's family shall not be treated as capital of the claimant.

Income treated as capital

31. (1) Any bounty derived from employment to which paragraph 6 of Schedule 3 applies and paid at intervals of at least one year shall be treated as capital.

(2) Any amount by way of a refund of income tax deducted from profits or emoluments chargeable to income tax under Schedule D or E shall be treated as capital.

(3) Any holiday pay which is not earnings under regulation 19(1)(d) (earnings of employed earners) shall be treated as capital.

(4) Except any income derived from capital disregarded under paragraphs 1, 2, 4, 7, 13 or 24 to 27 of Schedule 5, any income derived from capital shall be treated as capital but only from the date it is normally due to be credited to the claimant's account.

(5) In the case of employment as an employed earner, any advance of earnings or any loan made by the claimant's employer shall be treated as capital.

(6) Any charitable or voluntary payment which is not made or due to be made at regular intervals, other than a payment which is made under the Trusts, the Fund or the Independent Living Fund, shall be treated as capital.

Calculation of capital in the United Kingdom

32. Capital which a claimant possesses in the United Kingdom shall be calculated—

 (a) except in a case to which sub-paragraph (b) applies, at its current market or surrender value less—

   (i) where there would be expenses attributable to sale, 10 per cent, and
   (ii) the amount of any incumbrance secured on it;

 (b) in the case of a National Savings Certificate—

   (i) if purchased from an issue the sale of which ceased before 1st July last preceding the date on which the claim is made or treated as made, or the date of any subsequent review, at the price which it would have realised on that 1st July had it been purchased on the last day of that issue;
   (ii) in any other case, at its purchase price.

Calculation of capital outside the United Kingdom

33. Capital which a claimant possesses in a country outside the United Kingdom shall be calculated—

 (a) in a case where there is no prohibition in that country against the transfer to the United Kingdom of an amount equal to its current market or surrender value in that country, at that value;
 (b) in a case where there is such a prohibition, at the price which it would realise if sold in the United Kingdom to a willing buyer,

less, where there would be expenses attributable to sale, 10 per cent. and the amount of any incumbrance secured on it.

Notional capital

34. (1) A claimant shall be treated as possessing capital of which he has deprived himself for the purposes of securing entitlement to council tax benefit or increasing the amount of such benefit except to the extent that that capital is reduced in accordance with regulation 35 (diminishing notional capital rule).

(2) Except in the case of—

 (a) a discretionary trust; or
 (b) a trust derived from a payment made in consequence of a personal injury; or

(c) any loan which would be obtained only if secured against capital disregarded under Schedule 5,

any capital which would become available to the claimant upon application being made, but which has not been acquired by him, shall be treated as possessed by him but only from the date on which it could be expected to be acquired were an application made.

(3) Any payment of capital, other than a payment of capital made under the Trusts, the Fund or Independent Living Fund, made—

(a) to a third party in respect of a single claimant or in respect of a member of the family (but not a member of the third party's family) shall be treated as possessed by that single claimant or by that member to the extent that it is used for the food, ordinary clothing or footwear, household fuel or, eligible rent to which regulation 10 of the Housing Benefit (General) Regulations 1987 refers, of that single claimant or, as the case may be, of any member of that family or is used for any council tax, or water charges for which that claimant or member is liable;

(b) to a single claimant or a member of the family in respect of a third party (but not in respect of another member of that family) shall be treated as possessed by that single claimant or, as the case may be, that member of the family to the extent that it is kept or used by him by or on behalf of any member of the family.

(4) Where a claimant stands in relation to a company in a position analogous to that of a sole owner or partner in the business of that company, he may be treated as if he were such sole owner or partner and in such a case—

(a) the value of his holding in that company shall, notwithstanding regulation 29 (calculation of capital) be disregarded; and

(b) he shall, subject to paragraph (5), be treated as possessing an amount of capital equal to the value or, as the case may be, his share of the value of the capital of that company and the foregoing provisions of this Chapter shall apply for the purposes of calculating that amount as if it were actual capital which he does possess.

(5) For so long as the claimant undertakes activities in the course of the business of the company, the amount which he is treated as possessing under paragraph (4) shall be disregarded.

(6) Where a claimant is treated as possessing capital under any of paragraphs (1) to (3) the foregoing provisions of this Chapter shall apply for the purposes of calculating its amount as if it were actual capital which he does possess.

(7) In paragraph (3) the expression "ordinary clothing or footwear" means clothing or footwear for normal daily use but does not include school uniforms, or clothing or footwear used solely for sporting activities.

Diminishing notional capital rule

35. (1) Where a claimant is treated as possessing capital under regulation 34(1) (notional capital), the amount which he is treated as possessing—

(a) in the case of a week that is subsequent to—

  (i) the relevant week in respect of which the conditions set out in paragraph (2) are satisfied, or

  (ii) a week which follows that relevant week and which satisfies those conditions,

shall be reduced by an amount determined under paragraph (3);

 (b) in the case of a week in respect of which paragraph (1)(a) does not apply but where—

  (i) that week is a week subsequent to the relevant week, and

  (ii) that relevant week is a week in which the condition in paragraph (4) is satisfied,

shall be reduced by the amount determined under paragraph (4).

(2) This paragraph applies to a benefit week or part week where the claimant satisfies the conditions that—

 (a) he is in receipt of council tax benefit; and

 (b) but for regulation 34(1), he would have received an additional amount of council tax benefit in that week.

(3) In a case to which paragraph (2) applies, the amount of the reduction for the purposes of paragraph (1)(a) shall be equal to the aggregate of—

 (a) the additional amount to which sub-paragraph (2)(b) refers;

 (b) where the claimant has also claimed housing benefit, the amount of any housing benefit or any additional amount of that benefit to which he would have been entitled in respect of the whole or part of the benefit week to which paragraph (2) refers but for the application of regulation 43(1) of the Housing Benefit (General) Regulations 1987 (notional capital);

 (c) where the claimant has also claimed family credit, the amount of family credit or any additional amount of that benefit to which he would have been entitled in respect of the whole or part of the benefit week to which paragraph (2) refers but for the application of regulation 34(1) of the Family Credit (General) Regulations 1987 (notional capital);

 (d) where the claimant has also claimed income support, the amount of income support to which he would have been entitled in respect of the whole or part of the benefit week to which paragraph (2) refers but for the application of regulation 51(1) of the Income Support (General) Regulations 1987 (notional capital).

(4) Subject to paragraph (5), for the purposes of paragraph (1)(b) the condition is that the claimant would have been entitled to council tax benefit in the relevant week but for regulation 34(1), and in such a case the amount of the reduction shall be equal to the aggregate of—

 (a) the amount of council tax benefit to which the claimant would have been entitled in the relevant week but for regulation 34(1); and for the purposes of this sub-paragraph if the amount is in respect of a part-week that amount shall be determined by dividing the amount of council tax benefit to which he would have been so entitled by the number equal to the number of days in the part-week and multiplying the quotient so obtained by 7;

 (b) if the claimant would, but for regulation 43(1) of the Housing Benefit (General) Regulations 1987 have been entitled to housing benefit or to an additional amount of housing benefit in respect of the benefit week which includes the last day of the relevant week the amount which is equal to—

    (i) in a case where no housing benefit is payable, the amount to which he would have been entitled, or

    (ii) in any other case, the amount equal to the additional amount of housing benefit to which he would have been entitled,

and, for the purposes of this sub-paragraph, if the amount is in respect of a part-week, that amount shall be determined by dividing the amount of housing benefit to which he would have been so entitled by the number equal to the number of days in the part-week and multiplying the quotient so obtained by 7;

(c) if the claimant would, but for regulation 34(1) of the Family Credit (General) Regulations 1987, have been entitled to family credit or to an additional amount of that benefit in respect of the benefit week within the meaning of regulation 34A(8)(a) of those Regulations (diminishing notional capital rule), which includes the last day of the relevant week,

    (i) in a case where no family credit is payable, the amount to which he would have been entitled, or

    (ii) in any other case, the amount equal to the additional amount of family credit to which he would have been entitled; and

(d) if the claimant would, but for regulation 51(1) of the Income Support (General) Regulations 1987, have been entitled to income support in respect of the benefit week, within the meaning of regulation 2(1) of these Regulations (interpretation), which includes the last day of the relevant week the amount to which he would have been entitled and, for the purposes of this sub-paragraph, if the amount is in respect of a part-week, that amount shall be determined by dividing the amount of the income support to which he would have been so entitled by the number equal to the number of days in the part-week and multiplying the quotient so obtained by 7.

(5) The amount determined under paragraph (4) shall be re-determined under that paragraph if the claimant makes a further claim for council tax benefit and the conditions in paragraph (6) are satisfied, and in such a case—

(a) sub-paragraphs (a) and (b) of paragraph (4) shall apply as if for the words "relevant week" there were substituted the words "relevant subsequent week"; and

(b) subject to paragraph (7), the amount as re-determined shall have effect from the first week following the relevant subsequent week in question.

(6) The conditions are that—

(a) a further claim is made 26 or more weeks after—

    (i) the date on which the claimant made a claim for council tax benefit in respect of which he was first treated as possessing the capital in question under regulation 34(1),

    (ii) in a case where there has been at least one re-determination in accordance with paragraph (5), the date on which he last made a claim for council tax benefit which resulted in the weekly amount being re-determined, or

    (iii) the date on which he last ceased to be entitled to council tax benefit,

whichever last occurred; and

(b) the claimant would have been entitled to council tax benefit but for regulation 34(1).

"sandwich course" has the meaning prescribed in paragraph 1(1) of Schedule 5 to the Education (Mandatory Awards) Regulations 1991;

"standard maintenance grant" means—

(a) in the case of a student attending a course of study at the University of London or an establishment within the area comprising the City of London and the Metropolitan Police District, the amount specified for the time being in paragraph 2(2)(a) of Schedule 2 to the Education (Mandatory Awards) Regulations 1991 for such a student; and

(b) in any other case the amount specified in paragraph 2(2) of Schedule 2 other than in sub-paragraph (a) or (b) thereof;

"student" means a person, other than a person in receipt of a training allowance, who is attending a course of study at an educational establishment and a person who has started on such a course shall be treated as attending it throughout any period of term or vacation within it, until the last day of the course or such earlier date as he abandons it or is dismissed from it;

"year" in relation to a course means the period of 12 months beginning on 1st January, 1st April or 1st September according to whether the academic year of the course in questions begins in the spring, the summer or the autumn respectively.

Treatment of students

39. These Regulations shall have effect in relation to students subject to the following provisions of this Part.

Students who are excluded from entitlement to council tax benefit

40.—(1) Except to the extent that a student may be entitled to an alternative maximum council tax benefit by virtue of section 131(3) and (6) of the Contributions and Benefits Act 1992, a student to whom paragraph (2) applies is a person of a prescribed class for the purposes of section 131(3)(b) of that Act (persons excluded from entitlement to council tax benefit).

(2) Subject to paragraph (3), this paragraph applies to a full-time student and students to whom regulation 41(1) refers (students from abroad).

(3) Except with respect to students to whom regulation 41(2) refers, paragraph (2) shall not apply to a student—

(a) who is a person on income support;

(b) whose applicable amount would, but for this regulation, include the lone parent premium, pensioner premium for persons under 75 or, as the case may be, persons 75 or over, higher pensioner premium, disability premium or severe disability premium;

(c) who has a partner who is also a full-time student, if he or that partner is treated as responsible for a child or young person;

(d) who is a single claimant with whom a child is placed by a local authority or voluntary organisation within the meaning of the Children Act 1989 or, in Scotland, boarded out within the meaning of the Social Work (Scotland) Act 1968;

(e) who is aged under 19 and whose course of study is not a course of higher education;

(f) in respect of whom—

    (i) a supplementary requirement has been determined under paragraph 15 of Schedule 2 to the Education (Mandatory Awards) Regulations 1987 or the Education (Mandatory Awards) Regulations 1988, paragraph 12 of Schedule 2 to the Education (Mandatory Awards) Regulations 1989, paragraph 12 of Schedule 2 to the Education (Mandatory Awards) Regulations 1990 or paragraph 12 of Schedule 2 to the Education (Mandatory Awards) Regulations 1991; or

    (ii) an allowance or, as the case may be, bursary has been granted which includes a sum under paragraph (1)(d) of regulation 6 of the Students' Allowances (Scotland) Regulations 1987 or, as the case may be, the Education Authority Bursaries (Scotland) Regulations 1988 in respect of expenses incurred; or

    (ii) a payment has been made under section 2 of the Education Act 1962; or

    (iv) a supplementary requirement has been determined under paragraph 15 of Schedule 7 to the Students Awards Regulations (Northern Ireland) 1987, paragraph 15 of Schedule 7 to the Students Awards Regulations (Northern Ireland) 1988, paragraph 12 of Schedule 7 to the Students Awards Regulations (Northern Ireland) 1990 or paragraph 12 of Schedule 7 to the Students Awards (No. 2) Regulations (Northern Ireland) 1990 or a payment has been made under Article 50(3) of the Education and Libraries (Northern Ireland) Order 1986,

on account of his disability by reason of deafness.

(4) In paragraph (3)(e) reference to a course of higher education is a reference to a course of any description mentioned in Schedule 6 to the Education Reform Act 1988 or any course to which Schedule 1 to the Education (Student Loans) Act 1990 refers.

(5) A full-time student to whom sub-paragraph (f) of paragraph (3) applies, shall be treated as satisfying that sub-paragraph from the date on which he made a request for the supplementary requirement, allowance, bursary or payment as the case may be.

Further provision with respect to students entering the United Kingdom from abroad

41. (1) Except in the case of a student who is a person on income support, a student with limited leave or without leave to enter or remain in the United Kingdom is a prescribed person for the purposes of section 131(6) of the Contributions and Benefits Act 1992 (persons not entitled to council tax benefit).

(2) For the purposes of paragraph (1) "student with limited leave or without leave to enter or remain in the United Kingdom" means a person who is present in the United Kingdom for the purpose of attending a course of education, whether or not he is for the time being engaged in a programme of studies, and who—

(a) is a person other than a national of a member State or a person to whom the European Convention on Social and Medical Assistance done in Paris on 11th December 1953 applies, who has a limited leave (as defined in section 33(1) of the Immigration Act 1971) to enter or remain in the United Kingdom which has been given in accordance with any provision of immigration rules (as defined in section 33(1) of that Act) which refers to there being, or to there needing to be, no recourse to public funds, or to there being no charge on public funds, during that limited leave; or

(b) having a limited leave (as defined in section 33(1) of the Immigration Act 1971) to enter or remain in the United Kingdom, has remained without further leave under that Act beyond the time limited by the leave; or

(c) is the subject of a deportation order, that is to say an order within section 5(1) of the Immigration Act 1971 (procedure relating to deportation) requiring him to leave and prohibiting him from entering the United Kingdom; or

(d) is adjudged by the immigration authorities to be an illegal entrant (as defined in section 33(1) of the Immigration Act 1971) who has not subsequently been given leave under that Act to enter or remain in the United Kingdom.

Chapter II. Income

Calculation of grant income

42. (1) The amount of a student's grant income to be taken into account shall, subject to paragraphs (2) and (3), be the whole of his grant income.

(2) There shall be excluded from a student's grant income any payment—

(a) intended to meet tuition fees or examination fees;

(b) intended to meet the cost of special equipment for a student on a course which began before 1st September 1986 in architecture, art and design, home economics, landscape architecture, medicine, music, ophthalmic optics, orthoptics, physical education, physiotherapy, radiography, occupational therapy, dental hygiene, dental therapy, remedial gymnastics, town and country planning and veterinary science or medicine;

(c) in respect of the student's disability;

(d) intended to meet additional expenditure connected with term time residential study away from the student's educational establishment;

(e) on account of the student maintaining a home at a place other than that at which he resides during his course;

(f) on account of any other person but only if that person is residing outside of the United Kingdom and there is no applicable amount in respect of him;

(g) intended to meet the cost of books and equipment (other than special equipment) or, in the case of a full-time student, if not so intended an amount equal to £257 towards such costs;

(h) intended to meet travel expenses incurred as a result of his attendance on the course.

(3) Where in pursuance of an award a student is in receipt of a grant in respect of maintenance under regulation 17(b) of the Education (Mandatory Awards) Regulations 1991 (payments), there shall be excluded from his grant income a sum equal to the amount specified in paragraph 7(4) of Schedule 2 to those Regulations (disregard of travel costs) being the amount to be disregarded in respect of travel costs in the particular circumstances of his case.

(4) A student's grant income shall be apportioned—

(a) subject to paragraph (4), in a case where it is attributable to the period of study, equally between the weeks in that period;

(b) in any other case, equally between the weeks in the period in respect of which it is payable.

(5) In the case of a student on a sandwich course, any periods of experience within the period of study shall be excluded and the student's grant income shall be apportioned equally between the remaining weeks in that period.

Calculation of covenant income where a contribution is assessed

43. (1) Where a student is in receipt of income by way of a grant during a period of study and a contribution has been assessed, the amount of his covenant income to be taken into account for that period and any summer vacation immediately following shall be the whole amount of the covenant income less, subject to paragraph (3), the amount of the contribution and the amount deducted by way of tax in respect of that income.

(2) The weekly amount of the student's covenant income shall be determined—

(a) by dividing the amount of income which falls to be taken into account under paragraph (1) by 52 or 53, whichever is reasonable in the circumstances; and
(b) by disregarding from the resulting amount, £5.

(3) For the purposes of paragraph (1), the contribution shall be treated as increased by the amount (if any) by which the amount excluded under regulation 42(2)(h) (calculation of grant income) falls short of the amount specified in paragraph 7(4)(i) of Schedule 2 to the Education (Mandatory Awards) Regulations 1991 (travel expenditure).

Covenant income where no grant income or no contribution is assessed

44. (1) Where a student is not in receipt of income by way of a grant the amount of his covenant income shall be calculated as follows—

(a) any sums intended for any expenditure specified in regulation 42(2)(a) to (f) (calculation of grant income) necessary as a result of his attendance on the course shall be disregarded;
(b) any covenant income, up to the amount of the standard maintenance grant, which is not so disregarded, shall be apportioned equally between the weeks of the period of study;
(c) there shall be disregarded from the amount so apportioned the amount which would have been disregarded under regulation 42(2)(g) and (h) (calculation of grant income) had the student been in receipt of the standard maintenance grant;
(d) there shall be deducted from any amount in excess of the sums in sub-paragraphs (a) and (b) the amount deducted by way of tax in respect of the covenanted income; and
(e) the balance, if any, shall be divided by 52 or 53 whichever is reasonable in the circumstances and treated as weekly income of which £5 shall be disregarded.

(2) Where a student is in receipt of income by way of a grant and no contribution has been assessed, the amount of his covenanted income shall be calculated in accordance with sub-paragraphs (a) to (e) of paragraph (1), except that—

(a) the value of the standard maintenance grant shall be abated by the amount of such grant income less an amount equal to the amount of any sums disregarded under regulation 42(2)(a) to (f); and

(b) the amount to be disregarded under paragraph (1)(c) shall be abated by an amount equal to the amount of any sums disregarded under regulation 42(2)(g) and (h) and (3).

Relationship with amounts to be disregarded under Schedule 4

45. No part of a student's covenant income or grant income shall be disregarded under paragraph 13 of Schedule 4 and any other income shall be disregarded thereunder to the extent that the amount disregarded under regulation 43(2)(b) (calculation of covenant income where a contribution is assessed) or, as the case may be, 44(1)(e) (covenant income where no grant income or no contribution is assessed) is less than £10.

Other amounts to be disregarded

46. For the purposes of ascertaining income other than grant income and covenant income, any amounts intended for any expenditure specified in regulation 42(2) (calculation of grant income), necessary as a result of his attendance on the course shall be disregarded but only if, and to the extent that, the necessary expenditure exceeds or is likely to exceed the amount of the sums disregarded under regulation 42(2), 43(3) or 44(1)(a) or (c) (calculation of grant and covenant income) on like expenditure.

Treatment of student loans

47. (1) A loan which is made to a student pursuant to arrangements made under section 1 of the Education (Student Loans) Act 1990(**a**) or Article 3 of the Education (Student Loans) (Northern Ireland) Order 1990(**b**) shall be treated as income.

(2) In calculating the weekly amount of the loan to be taken into account as income—

(a) except where sub-paragraph (b) applies, the loan shall be apportioned equally between the weeks in the academic year in respect of which the loan is payable;

(b) in the case of a loan which is payable in respect of the final academic year of the course or, if the course is only of one academic year's duration, in respect of that year, the loan shall be apportioned equally between the weeks in the period beginning with the start of the final academic year or, as the case may be, the single academic year and ending with the last day of the course,

and from the weekly amount so apportioned there shall be disregarded £10.

(3) Any loan for which a student is eligible in respect of an academic year under the arrangements mentioned in paragraph (1) but which has not been acquired by him shall be treated as possessed by him and paragraphs (1) and (2) shall apply accordingly; and for the purposes of this paragraph the loan for which a student is eligible is the maximum amount payable to him under those arrangements.

Disregard of contribution

48. Where the claimant or his partner is a student and the income of one is taken into account for the purposes of assessing a contribution to the student's grant, an amount equal to the contribution shall be disregarded for the purposes of calculating the income of the one liable to make that contribution.

Income treated as capital

49. Any amount by way of a refund of tax deducted from a student's covenant income shall be treated as capital.

Disregard of changes occurring during summer vacation

50. In calculating a student's income the appropriate authority shall disregard any change in the standard maintenance grant occurring in the recognised summer vacation appropriate to the student's course, if that vacation does not form part of his period of study from the date on which the change occurred to the end of that vacation.

Part VI. Amount of Benefit

Maximum council tax benefit

51. (1) Subject to paragraphs (2) to (4), the amount of a person's maximum council tax benefit in respect of a day for which he is liable to pay council tax, shall be 100 per cent. of the amount $\frac{A}{B}$ where—

(a) A is the amount set by the appropriate authority as the council tax for the relevant financial year in respect of the dwelling in which he is a resident and for which he is liable, subject to any discount which may be appropriate to that dwelling under section 11 or 79 of the 1992 Act; and

(b) B is the number of days in that financial year,

less any deductions in respect of non-dependants which fall to be made under regulation 52 (non-dependant deductions).

(2) In calculating a person's maximum council tax benefit—

(a) any reduction in the amount that person is liable to pay in respect of council tax in consequence of regulations made under sections 13 and 80 of the 1992 Act (reduced amounts of council tax) shall be taken into account;

(b) any reduction in the amount that person is liable to pay in respect of council tax by virtue of Schedule 2 paragraph 6 of the 1992 Act (reductions for lump sum payments), shall be disregarded.

(3) Subject to paragraph (4), where a claimant is jointly and severally liable for council tax in respect of a dwelling in which he is resident with one or more other persons, in determining the maximum council tax benefit in his case in accordance with paragraph (1), the amount A shall be divided by the number of persons who are jointly and severally liable for that tax.

(4) Where a claimant is jointly and severally liable for council tax in respect of a dwelling with only his partner, paragraph (3) shall not apply in his case.

Non-dependant deductions

52. (1) Subject to the following provisions of this regulation, the non-dependant deductions in respect of a day referred to in regulation 51 (maximum council tax benefit) shall be—

(a) in respect of a non-dependant aged 18 or over in remunerative work, £2.00 x ⅐;
(b) in respect of a non-dependant aged 18 or over to whom sub-paragraph (a) does not apply, £1.00 x ⅐.

(2) In the case of a non-dependant aged 18 or over to whom paragraph (1)(a) applies, where it is shown to the appropriate authority that his normal gross weekly income is less than £100.00, the deduction to be made under this regulation shall be that specified in paragraph (1)(b).

(3) Only one deduction shall be made under this regulation in respect of a married or unmarried couple or, as the case may be, members of a polygamous marriage and, where, but for this paragraph, the amount that would fall to be deducted in respect of one member of a couple or polygamous marriage is higher than the amount (if any) that would fall to be deducted in respect of the other, or any other, member, the higher amount shall be deducted.

(4) In applying the provisions of paragraph (2) in the case of a married or unmarried couple or, as the case may be, a polygamous marriage, regard shall be had, for the purpose of that paragraph, to the couple's or, as the case may be, all members of the polygamous marriage's joint weekly gross income.

(5) Where in respect of a day—

(a) a person is a resident in a dwelling but is not himself liable for council tax in respect of that dwelling and that day;
(b) other residents in that dwelling (the liable persons) have joint and several liability for council tax in respect of that dwelling and that day otherwise than by virtue of section 9 or 77 of the 1992 Act (liability of spouses); and
(c) the person to whom sub-paragraph (a) refers is a non-dependant of two or more of the liable persons,

the deduction in respect of that non-dependant shall be apportioned equally between those liable persons.

(6) No deduction shall be made in respect of any non-dependants occupying a claimant's dwelling if the claimant or his partner is—

(a) blind or treated as blind by virtue of paragraph 13 of Schedule 1 (additional condition of the higher pensioner and disability premiums); or
(b) receiving in respect of himself either—

(i) attendance allowance; or
(ii) the care component of the disability living allowance.

(7) No deduction shall be made in respect of a non-dependant if—

(a) although he resides with the claimant, it appears to the appropriate authority that his normal home is elsewhere; or

(b) he is in receipt of a training allowance paid in connection with a Youth Training Scheme established under section 2 of the Employment and Training Act 1973 or section 2 of the Enterprise and New Towns (Scotland) Act 1990; or

(c) he is a full-time student within the meaning of Part V (Students); or

(d) he is not residing with the claimant because he has been a patient for a period in excess of six weeks, and for these purposes—

    (i) "patient" has the meaning given in regulation 10(2) (patients), and

    (ii) the period of six weeks shall be calculated by reference to paragraph (3) of that regulation as if that paragraph applied in his case.

(8) No deduction shall be made in respect of a non-dependant—

(a) who is on income support; or

(b) to whom Schedule 1 of the 1992 Act applies (persons disregarded for purposes of discount) but this sub-paragraph shall not apply to a non-dependant who is a student to whom paragraph 4 of that Schedule refers.

(9) In the application of paragraph (2) there shall be disregarded from his weekly gross income any attendance allowance or any disability living allowance received by him.

Council tax benefit taper

53. The prescribed percentage for the purpose of sub-section (5)(c)(ii) of section 131 of the Contributions and Benefits Act 1992 as it applies to council tax benefit, (percentage of excess of income over the applicable amount which is deducted from maximum council tax benefit), shall be $2\frac{5}{7}$ per cent.

Alternative maximum council tax benefit

54. (1) Subject to paragraphs (2) and (3), the alternative maximum council tax benefit where the conditions set out in section 131(3) and (6) of the Contributions and Benefits Act 1992 are fulfilled, shall be the amount determined in accordance with Schedule 2.

(2) Subject to paragraph (3), where a claimant is jointly and severally liable for council tax in respect of a dwelling in which he is resident with one or more other persons, in determining the alternative maximum council tax benefit in his case, the amount determined in accordance with Schedule 2 shall be divided by the number of persons who are jointly and severally liable for that tax.

(3) Where a claimant is jointly and severally liable for council tax in respect of a dwelling with only his partner, solely by virtue of section 9 or 77 of the 1992 Act (liability of spouses), paragraph (2) shall not apply in his case.

Residents of a dwelling to whom section 131(6) of the Contributions and Benefits Act 1992 does not apply

55. Subsection (6) of section 131 of the Contributions and Benefits Act 1992 (residents of a dwelling in respect of whom entitlement to an alternative maximum council tax benefit may arise) shall not apply in respect of any person referred to in the following paragraphs namely—

(a) a person who is liable for council tax solely in consequence of the provisions of sections 9 or 77 of the 1992 Act (spouse's joint and several liability for tax);

(b) a person who is residing with a married or unmarried couple or with the members of a polygamous marriage where the claimant for council tax benefit is a member of that couple or of that marriage and neither member of that couple or in the case of a polygamous marriage no member or only one member of that marriage is a person who, in accordance with Schedule 1 of the 1992 Act, falls to be disregarded for the purposes of discount;

(c) a person who jointly with the claimant for benefit falls within the same paragraph of sections 6(2)(a) to (e) or 75(2)(a) to (e) of the 1992 Act (persons liable to pay council tax) as applies in the case of the claimant;

(d) a person who is residing with two or more persons both or all of whom fall within the same paragraph of sections 6(2)(a) to (e) or 75(2)(a) to (e) of the 1992 Act where none or only one of those persons is a person who in accordance with Schedule 1 of the 1992 Act falls to be disregarded for the purposes of discount.

PART VII. BENEFIT PERIODS, CHANGES OF CIRCUMSTANCES AND INCREASES FOR EXCEPTIONAL CIRCUMSTANCES

Date on which entitlement is to begin

56. (1) Subject to paragraph (2) and to regulation 62(13) to (15) (renewal claims) any person by whom or in respect of whom a claim for council tax benefit is made and who is otherwise entitled to that benefit shall be so entitled from the benefit week following the date on which that claim is made or is treated as made.

(2) Where a person is otherwise entitled to council tax benefit and becomes liable for the first time for an appropriate authority's council tax in respect of a dwelling of which he is a resident in the benefit week in which his claim is made or is treated as made, he shall be so entitled from that benefit week.

Benefit period

57.—(1) Where a person is entitled to council tax benefit the appropriate authority shall make an award for a specified period ("the benefit period") commencing with—

(a) the first benefit week in respect of which he is so entitled; or if later
(b) the benefit week in which the claim is received at the designated office.

(2) The benefit period shall be such number of benefit weeks as the appropriate authority shall determine having regard in particular to any relevant circumstances which the appropriate authority reasonably expects may affect entitlement in the future.

(3) Subject to paragraph (4), the benefit period shall not exceed 60 benefit weeks.

(4) Where a claimant either is on income support or, although not in receipt thereof, has included in the calculation of his applicable amount the disability premium, the severe disability premium or the higher pensioner premium, and a claim for a further award of council tax benefit has not been made by the last benefit week of his benefit period, the appropriate authority may extend the current benefit period by not more than 4 benefit weeks.

Date on which benefit period is to end

58. The benefit period shall end with the last day of the final week of that period, determined by the appropriate authority in accordance with regulation 57(2) to (4) (benefit period) unless—

(a) the claimant is a person on income support and he ceased to be so entitled except in cases to which sub-paragraph (b) refers, when the benefit period will end with the last day of the benefit week in which the cessation of his entitlement takes effect in accordance with regulation 59 (date when change of circumstances is to take effect);

(b) the claimant is a person on income support and he ceases to be so entitled on account of an award of benefit under the Contributions and Benefits Act 1992, when the benefit period will end at the end of the benefit week in which the payment of income support ceases; or

(c) the appropriate authority determines that some other change of circumstances has occurred which should result in the benefit period ending with an earlier week, when the benefit period will end with the last day of that week.

Date on which change of circumstances is to take effect

59. (1) Except in cases where regulation 18 (disregard of changes in tax, contributions, etc) applies and subject to paragraphs (2) to (7), a change of circumstances which affects entitlement to, or the amount of, council tax benefit ("change of circumstances"), shall take effect from the first day of the benefit week following the date on which the change actually occurs, and where that change is cessation of entitlement to any benefit under the Contribution and Benefits Act 1992, the date on which the change actually occurs shall be the day immediately following the last day of entitlement to that benefit.

(2) Subject to paragraph (3), where the change of circumstances is a change in the amount of council tax payable, it shall take effect from the day on which it actually occurs.

(3) Where the change of circumstances is a change in the amount a person is liable to pay in respect of council tax in consequence of regulations under section 13 or 80 of the 1992 Act (reduced amounts of council tax) or changes in the discount to which a dwelling may be subject under sections 11, 12 or 79 of that Act, it shall take effect from the day on which the change in amount has effect.

(4) Where the change of circumstances is an amendment to these Regulations, it shall take effect from the date on which the amendment to these Regulations comes into force.

(5) Where the change of circumstances is the claimant's acquisition of a partner, the change shall have effect on the day on which the acquisition takes place.

(6) Where the change of circumstances is the death of a claimant's partner or their separation, it shall have effect on the day the death or separation occurs.

(7) If two or more changes of circumstances occurring in the same benefit week would, but for this paragraph, take effect in different benefit weeks in accordance with paragraphs (1) to (6) they shall take effect from the day to which paragraph (2), (3), (5) or (6) above refers, or, where more than one day is concerned, from the earlier day.

Increases of weekly amounts for exceptional circumstances

60. The appropriate authority may modify the provisions of Part VI of these Regulations (amount of benefit) so that, if it considers the circumstances of a person for whom a claim for council tax benefit has been made to be exceptional, the amount of any council tax benefit to be allowed or paid in his case may be increased to an extent which does not cause the total council tax benefit to be allowed or paid to him in any week to exceed—

    (a) the amount $\frac{A}{B}$ to which regulation 51(1) refers (maximum council tax benefit);

or

    (b) in the case of an alternative maximum council tax benefit the highest of the amounts specified in respect of a day in Schedule 2 (alternative maximum council tax benefit),

multiplied by 7.

Part VIII. Claims

Who may claim

61. (1) In the case of a married or unmarried couple or members of a polygamous marriage a claim shall be made by whichever one of them they agree should so claim or, in default of agreement, by such one of them as the appropriate authority shall determine.

(2) Where a person who is liable to pay council tax in respect of a dwelling is unable for the time being to act, and—

    (a) a receiver has been appointed by the Court of Protection with power to claim, or as the case may be, receive benefit on his behalf; or

    (b) in Scotland, his estate is being administered by a curator, judicial factor or other guardian acting or appointed in terms of law; or

    (c) an attorney with a general power or a power to claim or, as the case may be, receive benefit, has been appointed by that person under the Powers of Attorney Act 1971 or the Enduring Powers of Attorney Act 1985 or otherwise,

that receiver, curator, other guardian or attorney, as the case may be, may make a claim on behalf of that person.

(3) Where a person who is liable to pay council tax in respect of a dwelling is unable for the time being to act and paragraph (2) does not apply to him, the appropriate authority may, upon written application made to them by a person who, if a natural person, is over the age of 18, appoint that person to exercise on behalf of the person who is unable to act, any right to which that person might be entitled under the Contributions and Benefits Act 1992 and to receive and deal on his behalf with any sums payable to him.

(4) Where the appropriate authority has made an appointment under paragraph (3)—

    (a) it may at any time revoke the appointment;

    (b) the person appointed may resign his office after having given 4 weeks notice in writing to the appropriate authority of his intention to do so;

    (c) any such appointment shall terminate when the appropriate authority is notified of the appointment of a person mentioned in paragraph (2).

(5) Where a person who is liable to pay council tax in respect of a dwelling is for the time being unable to act and the Secretary of State has appointed a person to act on his behalf for the purposes of section 6(1)(g) of the Administration Act 1992, the appropriate authority may if that person so requests in writing, treat him as if he had been appointed by them under paragraph (3).

(6) Anything required by these Regulations to be done by or to any person who is for the time being unable to act may be done by or to the person mentioned in paragraph (2) above or by or to the person appointed or treated as appointed under this regulation and the receipt of any such person so appointed shall be a good discharge to the appropriate authority for any sum paid.

Time and manner in which claims are to be made

62. (1) Every claim shall be in writing and made on a properly completed form approved for the purposes by the appropriate authority or in such written form as the appropriate authority may accept as sufficient in the circumstances of any particular case or class of cases and be accompanied by or supplemented by such certificates, documents, information and evidence as are required in accordance with regulation 63(1) (evidence and information).

(2) The forms approved for the purpose of claiming shall be provided free of charge by the appropriate authority or such persons as they may authorise or appoint for the purpose.

(3) Each appropriate authority shall notify the Secretary of State of the address to which claims delivered or sent to the appropriate social security office are to be forwarded.

(4) A claim—

  (a) may be sent or delivered to the appropriate social security office where the claimant or his partner is also claiming income support;
  (b) where it has not been sent or delivered to the appropriate social security office, shall be sent or delivered to the designated office;
  (c) sent or delivered to the appropriate social security office shall be forwarded to the appropriate authority within two working days of the date of either the date of determination of the claim for income support or the receipt of the claim at the appropriate social security office, whichever is the later, or as soon as reasonably practicable thereafter.

(5) Subject to paragraph (12) the date on which a claim is made shall be—

  (a) in a case where an award of income support has been made to the claimant or his partner and the claim is made within 4 weeks of the date on which the claim for that income support was received at the appropriate social security office, the first day of entitlement to that income support;
  (b) in a case where the claimant or his partner claimed income support but there is no entitlement to income support, the date on which the claim for council tax benefit is received at the appropriate social security office or the designated office whichever is the earlier;
  (c) in a case where a claimant or his partner is a person on income support and he becomes liable for the first time to pay council tax in respect of the dwelling he occupies as his home, where the claim to the authority is received at the designated office or appropriate social security office within 4 weeks of the date of the change, the date on which the change takes place;

(d) in any other case, the date on which the claim is received at the designated office.

(6) Where a claim received at the designated office has not been made in the manner prescribed in paragraph (1), that claim is for the purposes of these Regulations defective.

(7) Where a claim is defective because—

(a) it was made on the form approved for the purpose but that form is not accepted by the appropriate authority as being in a written form sufficient in the circumstances of the case; or
(b) it was made in writing but not on the form approved for the purpose and the appropriate authority does not accept the claim as being in a written form which is sufficient in the circumstances of the case,

the appropriate authority may, in a case to which sub-paragraph (a) applies, refer the defective claim to the claimant or, in a case to which sub-paragraph (b) applies, supply the claimant with the approved form.

(8) The appropriate authority shall treat a defective claim as if it had been made in the first instance where the approved form referred or sent to the claimant in accordance with paragraph (7) is received at the designed office properly completed within 4 weeks of it having been referred or sent to him, or such longer period as the appropriate authority may consider reasonable.

(9) A claim which is made on an approved form for the time being is, for the purposes of this regulation, properly completed if completed in accordance with the instructions on the form.

(10) Where a person has not yet become liable for council tax to an appropriate authority but it is anticipated that he will become so liable within a period of 8 weeks (the relevant period), he may claim council tax benefit at any time in that period in respect of that tax and, provided that liability arises within the relevant period, the authority shall treat the claim as having been made on the day on which the liability for the tax arises.

(11) Where, exceptionally, an appropriate authority has not set or imposed its council tax by the beginning of the financial year, if a claim for council tax benefit is properly made or treated as properly made and—

(a) the date on which the claim is made or treated as made is in the period from the 1st April of the current year and ending 4 weeks after the date on which the authority sets or imposes the tax; and
(b) if the tax had been determined, the claimant would have been entitled to council tax benefit either from—

(i) the benefit week in which the 1st April of the current year fell, or
(ii) a benefit week falling after the date specified in head (i) but before the claim was made,

the appropriate authority shall treat the claim as made in the benefit week immediately preceding the benefit week in which such entitlement would have commenced.

(12) Where the claimant is not entitled to council tax benefit in the benefit week immediately following the date of his claim but the appropriate authority is of the opinion that unless there is a change of circumstances he will be entitled to council tax benefit for a period beginning not later than the thirteenth benefit week follow-

ing the date on which the claim is made, the appropriate authority may treat the claim as made on a date in the benefit week immediately preceding the first benefit week of that period of entitlement and award benefit accordingly.

(13) A person to whom council tax benefit has been granted, or the partner of such a person, may make a claim to the appropriate authority for a further grant of that benefit, for a period beginning immediately after the end of his current benefit period, not more than 13 weeks before the end of that period.

(14) A person may make a further claim not more than 4 weeks after the end of his benefit period or the benefit period of his partner or former partner for a further grant of such benefit, for a period beginning immediately after the end of that benefit period.

(15) The appropriate authority shall invite a person to whom council tax benefit has been granted to make a claim for a further grant of that benefit where either—

    (a) the benefit period ended in circumstances to which regulation 58(a) and (b) refers (end of entitlement to income support); or

    (b) the benefit period is for a period exceeding 16 weeks and is due to end within 8 weeks in accordance with regulation 57(2) to (4) (benefit period) and no such claim has been received in accordance with paragraph (13),

and any claim received following that invitation, if made within 4 weeks of the end of the current benefit period, shall be treated as made for a period beginning immediately after the end of that benefit period in accordance with paragraph (13) or, as the case may be, paragraph (14).

(16) Where the claimant makes a claim in respect of any period before the date on which that claim was, or was treated as, made and he proves that there was good cause for his failure to make that claim throughout the period between any date in that earlier period and the date on which the claim was or was treated as made, his claim shall, subject to section 1(2) of the Administration Act 1992 (12 months limit on entitlement before the date of claim), be treated as made on the first day of that earlier period from which he can prove good cause.

Evidence and information

63. (1) A person who makes a claim shall furnish such certificates, documents, information and evidence in connection with the claim, or any question arising out of it, as may be reasonably required by the appropriate authority in order to determine that person's entitlement to council tax benefit, and shall do so within 4 weeks of being required to do so or such longer period as the appropriate authority may consider reasonable, but nothing in this regulation shall require a person to furnish any certificates, documents, information or evidence relating to a payment to which paragraph (3) applies.

(2) Where a request is made under paragraph (1), the appropriate authority shall—

    (a) inform the claimant of his duty under regulation 65 (duty to notify change of circumstances) to notify the designated office of any change of circumstances; and

    (b) without prejudice to the extent of the duty owed under regulation 65, indicate to him either orally or by notice or by reference to some other document available to him on application and without charge, the kind of change of circumstances which is to be notified.

(3) This paragraph applies to any of the following payments—

    (a) a payment which is—

        (i) disregarded under paragraph 22 (income in kind) of Schedule 4 or paragraph 32 of Schedule 5 (payments in kind made by a charity or under certain trusts), and

        (ii) made under the Trusts, or the Fund;

    (b) a payment which is disregarded under paragraph 35 of Schedule 4 or under paragraph 23 of Schedule 5 (payments made under certain trusts), other than a payment under the Independent Living Fund.

Amendment and withdrawal of claim

64. (1) A person who has made a claim may amend it at any time before a determination has been made on it, by a notice in writing delivered or sent to the designated office and any claim so amended shall be treated as if it had been amended in the first instance.

(2) A person who has made a claim may withdraw it at any time before a determination has been made on it, by notice to the designated office and any such notice of withdrawal shall have effect when it is received.

Duty to notify changes of circumstances

65. (1) Subject to paragraphs (2) and (4), if at any time between the making of a claim and its determination, or during the benefit period, there is a change of circumstances which the claimant or any person by whom or on whose behalf sums payable by way of council tax benefit are receivable might reasonably be expected to know might affect the claimant's right to, the amount of, or the receipt of council tax benefit, that person shall be under a duty to notify that change of circumstances by giving notice in writing to the designated office.

(2) The duty imposed on a person by paragraph (1) does not extend to notifying changes—

    (a) in the amount of a council tax payable to the appropriate authority;

    (b) in the age of the claimant or that of any member of his family;

    (c) in these Regulations; or

    (d) in the case of a claimant on income support, any changes in circumstances which affect the amount of income support but not the amount of council tax benefit to which he is entitled, other than the cessation of that entitlement to income support.

(3) Notwithstanding paragraph (2)(b) or (d) a claimant shall be required by paragraph (1) to notify the designated office of any change in the composition of his family arising from the fact that a person who was a member of his family is now no longer such a person because he ceases to be a child or young person.

(4) Where the amount of a claimant's council tax benefit is the alternative maximum council tax benefit in his case, the claimant shall be under a duty to give written notice to the designated office of changes which occur in the number of adults in the dwelling or in their total gross incomes which might reasonably be expected to

change his entitlement to that council tax benefit and where any such adult ceases to be in receipt of income support the date when this occurs.

PART IX. DETERMINATION OF QUESTIONS

Who is to make a determination

66. (1) Unless provided otherwise by these Regulations, any matter required to be determined under these Regulations shall be determined in the first instance by the appropriate authority.

(2) An authority shall be under no duty to determine a claim—

(a) where the claim has not been made in accordance with regulation 62(1) (time and manner in which claims are to be made) or treated as so made by virtue of regulation 61(8);

(b) where the claimant has failed to satisfy the provisions of regulation 63 (evidence and information);

(c) where the claim has been or is treated as withdrawn under regulation 64 (amendment and withdrawal of claim);

(d) made more than 13 benefit weeks prior to the expiry of the claimant's current benefit period.

(3) Every claim shall be determined by the appropriate authority within 14 days of the provisions of regulations 62 and 63 being satisfied (time and manner for making claims and evidence and information required) or as soon as reasonably practicable thereafter.

Notification of determinations

67. (1) Except in cases to which paragraphs (a) and (b) of regulation 83 (excess benefit in consequence of a reduction of an appropriate authority's council tax) refer, an Authority shall notify in writing any person affected by a determination made by it under these Regulations—

(a) in the case of a determination on a claim, forthwith or as soon as reasonably practicable thereafter;

(b) in any other case, within 14 days of that determination or as soon as reasonably practicable thereafter,

and every notification shall include a statement as to the matters set out in Schedule 6.

(2) A person to whom an authority sends or delivers a notification of determination may request in writing the authority to provide a written statement setting out the reasons as to its determination of any matter set out in the notice.

(3) The written statement referred to in paragraph (2) shall be sent to the person requesting it within 14 days or as soon as is reasonably practicable thereafter.

Time and manner of making notifications, requests or representations

68. (1) Any notice or other document that is to be given or sent to an authority shall be deemed to have been given or sent on the day it is received at the designated office.

(2) Any notice or other document that is to be given or sent by an authority to any person shall be deemed to have been given or sent, if sent by post, to that person's last known or notified address, on the date it was posted.

(3) The times specified by regulations 69(2) (review of determinations), and 70 (further review of determinations) for making representations or a request for a further review may be extended for special reasons, by the appropriate authority or where relevant a Review Board, even though the time specified may have already expired.

(4) Any application for an extension of time shall be in writing, shall be sent or delivered to the designated office and shall be determined by the appropriate authority or where relevant decided by a Review Board.

(5) There shall be no review or further review of a determination or decision of a Review Board under paragraph (3) or (4).

Review of determinations

69. (1) Any determination or decision of a Review Board may be reviewed at any time by the appropriate authority if—

(a) there has been any relevant change of circumstances since the determination or decision was made; or

(b) the authority is satisfied and, in the case of a decision, satisfied by fresh evidence, that the determination or decision was made in ignorance of, or was based on a mistake as to, some material fact; or

(c) except in the case of a decision made by a Review Board, it is satisfied that the determination was based on a mistake as to the law.

(2) Notwithstanding paragraph (1), if a person makes written representations to an authority concerning a determination which it makes in relation to him within 6 weeks of the date of notification to him of the determination, the authority shall review the determination in the light of those representations within 14 days of receiving the representations or as soon as reasonably practicable thereafter.

(3) Subject to paragraph (5), where a determination is revised on review, the determination as revised shall have effect—

(a) in a case to which paragraph (1)(a) applies, from the date on which the relevant change of circumstances is to have effect, in accordance with regulation 59 (date on which change of circumstances is to take effect);

(b) in a case to which paragraph (1)(b) or (c) or (2) applies, in place of the original determination;

(c) in the case of a determination under regulation 62(16) (back dating of late claims), not to allow a claim to be treated as made on a date earlier than it was made, which is revised in favour of the claimant, from the date on which in accordance with regulation 62(16) that claim is treated as made.

(4) For the purposes of calculating the period of 6 weeks mentioned in paragraph (2) no account shall be taken of any period beginning with the receipt by an authority of a request for a statement under regulation 67(2) (notifications of determinations) and ending with the provision to that person of that statement.

(5) Except as provided by paragraph (3)(c) a determination or decision shall not be revised upon review so as to make council tax benefit payable or to increase the

amount of benefit payable in respect of any period which is more than 52 weeks before—

    (a) where written representations were made in accordance with paragraph (2), the date on which those written representations were made; or

    (b) in any other case, the date on which the determination was revised.

(6) Notwithstanding paragraph (1)(a), a determination or a decision shall not be reviewed where the change of circumstances is the repayment of a loan to which regulation 47 (treatment of student loans) applies.

(7) Regulations 67 to 69 shall apply to the revision of any determination as they apply to a determination.

Further review of determinations

70. (1) A person who has made representations under regulation 69(2) (review of determinations) may give or send to the appropriate authority written notice requesting a further review of the determination within 4 weeks of the date on which the determination on those representations was sent to him.

(2) The notice given under paragraph (1) shall set out the grounds on which a further review is requested.

(3) Subject to paragraph (4), the further review shall be conducted by a Review Board appointed by the appropriate authority and constituted in accordance with Schedule 7.

(4) Notwithstanding paragraph (3) where, under this regulation, a person has requested a further review of a determination and has also, in connection with a claim for housing benefit, requested a further review of a determination relating to housing benefit in accordance with regulation 81 of the Housing Benefit (General) Regulations 1987 (further reviews of determinations with respect to housing benefit), a Review Board appointed in accordance with that regulation may also be appointed under this regulation to conduct a further review of the determination in respect of council tax benefit at the same time, provided that the appropriate authority and the person who has made the representation against each determination and any affected partner agree to this course.

(5) Notice of any hearing by the Review Board shall be given by the Board to the persons concerned in accordance with regulation 71(3) (10 days notice of hearing) unless all such persons agree that such notice may be dispensed with.

Procedure on further review

71.—(1) Within 6 weeks of receipt by an authority of a notice under regulation 70(1) (further review of determinations) requesting a further review or, if that is not reasonably practicable as soon as possible thereafter, the Review Board shall hold an oral hearing in order to conduct a further review.

(2) Subject to the provisions of these Regulations—

    (a) the procedure in connection with a further review shall be such as the Chairman of the Review Board shall determine;

    (b) any person affected may make representations in writing in connection with the further review and such representations shall be considered by the Review Board;

    (c) at the hearing any person affected has the right—

        (i) to be heard, and may be accompanied and may be represented by another person whether that person is professionally qualified or not, and for the purposes of the proceedings at the hearing any representative shall have the rights and powers to which any person affected is entitled under these Regulations,

       (ii) to call persons to give evidence, and

     (iii) to put questions to any person who gives evidence;

    (d) the Review Board may call for, receive or hear representations and evidence from any person present as it considers appropriate.

(3) Reasonable notice (being not less than 10 days beginning on the day on which notice is given and ending on the day before the hearing of the further review) of the time and place of the oral hearing before the Review Board shall be given to any person affected, and if such notice has not been given the hearing may proceed only with the consent of every person affected or his representative.

(4) If any person affected should fail to appear at the hearing, notice having been given to him in accordance with paragraph (3), the Review Board may, having regard to all the circumstances including any explanations offered for the absence, proceed with the hearing notwithstanding his absence, or give such directions with a view to the conduct of the further review as it may think proper.

(5) Any person affected to whom notice has been given under paragraph (3) may apply in writing to the Chairman requesting a postponement of the hearing or withdrawing his application for a further review at any time before the decision on further review is given and either before or after the hearing has begun, and the Chairman may grant or refuse the application as he thinks fit.

(6) A hearing may be adjourned by the Review Board at any time during the hearing on the application of any person affected or of its own motion, and if a hearing is adjourned part heard and after the adjournment the Review Board is differently constituted, otherwise than through the operation on that occasion of paragraph (7), the proceedings shall be by way of a complete rehearing of the case.

(7) Any hearing may, with the consent of every person affected or his representative but not otherwise, be proceeded with in the absence of any member of the Review Board provided that at least two members are present and one member is present or acts as the Chairman of the Board.

(8) The decision of the majority of the Review Board shall be the decision of the Board, and where the Board consists of an even number, the Chairman shall have a second or casting vote.

(9) An authority may pay travelling expenses in respect of attendance at the hearing to any person affected and to one other person representing or accompanying him at the hearing.

Decisions upon further review

72. (1) Upon further review the Review Board shall decide whether to confirm or revise the determination of the appropriate authority and, where the determination has been reviewed and revised under regulation 69 (review of determinations), it shall decide whether to confirm or revise the determination so revised.

(2) In reaching its decision the Review Board shall apply the provisions of these Regulations as though any duty imposed on, or power or discretion conferred on, an authority were imposed or conferred upon the Review Board.

(3) In its application to a decision of a Review Board, the 52 week period referred to in regulation 69(5) (review of determinations) shall be calculated from the date that the appropriate authority either confirmed or revised its determination on review.

(4) The Chairman of the Review Board shall—

   (a) record in writing all its decisions; and
   (b) include in the record of every decision a statement of the reasons for such decisions and of its findings on questions of fact material thereto.

(5) Within 7 days of the Review Board's decision or, if that is not reasonably practicable, as soon as possible thereafter, a copy of the record of that decision made in accordance with this regulation shall be given or sent to every person affected.

Effect of revising a determination

73. Where a Review Board has decided that a determination or, as the case may be, a revised determination of an authority shall be revised, the authority shall alter its determination or, as the case may be, revised determination in accordance with that decision with effect from the date of determination or, as the case may be, revised determination.

Correction of accidental errors in determinations and decisions

74. (1) Subject to regulation 76 (provisions common to regulations 74 and 75), accidental errors in any determination or record of a decision may at any time be corrected by the determining authority who gave the determination or decision or by an authority of like status.

(2) A correction to a determination or to the record of a decision shall be deemed to be part of that determination or of that record and written notice of it shall be given as soon as practicable to any person affected.

Setting aside of determinations and decisions on certain grounds

75. (1) Subject to regulation 76 (provisions common to regulations 74 and 75), on an application made by any person affected by the determination or decision, a determination or decision may be set aside by the determining authority which gave the determination or decision or by an authority of like status, in a case where it appears just to set the determination or decision aside on the grounds that—

   (a) a document relating to the matters relevant to the determination or decision was not sent to, or was not received at an appropriate time by, any person affected by the determination or decision, his representative, or the determining authority which gave the determination or decision; or
   (b) in the case of a hearing before the Review Board, any person affected or his representative was not present; or
   (c) the interests of justice so require.

(2) An application under this regulation shall be made in writing and sent or delivered to the determining authority which gave the determination or decision, within 13 weeks of the day on which notice of that determination or decision was given.

(3) Where an application to set aside a decision of the Review Board is entertained under paragraph (1), any person affected shall be sent a copy of the application and shall be afforded a reasonable opportunity of making representations on it before the application is determined.

(4) Notice in writing of a determination or decision on an application to set aside a determination or decision shall be given to any person affected, as soon as may be practicable, and the notice shall contain a statement giving reasons for the determination or decision.

(5) For the purposes of determining under these Regulations an application to set aside a determination or decision there shall be disregarded regulation 68(2) (time and manner of making notifications, requests or representations) and any provision in any enactment or instrument to the effect that any notice or document required or authorised to be given or sent to any person shall be deemed to have been given or sent if it was sent by post to that person's last known or notified address.

Provisions common to regulations 74 and 75

76. (1) In regulations 74 and 75—
   "authority of like status" means a Review Board of different composition to that giving the decision where it is inexpedient for the same Review Board to correct or set aside its decision;
   "determining authority" means an appropriate authority or a Review Board.

(2) In calculating the time specified in regulations 69(2) (review of determinations), 70(1) (further review of determinations), and 75(2) (setting aside of determinations and decisions on certain grounds) there shall be disregarded any day before the day on which notice was given of a correction to a determination or to the record of a decision under regulation 74 (correction of accidental errors in determinations and decisions) or a refusal to make such a correction, or on which notice is given of a determination or decision that a determination or decision shall not be set aside following an application made under regulation 75 as the case may be.

(3) There shall be no review or further review of a correction made under regulation 74 or a refusal to make such a correction or against a determination or decision given under regulation 75.

PART X. AWARDS OR PAYMENTS OF BENEFIT

Time and manner of granting council tax benefit

77. (1) Subject to regulations 80, 81 and 82 (withholding of benefit, payments on death and offsetting), where a person is entitled to council tax benefit in respect of his liability for an appropriate authority's council tax as it has effect in respect of the relevant or any subsequent chargeable financial year, the appropriate authority shall discharge his entitlement—

   (a) by reducing, so far as possible, the amount of his liability to which regulation 20(2) of the Council Tax (Administration and Enforcement) Regulations

1992 (the English and Welsh Regulations) or regulation 20(2) of the Council Tax (Administration and Enforcement) (Scotland) Regulations 1992 (the Scottish Regulations) refers; or

(b) where—

(i) such a reduction is not possible, or

(ii) such a reduction would be insufficient to discharge the entitlement to council tax benefit, or

(iii) the person entitled to council tax benefit is jointly and severally liable for the tax and the appropriate authority determines that such a reduction would be inappropriate,

by making payments to him of the benefit to which he is entitled, rounded where necessary to the nearest penny.

(2) The appropriate authority, shall notify the person entitled to council tax benefit of the amount of that benefit and how his entitlement is to be discharged in pursuance of paragraph (1).

(3) In a case to which paragraph (1)(b) refers—

(a) if the amount of the council tax for which he remains liable in respect of the relevant chargeable financial year, after any reduction to which paragraph (1)(a) refers has been made, is insufficient to enable his entitlement to a council tax benefit in respect thereof to be discharged in that year, upon the final instalment of that tax becoming due any outstanding benefit—

(i) shall be paid to that person if he so requires; or

(ii) in any other case shall (as the appropriate authority determines) either be repaid or credited against any subsequent liability of the person to make a payment in respect of the authority's council tax as it has effect for any subsequent year;

(b) if that person has ceased to be liable for the appropriate authority's council tax and has discharged the liability for that tax, the outstanding balance (if any) of the council tax benefit in respect thereof shall be paid within 14 days or, if that is not reasonably practicable, as soon as practicable thereafter;

(c) in any other case, the council tax benefit shall be paid within 14 days of the receipt of the claim at the designated office or, if that is not reasonably practicable, as soon as practicable thereafter.

(4) For the purposes of this regulation "instalment" means any instalment of an appropriate authority's council tax to which regulation 19 of either the English and Welsh Regulations or as the case may be the Scottish Regulations refers (council tax payments).

Person to whom benefit is to be paid

78. (1) Subject to regulation 81 (payment on death) and paragraph (2), any payment of council tax benefit under regulation 77(1)(b) shall be made to that person.

(2) Where a person other than a person who is entitled to council tax benefit made the claim and that first person is a person acting pursuant to an appointment under regulation 61(3) (persons appointed to act for a person unable to act) or is treated as having been so appointed by virtue of regulation 61(5), benefit may be paid to that person.

Shortfall in benefit

79. (1) Except in cases to which paragraph (2) refers, where, on the review of a determination or a decision of a review board allowing council tax benefit to a person, it is determined that the amount allowed was less than the amount to which that person was entitled, the appropriate authority shall either—

   (a) make good any shortfall in benefit which is due to that person, by reducing so far as possible the next and any subsequent payments he is liable to make in respect of the council tax of the authority concerned as it has effect for the relevant chargeable financial year until that shortfall is made good; or

   (b) where this is not possible or the person concerned so requests, pay any shortfall in benefit due to that person within 14 days of the decision on review being made or if that is not reasonably practicable, as soon as possible afterwards.

(2) A shortfall in benefit need not be paid in any case to the extent that there is due from the person concerned to the appropriate authority any recoverable excess benefit to which regulation 84(1) refers.

Withholding of benefit

80. (1) Where it appears to an appropriate authority that a question has arisen in relation to a person's entitlement to council tax benefit or to the allowance or payment of such benefit it may withhold the allowance or payment of the benefit in whole or in part pending the determination of that question on review under regulation 69 (review of determinations).

(2) Where it appears to an authority that a question has arisen whether any amount allowed or paid to a person by way of, or in connection with, a claim for council tax benefit, constitutes excess benefits for the purposes of section 76 of the Administration Act 1992 or Part XI of these Regulations (excess benefit) it may withhold any allowance or payment of arrears of benefit to that person, in whole or in part, pending the determination of that question.

(3) Upon determination of a question to which paragraph (1) or (2) refers, any benefit withheld under those paragraphs shall be—

   (a) allowed to the person concerned by reducing, so far as possible, the next and any subsequent payments he is liable to make in respect of the council tax of the authority concerned as it has effect for the relevant chargeable financial year, until the benefit withheld is made good; or

   (b) where this is not possible or the person concerned so requests, paid to that person within 14 days of the determination of that question or, if this is not reasonably practicable, as soon as possible afterwards, except to the extent that there was no entitlement to that benefit or recoverable excess benefit remain due from the person from whom the benefit was withheld.

Payment on death of the person entitled

81. (1) Where the person entitled to any council tax benefit has died and it is not possible to award any council tax benefit which is due in the form of a reduction of the council tax for which he was liable, the appropriate authority shall make payment either to his personal representative or, where there is none, his next of kin if aged 16 or over.

(2) For the purposes of paragraph (1), "next of kin" means in England and Wales the persons who would take beneficially on an intestacy and in Scotland the person entitled to the moveable estate on intestacy.

(3) A payment under paragraph (1) may not be made unless the personal representative of the next of kin, as the case may be, makes written application for the payment of any sum of benefit to which the deceased was entitled, and such written application is sent to or delivered to the appropriate authority at its designated office within 12 months of the deceased's death or such longer period as the authority may allow in any particular case.

(4) The authority may dispense with strict proof of title of any person claiming under paragraph (3) and the receipt of such a person shall be a good discharge to the authority for any sum so paid.

Offsetting

82. (1) Where a person has been allowed or paid a sum of council tax benefit under a determination which is subsequently revised upon review or further review, any sum allowed or paid in respect of a period covered by the subsequent determination shall be offset against arrears of entitlement under the subsequent determination except to the extent that the sum exceeds the arrears and shall be treated as properly awarded or paid on account of them.

(2) No amount may be offset under paragraph (1) which has been determined to be excess benefit within the meaning of regulation 83 (meaning of excess benefit).

PART XI. EXCESS BENEFIT

Meaning of excess benefit

83. In this Part "excess benefit" means any amount which has been allowed by way of council tax benefit and to which there was no entitlement under these Regulations (whether on initial determination or as subsequently revised on review or further review) and includes any excess which arises by reason of—

    (a) a reduction in the amount a person is liable to pay in respect of council tax in consequence of—

        (i) regulations made under section 13 or 80 of the 1992 Act (reduction in the amount of a person's council tax); or

        (ii) any discount to which that tax is subject by virtue of section 11, or 79 of that Act;

    (b) a substitution under sections 31 or 60 or, in Scotland, section 94 of the 1992 Act (substituted amounts) of a lesser amount for an amount of council tax previously set by the appropriate authority under section 30 or, in Scotland section 93 of that Act (amount set for council tax).

Recoverable excess benefit

84. (1) Any excess benefit, except benefit to which paragraph (2) applies, shall be recoverable.

(2) Subject to paragraphs (4) and (5) and excepting any excess benefit arising in consequence of a reduction in tax or substitution to which regulation 83 refers, this

paragraph applies to excess benefit allowed in consequence of an official error, where the claimant or a person acting on his behalf or any other person to whom the excess benefit is allowed could not, at the time the benefit was allowed or upon the receipt of any notice relating to the allowance of that benefit, reasonably have been expected to realise that it was excess benefit.

(3) In paragraph (2), "excess benefit allowed in consequence of an official error" means excess benefit in consequence of a mistake made or something done or omitted to be done by the appropriate authority or by an officer or person acting for that authority or by an officer of the Department of Social Security or the Department of Employment acting as such where the claimant, a person acting on his behalf or any other person to whom the payment is allowed did not cause or materially contribute to that mistake, act or omission.

(4) Paragraph (2) shall not apply with respect to excess benefit to which regulation 83(a) and (b) refers.

(5) Where in consequence of an official error a person has been awarded excess benefit, upon the award being reviewed any excess benefit which remains credited to him by the appropriate authority in respect of a period after the date of the review, shall be recoverable.

Authority by which recovery may be made

85. The appropriate authority which allowed the recoverable excess benefit may recover it.

Person from whom recovery may be sought

86. (1) Subject to paragraph (2), recoverable excess benefit shall be due from the claimant or the person to whom the excess benefit was allowed.

(2) Where recoverable excess benefit is allowed to a claimant who has one or more partners, recovery of the excess may be made by deduction from any council tax benefit allowed to a partner, provided the claimant and that partner were members of the same household both at the time the excess benefit is allowed and when the deduction is made.

Methods of recovery

87. (1) Without prejudice to any other method of recovery an appropriate authority may recover any recoverable excess benefit due from any person referred to in regulation 86 (person from whom recovery may be sought) by any of the methods specified in paragraphs (2) and (3) or any combination of those methods.

(2) Excess benefit may be recovered either—

    (a) by payment by or on behalf of the person to whom regulation 86(1) refers, or

    (b) by an addition being made by the appropriate authority to any amount payable in respect of the council tax concerned.

(3) Where recoverable excess benefit due from any person cannot be recovered by either of the methods specified in paragraph (2), the appropriate authority may re-

quest the Secretary of State to recover the outstanding excess from the benefits prescribed in regulation 91 in accordance with the provisions of that regulation.

Further provision as to recovery of excess benefit

88. In addition to the methods for recovery of excess benefit which are specified in regulation 87, any sum or part of a sum which is due from the person concerned and which is not paid within 21 days of his being notified of the amount that is due, shall be recoverable in a court of competent jurisdiction by the authority to which the excess benefit is due.

Diminution of capital

89. (1) Where in the case of recoverable excess benefit, in consequence of a misrepresentation or failure to disclose a material fact (in either case whether fraudulent or otherwise) as to a person's capital, or an error, other than one to which regulation 84(2) (effect of official error) refers, as to the amount of a person's capital, the excess benefit was in respect of a period ("the excess benefit period") of more than 13 benefit weeks, the appropriate authority shall, for the purpose only of calculating the amount of the excess—

(a) at the end of the first 13 benefit weeks of the excess benefit period, treat the amount of the capital as having been reduced by the amount of excess council tax benefit allowed during those 13 weeks;

(b) at the end of each subsequent period of 13 benefit weeks, if any, of the excess benefit period, treat the amount of that capital as having been further reduced by the amount of excess council tax benefit allowed during the immediately preceding 13 benefit weeks.

(2) Capital shall not be treated as reduced over any period other than 13 benefit weeks or in any circumstances other than those, for which paragraph (1) provides.

Sums to be deducted in calculating recoverable excess benefit

90. In calculating the amount of recoverable excess benefit, the appropriate authority—

(a) if it determines that a lesser amount was properly allowable in respect of the whole or part of the excess benefit period, shall deduct that amount; and

(b) may deduct so much of any payment of council tax in respect of the excess benefit period which exceeds the amount, if any, which the claimant was liable to pay for that period under the original erroneous determination.

Recovery of excess benefit from prescribed benefits

91. (1) For the purposes of section 76(3)(c) of the Administration Act 1992 (deduction of excess council tax benefit from prescribed benefits), the benefits prescribed by this regulation are—

(a) any benefit under the Contributions and Benefits Act 1992, except guardian's allowance;

(b) any benefit payable under the legislation of any member State, other than the United Kingdom, concerning the branches of social security mentioned in article 4(1) of Regulation (EEC) No. 1408/71 on the application of social security schemes to employed persons, to self-employed persons and to members of their families moving within the Community, whether or not the benefit has been acquired by virtue of the provisions of that Regulation.

(2) Where the Secretary of State is satisfied that—

(a) recoverable excess benefit has been allowed in consequence of a misrepresentation of or failure to disclose a material fact (in either case where fraudulent or otherwise), by a claimant or any other person to whom council tax benefit has been allowed; and

(b) the person who misrepresented that fact or failed to disclose it is receiving a sufficient amount of one or more of the benefits prescribed in paragraph (1) to enable deductions to be made for the recovery of the excess,

he shall, if requested to do so by an appropriate authority under regulation 87 (methods of recovery) recover the excess by deduction from any of those benefits.

Part XII. Information

Information to be supplied by the Secretary of State to an appropriate authority

92. For the purposes of section 128(1) of the Administration Act 1992 (information which may be supplied by the Secretary of State where required by appropriate authorities in connection with the exercise of their functions relating to council tax benefit), the information prescribed by this regulation is—

(a) the name, date of birth and address of any person who is in receipt of income support and of any partner he may have;

(b) the date on which a claim for income support under Part VII of the Contributions and Benefits Act 1992 by a person was received by the appropriate social security office;

(c) that a person's claim for income support has been disallowed;

(d) where a person's claim for income support has been disallowed, the reason for the disallowance;

(e) where an award of income support has been made to a person, the first day of entitlement to that benefit;

(f) the date on which a person's entitlement to income support ended or is to end and the date on which the payment of income support ceased or is to cease;

(g) where a person's entitlement to income support ends, the reason for it ending;

(h) the national insurance number in respect of any person who is in receipt of income support and of any partner he may have;

(i) where a person or any partner of his is in receipt of income support and changes his residence from the area of one appropriate authority to that of another, the date on which a claim for council tax benefit by that person or his partner is received by the appropriate social security office;

(j) where—

　(i) a person in receipt of income support or any partner of his reports to an appropriate DSS office that another person is residing or has ceased to reside with him, and

(ii) that other person is a non-dependant,

the name and date of birth of that other person;

(k) any information not referred to in paragraphs (a) to (j) above which is required for the purpose of—

(i) the calculation and recovery of excess council tax benefit,
(ii) the investigation and prevention of offences relating to council tax benefit,
(iii) any proceedings for an offence relating to council tax benefit.

Information to be supplied by an appropriate authority to the Secretary of State

93. For the purposes of section 128(2) of the Administration Act 1992 (information which is to be supplied by an appropriate authority where required by the Secretary of State in connection with any of his functions under that Act or the Contributions and Benefits Act 1992), the information prescribed by this regulation is—

(a) that a claim for council tax benefit has been disallowed;
(b) the date on which a person's entitlement to council tax benefit ended or is to end;
(c) any information not referred to in paragraphs (a) and (b) above, which is required for the purpose of—

(i) the calculation and recovery of overpayments of benefits paid under the Contributions and Benefits Act 1992,
(ii) the investigation and prevention of offences relating to benefits under that Act,
(iii) any proceedings for offences relating to benefits under that Act.

SCHEDULE 1

APPLICABLE AMOUNTS

PART I. PERSONAL ALLOWANCES

1. The amounts specified in column (2) below in respect of each person or couple specified in column (1) shall be the amounts specified for the purposes of regulations 8(a) and 9(a) and (b)—

(1) *Person or Couple*	(2) *Amount*
(1) Single claimant aged—	
(a) not less than 18 but less than 25;	(1) (a) £33.60
(b) not less than 25.	(b) £42.45
(2) Lone parent	(2) £42.45
(3) Couple	(3) £66.60

2. The amounts specified in column (2) below in respect of each person specified in column (1) shall be the amounts specified for the purposes of regulations 8(b) and 9(c)—

(1)	(2)
Child or Young Person	*Amount*
Person aged—	
(a) less than 11;	(a) £14.55
(b) not less than 11 but less than 16;	(b) £21.40
(c) not less than 16 but less than 18;	(c) £25.55
(d) not less than 18.	(d) £33.60

Part II. Family Premium

3. The amount for the purposes of regulations 8(c) and 9(d) in respect of a family of which at least one member is a child or young person shall be £9.30.

Part III. Premiums

4. Except as provided in paragraph 5, the premiums specified in Part IV of this Schedule shall, for the purposes of regulations 8(d) and 9(e), be applicable to a claimant who satisfies the condition specified in paragraphs 8 to 16 in respect of that premium.

5. Subject to paragraph 6, where a claimant satisfies the conditions in respect of more than one premium in this Part of this Schedule, only one premium shall be applicable to him and, if they are different amounts, the higher or highest amount shall apply.

6. (1) The severe disability premium to which paragraph 14 applies may be applicable in addition to any other premium which may apply under this Schedule.

(2) The disabled child premium and the carer premium to which paragraphs 15 and 16 respectively apply may be applicable in addition to any other premium which may apply under this Schedule.

7. (1) Subject to sub-paragraph (2), for the purposes of this Part of this Schedule, once a premium is applicable to a claimant under this Part, a person shall be treated as being in receipt of any benefit for—

  (a) in the case of a benefit to which the Social Security (Overlapping Benefits) Regulations 1979 applies, any period during which, apart from the provisions of those Regulations, he would be in receipt of that benefit; and

  (b) any period spent by a person in undertaking a course of training or instruction provided or approved under section 2 of the Employment and Training Act 1973 or section 2 of the Enterprise and New Town (Scotland) Act 1990 for any period during which he is in receipt of a training allowance.

(2) For the purposes of the carer premium under paragraph 16, a person shall be treated as being in receipt of invalid care allowance by virtue of sub-paragraph (1)(a) only if and for

so long as the person in respect of whose care the allowance has been claimed remains in receipt of attendance allowance, or the care component of disability living allowance at the highest or middle rate prescribed in accordance with section 72(3) of the Contributions and Benefits Act 1992.

Lone Parent Premium

8. The condition is that the claimant is a lone parent.

Pensioner Premium for persons under 75

9. The condition is that the claimant—

    (a) is a single claimant or lone parent aged not less than 60 but less than 75; or

    (b) has a partner and is, or his partner is, aged not less than 60 but less than 75.

Pensioner Premium for persons 75 and over

10. The condition is that the claimant—

    (a) is a single claimant or lone parent aged not less than 75 but less than 80; or

    (b) has a partner and is, or his partner is, aged not less than 75 but less than 80.

Higher Pensioner Premium

11.—(1) Where the claimant is a single claimant or a lone parent, the condition is that—

    (a) he is aged not less than 80; or

    (b) he is aged less than 80 but not less than 60, and

        (i) the additional condition specified in paragraph 13(1)(a) is satisfied, or

        (ii) the claimant was in receipt of council tax benefit and the disability premium was applicable to him in respect of a benefit week within 8 weeks of his 60th birthday and he has, subject to sub-paragraph (3), remained continuously in receipt of council tax benefit since attaining that age.

(2) Where the claimant has a partner, the condition is that—

    (a) he or his partner is aged not less than 80; or

    (b) he or his partner is aged less than 80 but not less than 60 and either—

        (i) the additional condition specified in paragraph 13(1)(a) is satisfied, or

        (ii) the claimant was in receipt of council tax benefit and the disability premium was applicable to him in respect of a benefit week within 8 weeks of his 60th birthday and he has, subject to sub-paragraph (3), remained continuously in receipt of council tax benefit since attaining that age.

(3) For the purposes of this paragraph and paragraph 13—

    (a) once the higher pensioner premium is applicable to a claimant, if he then ceases, for a period of 8 weeks or less, to be entitled to council tax benefit, he shall, on becoming re-entitled to council tax benefit, thereafter be treated as having been continuously entitled to that benefit;

    (b) where sub-paragraphs (1)(b)(ii) and (2)(b)(ii) apply, if a claimant ceases to be entitled to council tax benefit for a period not exceeding 8 weeks which includes his 60th birthday, he shall, on becoming re-entitled to council tax benefit, thereafter be treated as having been continuously entitled to that benefit;

    (c) where the claimant or his partner—

(i)   was entitled to housing benefit at any time in the period of 8 weeks before be-
      coming entitled or re-entitled to council tax benefit, and

(ii) satisfied the conditions in respect of higher pensioner premium under paragraphs
      10 and 12 of Schedule 2 to the Housing Benefit (General) Regulations 1987,

for the purposes of establishing entitlement or re-entitlement for council tax benefit, he or his partner shall be treated as satisfying the equivalent conditions for higher
pensioner premium under this paragraph and paragraph 13.

Disability Premium

12. The condition is that—

(a)   where the claimant is a single claimant or lone parent, he is aged less than 60 and
      the additional condition specified in paragraph 13 is satisfied; or

(b)   where the claimant has a partner, either—

(i)   the claimant is aged less than 60 and the additional condition specified in para-
      graph 13(1)(a) or (b) is satisfied by him, or

(ii) his partner is aged less than 60 and the additional condition specified in para-
      graph 13(1)(a) is satisfied by his partner.

Additional Condition for the Higher Pensioner and Disability Premiums

13. (1) Subject to sub-paragraph (2) and paragraph 7, the additional condition referred to in
paragraphs 11 and 12 is that either—

(a)   the claimant or, as the case may be, his partner—

(i)   is in receipt of one or more of the following benefits: attendance allowance,
      disability living allowance, disability working allowance, mobility supplement,
      an invalidity pension under section 33 of the Contributions and Benefits Act
      1992 or severe disablement allowance under section 68 of that Act but, in the
      case of invalidity pension or severe disablement allowance, only where it is paid
      in respect of him, or

(ii) was in receipt of invalidity pension under section 33 of the Contributions and
      Benefits Act 1992 when entitlement to that benefit ceased on account of the
      payment of a retirement pension under that Act and the claimant has since re-
      mained continuously entitled to community charge benefit or, as the case may
      be, council tax benefit and, if the invalidity pension was payable to his partner,
      the partner is still a member of the family, or

(iii) except where paragraph (1)(a), (b), (c)(ii) or (d)(ii) of regulation 10 (patients)
      applies, was in receipt of attendance allowance, or disability living allowance
      but payment of the benefit has been suspended in accordance with regulations
      made under section 113(2) of the Contributions and Benefits Act 1992, or

(iv) is provided by the Secretary of State with an invalid carriage or other vehicle
      under section 5(2) of the National Health Service Act 1977 (other services) or,
      in Scotland, under section 46 of the National Health Service (Scotland) Act 1978
      (provision of services) or receives payments by way of grant from the Secre-
      tary of State under paragraph 2 of Schedule 2 to that 1977 Act (additional pro-
      visions as to vehicles) or under that section 46, or

(v)   is blind and in consequence registered in a register compiled by a local author-
      ity under section 29 of the National Assistance Act 1948 (welfare services) or
      has been certified as blind and in consequence he is registered in a register
      maintained by or on behalf of a regional or islands council; or

(b)   the circumstances of the claimant fall, and have fallen, in respect of a continuous
      period of not less than 28 weeks, within sub-paragraph (b) or, if he was in Northern
      Ireland for the whole or part of that period, within one or more comparable North-
      ern Irish provisions.

(2) For the purposes of sub-paragraph (1)(a)(v), a person who has ceased to be registered as blind on regaining his eyesight shall nevertheless be treated as blind and as satisfying the additional condition set out in that sub-paragraph for a period of 28 weeks following the date on which he ceased to be so registered.

(3) For the purposes of sub-paragraph (1)(b), once the higher pensioner premium or the disability premium is applicable to a claimant by virtue of his satisfying the additional condition specified in that provision, if he then ceases, for a period of 8 weeks or less, to be treated as incapable of work for the purposes of the provisions specified in that provision he shall, on again becoming so incapable of work, immediately thereafter be treated as satisfying the condition in sub-paragraph (1)(b).

(4) For the purposes of sub-paragraph (1)(a)(ii) and (iii), once the higher pensioner premium is applicable to the claimant by virtue of his satisfying the additional condition specified in those provisions, if he then ceases, for a period of 8 weeks or less, to be entitled to council tax benefit, he shall on again becoming so entitled to council tax benefit, immediately thereafter be treated as satisfying the additional condition in sub-paragraph (1)(a)(ii) and (iii).

(5) For the purposes of sub-paragraph (1)(b), once the disability premium is applicable to a claimant by virtue of his satisfying the additional condition specified in that provision, he shall continue to be treated as satisfying that condition for any period spent by him in undertaking a course of training provided under section 2 of the Employment and Training Act 1973 or section 2 of the Enterprise and New Towns (Scotland) Act 1990 or for any period during which he is in receipt of a training allowance.

(6) For the purposes of sub-paragraph (1)(b), the circumstances of a claimant fall within this sub-paragraph if—

    (a) he provides evidence of incapacity in accordance with regulation 2 of the Social Security (Medical Evidence) Regulations 1976 (evidence of incapacity for work) in support of a claim for sickness benefit, invalidity pension or severe disablement allowance within the meaning of sections 31, 33 or 68 of the Contributions and Benefits Act 1992, provided that an adjudication officer has not determined he is not incapable of work, or

    (b) he is in receipt of statutory sick pay within the meaning of Part XI of the Contributions and Benefits Act 1992.

(7) For the purposes of sub-paragraph (1)(b), once the disability premium is applicable to a claimant by virtue of his satisfying the additional condition specified in that provision, he shall continue to be treated as satisfying that condition for any period spent by him in undertaking a course of training provided under section 2 of the Employment and Training Act 1973 or section 2 of the Enterprise and New Towns (Scotland) Act 1990.

Severe Disability Premium

14. (1) The condition is that the claimant is a severely disabled person.

(2) For the purposes of sub-paragraph (1), a claimant shall be treated as being a severely disabled person if, and only if—

    (a) in the case of a single claimant or lone parent—

        (i)   he is in receipt of attendance allowance, or the care component of disability living allowance by at the highest or middle rate prescribed in accordance with section 72(3) of the Contributions and Benefits Act 1992, and

        (ii) subject to sub-paragraph (3), he has no non-dependants aged 18 or over residing with him, and

        (iii) an invalid care allowance under section 70 of the Contributions and Benefits Act 1992 is not in payment to anyone in respect of caring for him;

(b) in the case of a claimant who has a partner—

    (i) the claimant is in receipt of attendance allowance, or disability living allowance by virtue of entitlement to the care component at the highest or middle rate prescribed in accordance with section 72(3) of the Contributions and Benefits Act 1992, and

    (ii) his partner is also in receipt of such an allowance or, if he is a member of a polygamous marriage, all the partners of that marriage are in receipt of such an allowance, and

    (iii) subject to sub-paragraph (3), the claimant has no non-dependants aged 18 or over residing with him,

and either an invalid care allowance is in payment to someone in respect of caring for only one of a couple or, in the case of a polygamous marriage for one or more but not all the partners of the marriage, or else such an allowance is not in payment to anyone in respect of caring for either member of a couple or any partner of a polygamous marriage.

(3) For the purposes of sub-paragraph (2)(a)(ii) and (2)(b)(iii) no account shall be taken of either—

(a) a person receiving attendance allowance or disability living allowance by virtue of entitlement to the care component at the highest or middle rate prescribed in accordance with section 72(3) of the Contributions and Benefits Act 1992, or

(b) a boarder.

Disabled Child Premium

15. The condition is that a child or young person for whom the claimant or partner of his is responsible and who is a member of the claimant's household—

(a) has no capital or capital which, if calculated in accordance with Chapter VI of Part IV in like manner as for the claimant would not exceed £3,000; and

(b) is in receipt of disability living allowance or is no longer in receipt of such allowance because he is a patient, provided that the child or young person continues to be a member of the family; or

(c) is blind or treated as blind within the meaning of paragraph 13.

Carer Premium

16. (1) The condition is that the claimant or his partner is, or both of them are, in receipt of invalid care allowance under section 70 of the Contributions and Benefits Act 1992.

(2) If a claimant or his partner, or both of them, would be in receipt of invalid care allowance but for the provisions of the Social Security (Overlapping Benefits) Regulations 1979, where—

(a) the claim for that allowance was made on or after the 1st October 1990, and

(b) the person or persons in respect of whose care the allowance has been claimed remains or remain in receipt of attendance allowance, or the care component of disability living allowance at the highest or middle rate prescribed in accordance with section 72(3) of the Contributions and Benefits Act 1992,

he or his partner, or both of them, as the case may be, shall be treated for the purposes of sub-paragraph (1) as being in receipt of invalid care allowance.

(3) Where a carer premium is awarded but the person in respect of whom it is awarded either ceases to be in receipt of invalid care allowance or ceases to be treated as being in receipt of invalid care allowance, the condition for the award of the premium shall be treated

as satisfied for a period of 8 weeks from the date on which that person ceased to be in receipt of, or ceased to be treated as being in receipt of, invalid care allowance.

(4) Where a person who has been receiving, or who has been treated as receiving invalid care allowance, ceases to be in receipt of, or treated as being in receipt of that allowance and makes a claim for council tax benefit, the condition for the award of the carer premium shall be treated as satisfied for a period of 8 weeks from the date the person was last in receipt of, or was last treated as being in receipt of, invalid care allowance.

Persons in receipt of concessionary payments

17. For the purpose of determining whether a premium is applicable to a person under paragraphs 13 to 16, any concessionary payment made to compensate that person for the non-payment of any benefit mentioned in those paragraphs shall be treated as if it were a payment of that benefit.

Person in receipt of benefit for another

18. For the purposes of this Part of this Schedule, a person shall be regarded as being in receipt of any benefit if, and only if, it is paid in respect of him and shall be so regarded only for any period in respect of which that benefit is paid.

PART IV. AMOUNTS OF PREMIUMS SPECIFIED IN PART III

Premium	*Amount*
19. (1) Lone Parent Premium	(1) £10.60
(2) Pensioner Premium for persons under 75—	(2)
(a) where the claimant satisfies the condition in paragraph 9(a);	(a) £16.70
(b) where the claimant satisfies the condition in paragraph 9(b).	(b) £25.35
(3) Pensioner Premium for persons 75 or over—	(3)
(a) where the claimant satisfies the condition in paragraph 10(a);	(a) £18.65
(b) where the claimant satisfies the condition in paragraph 10(b).	(b) £28.00
(4) Higher Pensioner Premium—	(4)
(a) where the claimant satisfies the condition in paragraph 11(1)(a) or (b);	(a) £22.75
(b) where the claimant satisfies the condition in paragraph 11(2)(a) or (b).	(b) £32.55
(5) Disability Premium—	(5)
(a) where the claimant satisfies the condition in paragraph 12(a);	(a) £17.80
(b) where the claimant satisfies the condition in paragraph 12(b).	(b) £25.55
(6) Severe Disability Premium—	(6)
(a) where the claimant satisfies the condition in paragraph 14(2)(a);	(a) £32.55
(b) where the claimant satisfies the condition in paragraph 14(2)(b)—	
(i) in a case where there is someone in receipt of an invalid care allowance;	(b) (i) £32.55
(ii) in a case where there is no-one in receipt of such an allowance.	(ii) £65.10

(7) Disabled Child Premium	(7) £17.80 in respect of each child or young person in respect of whom the condition specified in paragraph 15 of Part III of this Schedule is satisfied.
(8) Carer Premium	(8) £11.55 in respect of each person who satisfies the condition specified in paragraph 16.

SCHEDULE 2

Regulation 54

AMOUNT OF ALTERNATIVE MAXIMUM
COUNCIL TAX BENEFIT

1. (1) Subject to paragraphs 2 and 3, the alternative maximum council tax benefit in respect of a day for the purpose of regulation 54 shall be determined in accordance with the following Table and in this Table "second adult" means any person or persons residing with the claimant to whom section 131(6) of the Contributions and Benefits Act 1992 applies.

(2) In this Schedule "council tax due in respect of that day" means the council tax payable under section 10 or 78 of the 1992 Act less any reductions made under section 13 or 80 (reduced amounts of council tax).

TABLE

(1) *Second adult*	(2) *Alternative maximum council tax benefit*
(a) Where the second adult or all second adults are in receipt of income support;	(a) 25 per cent. of the council tax due in respect of that day;
(b) Where the gross income of the second adult or, where there is more than one second adult, their aggregate gross income disregarding any income of persons on income support,	(b)
(i) does not exceed £100 per week;	(i) 15 per cent. of the council tax due in respect of that day;
(ii) exceeds £100 per week but does not exceed £130 per week;	(ii) 7.5 per cent. of the council tax due in respect of that day.

2. In determining a second adult's gross income for the purposes of this Schedule, there shall be disregarded from that income any attendance allowance, or any disability living allowance under section 71 of the Contributions and Benefits Act 1992.

3. Where there are two or more second adults residing with the claimant for benefit and any such second adult falls to be disregarded for the purposes of discount in accordance with Schedule 1 of the 1992 Act, his income shall be disregarded in determining the amount of any alternative maximum council tax benefit, unless that second adult is a member of a couple and his partner does not fall to be disregarded for the purposes of discount.

SCHEDULE 3 Regulations 20(2), 22(2) and 27(3)

SUMS TO BE DISREGARDED IN THE CALCULATION OF EARNINGS

1. In the case of a claimant who has been engaged in remunerative work as an employed earner or, had the employment been in Great Britain, would have been so engaged—

   (a) any earnings paid or due to be paid in respect of that employment which has been terminated—

   (i) by way of retirement but only if on retirement he is entitled to a retirement pension under the Contributions and Benefits Act 1992, or would be so entitled if he satisfied the contribution conditions,

   (ii) otherwise than by retirement except earnings to which regulation 19(1)(b) to (e) and (g) to (i) (earnings of employed earners) applies;

   (b) any earnings paid or due to be paid in respect of that employment which has been interrupted except earnings to which regulation 19(1)(d) and (e) applies.

2. In the case of a claimant who has been engaged in part-time employment as an employed earner or, had the employment been in Great Britain, would have been so engaged before he made a claim for council tax benefit, any earnings paid or due to be paid in respect of that employment which has been terminated or interrupted before the claim is made except earnings to which regulation 19(1)(e) applies.

3. (1) In a case to which this paragraph applies, £15; but notwithstanding regulation 11 (calculation of income and capital of members of a claimant's family and of a polygamous marriage) if this paragraph applies to a claimant it shall not apply to his partner except where, and to the extent that, the earnings of the claimant which are to be disregarded under this paragraph are less than £15.

(2) This paragraph applies where the claimant's applicable amount includes the amount by way of the disability premium or severe disability premium under Schedule 1 (applicable amounts).

(3) This paragraph applies where—

   (a) the claimant is a member of a couple and his applicable amount would, but for the higher pensioner premium under Schedule 1 being applicable, include an amount by way of the disability premium under that Schedule; and

   (b) he or his partner is under the age of 60 and at least one is engaged in employment.

(4) This paragraph applies where—

   (a) the claimant's applicable amount includes an amount by way of the higher pensioner premium under Schedule 1; and

   (b) the claimant or, if he is a member of a couple, either he or his partner has attained the age of 60; and

   (c) immediately before attaining that age he or, as the case may be, he or his partner was engaged in employment and the claimant was entitled by virtue of sub-paragraph (2) to a disregard of £15; and

   (d) he or, if he is a member of a couple, he or his partner has continued in employment.

(5) This paragraph applies where—

(a) the claimant is a member of a couple and his applicable amount would include an amount by way of the disability premium under Schedule 1, but for—

   (i)   the pensioner premium for persons aged 75 and over under that Schedule being applicable; or
   (ii) the higher pensioner premium under that Schedule being applicable; and

(b) he or his partner has attained the age of 75 but is under the age of 80 and the other is under the age of 60 and at least one member of the couple is engaged in employment.

(6) This paragraph applies where—

(a) the claimant is a member of a couple and he or his partner has attained the age of 75 but is under the age of 80 and the other has attained the age of 60; and
(b) immediately before the younger member attained that age either was engaged in employment and the claimant was entitled by virtue of sub-paragraph (5) to a disregard of £15; and
(c) either he or his partner has continued in employment.

(7) For the purposes of this paragraph, no account shall be taken of any period not exceeding eight consecutive weeks occurring on or after the date on which the claimant or, if he is a member of a couple, he or his partner attained the age of 60 during which either or both ceased to be engaged in employment or the claimant ceased to be entitled to any or all of the following benefits namely community charge benefit, council tax benefit or housing benefit.

4. If an amount by way of a lone parent premium under Schedule 1 (applicable amounts) is or, but for any pensioner premium, higher pensioner premium or disability premium being applicable to him, would be included in the calculation of the claimant's applicable amount, £25.

5. In a case where paragraph 3 does not apply to the claimant and he is one of a couple and a member of that couple is in employment, £10; but, notwithstanding regulation 11 (calculation of income and capital of members of claimant's family and of a polygamous marriage), if this paragraph applies to a claimant it shall not apply to his partner except where, and to the extent that, the earnings of the claimant which are to be disregarded under this paragraph are less than £10.

6. (1) In a case to which neither paragraph 3 nor 4 applies to the claimant, £15 of earnings derived from one or more employments as—

(a) a part-time fireman in a fire brigade maintained in pursuance of the Fire Services Acts 1947 to 1959;
(b) an auxiliary coastguard in respect of coast rescue activities;
(c) a person engaged part-time in the manning or launching of a life boat;
(d) a member of any territorial or reserve force prescribed in Part I of Schedule 3 to the Social Security (Contributions) Regulations 1979;

but, notwithstanding regulation 11 (calculation of income and capital of members of claimant's family and of a polygamous marriage), if this paragraph applies to a claimant it shall not apply to his partner except to the extent specified in sub-paragraph (2).

(2) If the claimant's partner is engaged in employment—

(a) specified in sub-paragraph (1), so much of his earnings as would not in aggregate with the amount of the claimant's earnings disregarded under this paragraph exceed £15;
(b) other than one specified in sub-paragraph (1), so much of his earnings from that employment up to £10 as would not in aggregate with the claimant's earnings disregarded under this paragraph exceed £15.

7. Where the claimant is engaged in one or more employments specified in paragraph 6(1), but his earnings derived from such employments are less than £15 in any week and he is also engaged in any other employment so much of his earnings from that other employment, up to £5, if he is a single claimant, or up to £10 if he has a partner, as would not in aggregate with the amount of his earnings disregarded under paragraph 6 exceed £15.

8. In a case to which none of the paragraphs 3 to 7 applies, £5.

9. Any amount or the balance of any amount which would fall to be disregarded under paragraph 17, 18 or 28 of Schedule 4 had the claimant's income which does not consist of earnings been sufficient to entitle him to the full disregard thereunder.

10. Where a claimant is on income support, his earnings.

11. Any earnings derived from employment which are payable in a country outside the United Kingdom for such period during which there is a prohibition against the transfer to the United Kingdom of those earnings.

12. Where a payment of earnings is made in a currency other than sterling, any banking charge or commission payable in converting that payment into sterling.

13. Any earnings of a child or young person except earnings to which paragraph 14 applies.

14. In the case of earnings of a young person who has ceased full-time education for the purposes of section 142 of the Contributions and Benefits Act 1992 (meaning of child) and who is engaged in remunerative work—

    (a) if an amount by way of a disabled child premium under Schedule 1 is included in the calculation of his applicable amount, £15;

    (b) in any other case, £5.

15. In this Schedule "part-time employment" means employment in which the person is engaged on average for less than 16 hours a week.

SCHEDULE 4

Regulation 24(2)

SUMS TO BE DISREGARDED IN THE CALCULATION OF INCOME OTHER THAN EARNINGS

1. Any amount paid by way of tax on income which is to be taken into account under regulation 24 (calculation of income other than earnings).

2. Any payment in respect of any expenses incurred by a claimant who is—

    (a) engaged by a charitable or voluntary body, or

    (b) a volunteer,

if he otherwise derives no remuneration or profit from the employment and is not to be treated as possessing any earnings under regulation 26(4) (notional income).

3. In the case of employment as an employed earner, any payment in respect of expenses wholly, exclusively and necessarily incurred in the performance of the duties of the employment.

4. Where a claimant is on income support, the whole of his income.

5. Any disability living allowance.

6. Any concessionary payment made to compensate for the non-payment of—

    (a) any payment specified in paragraph 5 or 8;

    (b) income support;

    (c) mobility allowance in section 37A of the Social Security Act 1975.

7. Any mobility supplement under article 26A of the Naval, Military and Air Forces etc (Disablement and Death) Service Pensions Order 1983 (including such a supplement by virtue of any other scheme or order) or under article 25A of the Personal Injuries (Civilians) Scheme 1983 or any payment intended to compensate for the non-payment of such a supplement.

8. Any attendance allowance.

9. Any payment to the claimant as holder of the Victoria Cross or of the George Cross or any analogous payment.

10. Any sum in respect of a course of study attended by a child or young person payable by virtue of Regulations made under section 81 of the Education Act 1944 (assistance by means of scholarships or otherwise), or by virtue of section 2(1) of the Education Act 1962 (awards for courses of further education), or section 49 of the Education (Scotland) Act 1980 (power to assist persons to take advantage of educational facilities).

11. In the case of a claimant participating in arrangements for training made under section 2 of the Employment and Training Act 1973 or section 2 of the Enterprise and New Towns (Scotland) Act 1990 or attending at an employment rehabilitation centre established under that section of the 1973 Act—

    (a)   any travelling expenses reimbursed to the claimant;

    (b)   if he receives an allowance under section 2(2)(d) of the 1973 Act or section 2(4)(c) of the 1990 Act, such amount, if any, of that allowance expressed to be a living away from home allowance;

    (c)   any training premium,

but this paragraph, except in so far as it relates to a payment under sub-paragraph (a), (b) or (c), does not apply to any part of any allowance under section 2(2)(d) of the 1973 Act or section 2(4)(c) of the 1990 Act.

12. Any Job Start Allowance payable under section 2(1) of the Employment and Training Act 1973.

13. (1) Except where sub-paragraph (2) applies and subject to sub-paragraph (3) and paragraphs 34 and 35, £10 of any charitable payment or of any voluntary payment made or due to be made at regular intervals.

(2) Subject to sub-paragraph (3) and paragraph 35, any charitable payment or voluntary payment made or due to be made at regular intervals which is intended and used for an item other than food, ordinary clothing or footwear, household fuel, eligible rent, council tax or water charges of a single claimant or, as the case may be, of the claimant or any other member of his family or is used for any council tax or water charges for which that claimant or member is liable.

(3) Sub-paragraphs (1) and (2) shall not apply to a payment which is made or due to be made by—

    (a)   a former partner of the claimant, or a former partner of any member of the claimant's family; or

    (b)   the parent of a child or young person where that child or young person is a member of the claimant's family.

(4) For the purposes of sub-paragraph (1) where a number of charitable or voluntary payments fall to be taken into account in any one week they shall be treated as though they were one such payment.

(5) For the purposes of sub-paragraph (2) the expression "ordinary clothing or footwear" means clothing or footwear for normal daily use, but does not include school uniforms, or clothing or footwear used solely for sporting activities.

14. Subject to paragraph 34, £10 of any of the following, namely—

(a) war disablement pension or war widow's pension or a payment made to compensate for the non-payment of such a pension;

(b) a pension paid by the government of a country outside Great Britain which is either

(i) analogous to a war disablement pension; or
(ii) analogous to a war widow's pension;

(c) a person paid under any special provision made by the law of Germany or any part of it, or of the Republic of Austria, to victims of National Socialist persecution.

15. (1) Any income derived from capital to which the claimant is or is treated under regulation 36 (capital jointly held) as beneficially entitled but, subject to sub-paragraph (2), not income derived from capital disregarded under paragraph 1, 2, 4, 7, 13 or 24 to 27 of Schedule 5.

(2) Income derived from capital disregarded under paragraph 2, 4 or 24 to 27 of Schedule 5 but only to the extent of—

(a) any mortgage payments made in respect of the dwelling and premises; or
(b) any—

(i) council tax, or
(ii) charges for water or services to which Schedule 11 paragraph 1(a) or (b) of the 1992 Act refer, which the claimant is liable to pay in respect of the dwelling or premises, in the period during which that income accrued.

16. Where a claimant receives income under an annuity purchased with a loan which satisfies the following conditions—

(a) that the loan was made as part of a scheme under which not less than 90% of the proceeds of the loan were applied to the purchase by the person to whom it was made of an annuity ending with his life or with the life of the survivor of two or more persons (in this paragraph referred to as "the annuitants") who include the person to whom the loan was made;

(b) that the interest on the loan is payable by the person to whom it was made or by one of the annuitants;

(c) that at the time the loan was made the person to whom it was made or each of the annuitants had attained the age of 65;

(d) that the loan was secured on a dwelling in Great Britain and the person to whom the loan was made or one of the annuitants owns an estate or interest in that dwelling; and

(e) that the person to whom the loan was made or one of the annuitants occupies the dwelling on which it was secured as his home at the time the interest is paid,

the amount, calculated on a weekly basis, equal to—

(i) where, or insofar as, section 369 of the Income and Corporation Taxes Act 1988 (mortgage interest payable under deduction of tax) applies to the payments of interest on the loan, the interest which is payable after deduction of a sum equal to income tax on such payments at the basic rate for the year of assessment in which the payment of interest becomes due,

(ii) in any other case the interest which is payable on the loan without deduction of such a sum.

17. Where the claimant makes a parental contribution in respect of a student attending a course at an establishment in the United Kingdom or undergoing education in the United Kingdom, which contribution has been assessed for the purposes of calculating—

(a) under regulations made in exercise of the powers conferred by section 1 of the Education Act 1962, that student's award under that section;

(b) that student's award under section 2 of that Act; or

(c)   under regulations made in exercise of the powers conferred by section 49 of the Education (Scotland) Act 1980, that student's bursary, scholarship, or other allowance under that section or under regulations made in exercise of the powers conferred by section 73 of that Act of 1980, any payment to that student under that section,

an amount equal to the weekly amount of that parental contribution, but only in respect of the period for which that contribution is assessed as being payable.

18. (1) Where the claimant is the parent of a student aged under 25 in advanced education who either—

(a)   is not in receipt of an award or grant in respect of that education; or
(b)   is in receipt of an award under section 2 of the Education Act 1962 (discretionary awards) or a bursary, scholarship or other allowance under section 49(1) of the Education (Scotland) Act 1980, or a payment under section 73 of that Act of 1980,

and the claimant makes payments by way of a contribution towards the student's maintenance, other than a parental contribution falling within paragraph 17, an amount specified in sub-paragraph (2) in respect of each week during the student's term.

(2) For the purposes of sub-paragraph (1), the amount shall be equal to—

(a)   the weekly amount of the payments; or
(b)   the amount by way of a personal allowance for a single claimant under 25 less the weekly amount of any award, bursary, scholarship, allowance or payment referred to in sub-paragraph (1)(b),

whichever is less.

19. Any payment made to the claimant by a child or young person or a non-dependant.

20. Where the claimant occupies a dwelling as his home which is also occupied by a person other than one to whom paragraph 19 refers and that person is contractually liable to make payments in respect of his occupation of the dwelling to the claimant-

(a)   £4 of any payment made by that person; and
(b)   a further £8.60 where the payment is inclusive of an amount for heating.

21. Where the claimant occupies a dwelling as his home which is also occupied by a boarder and payments are made by the boarder in respect of his occupation—

(a)   £20.00 of any payment made by that boarder; and
(b)   where any payment exceeds £20.00, 50% of the excess.

22. Any income in kind.

23. Any income which is payable in a country outside the United Kingdom for such period during which there is a prohibition against the transfer to the United Kingdom of that income.

24. (1) Any payment made to the claimant in respect of a person who is a member of his family—

(a)   in accordance with regulations made pursuant to section 57A of the Adoption Act 1976 (permitted allowances) or with a scheme approved by the Secretary of State under section 51 of the Adoption (Scotland) Act 1978 (schemes for payments of allowances to adopters);
(b)   which is a payment made by a local authority, in pursuance of section 15(1) of, and paragraph 15 of Schedule 1 to the Children Act 1989 (local authority contribution to a child's maintenance where the child is living with a person as a result of a residence order) or as the case may be, section 50 of the Children Act 1975 (payment towards maintenance of children),

to the extent specified in sub-paragraph (2).

(2) In the case of a child or young person—

    (a) to whom regulation 27(2) applies (capital in excess of £3,000), the whole payment;

    (b) to whom that regulation does not apply, so much of the weekly amount of the payment as exceeds the amount included under Schedule 1 in the calculation of the claimant's applicable amount for that child or young person by way of the personal allowance and disabled child premium, if any.

25. Any payment made by a local authority to the claimant with whom a person is accommodated by virtue of arrangements made under section 23(2)(a) of the Children Act 1989 or, as the case may be, section 21 of the Social Work (Scotland) Act 1968 or by a voluntary organisation under section 59(1)(a) of the 1989 Act or by a care authority under regulation 9 of the Boarding Out and Fostering of Children (Scotland) Regulations 1985 (provision of accommodation and maintenance for children by local authorities and voluntary organisations).

26. Any payment made by a health authority, local authority or voluntary organisation to the claimant in respect of a person who is not normally a member of the claimant's household but is temporarily in his care.

27. Any payment made by a local authority in accordance with section 17 or 24 of the Children Act 1989 or, as the case may be, section 12, 24 or 26 of the Social Work (Scotland) Act 1968 (provision of services for children and their families and advice and assistance to certain children).

28. An amount equal to any maintenance payment made by the claimant to his former partner or in respect of his children other than children who are members of his household.

29. Any payment received under an insurance policy taken out to insure against the risk of being unable to maintain repayments on a loan for the purchase of the dwelling which the claimant occupies as his home and secured on that dwelling to the extent that it does not exceed the amount calculated, on a weekly basis, of that repayment.

30. Any payment of income which by virtue of regulation 31 (income treated as capital) is to be treated as capital.

31. Any social fund payments made pursuant to Part VIII of the Contributions and Benefits Act 1992.

32. Any payment under section 148 of the Contributions and Benefits Act 1992 (pensioners' Christmas bonus).

33. Where a payment of income is made in a currency other than sterling, any banking charge or commission payable in converting that payment into sterling.

34. The total of claimant's income or, if he is a member of a family, the family's income and the income of any person which he is treated as possessing under regulation 11(3) (calculation of income and capital of members of claimant's family and of a polygamous marriage) to be disregarded under regulation 43(2)(b) and regulation 44(1)(e) (calculation of covenant income where a contribution is assessed, covenant income where no grant income or no contribution is assessed), regulation 47(2) (treatment of student loans) and paragraphs 13 and 14 shall in no case exceed £10 per week.

35. (1) Any payment made under the Trusts, the Fund or the Independent Living Fund.

(2) Any payment by or on behalf of a person who is suffering or who suffered from haemophilia or who is or was a qualifying person, which derives from a payment made under any of the Trusts to which sub-paragraph (1) refers and which is made to or for the benefit of—

    (a) that person's partner or former partner from whom he is not, or where that person has died was not, estranged or divorced;

    (b) any child who is a member of that person's family or who was such a member and who is a member of the claimant's family; or

(c) any young person who is a member of that person's family or who was such a member and who is a member of the claimant's family.

(3) Any payment by or on behalf of the partner or former partner of a person who is suffering or who suffered from haemophilia or who is or was a qualifying person provided that the partner or former partner and that person are not, or if either of them has died were not, estranged or divorced, which derives from a payment made under any of the Trusts to which sub-paragraph (1) refers and which is made to or for the benefit of—

(a) the person who is suffering from haemophilia or who is a qualifying person;
(b) any child who is a member of that person's family or who was such a member and who is a member of the claimant's family; or
(c) any young person who is a member of that person's family or who was such a member and who is a member of the claimant's family.

(4) Any payment by a person who is suffering from haemophilia or who is a qualifying person, which derives from a payment under any of the Trusts to which sub-paragraph (1) refers, where—

(a) that person has no partner or former partner from whom he is not estranged or divorced, nor any child or young person who is or had been a member of that person's family; and
(b) the payment is made either—

(i) to that person's parent or step-parent, or
(ii) where that person at the date of the payment is a child, a young person or a student who has not completed his full-time education and has no parent or step-parent, to his guardian,

but only for a period from the date of the payment until the end of two years from that person's death.

(5) Any payment out of the estate of a person who suffered from haemophilia or who was a qualifying person, which derives from a payment under any of the Trusts to which sub-paragraph (1) refers, where—

(a) that person at the date of his death (the relevant date) had no partner or former partner from whom he was not estranged or divorced, nor any child or young person who was or had been a member of his family; and
(b) the payment is made either—

(i) to that person's parent or step-parent, or
(ii) where that person at the relevant date was a child, a young person or a student who had not completed his full-time education and had no parent or step-parent, to his guardian,

but only for a period of two years from the relevant date.

(6) In the case of a person to whom or for whose benefit a payment referred to in this paragraph is made, any income which derives from any payment of income or capital made under or deriving from any of the Trusts.

(7) For the purposes of sub-paragraphs (2) to (6), any reference to the Trusts shall be construed as including a reference to the Fund.

36. Any housing benefit.

37. Any payment made by the Secretary of State to compensate for the loss (in whole or in part) of entitlement to housing benefit.

38. Any payment by the Secretary of State to compensate for the loss of housing benefit supplement under regulation 19 of the Supplementary Benefit (Requirements) Regulations 1983.

39. Any resettlement benefit which is paid to the claimant by virtue of regulation 3 of the Social Security (Hospital In-Patients) Amendment (No. 2) Regulations 1987.

40. Any payment to a juror or witness in respect of attendance at a court other than compensation for loss of earnings or for the loss of a benefit payable under the Contributions and Benefits Act 1992.

41. Any payment in consequence of a reduction of a personal community charge pursuant to regulations under section 13A of the Local Government Finance Act 1988 or section 9A of the Abolition of Domestic Rates Etc (Scotland) Act 1987 (reduction of liability for personal community charges) or reduction of council tax either under section 13 or, as the case may be, section 80 of the 1992 Act.

42. Any special war widows payment made under—

- (a) the Naval and Marine Pay and Pensions (Special War Widows Payment) Order 1990 made under section 3 of the Naval and Marine Pay and Pensions Act 1865;
- (b) the Royal Warrant dated 19th February 1990 amending the Schedule to the Army Pensions Warrant 1977;
- (c) the Queen's Order dated 26th February 1990 made under section 2 of the Air Force (Constitution) Act 1917;
- (d) the Home Guard War Widows Special Payments Regulations 1990 made under section 151 of the Reserve Forces Act 1980;
- (e) the Orders dated 19th February 1990 amending orders made on 12th December 1980 concerning the Ulster Defence Regiment made in each case under Section 140 of the Reserve Forces Act 1980,

and any analogous payment made by the Secretary of State for Defence to any person who is not a person entitled under the provisions mentioned in sub-paragraphs (a) to (e) of this paragraph.

43. (1) Any payment or repayment made—

- (a) as respects England and Wales, under regulation 3, 5 or 8 of the National Health Service (Travelling Expenses and Remission of Charges) Regulations 1988 (travelling expenses and health services supplies);
- (b) as respects Scotland, under regulation 3, 5 or 8 of the National Health Service (Travelling Expenses and Remission of Charges) (Scotland) Regulations 1988 (travelling expenses and health services supplies).

(2) Any payment or repayment made by the Secretary of State for Health, the Secretary of State for Scotland or the Secretary of State for Wales which is analogous to a payment or repayment mentioned in sub-paragraph (1).

44. Any payment made under regulation 9 to 11 or regulation 13 of the Welfare Food Regulations 1988 (payments made in place of milk tokens or the supply of vitamins).

45. Any payment made by either the Secretary of State for the Home Department or by the Secretary of State for Scotland under a scheme established to assist relatives and other persons to visit persons in custody.

46. (1) Where a claimant's applicable amount includes an amount by way of the family premium, £15 of any payment of maintenance, whether under a court order or not, which is made or due to be made by—

- (a) the claimant's former partner, or the claimant's partner's former partner; or
- (b) the parent of a child or young person where that child or young person is a member of the claimant's family except where that parent is the claimant or the claimant's partner.

(2) For the purposes of sub-paragraph (1), where more than one maintenance payment falls to be taken into account in any week, all such payments shall be aggregated and treated as if they were a single payment.

47. Any payment made by the Secretary of State to compensate a person who was entitled to supplementary benefit in respect of a period ending immediately before 11th April 1988 but who did not become entitled to income support in respect of a period beginning with that day.

48. Any payment (other than a training allowance) made, whether by the Secretary of State or any other person, under the Disabled Persons Employment Act 1944 or in accordance with arrangements made under section 2 of the Employment and Training Act 1973 to assist disabled persons to obtain or retain employment despite their disability.

SCHEDULE 5

Regulation 29(2)

CAPITAL TO BE DISREGARDED

1. The dwelling together with any garage, garden and outbuildings, normally occupied by the claimant as his home including any premises not so occupied which it is impracticable or unreasonable to sell separately, in particular any croft land on which the dwelling is situated; but, notwithstanding regulation 11 (calculation of income and capital of members of claimant's family and of a polygamous marriage), only one dwelling shall be disregarded under this paragraph.

2. Any premises acquired for occupation by the claimant which he intends to occupy as his home within 26 weeks of the date of acquisition or such longer period as is reasonable in the circumstances to enable the claimant to obtain possession and commence occupation of the premises.

3. Any sum directly attributable to the proceeds of sale of any premises formerly occupied by the claimant as his home which is to be used for the purchase of other premises intended for such occupation within 26 weeks of the date of sale or such longer period as is reasonable in the circumstances to enable the claimant to complete the purchase.

4. Any premises occupied in whole or in part—

  (a) by a partner or relative of a single claimant or any member of the family as his home where that person is either aged 60 or over or incapacitated;
  (b) by the former partner of the claimant as his home; but this provision shall not apply where the former partner is a person from whom the claimant is estranged or divorced.

5. Where a claimant is on income support, the whole of his capital.

6. Any reversionary interest.

7. (1) The assets of any business owned in whole or in part by the claimant and for the purposes of which he is engaged as a self-employed earner, or if he has ceased to be so engaged, for such period as may be reasonable in the circumstances to allow for disposal of any such asset.

(2) The assets of any business owned in whole or in part by the claimant where—

  (a) he is not engaged as a self-employed earner in that business by reason of some disease or bodily or mental disablement; but
  (b) he intends to become engaged or, as the case may be, re-engaged as a self-employed earner in that business as soon as he recovers or is able to become engaged, or re-engaged, in that business;

a period of 26 weeks from the date on which the claim for council tax benefit is made, or is treated as made, or, if it is unreasonable to expect him to become engaged or re-engaged in that business within that period, for such longer period as is reasonable in the circumstances to enable him to become so engaged or re-engaged.

8. Any arrears of, or any concessionary payment made to compensate for arrears due to the non-payment of—

(a) any payment specified in paragraph 5, 7 or 8 of Schedule 4;
(b) an income-related benefit or supplementary benefit, family income supplement under the Family Income Supplements Act 1970 or housing benefit under Part II of the Social Security and Housing Benefits Act 1982,

but only for a period of 52 weeks from the date of the receipt of arrears or of the concessionary payment.

9. Any sum—

(a) paid to the claimant in consequence of damage to, or loss of the home or any personal possession and intended for its repair or replacement; or
(b) acquired by the claimant (whether as a loan or otherwise) on the express condition that it is to be used for effecting essential repairs or improvement to the home,

which is to be used for the intended purpose for a period of 26 weeks from the date on which it was so paid or acquired or such longer period as is reasonable in the circumstances to effect the repairs, replacement or improvement.

10. Any sum—

(a) deposited with a housing association as defined in section 1(1) of the Housing Associations Act 1985 or section 338(1) of the Housing (Scotland) Act 1987 as a condition of occupying the home;
(b) which was so deposited and which is to be used for the purchase of another home, for the period of 26 weeks or such longer period as may be reasonable in the circumstances to enable the claimant to complete the purchase.

11. Any personal possessions except those which have been acquired by the claimant with the intention of reducing his capital in order to secure entitlement to council tax benefit or to increase the amount of that benefit.

12. The value of the right to receive any income under an annuity or the surrender value (if any) of such a annuity.

13. Where the funds of a trust are derived from a payment made in consequence of any personal injury to the claimant the value of the trust fund and the value of the right to receive any payment under that trust.

14. The value of the right to receive any income under a life interest or from a liferent.

15. The value of the right to receive any income which is disregarded under paragraph 11 of Schedule 3 or paragraph 23 of Schedule 4.

16. The surrender value of any policy of life insurance.

17. Where any payment of capital falls to be made by instalments, the value of the right to receive any outstanding instalments.

18. Any payment made by a local authority in accordance with section 17 or 24 of the Children Act 1989 or, as the case may be, section 12, 24 or 26 of the Social Work (Scotland) Act 1968 (provision of services for children and their families and advice and assistance to certain children).

19. Any social fund payment made pursuant to Part VIII of the Contributions and Benefits Act 1992.

20. Any refund of tax which falls to be deducted under section 369 of the Income and Corporation Taxes Act 1988 (mortgage interest payable under deduction of tax) on a payment of relevant loan interest for the purpose of acquiring an interest in the home or carrying out repairs or improvements to the home.

21. Any capital which by virtue of regulation 25 or 47 (capital treated as income or treatment of student loans) is to be treated as income.

22. Where any payment of capital is made in a currency other than sterling, any banking charge or commission payable in converting that payment into sterling.

23. (1) Any payment made under the Trusts, the Fund or the Independent Living Fund.

(2) Any payment by or on behalf of a person who is suffering or who suffered from haemophilia or who is or was a qualifying person, which derives from a payment made under any of the Trusts to which sub-paragraph (1) refers and which is made to or for the benefit of—

    (a)   that person's partner or former partner from whom he is not, or where that person has died was not, estranged or divorced;

    (b)   any child who is a member of that person's family or who was such a member and who is a member of the claimant's family; or

    (c)   any young person who is a member of that person's family or who was such a member and who is a member of the claimant's family.

(3) Any payment by or on behalf of the partner or former partner of a person who is suffering or who suffered from haemophilia or who is or was a qualifying person provided that the partner or former partner and that person are not, or if either of them has died were not, estranged or divorced, which derives from a payment made under any of the Trusts to which sub-paragraph (1) refers and which is made to or for the benefit of—

    (a)   the person who is suffering from haemophilia or who is a qualifying person;

    (b)   any child who is a member of that person's family or who was such a member and who is a member of the claimant's family; or

    (c)   any young person who is a member of that person's family or who was such a member and who is a member of the claimant's family.

(4) Any payment by a person who is suffering from haemophilia or who is a qualifying person, which derives from a payment under any of the Trusts to which sub-paragraph (1) refers, where—

    (a)   that person has no partner or former partner from whom he is not estranged or divorced, nor any child or young person who is or had been a member of that person's family; and

    (b)   the payment is made either—

        (i)   to that person's parent or step-parent, or

        (ii)   where that person at the date of the payment is a child, a young person or a student who has not completed his full-time education and has no parent or step-parent, to his guardian, but only for a period from the date of the payment until the end of two years from that person's death.

(5) Any payment out of the estate of a person who suffered from haemophilia or who was a qualifying person, which derives from a payment under any of the Trusts to which sub-paragraph (1) refers, where—

    (a)   that person at the date of his death (the relevant date) had no partner or former partner from whom he was not estranged or divorced, nor any child or young person who was or had been a member of his family; and

    (b)   the payment is made either—

        (i)   to that person's parent or step-parent, or

        (ii)   where that person at the relevant date was a child, a young person or a student who had not completed his full-time education and had no parent or step-parent, to his guardian,

but only for a period of two years from the relevant date.

(6) In the case of a person to whom or for whose benefit a payment referred to in this paragraph is made, any capital resource which derives from any payment of income or capital made under or deriving from any of the Trusts.

(7) For the purpose of sub-paragraphs (2) to (6), any reference to the Trusts shall be construed as including a reference to the Fund.

24. (1) Where a claimant has ceased to occupy what was formerly the dwelling occupied as the home following his estrangement or divorce from his former partner, that dwelling for a period of 26 weeks from the date on which he ceased to occupy that dwelling, or where the dwelling is occupied as the home by the former partner who is a lone parent, for so long as it is so occupied.

(2) In this paragraph "dwelling" includes any garage, garden and outbuildings, which were formerly occupied by the claimant as his home and any premises not so occupied which it is impracticable or unreasonable to sell separately, in particular any croft land on which the dwelling is situated.

25. Any premises where the claimant is taking reasonable steps to dispose of those premises, for a period of 26 weeks from the date on which he first took such steps, or such longer period as is reasonable in the circumstances to enable him to dispose of those premises.

26. Any premises which the claimant intends to occupy as his home and in respect of which he is taking steps to obtain possession and has sought legal advice, or has commenced legal proceedings, with a view to obtaining possession, for a period of 26 weeks from the date on which he first sought such advice or first commenced such proceedings whichever is the earlier, or such longer period as is reasonable in the circumstances to enable him to obtain possession and commence occupation of those premises.

27. Any premises which the claimant intends to occupy as his home to which essential repairs or alterations are required in order to render them fit for such occupation, for such period as is necessary to enable those repairs or alterations to be carried out.

28. Any payment made by the Secretary of State to compensate for the loss (in whole or in part) of entitlement to housing benefit.

29. Any payment made by the Secretary of State to compensate for the loss of housing benefit supplement under regulation 19 of the Supplementary Benefit (Requirements) Regulations 1983.

30. The value of the right to receive an occupational or personal pension.

31. The value of the right to receive any rent.

32. Any payment in kind made by a charity or under the Trusts or the Fund.

33. Any payment not exceeding £200 made under section 2 of the Employment and Training Act 1973 (functions of the Secretary of State) or section 2 of the Enterprise and New Towns (Scotland) Act 1990 as a training bonus to a person participating in arrangements for training made under either of those sections, but only for a period of 52 weeks from the date of the receipt of that payment.

34. Any housing benefit.

35. Any payment in consequence of a reduction of a personal community charge pursuant to regulations under section 13A of the Local Government Finance Act 1988 or section 9A of the Abolition of Domestic Rates Etc (Scotland) Act 1987 (reduction of liability for personal community charge) or reduction of council tax under section 13 or, as the case may be section 80 of the 1992 Act, but only for a period of 52 weeks from the date of the receipt of the payment.

36. Any grant made in accordance with a scheme made under section 129 of the Housing Act 1988 or section 66 of the Housing (Scotland) Act 1988 (schemes for payments to assist local housing authority and local authority tenants to obtain other accommodation) which is to be used—

    (a) to purchase premises intended for occupation as his home; or

(b) to carry out repairs or alterations which are required to render premises fit for occupation as his home,

for a period of 26 weeks from the date on which he received such a grant or such longer period as is reasonable in the circumstances to enable the purchase, repairs or alterations to be completed and the claimant to commence occupation of those premises as his home.

37. Any arrears of special war widows payment which is disregarded under paragraph 42 of Schedule 4 (sums to be disregarded in the calculation of income other than earnings), but only for a period of 52 weeks from the date of the receipt of the arrears.

38. (1) Any payment or repayment made—

(a) as respects England and Wales, under regulation 3, 5 or 8 of the National Health Service (Travelling Expenses and Remission of Charges) Regulations 1988 (travelling expenses and health service supplies);
(b) as respects Scotland, under regulation 3, 5 or 8 of the National Health Service (Travelling Expenses and Remission of Charges) (Scotland) Regulations 1988 (travelling expenses and health service supplies);

but only for a period of 52 weeks from the date of the receipt of the payment or repayment.

(2) Any payment or repayment by the Secretary of State for Health, the Secretary of State for Scotland or the Secretary of State for Wales which is analogous to a payment or repayment mentioned in sub-paragraph (1); but only for a period of 52 weeks from the date of the receipt of the payment or repayment.

39. Any payment made under regulation 9 to 11 or regulation 13 of the Welfare Food Regulations 1988 (payments made in place of milk tokens or the supply of vitamins), but only for a period of 52 weeks from the date of the receipt of the payment.

40. Any payment made either by the Secretary of State for the Home Department or by the Secretary of State for Scotland under a scheme established to assist relatives and other persons to visit persons in custody, but only for a period of 52 weeks from the date of the receipt of the payment.

41. Any payment made by the Secretary of State to compensate a person who was entitled to supplementary benefit in respect of a period ending immediately before 11th April 1988 but who did not become entitled to income support in respect of a period beginning with that day.

42. Any payment (other than training allowance, or training bonus under section 2 of the Employment and Training Act 1973) made, whether by the Secretary of State or any other person under the Disabled Persons (Employment) Act 1944 or in accordance with arrangements made under section 2 of the Employment and Training Act 1973 to assist disabled persons to obtain or retain employment despite their disability.

43. Any payment made by a local authority under section 3 of the Disabled Persons (Employment) Act 1958 to homeworkers assisted under the Blind Homeworkers' Scheme.

SCHEDULE 6   Regulation 67

MATTERS TO BE INCLUDED IN THE NOTICE OF DETERMINATION

PART I. GENERAL

1. The statement of matters to be included in any notice of determination issued by an appropriate authority to a person, and referred to in regulation 67 (notification of determinations) and 69 (review of determinations) are those matters set out in the following provisions of this Schedule.

2. Every notice of determination shall include a statement as to the right of any person affected by that determination to request a written statement under regulation 67(2) (requests for statement of reasons) and the manner and time in which to do so.

3. Every notice of determination shall include a statement as to the right of any person affected by that determination to make written representations in accordance with regulation 69(2) and the manner and time in which to do so.

4. Every notice of determination following written representations in accordance with regulation 69(2) (review of determinations) shall include a statement as to whether the original determination in respect of which the person made his representations has been confirmed or revised and where the appropriate authority has not revised the determination the reasons why not.

5. Every notice of determination following written representations in accordance with regulation 69(2) (review of determinations) shall include a statement as to the right of any person affected by that determination to request a further review in accordance with regulation 70 (further review of determinations) and of the manner and time in which to do so.

6. An authority may include in the notice of determination any other matters not prescribed by this Schedule which it sees fit, whether expressly or by reference to some other document available without charge to the person.

7. Parts II, III and IV of this Schedule shall apply only to the notice of determination given on a claim.

8. Where a notice of determination is given following a review of an earlier determination—

  (a) made of the authority's own motion which results in a revision of that earlier determination; or
  (b) made following written representations in accordance with regulation 69(2) (review of determinations), whether or not resulting in a revision of that earlier determination,

that notice shall, subject to paragraph 6, contain a statement only as to all the matters reviewed.

PART II. AWARDS WHERE INCOME SUPPORT IS PAYABLE

9. Where a person on income support is awarded council tax benefit, the notice of determination shall include a statement as to—

  (a) the normal weekly amount of council tax which may be rounded to the nearest penny;
  (b) the normal weekly amount of the council tax benefit, which amount may be rounded to the nearest penny;
  (c) the amount of and the category of non-dependant deductions made under regulation 52, if any;
  (d) the first day of entitlement to the council tax benefit;
  (e) the date on which his benefit period will end if it is not terminated earlier; and
  (f) his duty to notify any change of circumstances which might affect his entitlement to, or the amount of council tax benefit and, without prejudice to the extent of the duty owed under regulation 65 (duty to notify changes of circumstances), the kind of change of circumstances which is to be notified, either upon the notice or by reference to some other document available to him on application without charge

and in any case where the amount to which sub-paragraph (a) or (b) refers disregards fractions of a penny, the notice shall include a statement to that effect.

Part III. Awards Where No Income Support is Payable

10. Where a person is not on income support but is awarded council tax benefit, the notice of determination shall include a statement as to—

(a) the matters set out in paragraph 9;
(b) his applicable amount and how it is calculated;
(c) his weekly earnings; and
(d) his weekly income other than earnings.

Part IV. Notice Where Income of Non-dependant is Treated as Claimant's Income

11. Where an authority makes a determination under regulation 12 (circumstances in which income and capital of a non-dependant is to be treated as the claimant's) the notice of determination shall contain a statement as to—

(a) the fact that a determination has been made by reference to the income and capital of the claimant's non-dependant; and
(b) the appropriate authority's reasons for making that determination.

Part V. Notice Where No Award is Made

12. Where a person is not awarded council tax benefit under regulation 51 (maximum council tax benefit)—

(a) on grounds of income, the notice of determination shall include a statement as to—

(i)   the matters set out in paragraph 9(a), and
(ii) the matters set out in paragraph 10(b) to (d) where the person is not on income support;

(b) on the grounds that the amount of the alternative maximum council tax benefit exceeds the appropriate maximum council tax benefit, the matters set out in paragraph 15;
(c) for any reason other than those mentioned in sub-paragraphs (a) or (b), the notice of determination shall include a statement as to the reason why no award has been made.

Part VI. Awards Where Alternative Maximum Council Tax Benefit is Payable in Respect of a Day

13. Where a person is awarded council tax benefit determined in accordance with regulation 54 and Schedule 2 (alternative maximum council tax benefit) the notice of determination shall include a statement as to—

(a) the normal weekly amount of council tax, which amount may be rounded to the nearest penny;
(b) the normal weekly amount of the alternative maximum council tax benefit, which amount may be rounded to the nearest penny;
(c) the gross income or incomes and the rate of benefit which apply under Schedule 2;
(d) the first day of entitlement to benefit;
(e) the date on which the benefit period will end if it is not terminated earlier;
(f) the gross income of any second adult used to determine the rate of the alternative maximum council tax benefit or if any such adult is on income support;
(g) the claimant's duty to notify any change of circumstances which might affect his entitlement to, or the amount of the alternative maximum council tax benefit and,

without prejudice to the extent of the duty owed under regulation 65 (duty to notify changes of circumstances) the kind of change of circumstances which are to be notified, either upon the notice or by reference to some other document available to the claimant free of charge on application,

and in any case where the amount to which sub-paragraph (a) or (b) refers disregards fractions of a penny, the notice shall include a statement to that effect.

Notice where no award of alternative maximum council tax benefit is made

14. Where a person is not awarded council tax benefit in accordance with regulation 54 and Schedule 2 (alternative maximum council tax benefit)—

(a) on the grounds that the gross income or as the case may be the aggregate gross incomes, of any second adult or adults in the claimant's dwelling is too high, the notice of determination shall include a statement as to the matters set out in paragraphs 13(a), (c) and (f).

(b) on the grounds that the appropriate maximum council tax benefit is higher than the alternative maximum council tax benefit, the matters set out in paragraph 15 below;

(c) for any reason not referred to in sub-paragraphs (a) and (b), the notice of determination shall include a statement as to why no award has been made.

Notice where council tax benefit is awarded and section 131(9) of the Contributions and Benefits Act 1992 applies

15. Where the amount of a claimant's council tax benefit in respect of a day, is the greater of the appropriate maximum council tax benefit and the alternative maximum council tax benefit in his case the notice shall in addition to the matters set out in paragraphs 9, 10 or 13, as the case may be, include a statement as to—

(a) the amount of whichever is the lesser of the appropriate maximum council tax benefit or the alternative maximum council tax benefit in his case, which amount may be rounded to the nearest penny; and

(b) that this amount has not been awarded in consequence of the award of council tax benefit at a higher rate,

and in any case where the amount to which sub-paragraph (a) refers disregards fractions of a penny, the notice shall include a statement to that effect.

PART VII. NOTICE WHERE THERE IS RECOVERABLE EXCESS BENEFIT

16. Except in cases to which paragraphs (a) and (b) of regulation 83 (excess benefit in consequence of a reduction in an appropriate authority's council tax) refer, where the appropriate authority makes a determination that there is recoverable excess benefit within the meaning of regulation 84 (recoverable excess benefit), the notice of determination shall include a statement as to—

(a) the fact that there is recoverable excess benefit;
(b) the reason why there is recoverable excess benefit;
(c) the amount of the recoverable excess benefit;
(d) how the amount of the recoverable excess benefit was calculated;
(e) the benefit weeks to which the recoverable excess benefit relates in each benefit period or, where the recoverable excess benefit relates to a past period of entitlement as a result of backdating a claim under regulation 62(16) (back dating of late claims), in that past period; and
(f) the method or combination of methods by which the authority intends to recover the recoverable excess benefit, including—

(i)   payment by or on behalf of the person concerned of the amount due by the speci-
      fied date,
(ii) addition of the amount due to any amount in respect of the tax concerned for
      payment whether by instalments or otherwise by the specified date or dates, or
(iii) if recovery cannot be effected in accordance with heads (i) or (ii), requesting
      the Secretary of State to recover the excess benefits by deduction from the ben-
      efit prescribed in regulation 91 (recovery of excess benefit from prescribed
      benefits).

SCHEDULE 7

Regulation 70(3)

CONSTITUTION OF REVIEW BOARDS

1. A Review Board appointed by an authority listed in column (1) of the Table below shall consist of not less than three of the persons specified in relation to that authority in column (2) of that Table.

Table

(1)	(2)
Authority	*Composition of Board*
1. A billing authority other than the Common Council of the City of London.	**1.** Councillors of that Authority.
2. The Common Council of the City of London.	**2.** Persons who are mayor, aldermen or common councilmen.
3. In Scotland, a levying or district council.	**3.** Councillors of that authority or council.
4. In Scotland, a Development Corporation.	**4.** Members of a Development Corporation established for the purposes of a new town by Order made, or having effect as made under section 2(1) of the New Towns (Scotland) Act 1968.
5. Scottish Homes.	**5.** Members of the Scottish Homes.

2. The members of a Review Board shall appoint one of their number to be the Chairman.

The Council Tax Benefit (Transitional) Order 1992

(SI 1992/1909)

NOTES
Made: 3rd August 1992
Laid before Parliament: 10th August 1992
Coming into force: 31 August 1992

Citation, commencement and interpretation

1. (1) This Order may be cited as the Council Tax Benefit (Transitional) Order 1992 and shall come into force on 31st August 1992.

(2) In this Order unless the context otherwise requires—
"the Administration Act" means the Social Security Administration Act 1992;
"the Contributions and Benefits Act" means the Social Security Contributions and Benefits Act 1992;
"the 1992 Regulations" means the Council Tax Benefit (General) Regulations 1992;
"the 1989 Regulations" means the Community Charge Benefits (General) Regulations 1989;
"the 1987 Regulations" means the Housing Benefit (General) Regulations 1987;
"appropriate authority" means—

(a) in England and Wales, the billing authority to which Part I of the Local Government Finance Act 1992 refers,
(b) in Scotland, the levying authority to which Part II of that Act refers;

"community charge benefits" means the benefits of that name to which section 123(1) of the Contributions and Benefits Act refers;
"council tax benefit" means the benefit of that name to which section 123(1) of the Contributions and Benefits Act refers;
"housing benefit" means the benefit of that name to which section 123(1) of the Contributions and Benefits Act refers;
"the relevant date" means 1st April 1993;

and other expressions have the same meanings as in the 1992 Regulations.

(3) Unless the context otherwise requires, in this Order a reference in an article to a numbered paragraph is a reference to the paragraph in that article bearing that number.

Transitional provision for claims

2. (1) A claim for housing benefit under the 1987 Regulations or for community charge benefits under the 1989 Regulations made to the appropriate authority at any time in the period beginning with 31st August 1992 and ending with 31st March 1993, may in addition be treated as a claim for council tax benefit.

(2) Except in cases to which article 3 applies, where an appropriate authority is of the opinion that unless there is a change of circumstances a person will satisfy the conditions of entitlement for council tax benefit on the relevant date, it may invite him to claim council tax benefit from that date.

(3) Any claim for council tax benefit made under this Order or under the 1992 Regulations in the period prior to 1st April 1993, shall be treated as made in respect of a benefit period beginning on the relevant date, except where the claim is in respect of a period beginning on a later date, and regulation 62(10) of the 1992 Regulations (8 week time limit on claims in advance of entitlement) shall not apply to a claim so treated.

(4) A claim for community charge benefits under the 1989 Regulations made but not determined before the relevant date—

   (a)   shall remain effective, in respect of any period before that date, as a claim for benefit under those Regulations; and
   (b)   shall be treated, in respect of any later period, as a claim for council tax benefit under the 1992 Regulations.

(5) Subject to the provisions of this Order, any claim for council tax benefit under the 1992 Regulations made or treated as made in accordance with paragraphs (3) or (4)(b) may be determined before the relevant date in accordance with those Regulations.

(6) A determination which is made awarding council tax benefit under the 1992 Regulations in accordance with paragraph (5)—

   (a)   may award that benefit from the relevant date if it appears probable to the appropriate authority that the conditions for entitlement will be satisfied from that date;
   (b)   shall be subject to the conditions for entitlement satisfied on the relevant date; and
   (c)   may be reviewed if any question arises as to the satisfaction of those conditions.

(7) Regulation 66(3) of the 1992 Regulations (time within which claims are to be determined) shall not apply to claims for council tax benefit made or treated as made under this article until 14 days before the relevant date.

(8) To determine a person's entitlement to council tax benefit under the 1992 Regulations for the purposes of this Order, the appropriate authority may require that person to furnish such certificates, documents, information and evidence as it may reasonably require.

Waiver of claims

3. (1) Notwithstanding the provisions of section 1 of the Administration Act (necessity of claims for entitlement to benefit), the appropriate authority may determine that, with respect to any person who has been awarded either housing benefit or community charge benefits for a benefit period which includes 31st March 1993, it shall not be a condition of entitlement to council tax benefit under the 1992 Regulations that a claim for that benefit has been made; and where it so determines the provisions of the Administration Act and the Contributions and Benefits Act and regulations made thereunder shall apply, subject to the following provisions of this Order, as if a claim for that benefit had been duly made by or on behalf of a person to whom this paragraph applies in respect of a period beginning on the relevant date.

(2) Where by virtue of paragraph (1) a person's entitlement to council tax benefit falls to be determined as if a claim for it has been made, his entitlement may be determined at an earlier date than the relevant date if that person is entitled to either housing benefit or community charge benefit at that earlier date; and any entitlement to council tax benefit shall be determined in accordance with the 1992 Regulations as if the whole of those Regulations were in force.

(3) A determination which is made awarding council tax benefit under the 1992 Regulations in accordance with paragraph (2)—

(a) may award benefit from the relevant date if it appears probable to the appropriate authority that the conditions for entitlement will be satisfied from that date;

(b) shall be subject to the conditions for entitlement being satisfied on the relevant date; and

(c) may be reviewed if any question arises as to the satisfaction of those conditions.

Further provision for initial claims

4. (1) Subject to paragraph (2), where—

(a) a person is liable for council tax from the relevant date; and

(b) a claim for council tax benefit in respect of that tax is received by the designated office of the appropriate authority either—

(i) not more than 56 days after the relevant date, or

(ii) where the claimant does not receive his first council tax demand notice stating the payment he is required to make until after the relevant date, not more than 56 days from the date he receives that notice;

the claim for council tax benefit shall be treated as having been made on the relevant date.

(2) Where the claimant does not receive his first council tax demand notice until after the relevant date but the delay in the issue of the notice is due to his own act or omission, paragraph (1)(b)(ii) shall not apply in his case.

Determinations

5. (1) Where a determination, which is made by the appropriate authority before the relevant date in order that it may be effective from that date, is notified to a person before that date, regulation 69(2) of the 1992 Regulations (representations on reviews) shall have effect as though for the reference in that provision to a period of 6 weeks from the notification of the determination there were substituted a reference to a period of 6 weeks beginning on the relevant date.

(2) A determination under this Order shall be treated for the purposes of regulations 69 to 76 (reviews) as if it were a determination under those Regulations.

Recovery of overpayments of community charge benefits

6. Without prejudice to any other method of recovery, an overpayment of community charge benefits made to a person by an appropriate authority under the 1989 Regulations, which is recoverable under those Regulations by that authority, may be recovered by that authority, where council tax benefit is due from that authority to the person concerned, in the same manner as excess benefits may be recovered under the 1992 Regulations.

Outstanding community charge benefits

7. Where, on or after the relevant date, outstanding community charge benefit remains due to a person from an appropriate authority in respect of a benefit period ending on or before 31st March 1993, that authority may discharge that person's entitlement to the community charge benefit by a reduction in the amount that that person is or becomes liable to pay to that authority in respect of council tax for the financial year beginning on the relevant date.

Information to be supplied by an appropriate authority to the Secretary of State with respect to claimants for council tax benefit

8. In the period from 31st August 1992 to 31st March 1993, in addition to the information which is to be supplied by an appropriate authority to the Secretary of State in accordance with regulation 93 of the 1992 Regulations, an appropriate authority shall inform the Secretary of State of the name and national insurance number of any claimant or claimants for council tax benefit who are in receipt of income support and in respect of whom a determination has been made under this Order as to their entitlement to council tax benefit, provided that that information is required by the Secretary of State in connection with his functions under the Administration Act 1992 and the Contributions and Benefits Act 1992.

The Non-Domestic Rating (Payment of Interest) (Scotland) Regulations 1992

(SI 1992/2184)

NOTES
Made: 9th September 1992
Laid before Parliament: 10th September 1992
Coming into force: 1st October 1992

Citation and commencement

1. These Regulations may be cited as the Non-Domestic Rating (Payment of Interest) (Scotland) Regulations 1992 and shall come into force on 1st October 1992.

Interpretation

2. (1) In these Regulations, except where the context otherwise requires,-
    "the first payment date" means the earliest date on which any part of an amount being repaid by a rating authority was paid to them;

"liability" means a person's liability for rates in respect of the lands and heritages in question;

"overpayment" means—

    (a) in relation to the first (or only) relevant period, the amount by which the total of the sums paid in respect of rates by the ratepayer's in that relevant period exceeds his liability for that period, increased, in the case of an overpayment in error for which the first payment date was prior to 1st April 1990, by the amount by which the total of the sums so paid in error between the first payment date and 1st April 1990 exceeds his liability for the period between those dates; and

    (b) in relation to any other relevant period, the amount by which the total of the sums paid in respect of rates by the ratepayer—

        (i) in that relevant period;
        (ii) in each earlier relevant period; and
        (iii) in the case of an overpayment in error for which the first payment date was prior to 1st April 1990, in the period between the first payment date and 1st April 1990;

exceeds his liability for those periods, disregarding any amount constituting an overpayment in relation to any earlier relevant period;

"relevant date" means—

    (a) in the case of a repayment arising from a payment of rates made in error, the later of—

        (i) the first payment date; and
        (ii) 1st April 1990; and

    (b) in any other case, the effective date of the alteration of a valuation on a valuation roll which gave rise to the repayment in question;

"repayment" means the repayment, or as the case may be the crediting, by a rating authority of an amount in respect of overpaid rates;

"repayment day" means the day on which a repayment is or was made;

"the repealed provision" means section 9A of the Local Government (Scotland) Act 1975 as in force immediately prior to 1st October 1992;

"year" means any period of twelve months beginning with 1st April.

(2) For the purposes of these Regulations—

    (a) (i) the period commencing on 1st April of the year in which the repayment day falls and ending with the day immediately before that day is a relevant period if the person's liability subsists for the whole of that period;

        (ii) where the person's liability subsists only for part of that period, that part is a relevant period;

        (iii) any other complete year within the period beginning with the first day of the year in which the relevant date falls and ending on the day immediately preceding the repayment day is a relevant period if the person's liability subsists for the whole of that year; and

        (iv) where the person's liability subsists only for a part of such a year, that part is a relevant period; and

(b) (i) any complete year within the period beginning with the day after the end of the relevant period and ending on the day immediately preceding the repayment day; and

(ii) any part of any other year within that period;

are each subsequent periods in relation to that relevant period.

Entitlement to interest

3. (1) Subject to paragraph (2), where any amount has been paid to a rating authority in respect of rates either—

(a) in error; or

(b) in consequence of the entry on to a valuation roll in force on or after 1st April 1990 of a valuation which has subsequently been reduced;

and the rating authority make, or have after that date made, a repayment of the amount, the authority shall also pay to the person to whom the repayment is or was made interest on the amount, calculated in accordance with regulation 4 or, as the case may be, regulation 5 or 6.

(2) Where—

(a) such a repayment as is referred to in paragraph (1) is, or has been, made to a person by a rating authority;

(b) the rating authority have obtained against that person a summary warrant or a decree in an action for payment in respect of rates for a year, or part of a year, payable as regards the same lands and heritages as those by reference to which the overpayment of rates was made; and

(c) that year was, or included, a relevant period;

paragraph (1) shall not apply in respect of such part of the repayment as is referable to the overpayment in relation to that relevant period.

Calculation of interest — repayment on or after 1st October 1992

4. (1) Where such a repayment as is referred to in paragraph (1) of regulation 3 is made by a rating authority on or after 1st October 1992, the amount of interest payable shall be calculated—

(a) in a case where the repayment day falls within the same year as the relevant date and liability subsists on the day before the repayment day, in accordance with the formula—

$$\frac{A \times B \times R}{2 \times C \times 100} \quad \text{where—}$$

A is the amount of the overpayment in relation to the relevant period;

B is the number of days in the relevant period or, where the relevant date falls after the beginning of that period, the number of days in the period beginning on the relevant date and ending on the last day of the relevant period;

C is the number of days in the year; and

R   is the appropriate rate, expressed as a percentage;

(b) in any other case, by aggregating the amounts ascertained—

(i) in respect of each relevant period, in accordance with the formula—

$$\frac{D \times E \times R}{2 \times C \times 100} \quad \text{where—}$$

C   and R have the same meanings as in sub-paragraph (a);

D   is the amount of the overpayment in relation to the period in question; and

E   is the number of days in the relevant period or, where the period falls within the same year as the relevant date and that date falls after the beginning of that period, the number of days in the period beginning on the relevant date and ending on the last day of the relevant period; and

(ii) in respect of each subsequent period, in accordance with the formula—

$$\frac{F \times G \times R}{C \times 100} \quad \text{where—}$$

C   and R have the same meanings as in sub-paragraph (a);

F   is the amount of the overpayment in relation to the relevant period to which the subsequent period in question relates; and

G   is the number of days in the subsequent period in question.

(2) In paragraph (1), "the appropriate rate" means—

(a) in relation to a period constituting, or falling within, the year commencing on 1st April 1990, 14%;

(b) in relation to a period constituting, or falling within, the year commencing on 1st April 1991, 12%;

(c) in relation to a period constituting, or falling within, the year commencing on 1st April 1992, 9.5%;

(d) in relation to a period constituting, or falling within, the year commencing on 1st April 1993 or any subsequent year, the rate equivalent to one percentage point less than the base rate quoted by the reference banks and effective on 15th March (or, if that day is not a business day, the next business day) of the preceding year; or if different base rates are quoted and so effective, the rate equivalent to one percentage point less than the rate which, when the base rate quoted by each bank is ranked in a descending sequence of seven, is fourth in the sequence.

(3) In paragraph (2), "the reference banks", in relation to any 15th March, are the seven largest institutions—

(a) authorised by the Bank of England under the Banking Act 1987; and

(b) incorporated in and carrying on a deposit-taking business within the United Kingdom;

which quote a base rate in sterling effective as mentioned in sub-paragraph (d) of paragraph (2); and the size of an institution is to be determined by reference to the total gross assets of that institution together with any subsidiary (within the meaning of section 736 of the Companies Act 1985 denominated in sterling, as shown in its audited end-year accounts last published before the relevant 15th March.

Calculation of interest - repayment after 1st August 1991 and before 1st October 1992

5. (1) Where such a repayment as is referred to in paragraph (1) of regulation 3 was made by a rating authority after 1st August 1991 and before 1st October 1992, the amount of interest payable shall be calculated in accordance with paragraph (2) or, as the case may be, paragraph (3).

(2) Where the amount of interest in respect of a repayment would, if calculated in accordance with regulation 4, be less than the amount of interest in respect of that repayment paid by the rating authority under the repealed provision, no interest shall be payable in respect of that repayment under these Regulations.

(3) Where the amount of interest so calculated in respect of a repayment would be greater than the amount of interest in respect of that repayment paid by the authority under the repealed provision, the interest payable under these Regulations shall be calculated in accordance with the formula—

$(H-J) + K$ where—

H   is the amount of interest on the repayment calculated in accordance with regulation 4;

J   is the amount of interest in respect of that repayment paid under the repealed provision; and

K   is the product of the formula specified in paragraph (4).

(4) The formula specified in this paragraph is—

$$\frac{(H-J) \times L \times 12}{36,600} + \frac{(H-J) \times M \times 9.5}{36,500} \text{ where—}$$

H   and J have the same meanings as in paragraph (3);

L   is the number of days beginning on the repayment day and ending on 31st March 1992; and

M   is the number of days beginning on 1st April 1992 or, if the repayment day is later, on the repayment day and ending on the day on which interest payable in terms of this regulation is paid.

Calculation of interest - repayment on or before 1st August 1991

6. (1) Where such a repayment as is referred to in paragraph (1) of regulation 3 was made by a rating authority on or before 1st August 1991, the amount of interest payable shall be calculated in accordance with the formula—

$H + N$ where—

H has the same meaning as in paragraph (3) of regulation 5; and

N is the product of the formula specified in paragraph (2).

(2) The formula specified in this paragraph is—

$$\frac{H \times P \times 14}{36,500} + \frac{H \times Q \times 12}{36,600} + \frac{H \times R \times 9.5}{36,500} \quad \text{where}-$$

H   has the same meaning as in paragraph (1);

P   is the number of days beginning on the repayment day and ending on 31st March 1991;

Q   is the number of days beginning on 1st April 1991 or, if the repayment day is later, on the repayment day and ending on 31st March 1992; and

R   is the number of days beginning on 1st April 1992 and ending on the day on which interest payable in terms of this regulation is paid.

Recovery of interest

7. (1) Where—

(a) any amount in respect of rates is repaid, or has after 1st August 1991 been repaid, to any person by a rating authority either—

    (i)   in error; or
    (ii) in consequence of the entry on to the valuation roll of a valuation which is subsequently increased;

(b) any interest in respect of that amount is, or was, paid by the authority to the person under these Regulations or the repealed provision; and
(c) the authority recover the amount;

they may also recover interest in accordance with paragraph (2).

(2) The amount of interest which the rating authority may recover under paragraph (1) shall be equal to the amount of interest which would not have been paid had the amount of rates being recovered never been repaid to the person.

The Council Tax (Dwellings and Part Residential Subjects) (Scotland) Regulations 1992

(SI 1992/2955)

NOTES
Made: 23rd November 1992
Laid before Parliament: 7th December 1992
Coming into force: 28th December 1992

Citation and commencement

1. These Regulations may be cited as the Council Tax (Dwellings and Part Residential Subjects) (Scotland) Regulations 1992 and shall come into force on 28th December 1992.

Interpretation

2. In these Regulations, unless the context otherwise requires—
"the Act" means the Local Government Finance Act 1992;
"hostel" has the same meaning as in sub-paragraph (2) of paragraph 8 of Schedule 1 to the Act;
"nursing home" has the same meaning as in that sub-paragraph;
"private hospital" has the same meaning as in that sub-paragraph;
"pupils receiving school education" shall be construed in accordance with the Education (Scotland) Act 1980(c);
"relevant person" means, in relation to any lands and heritages—

   (a) subject to paragraphs (b) and (c) below, the owner;
   (b) subject to paragraph (c) below, if they are let for a period of 12 months or more, the tenant; or
   (c) if they are sublet for such a period, the subtenant;

"residential care home" has the same meaning as in sub-paragraph (2) of paragraph 8 of Schedule 1 to the Act;
"school boarding house" means any premises used for the boarding of pupils receiving school education;
"school dormitory accommodation" means any accommodation used for sleeping purposes by pupils receiving school education;
"student" has the same meaning as in sub-paragraph (2) of paragraph 4 of Schedule 1 to the Act;
"voluntary organisation" has the same meaning as in section 94(1) of the Social Work (Scotland) Act 1968.

Variation of definition of dwelling

3. The definition of dwelling in section 72(2) of the Act is hereby further varied(b) in accordance with regulations 4 and 5 below.

4. There shall be included as a dwelling any lands and heritages or parts thereof—

   (a) which fall within the classes specified in Schedule 1 to these Regulations; and
   (b) which would, but for the provisions of section 73(1) of the Act—

   (i)   be entered separately in the valuation roll; or
   (ii) in the case of parts of lands and heritages, form part of a separate entry in the valuation roll.

5. There shall be excluded from the definition of dwelling any lands and heritages or parts thereof which fall within the classes specified in Schedule 2 to these Regulations.

Definition of part residential subjects—exceptions

6. The classes of lands and heritages which are prescribed for the purposes of paragraph (b) of the definition of part residential subjects in section 99(1) of the Act (lands and heritages excluded from that definition) are—

   (a) any lands and heritages or parts thereof excluded from the definition of dwelling under paragraph 3 of Schedule 2 to these Regulations; and

(b) any part of—

    (i) a hostel;
    (ii) a nursing home;
    (iii) a private hospital; or
    (iv) a residential care home;

which is not used wholly or mainly as the sole or main residence of a person employed there.

Amendment of the Council Tax (Dwellings) (Scotland) Regulations 1992

[*Amends the Council Tax (Dwellings) (Scotland) Regulations 1992.*]

SCHEDULE 1   Regulation 4

DEFINITION OF DWELLING—INCLUSIONS

Bed and breakfast accommodation

1. Any lands and heritages—

(a) which are the sole or main residence of a person;
(b) which are intended by such a person to be made available for letting, on a commercial basis and with a view to the realisation of profits, as bed and breakfast accommodation to no more than 6 persons per night;
(c) which are not made available for letting over the limit specified in sub-paragraph (b) above; and
(d) which would, but for being available for letting as referred to in sub-paragraph (b) above, be such lands and heritages as are described in sub-paragraph (i) of section 72(2)(a) of the Act.

Student halls

2. Any lands and heritages—

(a) which are used (or, if not in use, were last used) predominantly as residential accommodation by students; and
(b) in which there are facilities which are available for sharing by some or all of the students.

Barracks

3. Any lands and heritages—

(a) of which the Secretary of State for Defence is the owner;
(b) which are held for the purposes of armed forces accommodation; and
(c) which are the sole or main residence of at least one member of the armed forces or, if unoccupied, are likely to be the sole or main residence of such a person when next occupied.

Communal residential establishments

4. Any lands and heritages which are used (or, if not in use, were last used) wholly as the sole or main residence of persons who reside there and in which there are facilities available for sharing by some or all of those persons, other than any part of—

$$\frac{(A - B) \times C}{C + D}$$

Where—

A   is the gross council tax income produced in the district for that year calculated in accordance with regulation 5 below;

B   is the aggregate of the deductions specified in regulation 6 below to be made from that gross council tax income for that year;

C   is the amount set for that year under paragraph (a) of section 93(1) of the Act by the council of the district; and

D   is the amount set for that year under the said paragraph (a) by the council of the region within which the district is situated.

Gross council tax income

5. For the purpose of the definition of A in regulation 4 above, the gross council tax income produced in the district for any financial year shall be calculated by aggregating the following amounts:—

(a)   the total amount of the regional and district council tax for that year in respect of dwellings within the district, payment of which has been demanded by or on behalf of the levying authority and which has been paid or remains payable to that authority;

(b)   the amount of any contributions for that year made by the Crown to the levying authority in lieu of council tax in respect of such dwellings;

(c)   the amount of council tax benefit for that year granted by or on behalf of the levying authority under the Council Tax Benefit (General) Regulations 1992 in respect of such dwellings;

(d)   the amount by which the total amount payable as council tax for that year in respect of such dwellings has been reduced by virtue of regulations under section 80 of the Act (other than the Council Tax (Reductions for Disabilities) (Scotland) Regulations 1992; and

(e)   any amount falling within paragraph (a) above which has been paid after being written off by the levying authority as irrecoverable.

Deductions from gross council tax income

6. For the purposes of the definition of B in regulation 4 above, the deductions to be made from the gross council tax income produced in the district for any financial year are as follows:-

(a)   any amount falling within paragraph (a) of regulation 5 above which has been paid to a levying authority by a person and which—

(i)   has subsequently been repaid to him; or

(ii)   has subsequently been credited in respect of a liability of his to pay an amount which does not fall within that paragraph; and

(b)   any amount falling within paragraph (a) of regulation 5 above which is written off by the levying authority as irrecoverable.

The Non-Domestic Rating Contributions (Scotland) Regulations 1992
(SI 1992/3061)

NOTES
Made: 7th December 1992
Laid before Parliament: 10th December 1992
Coming into force: 31st December 1992

Citation and commencement

1. These Regulations may be cited as the Non-Domestic Rating Contributions (Scotland) Regulations 1992 and shall come into force on 31st December 1992.

Interpretation

2. In these Regulations, unless the context otherwise requires—
"the Act" means the Local Government Finance Act 1992;
"the 1947 Act" means the Local Government (Scotland) Act 1947;
"the 1956 Act" means the Valuation and Rating (Scotland) Act 1956;
"the 1962 Act" means the Local Government (Financial Provisions etc.) (Scotland) Act 1962;
"the 1966 Act" means the Local Government (Scotland) Act 1966;
"the 1975 Act" means the Local Government (Scotland) Act 1975;
"authority" means a levying authority;
"provisional amount" means the provisional amount arrived at under paragraph 11(2) of Schedule 12 to the Act as regards an authority for a year, or the amount for the time being treated as that amount in accordance with regulation 6 of these Regulations:
"relevant day" means a day in a relevant year;
"relevant year" means a year for which a calculation of a non-domestic rating contribution or a calculation or recalculation of a provisional amount is being made;
"year" means a financial year.

Calculation of non-domestic rating contributions

3. The rules for the calculation under paragraph 11 of Schedule 12 to the Act of an authority's non-domestic rating contribution for a year are the rules contained in Schedule 1 to these Regulations.

Assumptions relating to provisional amounts

4. A calculation under paragraph 11(2) of Schedule 12 to the Act shall be made on the basis of the information before the Secretary of State at the time he makes the calculation and subject to the assumptions prescribed in Schedule 2 to these Regulations.

Recalculation of provisional amounts

5.—(1) Regulation 6 below applies as regards an authority for a year if—

(a) a provisional amount has been arrived at as regards the authority for the year; and

(b) the prescribed conditions are fulfilled.

(2) The prescribed conditions are—

(a) that the authority have on a day in the year calculated an amount, under paragraph (3) below, which is equal to or less than 97% of the provisional amount for the authority for the year;

(b) that the authority have notified the Secretary of State of the amount calculated under paragraph (3) below and of the day on which that amount was calculated; and

(c) that the Secretary of State believes that the amount calculated by the authority under paragraph (3) below is likely to have been calculated in accordance with that paragraph and informs the authority of his belief.

(3) The amount calculated under this paragraph is the total of the amounts calculated in accordance with Parts I and II of Schedule 3 to these Regulations.

6. Where this regulation applies, for the purposes of paragraph 11 of Schedule 12 to the Act the provisional amount for the authority for the year is to be treated as being the amount resulting from the calculation under regulation 5(3) above by virtue of which this regulation applies.

Repayments as a result of a recalculation

7.—(1) Where regulation 6 applies as regards an authority for a year, the Secretary of State shall repay to the authority at such time as he decides the amount calculated in accordance with paragraph (2) below.

(2) The amount is the difference between—

(a) the total of the amounts paid by the authority to the Secretary of State, under paragraph 11(4) of Schedule 12 to the Act, on relevant days preceding the day on which the calculation referred to in regulation 6 was made; and

(b) the amount calculated in accordance with the formula—

$$\frac{A}{B} \times C$$

where—

A is the amount being treated as the provisional amount for the authority under regulation 6;

B is the provisional amount having effect for the authority immediately prior to application of that regulation; and

C is the total of the amounts directed by the Secretary of State to be paid by the authority, under paragraph 11(4) of Schedule 12 to the Act, on relevant days preceding the day on which the calculation referred to in regulation 6 was made.

Reduced payments as a result of a recalculation

8. Where regulation 6 applies as regards an authority for a year, the amount of an instalment directed by the Secretary of State to be paid by the authority, under paragraph 11(4) of Schedule 12 to the Act, on or after the day on which the calculation referred to in regulation 6 was made shall be treated as being the amount calculated in accordance with the formula—

$$\frac{A}{B} \times C$$

where—

A and B have the same meanings as in regulation 7; and

C is the amount the Secretary of State directed to be paid by the authority in the instalment.

Information which may be left out of account in making a calculation

9. In making a calculation under paragraph 11(5)(a) of Schedule 12 to the Act, an authority may leave out of account any information which—

(a) it is not reasonably practicable for them to take into account; and
(b) was received by them after 31st May in the year immediately following that to which the calculation relates.

SCHEDULE 1

Regulation 3

RULES FOR THE CALCULATION OF NON-DOMESTIC RATING CONTRIBUTIONS

1.—(1) In relation to each authority, there shall be calculated for the year commencing on 1st April 1993 and each subsequent year the amounts described in paragraphs 2 to 10 of this Schedule.

(2) From the amount described in paragraph 2 there shall be deducted the amounts described in paragraphs 3 to 8, and to that amount there shall be added the amounts described in paragraphs 9 and 10.

(3) The amount calculated under sub-paragraph (2) above shall be the authority's non-domestic rating contribution for the year.

Gross amount due to the authority

2. The amount which is the total of—

(a) the amounts paid or payable to the authority in respect of non-domestic rates for the relevant year; and
(b) the amounts paid or payable to the authority by way of a contribution in aid for the relevant year made in respect of lands and heritages which, but for any rule of law relating to Crown exemption, would be liable to non-domestic rates (including amounts paid or payable under section 20 of the 1956 Act);

without taking into account—

(i)   any apportionment carried out by the assessor under section 243A(1) of the 1947 Act;

(ii) any relief granted by the authority under section 244 of that Act; or

(iii) any reduction or remission granted by the authority under section 4(5) of the 1962 Act.

Deductions from gross amount

3. The amount which is the difference between the amount calculated under paragraph 2 of this Schedule for the relevant year and the amount which would be so calculated if any apportionment carried out by the assessor under section 243A(1) of the 1947 Act were taken into account.

4. The amount which is the difference between the amount calculated under paragraph 2 of this Schedule for the relevant year and the amount which would be so calculated if any relief granted by the authority under section 244 of the 1947 Act were taken into account.

5. The amount which is the difference between the amount calculated under paragraph 2 of this Schedule for the relevant year and the amount which would be so calculated if any reduction or remission granted by the authority under section 4(5) of the 1962 Act were taken into account.

6. The amounts which—

(a)   are payable to the authority in respect of non-domestic rates for the relevant year or a preceding year commencing after 31st March 1993;

(b)   in the opinion of the authority are bad debts which should be written off or are doubtful debts for which provision should be made; and

(c)   have not been taken into account as amounts described in this paragraph in the calculation made under paragraph 11(5) of Schedule 12 to the Act for a preceding year.

7. The amounts which—

(a)   as amounts paid or payable to the authority in respect of non-domestic rates for a preceding year were taken into account by the authority in the calculation made under paragraph 11(5) of Schedule 12 to the Act for that year;

(b)   have since been repaid or are now repayable by the authority; and

(c)   have not been taken into account by the authority as amounts described in this paragraph in the calculation made for a preceding year under paragraph 11(5) of Schedule 12 to the Act.

8. The amounts which have been paid in the relevant year by the authority under the Non-Domestic Rating (Payment of Interest) (Scotland) Regulations 1992 as interest in respect of overpaid non-domestic rates.

Additions to gross amount

9. The amounts which—

(a)   have been taken into account by the authority as amounts described in paragraph 6 of this Schedule in the calculation made for a preceding year under paragraph 11(5) of Schedule 12 to the Act;

(b)   have now been paid or are now payable to the authority; and

(c)   have not been taken into account by the authority as amounts described in this paragraph in such a calculation.

10. The amounts which—

(a) were amounts payable to the authority in respect of non-domestic rates for a preceding year or by way of such a contribution for that year as is described in sub-paragraph (b) of paragraph 2 of this Schedule;

(b) were not taken into account by the authority as amounts described in that paragraph in the calculation made for that year under paragraph 11(5) of Schedule 12 to that Act;

(c) have now been paid or are now payable to the authority; and

(d) have not been taken into account by the authority as amounts described in this paragraph in the calculation made for any preceding year under paragraph 11(5) of Schedule 12 to the Act.

SCHEDULE 2 Regulation 4

ASSUMPTIONS RELATING TO PROVISIONAL AMOUNTS

1.—(1) The assumptions prescribed in relation to paragraph 2 of Schedule 1 to these Regulations are the assumptions prescribed in paragraph 2 below.

(2) The assumptions prescribed in relation to paragraphs 3, 4, 6, 7, 9 and 10 of that Schedule are the assumptions prescribed in paragraphs 3 to 5 below.

Assumptions as to gross amount

2.—(1) It shall be assumed that the lands and heritages to be shown on the authority's valuation roll for each relevant day will be the lands and heritages shown on that roll on 31st December in the immediately preceding year.

(2) Subject to sub-paragraph (3) below, it shall be assumed that the rateable value of the lands and heritages described in sub-paragraph (1) above will on each relevant day be the rateable value shown for those lands and heritages on the authority's valuation roll on 31st December in the immediately preceding year.

(3) The assumption specified in sub-paragraph (2) above shall not apply in respect of such lands as, on 31st December in the immediately preceding year in question, have their rateable values for that year prescribed in or under an order made under section 6 of the 1975 Act.

(4) Subject to sub-paragraph (5) below, it shall be assumed that the occupier of lands and heritages on each relevant day will be the occupier on 31st December in the immediately preceding year.

(5) In respect of each day in the year commencing on 1st April 1993, it shall be assumed that—

(a) the occupier of any lands and heritages which—

(i) are occupied by a local authority on 31st December 1992 for, or in connection with, the purposes of a college of further education specified in Schedule 1 to the Transfer of Colleges of Further Education (Scotland) Order 1992; and

(ii) if owned by a local authority immediately before 1st April 1993, will fall to be transferred to the board of management of such a college of further education in terms of section 16 of the Further and Higher Education (Scotland) Act 1992;

will be that board of management; and

(b) any rate leviable in respect of those lands and heritages will, in terms of subsection (2) of section 4 of the 1962 Act, not exceed one-fifth of the rate which would be leviable apart from the provisions of that subsection.

(6) Where on 31st December in the immediately preceding year lands and heritages are unoccupied, it shall be assumed that they will remain unoccupied on each relevant day.

(7) It shall be assumed that the authority will not, in respect of any relevant day, exercise the discretion available to them under section 24(1) of the 1966 Act to levy rates on lands and heritages in their area which are unoccupied.

(8) It shall be assumed that the total amount described in paragraph 2 of Schedule 1 to these Regulations is the amount calculated under that paragraph in accordance with the assumptions prescribed in sub-paragraphs (1) to (7) above, multiplied by 0.985.

Assumptions as to deductions from and additions to gross amount

3. Where on 31st December in the immediately preceding year an apportioned value is being treated, in terms of section 243A(2) of the 1947 Act, as the rateable value of any lands and heritages, it shall be assumed for the purpose of calculating the amount described in paragraph 3 of Schedule 1 to these Regulations that that apportioned value will be so treated as the rateable value of those lands and heritages on each relevant day.

4. It shall be assumed that the amount described in paragraphs 4, 7, 9 and 10 of Schedule 1 to these Regulations will be nil.

5.—(1) It shall be assumed that the amounts described in paragraph 6 of Schedule 1 to these Regulations will be 1% of the amount described in sub-paragraph (2) below.

(2) The amount referred to in sub-paragraph (1) above is the amount described in paragraph 2 of Schedule 1 to these Regulations (calculated in accordance with the provisions of paragraph 2 of this Schedule), less the deductions from that amount prescribed in paragraphs 3 and 5 of Schedule 1 to these Regulations (calculated in accordance with the provisions of paragraph 3 of this Schedule).

SCHEDULE 3   Regulation 5(3)

RECALCULATION OF PROVISIONAL AMOUNTS

PART I

DAYS PRECEDING THE DAY OF THE CALCULATION

1.—(1) The amount calculated in accordance with this Part of this Schedule is an amount calculated under regulation 3, as if it were a calculation under paragraph 11(5) of Schedule 12 to the Act of the authority's non-domestic rating contribution for the year.

(2) For the purposes of sub-paragraph (1) above, Schedule 1 to these Regulations shall have effect subject to the modification that references to the relevant year in that Schedule shall be treated as references to that part of the relevant year preceding the day on which the calculations in accordance with this Schedule are made.

PART II

DAYS ON AND AFTER THE DAY OF THE CALCULATION

2.—(1) The amount calculated in accordance with this Part of this Schedule is an amount calculated, under regulations 3 and 4, as if it were a calculation of the authority's non-domestic rating contribution for the year being made by them (rather than the Secretary of State) under paragraph 11(2) of Schedule 12 to the Act.

(2) For the purposes of sub-paragraph (1) above, Schedules 1 and 2 to these Regulations shall have effect subject to paragraph 3 of this Schedule.

3.—(1) The references in Schedule 1 to the relevant year shall be treated as references to that part of the relevant year after the day immediately preceding the day on which the calculations in accordance with the Schedule are made.

(2) The references in Schedule 2 to relevant days shall be treated as references to relevant days on and after the day on which the calculations in accordance with this Schedule are made.

(3) In paragraph 2 of Schedule 2—

(a) the references to 31st December in the immediately preceding year shall be treated as references to the day on which the calculations in accordance with this Schedule are made; and

(b) sub-paragraph (3) shall be disregarded.

The Council Tax (Transitional Reduction Scheme) (Scotland) Regulations 1993

(SI 1993/277)

NOTES
Made: 16th February 1993
Laid before Parliament: 19th February 1993
Coming into force: 1st April 1993

PART I
GENERAL

Citation and commencement

1. These Regulation may be cited as the Council Tax (Transitional Reduction Scheme) (Scotland) Regulations 1993 and shall come into force on 1st April 1993.

Interpretation

2.—(1) In these Regulations, except insofar as the context otherwise requires—

"the Act" means the Local Government Finance Act 1992;
"the 1987 Act" means the Abolition of Domestic Rates Etc. (Scotland) Act 1987;
"the Benefit Regulations" means the Council Tax Benefit (General) Regulations 1992;
"the Disabilities Regulations" means the Council Tax (Reduction for Disabilities) (Scotland) Regulations 1992;
"adjusted council tax", in relation to a local authority, means the amount determined in accordance with the following formula—

$$\frac{A}{B}$$

where—
A is the lower of—

  (a) the total amount which the authority, in determining their set council tax, have calculated as being that required to be raised from their council tax for the prescribed year to meet or cover the expenses and contingencies referred to in subsection (3) of section 93 of the Act; and

  (b) the amount appearing in column 2 of the Schedule to these Regulations opposite the name of the authority in column 1 of that Schedule; and

  B is the figure appearing in column 3 of the Schedule to these Regulations opposite the name of the authority in column 1 of that Schedule;

"alternative valuation band", in relation to a dwelling, means the valuation band which appears immediately above the relevant valuation band in the Table set out in section 74(2) of the Act;

"applicable council tax" means—

(a) in a case where a local authority have set (or are deemed to have set) a substituted or reduced amount of council tax in respect of the prescribed year, the lower of—

  (i) that substituted or reduced amount; and

  (ii) the authority's adjusted council tax; and

(b) in any other case, the lower of—

  (i) the authority's set council tax; and

  (ii) the authority's adjusted council tax;

"chargeable amount", in relation to a person, a dwelling and a day, means the amount which (but for these Regulations) the person would be liable to pay as council tax in respect of that dwelling and day, having taken account of section 79 of the Act and the Disabilities Regulations but leaving out of account any reduction attributable to the Benefit Regulations;

"prescribed year" means the financial year beginning on 1st April 1993;

"qualifying dwelling" means a dwelling—

(a) in which at the end of 31st March 1993 a person is solely or mainly resident; and

(b) which is not, in respect of 1st April 1993, an exempt dwelling in terms of section 72(6) of the Act;

"register" means a Community Charges Register established under section 13 of the 1987 Act;

"relevant valuation band", in relation to a dwelling, means the valuation band shown as applicable to the dwelling in the levying authority's valuation list;

"set council tax" means the amount first set under paragraph (a) of section 93(1) of the Act by a local authority in respect of the prescribed year.

(2) Any reference in these Regulations to the scheme council tax for dwellings listed in a valuation band is a reference to—

  (a) in the case of a dwelling situated within the area of an islands council, the amount which would have been set or determined under subsection (1) of section 93 of the Act for the prescribed year in respect of dwellings in that band if that council had set an amount under paragraph (a) of that subsection equal to their applicable council tax;

  (b) in any other case, the total of the amounts which would have been set or determined under that subsection for the prescribed year in respect of dwellings in that band if both the regional and district councils within the areas of which the dwelling is situated had set amounts under that paragraph equal to their applicable council taxes.

(3) Any reference in these Regulations to a liable person is a reference to a person who is liable (whether solely or jointly and severally with another person or per-

sons) to pay to a levying authority an amount in respect of council tax for a particular dwelling; and references to an amount which a person is liable to pay shall be construed accordingly.

Prescribed year

3. The financial year beginning on 1st April 1993 is prescribed as the year for which these Regulations apply.

PART II
REDUCTIONS RELATED TO COMMUNITY CHARGES

Persons to whom Part II applies

4. A person is an eligible person for the purposes of this Part in respect of a particular day in the prescribed year if, as regards that day—
   (a) he is a liable person in respect of a qualifying dwelling; and
   (b) the dwelling is the sole or main residence of any person.

Calculation of amount payable

5.—(1) Where a person is an eligible person in respect of a day, the amount which he is liable to pay as council tax in respect of that day and the qualifying dwelling in question shall, subject to paragraphs (4) to (6), be equal to the difference between—
   (a) the chargeable amount; and
   (b) the amount determined in accordance with the following formula—

$$\frac{(T \times P) - (C + S)}{365}$$

(2) In paragraph (1)—
   (a) T is an amount equal to the scheme council tax for—
      (i)   in the case of a dwelling in respect of which, as regards 1st April 1993, a person is an eligible person for the purposes of the Disabilities Regulations, dwellings listed in the alternative valuation band; or
      (ii) in any other case, dwellings listed in the relevant valuation band;
   (b) P is the percentage which is obtained by deducting from 100 per cent the percentage discount (if any) applicable, in terms of section 79 of the Act, to the council tax payable in respect of the dwelling in question and 1st April 1993;
   (c) C is the product of the formula—

   $(A \times N) - R,$

   Where—

      A is—
      (i)   the personal community charge determined in respect of the financial year beginning on 1st April 1992 by the islands council within the area of which the dwelling in question is situated; or
      (ii) the aggregate of the personal community charges determined in respect of that financial year by the regional and district councils within the areas of which the dwelling in question is situated;

N is the number of persons who—

(i) are entered in the register as being solely or mainly resident on 31st March 1993 at the address of the dwelling in question and are liable on that date to pay the personal community charge; or

(ii) by virtue of being solely or mainly resident in that dwelling on that date, are liable to pay an amount by way of contribution under section 11(11) of the 1987 Act (collective community charge contributions); and

R is an amount equal to the difference (if any) between—

(i) the aggregate of the amounts which, on the assumptions specified in paragraph (3), would have been payable to the levying authority in question in respect of personal community charge by persons entered in the register as being solely or mainly resident at the address of the dwelling in question on 31st March 1993 and liable to pay that charge on that date, as regards days in the financial year ending on that date on which they were entered in the register as being solely or mainly resident there; and

(ii) the aggregate of the amounts which would have been so payable by those persons, but for section 8(5) and (6A) of the 1987 Act and regulations under section 9A of that Act; and

(d) S is the amount specified in column (2) of the following Table in relation to such valuation band shown in column (1) of that Table as is—

(i) in the case of a dwelling in respect of which, as regards 1st April 1993, a person is an eligible person for the purposes of the Disabilities Regulations, the alternative valuation band;

(ii) in any other case, the relevant valuation band;

TABLE

(1)	(2)
Valuation band	Amount
A	£ 91
B	£104
C	£117
D	£130
E	£143
F	£156
G	£169
H	£182.

(3) The assumptions referred to in the definition of "R" in paragraph (2)(c) are that—

(a) so far as relevant for the purposes of section 8(5) or (6A), or regulations under section 9A, of the 1987 Act, the circumstances of an individual and a state of affairs on 31st March 1993 had been his circumstances and the state of affairs on each day of the financial year ending on that day; and

(b) any reduction in the amounts referred to in paragraph (i) of that definition attributable to the Community Charge Benefits (General) Regulations 1989 had not been applied.

(4) Where the amount determined in any case under sub-paragraph (b) of paragraph (1) is a negative amount, there shall be no reduction applicable under these Regulations in the amount payable as council tax in that case.

(5) Where the amount determined in any case under sub-paragraph (b) of paragraph (1) is equal to or greater than the amount under sub-paragraph (a) of that paragraph, the amount payable as council tax in that case shall be nil.

(6) Where a person—

(a) is, by virtue of paragraph (1), liable to pay a smaller amount as council tax in respect of a dwelling and a day than he would otherwise have been; and

(b) is entitled under the Benefit Regulations to council tax benefit in respect of that dwelling and day;

the amount which he is liable to pay in respect of that dwelling and day shall be the amount ascertained in accordance with paragraph (1) less the amount of his council tax benefit for that day.

PART III

APPEALS

Appeals

6.—(1) Where a levying authority make a decision relating to the application or operation of these Regulations in relation to a person, the authority shall, if requested in writing by the person so affected, provide him with a written statement of their decision and the reasons for it; and any such statement shall be dated and shall be sent within 14 days from the date on which it is requested or as soon as is reasonable practicable thereafter.

(2) No appeal may be made to a valuation appeal committee in respect of any decision of a levying authority relating solely to the application or operation of these Regulations; but a person aggrieved by such a decision may appeal to a review board appointed by the relevant levying authority and constituted as mentioned in regulation 70(3) of the Benefit Regulations.

Notice of appeal

7. The appellant shall give notice of appeal in writing to the levying authority.

Procedure for appeals.

8.—(1) Regulations 71(2) to (9) and 72(4) and (5) of the Benefit Regulations shall apply with the necessary modifications for the purposes of an appeal under these Regulations as they apply for the purposes of a further review.

(2) A levying authority shall comply with any decision of their review board.

SCHEDULE
ADJUSTED COUNCIL TAX

Regulation 2(1)

Column 1 Local Authority	Column 2 Amount £	Column 3 Figure
Regional Councils		
Borders	9,902,000	37,645
Central	32,593,000	89,710
Dumfries and Galloway	15,666,000	50,456
Fife	42,436,000	113,687
Grampian	54,011,000	178,470
Highland	23,315,000	70,971
Lothian	109,638,000	275,127
Strathclyde	227,919,000	739,592
Tayside	43,897,000	131,772
District Councils		
Berwickshire	1,139,000	7,047
Ettrick and Lauderdale	1,988,000	12,187
Roxburgh	1,999,000	12,159
Tweeddale	986,000	6,251
Clackmannan	2,181,000	15,194
Falkirk	5,456,000	44,539
Stirling	4,608,000	29,977
Annandale and Eskdale	2,081,000	12,670
Nithsdale	3,139,000	19,000
Stewartry	1,437,000	8,999
Wigtown	1,625,000	9,786
Dunfermline	5,000,000	40,822
Kirkcaldy	5,661,000	46,216
North East Fife	3,264,000	26,649
Aberdeen City	10,984,000	77,240
Banff and Buchan	3,147,000	25,689
Gordon	3,461,000	28,256
Kincardine and Deeside	2,561,000	20,911
Moray	3,231,000	26,374
Badenoch and Strathspey	767,000	4,840
Caithness	1,374,000	7,758
Inverness	3,694,000	22,049
Lochaber	1,144,000	6,833
Nairn	659,000	4,000
Ross and Cromarty	2,786,000	16,363
Skye and Lochalsh	721,000	4,365
Sutherland	793,000	4,763

Column 1	Column 2	Column 3
Local Authority	*Amount*	*Figure*
	£	
East Lothian	4,108,000	32,014
Edinburgh City	32,438,000	173,785
Midlothian	3,163,000	25,826
West Lothian	5,329,000	43,502
Argyll and Bute	2,939,000	23,992
Bearsden and Milngavie	2,295,000	18,213
Clydebank	6,135,000	14,682
Clydesdale	3,152,000	17,369
Cumbernauld and Kilsyth	2,197,000	17,940
Cumnock and Doon Valley	1,487,000	11,527
Cunninghame	5,472,000	42,522
Dumbarton	5,222,000	27,140
East Kilbride	3,885,000	27,976
Eastwood	3,282,000	26,797
Glasgow City	50,357,000	225,253
Hamilton	4,640,000	31,312
Inverclyde	3,886,000	26,995
Kilmarnock and Loudoun	2,996,000	24,460
Kyle and Carrick	5,252,000	41,229
Monklands	5,272,000	27,288
Motherwell	5,156,000	38,768
Renfrew	12,026,000	66,688
Strathkelvin	4,604,000	29,441
Angus	3,766,000	30,744
Dundee City	9,446,000	55,320
Perth and Kinross	5,599,000	45,708
Islands Councils		
Orkney	2,604,000	6,019
Shetland	7,414,000	6,673
Western Isles	3,689,000	8,475

The Council Tax (Alteration of Lists and Appeals) (Scotland) Regulations 1993

(SI 1993/355)

NOTES
Made: 19th February 1993
Laid before Parliament: 4th March 1993
Coming into force: 1st April 1993

ARRANGEMENT OF REGULATIONS

PART I

PRELIMINARY

1. Citation and commencement.
2. Interpretation.

PART II

ALTERATION OF VALUATION LISTS

3. Interpretation of Part II.
4. Restrictions on alteration of valuation bands.
5. Circumstances and periods in which proposals may be made.
6. Manner of making proposals and information to be included.
7. Acknowledgement of proposals.
8. Proposals treated as invalid—lack of title or out of time.
9. Proposals treated as invalid—lack of information.
10. Proposals treated as invalid—appeals.
11. Withdrawal of proposals.
12. Joint proposals.
13. Valuations in connection with proposals.
14. Alterations agreed by assessor.
15. Disagreement as to proposed alteration.
16. Notification of alteration.
17. Effective date for alterations—additions or deletions of dwellings.
18. Effective date for alterations—corrections.
19. Effective date for alterations—other cases.
20. Service of notices.

PART III

NON-LIST APPEALS

21. Appeals in relation to estimates or benefit matters.
22. Appeals against levying authority decisions and calculations.

23. Appeals against penalties.
24. Appeals against completion notices.

PART IV

APPEAL PROCEDURE

25. Interpretation of Part IV.
26. Withdrawal of appeals.
27. Disposal by written representations.
28. Notice of hearing.
29. Statement of evidence.
30. Power to require attendance of witnesses and to order recovery of documents.
31. Failure to appear or be represented at hearing.
32. Arrangements at hearing.
33. Procedure at hearing.
34. Representation at hearing.
35. Record of evidence.
36. Decisions.
37. Orders.

PART I

PRELIMINARY

Citation and commencement

1. These Regulations may be cited as the Council Tax (Alteration of Lists and Appeals) (Scotland) Regulations 1993 and shall come into force on 1st April 1993.

Interpretation

2. In these Regulations—

"the Act" means the Local Government Finance Act 1992;

"the Administration Regulations" means the Council Tax (Administration and Enforcement) (Scotland) Regulations 1992;

"assessor", in relation to a list, means the local assessor charged with its maintenance under section 84(1) of the Act;

"levying authority", in relation to a dwelling, means the levying authority in whose area the dwelling is situated;

"list" means a valuation list compiled under section 84 of the Act;

"local valuation panel" means the panel for an area constituted in accordance with the Valuation (Local Panels and Appeals Committees Model Scheme) (Scotland) Order 1975;

"proposal" means a proposal for the alteration of a list;

"the relevant local valuation panel", in relation to an appeal, means the local valuation panel for the area of the levying authority—

(a) whose decision or calculation is the subject of the appeal; or

(b) in whose area is situated the dwelling which is the subject of the appeal.

PART II

ALTERATION OF VALUATION LISTS

Interpretation of Part II

3.—(1) In this Part—

"alteration" means alteration of a list in relation to a particular dwelling, and "alter" shall be construed accordingly;

"company" and "subsidiary" have the same meanings as in sections 736 and 736A of the Companies Act 1985;

"demand notice" means a notice served under Part V of the Administration Regulations;

"interested person", in relation to a proposal, means a person who is or was—

   (a) the owner; or
   (b) a taxpayer,

as regards the dwelling and any part of the period to which the proposal relates;

"proposer", in relation to a proposal, means—

   (a) the person who made the proposal; and
   (b) any person who is, in terms of regulation 11(3) or 12(2), to be treated as having made the proposal;

"secretary", in relation to a local valuation panel, means the secretary or assistant secretary to that panel;

"taxpayer", in relation to a dwelling and a day, means—

   (a) a person who is liable (whether solely or jointly and severally) to pay council tax in respect of the dwelling and the day; or
   (b) a person who would be so liable if the dwelling were not—
      (i)   an exempt dwelling; or
      (ii) a dwelling in respect of which the amount or amounts set under section 93 of the Act for the financial year in which the day falls were nil.

(2) For the purposes of this Part, an appeal decision is a "relevant decision" in respect of a dwelling if—

   (a) it was made by—
      (i)   a valuation appeal committee for the area in which the dwelling is situated;
      (ii) the Court of Session; or
      (iii) the House of Lords; and

   (b) either because of a general principle stated in it or because it relates to a comparable dwelling, the decision provides reasonable grounds for contending that the valuation band shown on the list in respect of the dwelling is not the one which should be shown.

Restrictions on alteration of valuation bands

4.—(1) No alteration shall be made of a valuation band shown in the list as applicable to any dwelling unless—

   (a) since the valuation band was first shown in the list as applicable to the dwelling—

      (i) there has been a material increase in the value of the dwelling and it, or any part of it, has subsequently been sold; or

      (ii) subject to paragraph (2), there has been a material reduction in the value of the dwelling;

   (b) the local assessor is satisfied that—

      (i) a different valuation band should have been determined by him as applicable to the dwelling; or

      (ii) the valuation band shown in the list is not that determined by him as so applicable;

   (c) the assessor has, under Schedule 5 to the Act, added, amended or deleted an apportionment note relating to any lands and heritages included in the valuation roll; or

   (d) there has been a successful appeal under the Act against the valuation band shown in the list.

(2) Where a material reduction in the value of a dwelling is caused wholly by the demolition of any part of the dwelling, the valuation band shall not be altered if—

   (a) the works of demolition are part of, or connected with, a building, engineering or other operation which—

      (i) has been carried out;

      (ii) is in progress; or

      (iii) is proposed to be carried out,

   in relation to the dwelling; and

   (b) the market value of the dwelling immediately before the commencement of the relevant works is less than it would have been had the dwelling then been in the same physical state as it is in immediately after completion of those works.

(3) In paragraph (2)(b)—

   "market value" means the amount which the dwelling might reasonably have been expected to realise if it had been sold in the open market by a willing seller; and

   "relevant works" means the works of demolition and the building, engineering or other operation of which those works of demolition are part or with which they are connected.

Circumstances and periods in which proposals may be made

5.—(1) Subject to paragraphs (2), (7), (8) and (10), an interested person may at any time on or after 1st April 1993 make a proposal for alteration of the list so as to—

   (a) show with effect from a particular date a dwelling which is not or was not shown on the list;

   (b) delete with effect from a particular date a dwelling which is or was shown on the list; or

   (c) change with effect from a particular date a valuation band which is or was shown on the list in respect of a dwelling.

(2) Where a dwelling is shown on the list as compiled, no proposal for alteration of the valuation band first shown in respect of the dwelling on the grounds that it is not the band which should have been so shown may be made after 30th November 1993 unless it is such a proposal as is described in paragraph (3), (4), (5) or (6).

(3) Where—

(a) the valuation band shown in respect of a dwelling on the list as compiled is not the same valuation band as was shown in respect of that dwelling on the copy of the proposed list sent to the levying authority in terms of section 85 (1)(b) of the Act; and

(b) that dwelling is not one in respect of which notification has been given by the authority in terms of regulation 6(3) of the Administration Regulations;

a proposal in relation to that dwelling may be made within 6 months of issue by the levying authority of the first demand notice showing in respect of the dwelling the valuation band which appears on the list as compiled.

(4) Where notification has been given by a levying authority in respect of a dwelling in terms of paragraph (2) or (3) of regulation 6 of the Administration Regulations, a proposal in relation to that dwelling may be made within 6 months of that notification.

(5) Where a person first becomes a taxpayer in respect of a dwelling after 31st May 1993, that person may, unless any of the circumstances specified in paragraph (9) apply, make a proposal in relation to that dwelling within 6 months of becoming a taxpayer.

(6) Where an appeal decision which is a relevant decision in respect of a dwelling has been made, a proposal in relation to that dwelling may be made within 6 months of that decision.

(7) Where a list is altered so as to show a dwelling which was not shown on the list as compiled, no proposal for alteration of the valuation band first shown in respect of that dwelling on the grounds that it is not the band which should have been so shown may be made unless—

(a) the proposal is made before 1st December 1993;

(b) the proposal is made within 6 months of—

(i) the date on which the only or last notice in respect of that alteration was served under regulations 14 and 16; or

(ii) where no such notice was served, the date of the appeal decision to which the alteration gives effect;

(c) the proposal is made by a person who has within the last 6 months first become a taxpayer in respect of the dwelling and none of the circumstances specified in paragraph (9) apply; or

(d) the proposal is made within 6 months of an appeal decision which is a relevant decision in respect of the dwelling.

(8) Where the valuation band shown in respect of a dwelling on the list is altered, no proposal for a further alteration of that band (whether involving a restoration to the original band or otherwise) may be made unless—

(a) the proposal is made before 1st December 1993;

(b) the proposal is made within 6 months of—

(i) the date on which the only or last notice in respect of that alteration was served under regulations 14 and 16; or

(ii) where no such notice was served, the date of the appeal decision to which the alteration gives effect;

(c) the proposal is made by a person who has within the last 6 months first become a taxpayer in respect of the dwelling and none of the circumstances specified in paragraph (9) apply;

(d) the proposal is made within 6 months of an appeal decision which is a relevant decision in respect of the dwelling; or

(e) the grounds of the proposal are that, since the effective date of the alteration—

(i) there has been a material increase in the value of the dwelling and it, or any part of it, has subsequently been sold;

(ii) there has been a material reduction in the value of the dwelling; or

(iii) the assessor has, under Schedule 5 to the Act, added, amended or deleted an apportionment note relating to any lands and heritages of which the dwelling forms or formed part.

(9) The circumstances referred to in paragraphs (5), (7)(c) and (8)(c) are that—

(a) a proposal to alter the list in relation to the same dwelling and arising from the same facts has been considered and determined by a valuation appeal committee or on appeal from such a committee;

(b) the new taxpayer is a company which is a subsidiary of the immediately preceding taxpayer;

(c) the immediately preceding taxpayer was a company which is a subsidiary of the new taxpayer;

(d) both the new and immediately preceding taxpayers are companies which are subsidiaries of the same company; or

(e) both the new and immediately preceding taxpayers are partnerships and at least one member of the partnership which is the new taxpayer was a member of the other partnership.

(10) No proposal may be made at any time to alter the valuation band shown in the list in respect of a dwelling falling within either of the classes of lands and heritages specified in paragraphs (2) and (3) of regulation 2 of the Council Tax (Dwellings) (Scotland) Regulations 1992.

Manner of making proposals and information to be included

6.—(1) A proposal shall—

(a) be made in writing;

(b) state the name and address of the person making it, and the capacity in which he does so;

(c) identify the dwelling to which it relates;

(d) identify the manner in which it is proposed that the list be altered and the date from which it is proposed that the alteration have effect;

(e) include a statement of the reasons why the person making the proposal believes that the list should be altered; and

(f) where it is a proposal which, but for any appeal decision which is a relevant decision in respect of the dwelling to which the proposal relates, would be out of time in terms of regulation 5, identify that appeal decision.

(2) Every proposal shall be served on the assessor.

Acknowledgement of proposals

7.—(1) Within the period of 14 days beginning on the day on which he receives a proposal, the assessor shall acknowledge its receipt by notice served on the proposer.

(2) A notice under paragraph (1) shall specify the date of receipt of the proposal and shall be accompanied by a statement of the effect of regulations 11, 12, 14 and 15.

Proposals treated as invalid—lack of title or out of time

8.—(1) Where the assessor is of the opinion that a proposal has not been validly made because the proposer is not a person who, at the time of making the proposal, is entitled to do so in terms of regulation 5, he may within six weeks of its service on him serve notice on the proposer that he is of that opinion, and stating—

(a) his reasons for that opinion; and
(b) the effect of paragraphs (2) and (3).

(2) If the proposer disagrees with the opinion of the assessor stated in a notice under paragraph (1), the proposer may appeal against the notice no later than four weeks after the date of its service.

(3) Where the assessor has served a notice under paragraph (1) and the proposer has not timeously appealed against it under paragraph (2), the assessor shall be entitled to treat the proposal as invalidly made and shall not require to take any further action in relation to it.

(4) Failure by the assessor to serve a notice under paragraph (1) in respect of a proposal shall not preclude him from contending in any appeal following a referral under regulation 15 that the proposal was not validly made for the reason mentioned in that paragraph.

Proposals treated as invalid—lack of information

9.—(1) Where the assessor is of the opinion that a proposal has not been validly made because it does not include all the information specified in paragraph (1) of regulation 6, he may within six weeks of the date of service of the proposal on him serve on the proposer a notice complying with paragraph (2).

(2) A notice under paragraph (1) shall—

(a) state the opinion of the assessor that the proposal has not been validly made;
(b) specify which of the information required by paragraph (1) of regulation 6 has not been supplied to him;
(c) state that the information must be supplied to him no later than four weeks after the date of service of the notice; and

(d) advise the proposer of his right of appeal under paragraph (3) and of the effect of paragraph (4).

(3) If the proposer disagrees with the opinion of the assessor stated in a notice under paragraph (1), the proposer may appeal against the notice no later than four weeks after the date of its service.

(4) Where the assessor has served a notice under paragraph (1) and the proposer has not—

(a) timeously appealed against it under paragraph (3); or
(b) timeously supplied to the assessor the information specified in the notice;

the assessor shall be entitled to treat the proposal as invalidly made and shall not require to take any further action in relation to it.

Proposals treated as invalid—appeals

10.—(1) An appeal under regulation 8(2) or 9(3) shall be initiated by serving notice of appeal on the assessor.

(2) Unless the assessor withdraws the notice against which the appeal is being made, he shall within four weeks of service of the notice of disagreement under paragraph (1) transmit to the secretary of the relevant local valuation panel notice that an appeal has been made, together with details of the contents of the proposal and of the reasons for his opinion that it has not been validly made.

Withdrawal of proposals

11.—(1) Subject to paragraphs (2) and (3), a proposal may be withdrawn by notice in writing served on the assessor by or on behalf of each proposer.

(2) Where, after reasonable inquiry, the assessor believes that none of the proposers are taxpayers in respect of the relevant dwelling at the time of seeking to withdraw the proposal, the assessor shall serve notice of proposed withdrawal on at least one current taxpayer in respect of that dwelling.

(3) Where, within the period of six weeks beginning on the day on which a notice under paragraph (2) is served, an interested person intimates to the assessor that he wishes to adopt the proposal, the proposal shall from the date of that intimation be treated for the purposes of these Regulations as having been made by that person.

Joint proposals

12.—(1) Where a person has made a proposal to the assessor, any other person who is an interested person in respect of that proposal may, so long as the proposal has not been withdrawn nor a referral in respect of it made under regulation 15, by notice indicate to the assessor that he wishes to support the proposal.

(2) Where a person has served notice under paragraph (1), the proposal shall from the date of service of the notice be treated for the purposes of these Regulations as having been made jointly by the original proposer and that person.

Valuations in connection with proposals

13. Any valuation of a dwelling carried out in connection with a proposal for the alteration of the list shall be carried out in accordance with section 86(2) of the Act.

Alterations agreed by assessor

14. Where the assessor is of the opinion that a proposal is well-founded, he shall—

(a) serve notice on each proposer that he intends to alter the list accordingly; and
(b) within six weeks of the date of the notice so alter the list.

Disagreement as to proposed alteration

15.—(1) Where the assessor is of the opinion that a proposal is not well-founded and it is not withdrawn, he shall in accordance with paragraphs (2) to (6) refer the disagreement between him and the proposer as an appeal to the relevant local valuation panel.

(2) Subject to paragraphs (3) to (5), a referral under paragraph (1) shall be made within the period of six months beginning on the day on which the proposal was served on the assessor.

(3) Where the assessor has served a notice under regulation 8(1) in respect of a proposal, a referral under paragraph (1) shall, subject to paragraph (5), be made within the period of six months beginning on the date on which—

(a) the assessor withdrew that notice; or
(b) the proposer's appeal against that notice was finally resolved in his favour.

(4) Where the assessor has served a notice under regulation 9(1) in respect of a proposal, a referral under paragraph (1) shall, subject to paragraph (5), be made within the period of six months beginning—

(a) where the assessor has been satisfied that he has been supplied with all the information specified in that notice, on the last date on which any of that information was supplied to him; or
(b) in any other case, on the date on which the proposer's appeal against that notice was finally resolved in his favour.

(5) Where a proposal has been adopted by a person under regulation 11(3), a referral under paragraph (1) shall be made within the period of six months beginning on the date on which that person intimated to the assessor his wish to adopt the proposal.

(6) A referral under paragraph (1) shall take place by means of the assessor transmitting to the secretary of the panel a notice of appeal together with a statement of the following matters:—

(a) the proposed alteration of the list;
(b) the date of service of the proposal;
(c) the name and address of the proposer; and
(d) the grounds on which the proposal was made.

Notification of alteration

16.—(1) Within six weeks of altering a list, an assessor shall notify the levying authority stating the effect of the alteration, and the levying authority shall as soon as is reasonably practicable alter the copy of the list deposited by them at their principal office under section 85(5) of the Act.

(2) Where a list is altered in the circumstances described in regulation 14 and the assessor, after reasonable inquiry, believes that none of the persons receiving notice under that regulation were taxpayers in respect of the relevant dwelling at the date of the alteration being made, he shall within six weeks of that date serve notice of the alteration on at least one such taxpayer.

(3) Where a list is altered so as to give effect to an appeal decision and the assessor, after reasonable inquiry believes that no party to the appeal was a taxpayer in respect of the relevant dwelling at the date of the alteration being made, he shall within six weeks of that date serve notice of the alteration on at least one such taxpayer.

(4) Where a list is altered otherwise than as described in paragraph (2) or (3), the assessor shall within six weeks of making the alteration serve notice of it on—

(a) at least one taxpayer in respect of the relevant dwelling; and
(b) the owner of that dwelling if the assessor, after reasonable inquiry, believes that he is not a taxpayer and the alteration involves the addition of the dwelling to the list.

(5) The assessor shall—

(a) serve with any notice under paragraph (2), (3) or (4), as the case may be, a statement of the effect of regulation 5 as it relates to the alteration in question; and
(b) take such steps as are reasonably practicable to secure that any such notice is served not later than notification is given under paragraph (1).

Effective date for alterations—additions or deletions of dwellings

17.—(1) Any alteration of the list effected so as to show a dwelling which is not or was not shown on the list shall have effect from the later of—

(a) the day on which the dwelling came into existence as a dwelling; and
(b) 1st April 1993.

Effective date for alterations—corrections

18.—(1) Any alteration of the list effected so as to show, in respect of a dwelling, the correct valuation band applicable to the dwelling on the day on which the dwelling was first shown on the list shall have effect from that day.

(2) Any alteration of the list effected so as to correct an inaccuracy resulting from an earlier alteration which was—

(a) intended to reflect a material increase or material reduction in the value of a dwelling; or

(b) a consequence of the assessor, under Schedule 5 to the Act, adding, amending or deleting an apportionment note relating to any lands and heritages included in the valuation roll,

shall have effect from the effective date of that earlier alteration.

Effective date for alterations—other cases

19.—(1) Any alteration of the list effected so as to reflect a material increase in the value of a dwelling shall have effect from the day on which the first sale of the dwelling, or any part of it, subsequent to the material increase was completed.

(2) For the purposes of paragraph (1), a sale of a dwelling, or part of a dwelling, shall be deemed to be completed on the date specified as the date of entry in the deed conveying the dwelling or part, as the case may be.

(3) Any alteration of the list which is—

(a) effected so as to reflect a material reduction in the value of a dwelling; and
(b) made without a proposal relating to that material reduction having been made to the assessor;

shall have effect from the later of—

(i)   the first day of the financial year in which the alteration is made; and
(ii) the operative date.

(4) Any alteration of the list which is—

(a) effected so as to reflect a material reduction in the value of a dwelling; and
(b) made in response to a proposal relating to that material reduction (whether or not the alteration is exactly that requested in the proposal).

shall have effect from the later of—

(i)   the first day of the financial year in which the proposal is made; and
(ii) the operative date.

(5) In paragraphs (3) and (4), "the operative date" means the first day on which the material reduction in the value of the dwelling was such that a valuation of it, carried out in accordance with section 86(2) of the Act and on the assumptions and in accordance with the principles prescribed thereunder in respect of valuations for compiling the list, would have placed the dwelling in a valuation band appearing in the Table set out in section 74(2) of the Act above the band shown in the valuation list in respect of the dwelling for that day.

(6) Any alteration of the list effected as a consequence of the assessor, under Schedule 5 to the Act, adding, amending or deleting an apportionment note relating to any lands and heritages included in the valuation roll shall have effect from the same date as that addition, amendment or deletion, as the case may be.

Service of notices

20. If the assessor has not, after reasonable inquiry, been able to ascertain the identity of any person upon whom a notice under this Part requires to be served by him, he may serve that notice by addressing it to "The Council Tax Payer" or "The Owner" (as the case may be) of the dwelling concerned (naming the dwelling) without further name or designation.

PART III

NON-LIST APPEALS

Appeals in relation to estimates or benefit matters

21. Section 81(1) of the Act shall not apply where the grounds on which the person concerned is aggrieved are that—

(a) any assumption as to the future that is required by Part V of the Administration Regulations to be made in the calculation of an amount payable as council tax or council water charge may prove to be inaccurate; or

(b) the calculation of an amount payable as council tax fails to take proper account of the provisions of the Council Tax Benefit (General) Regulations 1992.

Appeals against levying authority decision and calculations

22.—(1) An appeal under section 81(1) of the Act shall be initiated by serving a written notice of appeal on the levying authority.

(2) Any notice served under paragraph (1) shall contain the following information:—

(a) the grounds on which the appeal is made; and

(b) the date on which the aggrieved person's notice under section 81(4) of the Act was served on the levying authority.

(3) Where a person is aggrieved as mentioned in sub-section (1) of section 81 of the Act, any notice of appeal under paragraph (1) shall require to be served within 4 months of the date of service by him of the first notice under subsection (4) of that section bringing the grievance in question to the attention of the levying authority.

(4) On receipt of a notice under paragraph (1), the levying authority shall transmit it to the secretary or assistant secretary of the relevant local valuation panel.

Appeals against penalties

23.—(1) An appeal under paragraph 3 of Schedule 3 to the Act shall be initiated by serving a written notice of appeal on the levying authority.

(2) Any notice served under paragraph (1) shall—

(a) contain the following information:—

(i) the grounds on which the appeal is made; and

(ii) the date on which the penalty was imposed; and

(b) require to be served within 2 months of the later of—

(i) that date; and

(ii) 1st April 1993.

(3) On receipt of a notice under paragraph (1), the levying authority shall transmit it to the secretary or assistant secretary of the relevant local valuation panel.

Appeals against completion notices

24.—(1) An appeal under paragraph 2 of Schedule 6 to the Act shall be initiated by serving a written notice of appeal on the assessor.

(2) Any notice of appeal served under paragraph (1) shall—

    (a) contain a statement of the grounds on which the appeal is made; and

    (b) be accompanied by a copy of the completion notice which is the subject of the appeal.

(3) On receipt of a notice under paragraph (1), the assessor shall transmit it to the secretary or assistant secretary of the relevant local valuation panel.

PART IV

APPEAL PROCEDURE

Interpretation of Part IV

25.—(1) In this Part, unless the context otherwise requires—

    "appeal" means an appeal under—

        (a) Part II of these Regulations;

        (b) section 81(1) of the Act;

        (c) paragraph 3 of Schedule 3 to the Act; or

        (d) paragraph 2 of Schedule 6 to the Act;

    "committee" means a valuation appeal committee for a valuation area constituted in accordance with the Valuation (Local Panels and Appeal Committees Model Scheme) (Scotland) Order 1975;

    "secretary" means the secretary or assistant secretary to the local valuation panel from which the committee is constituted, or any other person for the time being authorised by that panel to act as secretary or assistant secretary to the committee.

(2) Any reference in this Part to a party to an appeal means the person or persons who made the appeal and—

    (a) in the case of an appeal under Part II of these Regulations or under paragraph 2 of Schedule 6 to the Act, the assessor;

    (b) in the case of any other appeal, the levying authority.

Withdrawal of appeals

26.—(1) An appeal may be withdrawn—

    (a) by notice in writing to that effect being given to the secretary of the committee by or on behalf of each appellant; or

    (b) with leave of the committee, by an appellant giving intimation to that effect at a hearing.

(2) Where, after an appeal under Part II of these Regulations has been lodged, the assessor decides that the proposal to which the appeal relates is well-founded, he shall—

(a) proceed in accordance with regulation 14; and

(b) inform the secretary of the committee accordingly;

and the appeal shall be deemed to be withdrawn.

Disposal by written representations

27.—(1) An appeal may be disposed of on the basis of written representations if all the parties have given their agreement in writing.

(2) Where all the parties have given their agreement as mentioned in paragraph (1), the secretary shall serve notice on the parties accordingly and each party may, within four weeks of service of such a notice, serve on the secretary a notice stating—

(a) his reasons or further reasons for the disagreement giving rise to the appeal; or

(b) that he does not intend to make further representations.

(3) A copy of any notice served in pursuance of paragraph (2) shall be served by the secretary on the other party or parties to the appeal, and shall be accompanied by a statement of the effect of paragraphs (4) and (5).

(4) Any party on whom a notice is served under paragraph (3) may, within four weeks of service of such a notice, serve on the secretary a further notice stating—

(a) his response to the other party's statement; or

(b) that he does not intend to make further representations;

and the secretary shall serve a copy of any such further notice on the other party or parties.

(5) After expiry of the period of four weeks referred to in paragraph (4), the secretary shall submit to the committee—

(a) any information transmitted to him under these Regulations; and

(b) any notice under paragraph (2) or (4).

(6) Following receipt of the documents referred to in paragraph (5), the committee may—

(a) require any party to furnish in writing further particulars of the grounds relied on and of any relevant facts or contentions; or

(b) order that the appeal be disposed of on the basis of a hearing.

(7) Where further particulars are supplied by a party in response to a requirement under paragraph (6)(a), the secretary shall serve a copy of those particulars on every other party and each such party may, within four weeks of such service, serve on the secretary any further statement he wishes to make in response.

(8) Any party may, at any time before an appeal is determined under this regulation, withdraw his agreement under paragraph (1) by serving notice on the secretary.

Notice of hearing

28.—(1) Where—

(a) an appeal has been made to the committee and the notice of appeal has not been withdrawn or deemed to be withdrawn; and

(b) the appeal is not one which is to be disposed of on the basis of written representations; the secretary shall issue to each party a notice for the hearing of
the appeal by the committee.

(2) The secretary shall give to each party not less than 35 days' notice of the date,
time and place set for the hearing of the appeal.

(3) The secretary shall advertise the date, time and place appointed for any hearing
by causing a notice giving such information to be conspicuously displayed—

(a) at an office of the levying authority for the area of the relevant local valuation panel; and
(b) at the place appointed for the hearing (unless that place is such an office as
is referred to in sub-paragraph (a)).

(4) The notice required by paragraph (3) shall name a place where a list of the appeals to be heard may be inspected

Statement of evidence

29.—(1) The committee may require a party, before such date as the committee may
specify—

(a) to provide any other party to the appeal with a written statement outlining
the evidence which he proposes to lead at the hearing; or
(b) to furnish any other party to the appeal with a copy of all productions on which
he proposes to found at the hearing.

(2) Where the committee makes any requirement under paragraph (1), it shall not
be competent, unless the committee so allows, for a party to lead evidence other than
in accordance with the material previously provided by him.

Power to require attendance of witnesses and to order recovery of documents

30.—(1) Except in a case which is to be disposed of on the basis of written representations and subject to paragraphs (2) and (3), the committee may, on the motion
of any party to the proceedings or *ex proprio motu*, by notice in writing—

(a) grant to a party such commission and diligence for the recovery of documents,
or provide such other means of recovery thereof, as could be granted or provided by the Court of Session in a cause before them, such recovery being
effected, where a commission and diligence has been granted, by execution
thereof or in that or any other case in any manner in which recovery could be
provided for by the Court of Session in such a cause; and
(b) require the attendance of any person as a witness or require the production
of any document relating to the question to be determined;

and may appoint the time at or within which or the place at which any act required
in pursuance of this regulation is to be done.

(2) No person shall be required in obedience to a requirement imposed under paragraph (1) to attend at any place which is more than 10 miles from the place where he
resides unless the necessary expenses are paid or tendered to him by the party at
whose instance his attendance has been required or by the committee, as the case
may be.

(3) Nothing in this regulation shall empower the committee to require any person to produce any book or document or to answer any question which he would be entitled, on the ground of privilege or confidentiality, to refuse to produce or to answer if the proceedings were proceedings in a court of law.

(4) Any notice given under paragraph (1) shall contain a reference to the provisions of section 82(3) of the Act (by which any person who fails to comply with any such notice shall be liable on summary conviction to a fine not exceeding level 1 on the standard scale).

Failure to appear or be represented at hearing

31.—(1) If no appellant appears or is represented at the hearing of an appeal, the committee may dismiss the appeal and shall, in that event, notify the appellant or appellants of the decision to dismiss the appeal.

(2) An appellant may, within 14 days from such notification or such longer period as the committee may in special circumstances allow, represent in writing to the committee that there was reasonable excuse for his absence and the committee may, if satisfied that there was such excuse, recall the said decision and appoint a further date, time and place for the hearing of the appeal, of which it shall give the parties not less than 7 days' notice.

Arrangements at hearing

32.—(1) The hearing shall be in public unless the committee with reasonable cause otherwise decides, but nothing in these Regulations shall prevent a member of the Council on Tribunals or of its Scottish Committee from attending any hearing in that capacity.

(2) The committee may at its discretion consider on the day of the hearing representations from parties as to the order of that day's list of appeal cases, and may thereafter alter that order.

(3) The committee may at its discretion—

(a) at any time postpone or adjourn a hearing, giving parties such intimation as it considers reasonable; or
(b) consider—

(i) any request for adjournment of a hearing made by a party; and
(ii) representations by any other party as to that request;

and, if it thinks fit, adjourn the hearing.

(4) In any case where a hearing has been adjourned before it has commenced, the date set for the adjourned hearing shall, for the purposes of regulation 28(2), be deemed to be the date set for the hearing.

Procedure at hearing

33. At the hearing of an appeal—

(a) the committee shall decide the order in which the parties shall be heard and may consider submissions by parties as to that order before reaching its decision;

(b) a party may call and examine witnesses, give evidence on his own behalf, and cross-examine—

  (i) any other party to the appeal who gives evidence; and
  (ii) any witness called by another party;

(c) the committee may require any witness to give evidence on oath or affirmation and for that purpose there may be administered an oath or affirmation in due form; and

(d) any written statement (including an affidavit) admissible under section 2(1)(b) of the Civil Evidence (Scotland) Act 1988 may be received in evidence without being spoken to by a witness if—

  (i) all parties to the appeal so agree; or
  (ii) in the absence of such agreement, the committee at its discretion so decides.

Representation at hearing

34.—(1) At the hearing of an appeal, a party may—

(a) conduct his own case; or
(b) subject to paragraphs (2) and (3), be represented by any person whether or not legally qualified.

(2) A member of the local valuation panel from which the committee is constituted shall not be entitled to represent any party to an appeal.

(3) The committee may, if satisfied that there are good and sufficient reasons for doing so, refuse to permit a particular person to represent a party at a hearing.

Record of evidence

35. Where a party requires a record to be made of the evidence led at the hearing, he—

(a) may make arrangements for the taking, at his expense, of such a record; and
(b) shall inform the committee accordingly.

Decisions

36.—(1) The decision of the committee on an appeal may be given—

(a) orally at the end of a hearing;
(b) orally at an adjourned sitting of a hearing; or
(c) in writing.

(2) A written statement of the reasons for the decision shall be given to all parties in every case and, where the decision is given orally, such a written statement shall be issued by the committee to all parties within seven days of the decision being given.

Orders

37.—(1) On deciding an appeal, other than an appeal under Part II of these Regulations, the committee may in consequence of the decision by order require—

(a) the reversal of a decision of a levying authority;

(b) the quashing of a calculation of an amount payable as council tax or council water charge;

(c) where the calculation of an amount has been quashed, the re-calculation of that amount;

(d) the quashing of a penalty imposed under paragraph 2 of Schedule 3 to the Act;

(e) the alteration of a list (prospectively or retrospectively).

(2) On deciding an appeal under Part II of these Regulations, the committee may in consequence of the decision by order require an assessor to alter a list in accordance with any provision made by or under the Act.

(3) The assessor shall comply with any order under sub-paragraph (e) of paragraph (1) or under paragraph (2) within six weeks beginning on the day of its making.

(4) An order under this regulation may require any matter ancillary to its subject-matter to be attended to.

The Council Tax (Deductions from Income Support) Regulations 1993

(SI 1993/494)

NOTES
Made: 5th March 1993
Laid before Parliament: 11th March 1993
Coming into force: 1st April 1993

Citation, commencement and interpretation

1. (1) These Regulations may be cited as the Council Tax (Deductions from Income Support) Regulations 1993 and shall come into force on 1st April 1993.

(2) In these Regulations, unless the context otherwise requires—

"the Administration Act" means the Social Security Administration Act 1992;

"the adjudication officer" means an officer appointed in accordance with section 38(1) of the Administration Act;

"application" means an application made under regulation 2 or regulation 3 containing the information specified in regulation 4;

"appropriate appeal court" means the appropriate court as determined in accordance with regulation 10(9) and 10(10);

"authority" means—

(a) in relation to England and Wales, a billing authority, and

(b) in relation to Scotland, a levying authority;

"benefit week" has the meaning prescribed by regulation 2(1) of the Income Support (General) Regulations 1987;

"Claims and Payments Regulations" means the Social Security (Claims and Payments) Regulations 1987;

"Commissioner" means the Chief or any other Social Security Commissioner appointed in accordance with section 52(1) or (2) of the Administration Act, and includes a Tribunal of three Commissioners constituted in accordance with section 57(1) of that Act;

"debtor"—

(a) in relation to England and Wales, has the same meaning as in paragraph 6 of Schedule 4 to the Local Government Finance Act, and

(b) in relation to Scotland, has the same meaning as in paragraph 6 of Schedule 8 to that Act;

"5 per cent. of the personal allowance for a single claimant aged not less than 25" means, where the percentage is not a multiple of 5 pence, the sum obtained by rounding that 5 per cent. to the next higher such multiple;

"income support" means income support within the meaning of the Social Security Contributions and Benefit Act 1992;

"the Local Government Finance Act" means the Local Government Finance Act 1992;

"personal allowance for a single claimant aged not less than 25" means the amount specified in paragraph 1(1)(e) of column 2 of Schedule 2 to the Income Support (General) Regulations 1987;

"social security office" means an office of the Department of Social Security which is open to the public for the receipt of claims for income support and includes an office of the Department of Employment which is open to the public for the receipt of claims for unemployment benefit;

"tribunal", except in relation to a Tribunal of three Commissioners, means a social security appeal tribunal constituted in accordance with section 41 of the Administration Act.

(3) Unless the context otherwise requires, any reference in these Regulations to a numbered regulation or Schedule is a reference to the regulation or Schedule bearing that number in these Regulations and any reference in a regulation or Schedule to a numbered paragraph is a reference to the paragraph of that regulation or Schedule having that number.

Application for deductions from income support: England and Wales

2. Where a liability order has been made against a debtor by a magistrates' court and the debtor is entitled to income support the billing authority concerned may apply to the Secretary of State asking him to deduct sums from any amounts payable to the debtor by way of income support in order to secure the payment of any outstanding sum which is or forms part of the amount in respect of which the liability order was made.

Application for deductions from income support: Scotland

3. Where a levying authority has obtained a summary warrant or a decree against a debtor in respect of arrears of sums payable under paragraph 1(1) of Schedule 8 to the Local Government Act and the debtor is entitled to income support, the levying authority may, without prejudice to its right to pursue any other means of recovering such arrears, apply to the Secretary of State asking him to deduct sums from any amounts payable to the debtor by way of income support in order to secure the payment of any outstanding sum which is or forms part of the amount in respect of which the summary warrant or decree was granted.

Contents of application

4. (1) An application shall contain the following particulars—

  (a) the name and address of the debtor;
  (b) the name and address of the authority making the application;
  (c) the name and place of the court which made the liability order or granted the summary warrant, or decree as the case may be;
  (d) the date on which the liability order was made or the summary warrant or decree granted as the case may be;
  (e) the amount specified in the liability order, summary warrant or decree as the case may be;
  (f) the total sum which the authority wishes to have deducted from income support.

(2) An authority making an application shall serve it on the Secretary of State by sending or delivering it to a social security office.

(3) Where it appears to the Secretary of State that an application from an authority gives insufficient particulars to enable the debtor to be identified he may require the authority to furnish such further particulars as may reasonably be required for that purpose.

Reference to adjudication officer

5. (1) Where the Secretary of State receives an application from an authority he shall, subject to regulation 8(4), refer it forthwith to an adjudication officer who shall determine whether there is sufficient entitlement to income support to enable the Secretary of State to make any deduction.

(2) The adjudication officer shall determine there is sufficient entitlement to income support to enable the Secretary of State to make a deduction—

  (a) if the amount payable by way of income support after any deduction to be made under regulation 7 is 10 pence or more;
  (b) if the aggregate amount payable under one or more of the following provisions, namely paragraphs 3(2)(a), 5(6), 6(2)(a), 7(3)(a), 7(5)(a) of Schedule 9 and paragraph 3(5) of Schedule 9A to the Claims and Payments Regulations, together with the amount to be deducted under regulation 7, does not exceed an amount equal to 3 times 5 per cent. of the personal allowance for a single claimant aged not less than 25 years.

(3) The adjudication officer shall determine whether there is sufficient entitlement to income support to enable a deduction to be made, so far as is practicable, within 14 days of receipt of the reference from the Secretary of State.

Notification of decision

6. The Secretary of State shall notify the debtor and the authority concerned in writing of the adjudication officer's decision so far as is practicable within 14 days from the date on which he receives that decision and at the same time he shall notify the debtor of his right of appeal.

Deductions from debtor's income support

7. Where the adjudication officer has determined that there is sufficient entitlement to income support the Secretary of State may deduct a sum equal to 5 per cent. of the personal allowance for a single claimant aged not less than 25 and pay that sum to the authority towards satisfaction of any outstanding sum which is or forms part of the amount in respect of which the liability order was made or the summary warrant or the decree was granted.

Circumstances, time of making and termination of deductions

8.—(1) The Secretary of State shall make deductions from income support under regulation 7 only if—

    (a) the debtor is entitled to income support throughout any benefit week;

    (b) no deductions are being made in respect of the debtor under any other application; and

    (c) no payments are being made under regulation 2 of the Community Charge (Deductions from Income Support) (Scotland) Regulations 1989 or regulation 2 of the Community Charge (Deductions from Income Support) (No. 2) Regulations 1990.

(2) The Secretary of State shall make deductions from income support by reference to the times at which payment of income support is made to the debtor.

(3) The Secretary of State shall cease making deductions from income support if—

    (a) there is no longer sufficient entitlement to income support to enable him to make the deduction;

    (b) an authority withdraws its application for deductions to be made; or

    (c) the debt in respect of which he was making the deductions is discharged.

(4) Where at any time during which the Secretary of State is making deductions in respect of an application he receives one or more further applications in respect of the debtor from whom the deductions are being made, he shall refer those further applications to the adjudication officer in accordance with the following order or priority, namely, the one bearing the earliest date shall be referred first and each subsequent application shall be referred, one at a time and in date order, only after deductions under any earlier application have ceased.

(5) Payments of sums deducted from income support by the Secretary of State under these Regulations shall be made to the authority concerned, as far as is practicable, at intervals not exceeding 13 weeks.

(6) Where the whole of the amount to which the application relates has been paid, the authority concerned shall, so far as is practicable, give notice of that fact within 21 days to the Secretary of State.

(7) The Secretary of State shall notify the debtor in writing of the total sums deducted by him under any application—

    (a) on receipt of a written request for such information from the debtor; or

    (b) on the termination of deductions made under any such application.

Withdrawal of application

9. An authority may withdraw an application at any time by giving notice in writing to the social security office to which the application was sent or delivered.

Appeal

10. (1) Where the adjudication officer has decided a question under regulation 5, the debtor may appeal to a tribunal.

(2) Subject to paragraph (5), an appeal lies to a Commissioner from any decision of a tribunal on the grounds that the decision of that tribunal was erroneous in point of law and the persons who may appeal are the debtor and the adjudication officer.

(3) If it appears to the Chief Commissioner or, in the case of his inability to act, to such other of the Commissioners as he may have nominated to act for that purpose, that an appeal falling to be heard by one of the Commissioners involves a question of law of special difficulty, he may direct that the appeal be dealt with, not by that Commissioner alone but by a tribunal consisting of three Commissioners and, if the decision is not unanimous, the decision of the majority shall be the decision of the tribunal.

(4) Subject to paragraph (5), an appeal on a question of law lies to the appropriate appeal court from any decision of a Commissioner and the persons who may appeal are—

    (a) the debtor;
    (b) the adjudication officer; and
    (c) the Secretary of State.

(5) No appeal lies—

    (a) to the Commissioner from a decision of a tribunal without the leave of the chairman of the tribunal which gave the decision or, if he refuses leave, without the leave of a Commissioner, or
    (b) to the appropriate appeal court from a decision of a Commissioner, without the leave of the Commissioner who decided the case, or if he refuses, without the leave of the appropriate appeal court.

(6) Where in any case it is impracticable, or it would be likely to cause undue delay, for an application for leave to appeal against a decision of a tribunal to be determined by the person who was the chairman of that tribunal, that application shall be determined by any other person qualified under section 41(4) of the Administration Act to act as a chairman of tribunals.

(7) In a case where the Chief Commissioner considers that it is impracticable, or would be likely to cause undue delay, for an application for leave to appeal to the appropriate appeal court to be determined by the Commissioner who decided the case, that application shall be determined—

    (a) where the decision was a decision of an individual Commissioner, by the Chief Commissioner or a Commissioner selected by the Chief Commissioner, and
    (b) where the decision was a decision of a Tribunal of Commissioners, by a differently constituted Tribunal of Commissioners selected by the Chief Commissioner.

(8) If the office of Chief Commissioner is vacant, or if the Chief Commissioner is unable to act, paragraph (7) shall have effect as if the expression "the Chief Commissioner" referred to such other of the Commissioners as may have been nominated to act for the purpose either by the Chief Commissioner or, if he has not made such a nomination, by the Lord Chancellor.

(9) On an application to a Commissioner for leave under this regulation it shall be the duty of the Commissioner to specify as the appropriate court—

(a) the Court of Appeal if it appears to him that the relevant place is in England and Wales; and
(b) the Court of Session if it appears to him that the relevant place is in Scotland;

except that if it appears to him, having regard to the circumstances of the case and in particular to the convenience of the persons who may be parties to the proposed appeal, that he should specify a different court mentioned in paragraphs (a) and (b) above as the appropriate court, it shall be his duty to specify that court as the appropriate court.

(10) In paragraph (9) "the relevant place", in relation to an application for leave to appeal from a decision of a Commissioner, means the premises where the tribunal whose decision was the subject of the Commissioner's decision usually exercises its functions.

Review

11. (1) Any decision under these Regulations of an adjudication officer, a tribunal or a Commissioner may be reviewed at any time by an adjudication officer if—

(a) the officer is satisfied that the decision was given in ignorance of, or was based on a mistake as to, some material fact; or
(b) there has been a relevant change of circumstances since the decision was given.

(2) Any decision of an adjudication officer may be reviewed by an adjudication officer on the grounds that the decision was erroneous in point of law.

(3) A question may be raised with a view to review under this regulation by means of an application in writing to an adjudication officer, stating the grounds of the application.

(4) On receipt of any such application, the adjudication officer shall take it into consideration and, so far as is practicable, dispose of it within 14 days of its receipt.

(5) A decision given by way of revision or a refusal to review under this regulation shall be subject to appeal in the same manner as the original decision and regulation 10(1) and Schedule 2 shall apply with the necessary modification in relation to a decision given on review as they apply to the original decision on a question.

Correction of accidental errors

12. (1) Subject to regulation 14, accidental errors in any decision or record of a decision made under regulations 5, 10 and 11 and Schedule 2 may at any time be cor-

rected by the person or tribunal by whom the decision was made or a person or tribunal of like status.

(2) A correction made to, or to the record of, a decision shall be deemed to be part of
the decision, or of that record, and written notice of it shall be given as soon as is
practicable to every party to the proceedings.

Setting aside decisions on certain grounds

13. (1) Subject to regulation 14, on an application made by a party to the proceedings, a decision, made under regulations 5, 10 and 11 and Schedule 2 by an adjudication officer, a tribunal or a Commissioner ("the adjudicating authority"), together
with any determination given on an application for leave to appeal to a Commissioner, or the appropriate appeal court against such a decision may be set aside by
the adjudicating authority which gave the decision or an authority of like status, in
a case where it appears just to set that decision aside on the grounds that

(a) a document relating to the proceedings in which the decision was given was
not sent to, or was not received at an appropriate time by a party to the proceedings or the party's representative or was not received at the appropriate
time by the person or tribunal who gave the decision;

(b) in the case of an appeal to a tribunal or an oral hearing before a Commissioner a party to the proceedings in which the decision was given or the party's representative was not present at the hearing relating to the proceedings;
or

(c) the interests of justice so require.

(2) An application under this regulation shall be made in accordance with regulation 15 and Schedule 1.

(3) Where an application to set aside is made under paragraph (1) every party to the
proceedings shall be sent a copy of the application and shall be afforded a reasonable opportunity of making representations on it before the application is determined.

(4) Notice in writing of a determination on an application to set aside a decision shall
be given to every party to the proceedings as soon as may be practicable and the
notice shall contain a statement giving the reasons for the determination.

(5) For the purpose of determining under these Regulations an application to set aside
a decision, there shall be disregarded regulation 16(1) which deems any notice or
other document required or authorised to be given or sent to any person to have been
given or sent if it was sent by post to that person's last known notified address.

Provisions common to regulations 12 and 13

14. (1) In calculating any time specified in Schedule 1 there shall be disregarded
any day falling before the day on which notice was given of a correction of a decision or the record thereof pursuant to regulation 12 or on which notice is given that
a determination of a decision shall not be set aside following an application under
regulation 13, as the case may be.

(2) There shall be no appeal against a correction made under regulation 12 or a refusal to make such a correction or against a determination under regulation 13.

(3) Nothing in regulation 12 or 13 shall be construed as derogating from any inherent or other power to correct errors or set aside decisions which is exercisable apart from these Regulations.

Manner of making applications or appeals and time limits

15. (1) Any application or appeal set out in Column (1) of Schedule 1 shall be made or given by sending or delivering it to the appropriate office within the specified time.

(2) In this regulation—

- (a) "appropriate office" means the office specified in Column (2) of Schedule 1 opposite the description of the relevant application or appeal listed in Column (1); and
- (b) "specified time" means the time specified in Column (3) of that Schedule opposite the description of the relevant application or appeal so listed.

(3) The time specified by this regulation and Schedule 1 for the making of any application or appeal (except an application to the chairman of a tribunal for leave to appeal to a Commissioner) may be extended for special reasons, even though the time so specified may already have expired, and any application for an extension of time under this paragraph shall be made to and determined by the person to whom the application or appeal is sought to be made or, in the case of a tribunal, its chairman.

(4) An application under paragraph (3) for an extension of time (except where it is made to a Commissioner) which has been refused may not be renewed.

(5) Any application or appeal set out in Column (1) of Schedule 1 shall be in writing and shall contain:—

- (a) the name and address of the appellant or applicant;
- (b) the particulars of the grounds on which the appeal or application is to be made or given; and
- (c) his address for service of documents if it is different from that in sub-paragraph (a); and in the case of an appeal to the Commissioner, but subject to paragraph 21(2) of Schedule 2, the notice of appeal shall have annexed to it a copy of the determination granting leave to appeal and a copy of the decision against which leave to appeal has been granted.

(6) Where it appears to an adjudication officer, or chairman of a tribunal, or Commissioner that an application or appeal which is made to him, or to the tribunal, gives insufficient particulars to enable the question at issue to be determined, he may require, and in the case of a Commissioner, direct that the person making the application or appeal shall furnish such further particulars as may reasonably be required.

(7) The conduct and procedure in relation to any application or appeal shall be in accordance with Schedule 2.

Manner and time for the service of notices etc.

16. (1) Any notice or other document required or authorised to be given or sent to any person under these Regulations shall be deemed to have been given or sent if it was sent by post properly addressed and pre-paid to that person at his ordinary or last notified address.

(2) Any notice or other document required or authorised to be given or sent to an appropriate social security office or office of the clerk to a tribunal shall be treated as having been so given or sent on the day that it is received in the appropriate social security office or office of the clerk to the tribunal.

(3) Any notice or document required to be given, sent or submitted to, or served on, a Commissioner—

(a) shall be given, sent or submitted to an office of the Social Security Commissioners;

(b) shall be deemed to have been given, sent or submitted if it was sent by post properly addressed and pre-paid to an office of the Social Security Commissioners.

SCHEDULE 1   Regulation 15(1)

TIME LIMITS FOR MAKING APPLICATIONS OR APPEALS

(1)	(2)	(3)
Application or Appeal	*Appropriate office*	*Specified time*
1. Appeal to a tribunal from an adjudication officer's decision (regulation 10(1)).	An appropriate social security office.	3 months beginning with the date when notice in writing of the decision was given to the appellant.
2. Application to the Chairman for leave to appeal to a Commissioner from the decision of a tribunal (paragraph 16, (Schedule 2))	The office of the Clerk to the tribunal	3 months beginning with the date when a copy of the record of the decision was given to the applicant.
3. Application to— (a) an adjudication officer; (b) a tribunal; or (c) a Commissioner, to set aside decision (regulation 13)	(a) An appropriate social security office; (b) The office of the clerk to the tribunal; (c) An office of the Social Security Commissioners.	(a) and (b) 3 months beginning with the date when notice in writing of the decision was given to the applicant. (c) 30 days from the date on which notice in writing of the decision was given to the applicant by an office of the Social Security Commissioners.
4. Application for leave to appeal to the Commissioner where the chairman has refused leave (paragraph 17, Schedule 2).	An office of the Social Security Commissioners.	42 days beginning with the date when notice in writing of the decision by the chairman to refuse leave was given to the applicant.

(1)	(2)	(3)
Application or Appeal	*Appropriate office*	*Specified time*
5. Appeal to the Commissioner (regulation 10(2))	An office of the Social Security Commissioners.	42 days beginning with the date when notice in writing of the decision was given to the applicant.
6. Leave to appeal to the appropriate appeal court (regulation 10(4)).	An office of the Social Security Commissioners.	3 months beginning with the date when notice in writing of the decision was given to the applicant.

SCHEDULE 2 Regulation 15(7)

CONDUCT AND PROCEDURE IN RELATION TO APPEALS AND APPLICATIONS

PART I. COMMON PROVISIONS IN CONNECTION WITH APPEALS AND APPLICATIONS

1. Subject to the provisions of these Regulations—

(a)   the procedure in connection with the consideration of any appeal, or any application in relation to questions to which these Regulations relate, shall be such as the adjudication officer, chairman of the tribunal or the Commissioner may determine;

(b)   any person who by virtue of these Regulations has the right to be heard at a hearing may be accompanied and represented by another person whether having professional qualifications or not, and for the purposes of any proceedings at any hearing any such representative shall have all the rights and powers to which the person whom he represents is entitled under these Regulations.

(2) Nothing in these Regulations shall prevent a member of the Council on Tribunals or of the Scottish Committee of that Council in his capacity as such from being present at any oral hearing before a tribunal or a Commissioner, notwithstanding that the hearing is not in public.

2. Reasonable notice (being not less than 10 days beginning on the day on which notice is given and ending on the day before the hearing of the appeal) of the time and place of any oral hearing before the tribunal or the Commissioner shall be given to every party to the proceedings, and if such notice has not been given to a person to whom it should have been given under the provisions of this paragraph the hearing may proceed only with the consent of that person.

3. At any oral hearing any party to the proceedings shall be entitled to be present and be heard.

Postponements and adjournments

4. (1) Where a person to whom notice of an oral hearing has been given wishes to apply for that hearing to be postponed he shall do so in writing to the chairman of the tribunal or the Commissioner stating his reasons for the application and the chairman or the Commissioner may grant or refuse the application as he sees fit.

(2) An oral hearing may be adjourned at any time on the application of any party to the proceedings or on the motion of the tribunal or the Commissioner.

Striking out of proceedings for want of prosecution

5. (1) The chairman of a tribunal or the Commissioner may, subject to sub-paragraph (2), on the application of any party to the proceedings or of his own motion, strike out any appeal or application for want of prosecution.

(2) Before making an order under sub-paragraph (1) the chairman of a tribunal or the Commissioner, shall send a notice to the person against whom it is proposed that any order should be made giving him a reasonable opportunity to show cause why such an order should not be made.

(3) The chairman of a tribunal or the Commissioner, may, on application by the party concerned, give leave to reinstate any application or appeal which has been struck out in accordance with sub-paragraph (1).

PART II. APPLICATION AND APPEALS TO THE TRIBUNAL

Procedure in connection with determinations.

6. For the purposes of arriving at its decision a tribunal shall, and for the purpose of discussing any question of procedure may, notwithstanding anything in these Regulations, order all persons not being members of the tribunal other than its clerk to withdraw from the sitting of the tribunal except that—

 (a) a member of the Council on Tribunals or of the Scottish Committee of that Council, the President of Social Security Appeal Tribunals and any full time chairman of a social security appeal tribunal appointed under section 51(1) of the 1992 Act; and
 (b) with the leave of the chairman of the tribunal, if no person having the right to be heard objects, any person mentioned in paragraph 13(1)(b) and (d) (except a person undergoing training as an adjudication officer),

may remain present at any such sitting.

Oral Hearings

7. A tribunal shall hold an oral hearing of every appeal made to them.

8. If a party to the proceedings to whom notice has been given under paragraph 2 should fail to appear at the hearing, the tribunal may, having regard to all the circumstances, including any explanation offered for the absence, proceed with the case notwithstanding his absence or give such directions with a view to the determination of the case as they think fit.

9. Any oral hearing before a tribunal shall be in public except that the hearing shall be in private where the debtor requests a private hearing, or where the chairman is satisfied in the particular circumstances of the case that intimate personal or financial circumstances may have to be disclosed, or that considerations of public security are involved.

10. Any case may, with the consent of the debtor or his representative, but not otherwise, be proceeded with in the absence of any one member other than the chairman.

11. Where the oral hearing is adjourned and at the hearing after the adjournment the tribunal is differently constituted otherwise than through the operation of paragraph 10, the proceedings at that hearing shall be by way of a complete rehearing of the case.

12. (1) The decision of the majority of the tribunal shall be the decision of the tribunal but, where the tribunal consists of an even number, the chairman shall have a second or casting vote.

(2) The chairman of a tribunal shall—

    (a) record in writing all its decisions; and

    (b) include in the record of every decision a statement of the reasons for such decision and of their findings on questions of fact material thereto; and

    (c) if a decision is not unanimous, record a statement that one of the members dissented and the reasons given by him for so dissenting.

    (3) As soon as may be practicable after a case has been decided by a tribunal, a copy of the record of the decision made in accordance with this paragraph shall be sent to every party to the proceedings who shall also be informed of the conditions governing appeals to a Commissioner.

13. (1) The following persons shall be entitled to be present at an oral hearing (whether or not it is in private) but shall take no part in the proceedings—

    (a) the President of Social Security Appeal Tribunals and any regional or full-time chairman of a social security appeal tribunal appointed under section 51(1) of the 1992 Act;

    (b) any person undergoing training as a chairman or other member of a tribunal, or as a clerk to a tribunal, or as an adjudication officer;

    (c) any person acting on behalf of the President of the Social Security Appeal Tribunals, the Chief Adjudication Officer appointed under section 39 of the 1992 Act, or the Secretary of State, in the training or supervision of clerks to tribunals or adjudication officers or officers of the Secretary of State or in the monitoring of standards of adjudication by adjudication officers;

    (d) with the leave of the chairman of the tribunal and with the consent of every party to the proceedings actually present, any other person.

(2) Nothing in sub-paragraph (1) affects the rights of any person mentioned in heads (a) and (b) at any oral hearing where he is sitting as a member of the tribunal or acting as its clerk, and nothing in this paragraph prevents the presence at an oral hearing of any witness.

14. Any person entitled to be heard at an oral hearing may address the tribunal, may give evidence, may call witnesses and may put questions directly to any person called as a witness.

Withdrawal of appeals

15. Any appeal to the tribunal under these Regulations may be withdrawn by the person who made the appeal—

    (a) before the hearing begins by giving written notice of intention to withdraw to the tribunal and with the consent in writing of the adjudication officer who made the decision; or

    (b) after the hearing has begun with the leave of the chairman of the tribunal at any time before the determination is made.

Application to a chairman for leave to appeal from a tribunal to a Commissioner

16. (1) Subject to the following provisions of this paragraph, an application to the chairman of a tribunal for leave to appeal to a Commissioner from a decision of the tribunal shall be made—

    (a) orally at the hearing after the decision is announced by the tribunal; or

    (b) as provided by regulation 15 and Schedule 1.

(2) Where an application in writing for leave to appeal is made by an adjudication officer, the clerk to the tribunal shall, as soon as may be practicable, send a copy of the application to every other party to the proceedings.

(3) The decision of the chairman on an application for leave to appeal made under sub-paragraph (1)(a) shall be recorded in the record of the proceedings of the tribunal, and an application under sub-paragraph (1)(b) shall be recorded in writing and a copy shall be sent to each party to the proceedings.

(4) A person who has made an application to the chairman of a tribunal for leave to appeal to a Commissioner may withdraw his application at any time before it is determined by giving written notice to the chairman.

PART III. APPLICATIONS AND APPEAL TO A COMMISSIONER

Applications to a Commissioner for leave to appeal from a tribunal

17. Subject to paragraph 18, an application may be made to a Commissioner for leave to appeal against a decision of a tribunal only where the applicant has been refused leave to appeal by a person qualified to act as chairman of a tribunal.

18. Where there has been a failure to apply to the chairman for leave to appeal during the time specified in Schedule 1, an application for leave to appeal may be made to a Commissioner who may, if for special reasons he thinks fit, accept and proceed to consider and determine the application.

Notice of application

19. (1) Where the applicant has been refused leave to appeal by the chairman of a tribunal otherwise than by a decision recorded in the record of proceedings of the tribunal, the notice shall also have annexed to it a copy of the decision refusing leave and shall state the date on which the applicant was given notice in writing of the refusal of leave.

(2) Where the applicant has failed—

    (a) to apply within the specified time to the chairman of a tribunal for leave to appeal; or

    (b) to comply with paragraph 4 of Schedule 1;

the notice of application for leave to appeal shall, in addition to complying with regulation 15(5), state the grounds relied upon for seeking acceptance of the application notwithstanding that the relevant period has expired.

20. Where an application for leave to appeal is made by an adjudication officer the applicant shall, as soon as may be practicable, send the respondent a copy of the notice of application for leave to appeal.

Determination of applications for leave

21. (1) The office of the Social Security Commissioners shall notify the applicant and the respondent in writing of the determination by a Commissioner of the application.

(2) Subject to a direction by a Commissioner to the contrary, where a Commissioner grants leave to appeal on an application, notice of appeal shall be deemed to have been given on the date when notice of the determination is given to the applicant and the notice of application shall be deemed to be a notice of appeal duly served under paragraph 5 of Schedule 1.

(3) If on consideration of an application for leave to appeal to him from the decision of a tribunal the Commissioner grants leave he may, with the consent of the applicant and each respondent, treat the application as an appeal and determine any questions arising on the application as though it were a question arising on an appeal.

Acknowledgement of a notice of appeal and notification to each respondent

22. The office of the Social Security Commissioners shall send—

    (a)   to the appellant an acknowledgement of the receipt of a notice of appeal; and

    (b)   to each respondent a copy of the notice of appeal.

Respondent's written observations

23. (1) A respondent who wishes to submit to a Commissioner written observations on the appeal shall do so within 30 days of being given notice in writing of it.

(2) Any such written observations shall include—

    (a)   the respondent's name and address for service;

    (b)   in the case of observations on an appeal, a statement as to whether or not he opposes the appeal; and

    (c)   in any case, the grounds upon which the respondent proposes to rely,

and a copy of any written observations from a respondent shall be sent by the office of the Social Security Commissioners to the other parties.

Written observations in reply

24. Any party may, within 30 days of being sent written observations submitted in accordance with paragraph 23, submit to a Commissioner written observations in reply and a copy of any such observations shall be sent by the office of the Social Security Commissioners to the other parties.

Directions

25. (1) At any stage of the proceedings, a Commissioner may, either of his own motion or on application setting out the direction which the applicant is seeking, give such directions as he considers necessary or desirable for the efficient and effective despatch of the proceedings.

(2) Without prejudice to paragraphs 23 and 24 or to sub-paragraph (1) above, a Commissioner may direct any party to any proceedings before him to make such written observations as may seem to him necessary to enable the question at issue to be determined.

(3) An application under sub-paragraph (1) shall be made to a Commissioner in writing and shall set out the direction which the applicant is seeking to have made and the grounds for the application.

(4) Unless the Commissioner shall otherwise determine, an application made pursuant to sub-paragraph (1) above shall be copied by the office of the Social Security Commissioners to the other parties.

Requests for oral hearing

26. (1) Subject to sub-paragraphs (2) and (3), a Commissioner may determine an application for leave to appeal or an appeal without an oral hearing.

(2) Where, in any proceedings before a Commissioner, a request is made by any party for an oral hearing the Commissioner shall grant the request unless, after considering all the circumstances of the case and the reasons put forward in the request for the hearing, he is satisfied that the application or appeal can properly be determined without a hearing, in which

event he may proceed to determine the case without a hearing and he shall in writing either before giving his determination or decision, or in it, inform the person making the request that it has been refused.

(3) A Commissioner may of his own motion at any stage, if he is satisfied that an oral hearing is desirable, direct such a hearing.

Oral hearings

27. (1) If any party to the proceedings to whom notice of an oral hearing has been given under paragraph 2 shall fail to appear at the hearing, the Commissioner may, having regard to all the circumstances, including any explanation offered for the absence, proceed with the case notwithstanding his absence, or the Commissioner may give such directions with a view to the determination of the case as he thinks fit.

(2) Any oral hearing shall be in public except where the Commissioner is satisfied that intimate personal or financial circumstances may have to be disclosed or that considerations of public security are involved, in which case the hearing or any part of it shall be in private.

(3) Where a Commissioner holds an oral hearing the following persons shall be entitled to be present and be heard

- (a) the person making the application or appeal
- (b) the debtor;
- (c) an adjudication officer;
- (d) a representative of a trade union, employer's association or other associations which exists to promote the interest and welfare of its members; or
- (e) any other person with the leave of the Commissioner.

Summoning of witness

28. (1) A Commissioner may summon any person to attend as a witness, at such time and place as may be specified in the summons, at an oral hearing of an application to a Commissioner for leave to appeal or of an appeal, to answer any questions or produce any documents in his custody or under his control which relate to any matter in question in the proceedings:

Provided that no person shall be required to attend in obedience to such a summons unless he has been given at least 7 days' notice of the hearing or, if less than 7 days, has informed the Commissioner that he accepts such notice as he has been given.

(2) A Commissioner may upon the application of a person summoned under this paragraph set the summons aside.

Postponement and adjournment

29. A Commissioner may of his own motion postpone an oral hearing, or adjourn it at any time once it has begun.

Withdrawal of applications for leave to appeal and appeals

30. At any time before it is determined,

- (a) an application for leave to appeal may be withdrawn by the applicant by giving written notice to a Commissioner of his intention to do so,
- (b) an appeal may be withdrawn by the appellant with leave of the Commissioner,

and a Commissioner may, on application by the party concerned give leave to reinstate any application or appeal which has been withdrawn and on giving leave he may give such directions as he thinks fit.

Irregularities

31. Any irregularity resulting from failure to comply with the requirements of these Regulations before a Commissioner has determined the application or appeal shall not of itself invalidate any proceedings, and the Commissioner, before reaching his decision, may waive the irregularity or take such steps as he thinks fit to remedy the irregularity whether by amendment of any document, or the giving of any notice or directions or otherwise.

Determinations and decisions of a Commissioner

32. (1) The determination of a Commissioner on an application for leave to appeal shall be in writing and signed by him.

(2) The decision of a Commissioner on an appeal shall be in writing and signed by him and, except in respect of a decision made with the consent of the parties, he shall record reasons.

(3) A copy of the determination or decision and any reasons shall be sent to the parties by the office of the Social Security Commissioners.

(4) Without prejudice to sub-paragraphs (2) and (3) above, a Commissioner may announce his determination or decision at the conclusion of an oral hearing.

General powers of a Commissioner

33. A Commissioner may, if he thinks fit—

- (a) except where regulation 15(4) applies, extend the time specified in these Regulations for doing any act, notwithstanding that the time specified may have expired;
- (b) abridge the time specified in these Regulations for doing any act;
- (c) expedite the proceedings in such manner as he thinks fit.

Delegation of functions to nominated officers

34. (1) All or any of the following functions of a Commissioner may be exercised by a nominated officer authorised by the Lord Chancellor in accordance with section 58(6) of the Administration Act—

- (a) making a direction under regulation 15(6) and paragraph 25;
- (b) making orders for oral hearings under paragraphs 26(2) and (3);
- (c) summoning witnesses under paragraph 28 and setting aside any witness summons made by a nominated officer;
- (d) ordering a postponement of oral hearings under paragraph 4(1);
- (e) giving leave for withdrawal of any appeal under paragraph 30;
- (f) making any order for extension of time under regulation 15 or extension or abridgement of time, or expediting proceedings under paragraph 33;
- (g) making an order under sub-paragraph (2).

(2) Any party may, within 10 days of being given the decision of a nominated officer, in writing request a Commissioner to consider, and confirm or replace with his own, that decision but such a request shall not stop the proceedings unless so ordered by the Commissioner.

PART IV. APPLICATION TO A COMMISSIONER FOR LEAVE TO APPEAL

Application to a Commissioner for leave to appeal to an appropriate appeal court

35. (1) For the purposes of making an application for leave to appeal where—

(a)   a debtor is unable for the time being to act; and

(b)   no receiver has been appointed by the Court of Protection with power to claim or receive benefit on his behalf or as regards the application of these regulations in Scotland, his estate is not being administered by any tutor, curator, guardian or other judicial factor acting or appointed in terms of law,

the Secretary of State may, upon written application made to him by a person who, if a natural person, is over the age of 18, appoint that person to exercise, on behalf of the person who is unable to act, any right to which that person may be entitled.

(2) Where the Secretary of State has made an appointment under sub-paragraph (1)—

(a)   he may at any time revoke it;

(b)   the person appointed may resign his office after having given one month's notice in writing to the Secretary of State of his intention to do so;

(c)   any such appointment shall terminate when the Secretary of State is notified that a receiver has been appointed by the Court of Protection or, as regards the application of these Regulations in Scotland, any such appointment shall terminate when the Secretary of State is notified that such a person as is mentioned in sub-paragraph (1)(b) of this paragraph has been appointed to administer the offender's estate.

36. Paragraph 30 shall apply to an application for leave to appeal as it applies to the proceedings therein set out.